Pathologies of Love

Women and Gender in the Early Modern World

SERIES EDITORS
Allyson Poska
Abby Zanger

Pathologies of Love

MEDICINE AND THE
WOMAN QUESTION IN
EARLY MODERN FRANCE

JUDY KEM

UNIVERSITY OF NEBRASKA PRESS   LINCOLN

Portions of chapter 2 previously appeared as "'Malebouche,'
Metaphors of Misreadings, and the 'Querelle des femmes'
in Jean Molinet's *Romant de la rose moralisé* (1500),"
Fifteenth-Century Studies 31 (April 2006): 123–43. Portions
of chapter 5 previously appeared as "Fatal Lovesickness
in Marguerite de Navarre's *Heptaméron*," *Sixteenth-
Century Journal* 41, no. 2 (Summer 2010): 355–70.

Library of Congress Cataloging-in-Publication Data
Names: Kem, Judy, author.
Title: Pathologies of love: medicine and the woman
question in early modern France / Judy Kem.
Description: Lincoln: University of Nebraska Press,
[2019] | Series: Women and gender in the early modern
world | Includes bibliographical references and index. |
Summary: "Judy Kem looks at the writings of Christine
de Pizan, Jean Molinet, Symphorien Champier,
Jean Lemaire de Belges, and Marguerite de Navarre,
examining the role of received medical ideas in the
querelle des femmes"—Provided by publisher.
Identifiers: LCCN 2019015610
ISBN 9781496215208 (cloth)
ISBN 9781496216861 (mobi)
ISBN 9781496216854 (epub)
ISBN 9781496216878 (pdf)
Subjects: LCSH: Women—France—History—Renaissance,
1450–1600. | Women—Health and hygiene—France—
History—16th century. | Sex differences—History—16th
century. | Sex differences in literature—History—16th
century. | Sex role—France—History—16th century.
| Sex role in literature—History—16th century. |
Medicine—Philosophy—History—16th century.
Classification: LCC HQ1149.F8 K46 2019 |
DDC 305.40944/09031—dc23
LC record available at https://lccn.loc.gov/2019015610

Set in Arno by Mikala R. Kolander.
Designed by N. Putens.

For my sister, Janet Kem Ausbrooks

CONTENTS

ILLUSTRATIONS

TABLES

ACKNOWLEDGMENTS

The work on this volume began several years ago, and over those many years I have profited from the suggestions, ideas, and editing skills of many individuals. First, I would like to thank Marian Rothstein, who encouraged and offered me helpful comments all along the way. Her comments on the first draft of this manuscript were invaluable. I also owe much to Régine Reynolds-Cornell, who edited parts of my critical edition on Symphorien Champier's *Nef des dames* and made helpful suggestions throughout that long process. I consider both mentors, colleagues, and dear friends. Thanks also go to friend and Marguerite scholar Leanna Bridge Rezvani, who answered many of my Marguerite questions and kept me connected by repeatedly inviting me to participate in sessions she organized at conferences. Our collaboration and communication have been very important. I also owe a debt of gratitude to my Wake Forest colleague, Jane Albrecht, who has offered me her unfailing support as well as her inestimable editing skills over the last three decades.

I am deeply indebted to the first reader of the manuscript at Ashgate. Her comments led me to rewrite the manuscript and transform it into something I hope resembles a book now rather than separate articles. A special thank-you goes to Alysson Poska and Abby Zanger, who, despite the "transformation" at Ashgate that interrupted this process for a time, stayed with me and urged me to submit my work to their new home, the University of Nebraska Press. My thanks go to the second and third readers of the manuscript, who not only found an embarrassing number of typos but also offered invaluable advice that made the project better. I also appreciate Kenneth Wee's excellent copyediting skills. The errors that remain are solely my responsibility.

I have also benefited from William C. Archie grants and R. J. Reynolds leaves from Wake Forest University that allowed me access to libraries in France and Belgium and to time away from teaching and service duties in order to work on this project. I could not have completed this project without the aid and professionalism of several individuals in the Z. Smith Reynolds Library on Wake Forest's campus. They contributed their patient forbearance in the face of all my rush book orders, tardy requests for renewals of materials, and wide-ranging requests for interlibrary loans and articles. They are (in alphabetical order): Lauren Corbett, James Harper, Tara Hauser, Travis Manning, and Peter Romanov. I would also like to thank the patient librarians in the manuscript and rare-book rooms at the Bibliothèque Royale in Brussels and the Bibliothèque Nationale in Paris.

My final thanks go to my sister, Janet Kem Ausbrooks, who repeatedly took on extraordinary familial duties while I worked on this manuscript. Like Marguerite de Navarre, she serves as the "family nurse" but is much more than that. She is truly a "Renaissance woman." This book is dedicated to her.

Pathologies of Love

Introduction

Early Modern Medicine and the Querelle des Femmes

Reason: Certainly there are ignorant women, but many women are more intelligent and possess livelier and more perceptive minds than many men. . . .

Christine: Though that may be the case as far as female intelligence is concerned, everyone knows that women have weak bodies, delicate and lacking in strength, and that they are naturally fearful. That is what terribly diminishes the reputation and authority of the female sex among men, because men claim that the body's imperfection brings about a diminished and poor moral character. Consequently, women are thought less worthy of praise.

—Christine de Pizan, *City of Ladies*

In early modern France, questions of women's physical makeup and its psychological and moral consequences played an integral role in the querelle des femmes.[1] This debate on the status of women and their role in society began in the fifteenth century, continued through the sixteenth, and, as many critics would say, has persisted well beyond.[2] In querelle works, early modern medicine, women's sexual difference, literary reception, and gendered language often merged. Authors like Jean Lemaire de Belges and Marguerite de Navarre gave literary expression to such received medical ideas as the origin of the Great Pox and fatal lovesickness, while doctors, like Symphorien Champier and François Rabelais, published literary works. Doctors and natural philosophers participated in the debate and used literary examples to prove their contentions about women's true physical, moral, and psychological nature and to explain the physiology of love. For example, literary depictions of lovesickness were used in medical treatises to explain the principles of contagion,[3] while Marguerite de Navarre challenged its purportedly lethal effects in her poetry and prose.

WOMEN IN EARLY MODERN MEDICINE

In the last three decades, scholars like Nancy Siraisi, Evelyne Berriot-Salvadore, Katharine Park, Joan Cadden, and Monica Green have examined how doctors defined and used women's anatomy in medieval and early modern France to advance arguments for and against women.[4] Women's biological condition was thought to affect their minds as well as their bodies, as the quotation above from Christine de Pizan clearly demonstrates. In *Un corps, un destin: La femme dans la médecine de la Renaissance*, Berriot-Salvadore sums up this attitude with the popular adage: "What is woman? An imperfect animal, deceitful and subject to illness" (Quesse de femme? Une beste imparfaite, decepvable et sujecte à maladie).[5] Early modern medical authorities thought that women's physical imperfections and weaknesses made them vulnerable to moral failings as well as disease.

AN IMPERFECT ANIMAL: WOMEN'S ANATOMY

The Greek physician Hippocrates (460–370 BC) believed that illnesses as well as certain human moods, emotions, and behaviors were caused by an excess or imbalance of bodily fluids called "humors": blood, yellow bile, black bile, and phlegm. Galen (AD 131–200) developed the first typology of temperaments in his *De temperamentis*, also known as *De complexionibus*,[6] and searched for physiological reasons for different behaviors in humans. He based them on the four elements (air, fire, earth, and water) and classified them as hot or cold, dry or humid. Nine temperaments were adduced from various qualities. The word "temperament" comes from the Latin *temperare*, "to mix." In the ideal personality, the complementary characteristics of hot–cold and dry–humid were well balanced. In four less ideal types, one of the four qualities was dominant. In the remaining four types, one pair of qualities dominated the complementary pair; for example, hot and moist dominated cold and dry. These latter four were the temperamental categories Galen named "sanguine" (blood), "choleric" (yellow bile), "melancholic" (black bile), and "phlegmatic" (phlegm) after the bodily humors.

TABLE 1. The four humors

Elements	Humors	Qualities	Major temperaments
Air	Blood	Hot/humid	Sanguine
Fire	Yellow bile	Hot/dry	Choleric
Earth	Black bile	Cold/dry	Melancholic
Water	Phlegm	Cold/humid	Phlegmatic

Humoral medicine found women's bodies inferior since they were considered generally cold and humid (phlegmatic), while men were more often hot and dry (choleric). In his *On the Usefulness of the Parts of the Body* (*De usu partium*), Galen offered two "indisputable" medical proofs of woman's imperfection in comparison to man:

> The female is less perfect than the male for one, principal reason—because she is colder; for if among animals the warm one is the more active, a colder animal would be less perfect than a warmer. A second reason is one that appears in dissecting. . . . All the parts . . . that men have, women have too, the difference between them lying in only one thing, which must be kept in mind . . . that in women the parts are within [the body], whereas in men they are outside . . . the parts that are inside in woman are outside in man.[7]

According to Galen, women's insufficient heat, the first proof, offered an explanation for their inverted anatomy, the second proof of their imperfection:

Now just as mankind is the most perfect of all animals, so within mankind the man is more perfect than the woman, and the reason for his perfection is his excess of heat, for heat is Nature's primary instrument. Hence in those animals that have less of it, her workmanship is necessarily more imperfect, and so it is no wonder that the female is less perfect than the male by as much as she is colder than he . . . woman is less perfect than the man in respect to the generative parts. For the parts were formed within her when she was still a fetus, but could not because of the defect in the heat emerge and project on the outside, and this, though making the animal itself that was being formed less perfect than one that is complete in all respects, provided no small advantage (Χρεία) for the race; for there needs must be a female. Indeed you ought not to think that our Creator would purposely make half the whole race imperfect and, as it were, mutilated, unless there was to be some greater advantage in such a mutilation.[8]

The belief that women possessed an inverted anatomy held sway for centuries, and while it was challenged as early as 1543, it remained surprisingly persistent well into the sixteenth century.[9] For example, throughout his life (he died in 1590) and even in posthumous editions—for example, the fifth edition (1598) of his *Œuvres* cited here—the eminent physician Ambroise Paré refers to women's inverted anatomy:

The sexual organ is nothing but the difference between the male and the female: from that it must be understood that a woman always has less heat than a man, and that *she has parts only slightly different, and located in another place than the man*: also her sperm-producing parts are colder, softer, and less dry than those of a man, and natural actions are not as perfect in her as in man. One must include eunuchs (the castrated) as belonging to the nature of woman, because they degenerate as males and obtain a female nature, as one sees by their feminine voice and lack of hair because of their weaker heat. Yet, one must realize that some women approach a man's nature and have a virile voice, and sometimes they even have a beard on the chin. On the other hand, some men retain a woman's nature, and they are called effeminate. The hermaphrodite, because he possesses the nature of man and of woman, lies between the two and participates in both.[10]

He also claimed that women's sex organs remained internal due to a lack of heat.[11] Even when anatomical proof later surfaced that women's anatomy was indeed different, Galen remained a rarely questioned and often quoted authority. And, although woman was "mutilated" and "imperfect," she was still useful for the propagation of the species.

Ideas about woman's imperfection and her useful, though minimal, role in procreation appeared in many medical works, mostly in Latin. Galen posited that both women and men generated semen, but woman's was "imperfect" and "weak" and contributed less than the man's to the fetus.[12] Since he thought the arteries that supplied blood to the right side of the testes and the right side of the uterus were warmer, he theorized that the right sides of both organs produced boys, while the left sides were much colder and produced girls.[13] However, Aristotle (384–322 BC), considered both a natural philosopher and medical authority, posited that men contributed the seed, while women mostly contributed a hospitable or inhospitable environment for it; he judged "menstrual fluid" vastly inferior to semen since the fluid was not sufficiently cooked or "concocted" to produce an active seed.[14] This disagreement between the two ancient authorities, Aristotle and Galen, on the relative contributions of men and women to conception would be hotly debated throughout the Middle Ages and well into the Renaissance.

Medieval and early modern authorities saw women's menstrual cycle as a purging of excess, bad humors. Men's bodies were considered more efficient than women's since they could fully digest food, change it into blood, and then, in the fourth and final digestion, transform it, with the necessary heat, into what was considered in medical writings a more refined substance: sperm. Due to their insufficient heat and consequently imperfect anatomy, women were incapable of fully digesting food. According to the thirteenth-century *De secretis mulierum*, a work falsely attributed to Albertus Magnus (ca. 1200–1280), the menstrual cycle was a dangerous time.[15] Helen Rodnite Lemay explains that the work was widely thought to be Albertus's because it was consistent with the low opinion of women he voiced in other works, such as his commentary *De animalibus*, based on Aristotle's work of the same title, and especially his *Quaestiones de animalibus*, in which the following condemnation appears: "For woman is a failed male and has a defective nature and is lacking in respect to him, and for that reason differs naturally from him and what she cannot acquire for herself, she acquires through begging and diabolical deceptions. From whence, I shall say briefly, all must beware of every woman as one would avoid a poisonous serpent and a horned devil, and if it was right to tell you what I know about women, the whole world would be astonished."[16] Like Albertus Magnus, Lemay writes, "pseudo-Albertus uses the principle that the heat in woman is weaker than the heat in man to conclude that all her food cannot be converted into flesh because of this. The residue, menstrual blood, was thought a product of female inferiority," a harmful "superfluity."[17] According to pseudo-Albertus, contact with menstrual blood could harm male companions and children.[18] Amenorrhea, a condition also known as menstrual retention or the absence of the menstrual cycle, could harm the woman herself, causing nausea, lack of appetite, chills, pains, and fever.

Women were also blamed for infertility. While some enlightened medical authorities looked for the source of the condition in both sexes or the couple's physical incompatibility—for example, if the penis were too short or the vagina too "slippery"—prevailing attitudes generally found the woman at fault since she was responsible for creating a hospitable environment for the child and bringing it to term.[19] Indeed, women's health and their reproductive health were often synonymous in contemporary medical works.[20] In France, where the custom of primogeniture and the Salic law often prevented women from inheriting property and succeeding to the throne, producing a male heir was paramount, so medical authorities concentrated on the conditions necessary to do so.[21] In an attempt to explain multiple births, some authorities described the female womb as a seven-celled organ that accommodated sons in the three warmer cells to the right, daughters in the three cooler ones on the left, and "monstrous" hermaphrodites in the middle. Equipped with this knowledge, doctors offered to assist patients, male and female, in navigating the mysteries of conception and enhancing the possibility of producing a son.

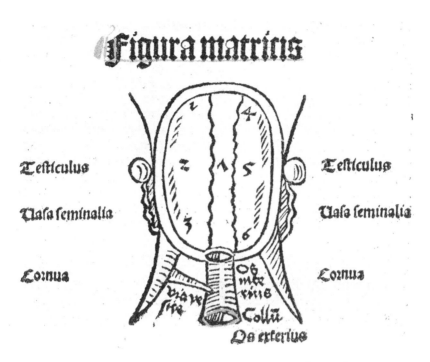

FIG. 1. The seven-celled uterus. Magnus Hundt, *Antropologium de hominis dignitate, natura, et proprietatibus; de elementis, partibus et membris humani corporis.* Leipzig: Wolfgang Monacensem, 1501. Image courtesy of the National Library of Medicine, Bethesda, Maryland.

AN ANIMAL SUBJECT TO ILLNESS: HYSTERIA, LOVESICKNESS, AND SYPHILIS

Since a woman's body was thought physiologically cold and humid and hence prone to putrefaction of the humors, especially if she suffered from infrequent periods or menstrual retention, she was particularly susceptible to diseases that arose from her uterus. Plato (ca. 429–347 BC) describes in the *Timaeus* the womb, or matrix, of women as an organ with a will of its own:

The animal within them [i.e., the womb] is desirous of procreating children, and when remaining unfruitful long beyond its proper time, gets discontented and angry, and wandering in every direction through the body, closes up the passages of the breath, and by obstructing respiration, drives them to extremity, causing all varieties of disease, until at length the desire and love of the man and the woman, bringing them together and as it were plucking the fruit from the tree, sow in the womb, as in a field, animals unseen by reason of their smallness and without form; these again are separated and matured within; they are then finally brought out into the light, and thus the generation of animals is completed.[22]

Although both men and women suffered from sexual deprivation, women purportedly suffered more. This wandering womb caused uterine suffocation and other conditions in women that Hippocrates would later call *hysteria*, after the word for uterus (ὑστέρα), ascribing to it agitation and various other symptoms, including toxic fumes. These poisons built up, especially if the uterus were deprived of the benefits of sex and procreation, which widened the woman's "passages," promoting the expulsion of bad humors and "cleansing" the body.[23] Hippocrates referred to the uterus as an animal within an animal, since he, like Plato, believed the sick womb, deprived of sex, wandered around the body and caused such disorders as anxiety, suffocation, tremors, and sometimes even convulsions, paralysis, and death. Hysteria affected virgins, widows, and single women in particular, so Hippocrates suggested that they marry so that they could enjoy a satisfactory sex life within the bonds of marriage. Galen's theories on hysteria were comparable. He recommended purges and the administering of hellebore, mint, laudanum, belladonna extract, valerian, and other herbs, but he too advised women to get married. Consequently, Berriot-Salvadore refers to hysteria as "an illness of women without men" (maladie des femmes sans hommes).[24]

In his *Viaticum*, Constantine the African (d. before 1098) described one disease that affected both men and women and became known by such names as *mal d'amor*, *amor heroycus*, love melancholy, erotomania, and lovesickness.[25] A long line of medieval and early modern physicians like Marsilio Ficino and Jacques Ferrand would describe its symptoms, causes, and cures.[26] It affected both men and women, and medical authorities hotly debated which gender suffered the most. Caused by unrequited love, it produced an excess of sperm, male and female, which led to a dangerous superfluity of black bile. Doctors prescribed remedies for their lovesick *male* patients, which included everything from having an old woman slander the loved one to therapeutic intercourse with another, or what Peter Lewis Allen refers to as the "coital cure."[27] The "coital cure" was out of the question for women; while doctors recommended it, at least for their male patients, theologians did not. A centuries-long battle ensued between those who would maintain the health of the body and those more concerned with the health of the soul.

Another illness, the opposite of lovesickness, was caused by excessive copulation and thought to affect only men. Several classical, medieval, and Renaissance medical authorities warned of the damage too-frequent coitus could cause men's health. It was especially harmful to eyesight, and could lead to sterility and even premature death. Through frequent coitus, a man's sperm became watery and devoid of *spiritus*. Aristotle claimed that watery sperm with "thin seed," the type often found in immature men, produced female children, while thicker semen generated males.[28] Men who engaged in excessive sexual activity risked literally drying up; consequently, too much sexual contact with women was to be avoided. Galen describes his remedy for one such dry male patient: "I was not wrong in thinking that a man in whom this humor [from the seminal vesicles] had been thoroughly dried up by frequent coitus . . . and who then, had difficulty in urinating would be cured if I ordered him to live temperately."[29] On the other hand, women, whose nature was moist, had less tendency to become dry, and, indeed, were thought to benefit physically from the heat of sexual intercourse. Women were also thought to be sexually insatiable and to need frequent sexual contact with hot, dry men to control their unhealthy moist nature.

Syphilis, or the Great Pox (la grosse vérole), was also blamed on women—or a class of women, at least: prostitutes. Early on, it was known to spread through sexual intercourse, and it reportedly surfaced in Italy during the French–Italian Wars, which began in 1494. The French named it the "mal de Naples," or the "Neapolitan disease," while Italians knew it as the *morbus gallicus*, or the "French disease." Some claimed that it was an old disease, reinvigorated through sin and debauchery, while others posited that it was new and a sign of divine vengeance for the sinful nature of the world.

Still others thought it originated in the New World. Most doctors blamed "loose women," such as the hundred or so prostitutes who followed Charles VIII into Italy, for its spread and urged men to avoid them at all costs. Their "moist humors" were considered an ideal breeding ground for disease.

One of the most common cures was mercury, which either killed the patient or, at the very least, caused terrible suffering. It was often administered externally, as in figure 2, considered the earliest depiction of the use of mercury for the treatment of syphilis, from a work titled *A malafranczos morbo Gallorum preservatio ac cura* (Prevention and care of the French illness, the disease of the Gauls), an eight-leaved quarto tract printed in Vienna in 1498 by Johann Winterburg. Leonardas Gerulaitis calls Bartholomaeus Steber's eight-leaved quarto tract the first work written by a professor of medicine on the new disease, but several other authors wrote about the disease as it spread across Europe around this time.[30] For example, J. David Oriel claims that Niccolò Leoniceno, a professor of medicine at Padua in Italy, published his *Libellus de epidemia, quam vulgo morbum gallicum vocent* (Notes on the epidemic commonly called the French disease) a year earlier than Steber.[31] Francisco Lopez de Villalobos (1473–1560), a physician in Salamanca, published *Tratado sobre las pestíferas bubas* (Treatise on the noxious pustules) the same year as Steber. The disease's origin, cause, and treatment were all hotly debated throughout the sixteenth century, long before and well after Fracastoro wrote his poem *Syphilis sive morbus gallicus* (Syphilis or the French disease), giving the disease the name "syphilis" in 1530, although the name most commonly used throughout Europe remained "the Great Pox" until the nineteenth century.

Although mercury was a commonly prescribed cure, Steber and others warned against its use. Physicians prescribed it as an external ointment in the early days. The physician at the top of figure 2 appears to be examining the woman patient's urine in a flask, while the physician at the bottom applies a mercury ointment with a spatula to the male patient; both patients are covered with characteristic lesions. Another typical mercury-based cure was the fumigation method, already used in the sixteenth century.

In the seventeenth-century depiction (fig. 3), the syphilitic patient is

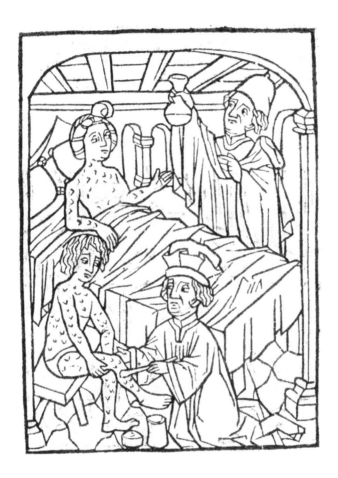

FIG. 2. External use of mercury to cure the "French illness." Woodcut from Bartholomäeus Steber, *A malafranczos morbo Gallorum praeservatio ac cura*. Vienna: Johann Winterburg, 1498. Image courtesy of the Austrian National Library, Vienna.

FIG. 3. The mercury fumigation method used to cure syphilis. Engraving by Jacques Lagniet, *Recueil des plus illustres proverbes divisés en trois livres*. Paris, 1663. Image courtesy of the Bibliothèque Nationale, Paris.

placed in an oven to inhale mercury fumes, and the caption on the outside of the oven makes it clear that the remedy was as much a punishment for sexual sin as a possible cure: "For one pleasure, a thousand pains; He is sweating out the pox." (Pour un plaisir, mil douleur[s]; Il sue la verolle.) The caption below reads:

For a little pleasure, I suffer a thousand pains
In one winter, I seem to suffer two summers
All over my body I sweat and my jaw trembles
I don't believe I'll ever see the end of my travails.[32]

These types of mercury sweat baths were thought to induce salivation and sweating, which were thought to eliminate the syphilitic poisons. However, many patients died of mercury poisoning or, if they survived, suffered greatly from its toxic effects. The treatment evidently remained for centuries, as much punishment for sexual sin as cure.

A DECEITFUL ANIMAL: WOMAN AS SEXUALLY
INSATIABLE AND LOQUACIOUS

The wandering womb, looking to be filled, was just one of the myths that contributed to the belief in women's sexual insatiability and inherent moral inferiority. According to the popular wisdom of the time, echoed in *De secretis mulierum* and its commentaries, "woman has a greater desire for sex than a man, for something foul is drawn to the good."[33] As previously noted, women's cold, moist nature benefited from the heat and dryness of sexual intercourse and also aided their monthly purgations by widening the channels; consequently, women who had sex regularly also menstruated regularly.

A woman's womb, characterized as "an animal within an animal," was thought out of control sexually, orally, and mentally. To get what they wanted (sex), promiscuous women were considered particularly eloquent. Proverbs 6:24 is just one example of that belief: "[A disciplined way of life] will keep you from the immoral woman, from the smooth tongue of an adulteress." A gossiping tongue was almost always female, especially in Paul's letters: "Women must likewise be dignified, not malicious gossips, but temperate, faithful in all things," and "Older women likewise are to be reverent in their behavior, not malicious gossips . . ."[34] Like the wandering womb and the penis, the tongue was considered to have a mind of its own: "And the tongue is a fire, a world of iniquity: so is the tongue among our members, that it defiles the whole body, and sets on fire the course of nature; and it is set on fire of hell. . . . But the tongue can no man tame; it is an unruly evil, full of deadly poison."[35] In *The Renaissance Notion of Woman*, Ian Maclean numbers garrulity among women's vices and associates it with the Fall: "Woman is debarred from speaking (because Eve's words beguiled Adam), from teaching and preaching."[36] According to Maclean, women's talkative nature was also said to be one effect of hysteria.[37] In general, all vices were held to have greater sway over women than men.

Humoral theory also contributed to assigning certain temperaments or personalities to women. For instance, women were thought more prone to exhibit phlegmatic or melancholic temperaments due to their coldness and supposedly more sedentary lifestyles. Hard labor and strenuous exercise were considered particularly harmful to them.[38] Their coldness, humidity, and inaction also indicated a slow wit or intellect. A rigorous program of study was just as deleterious to their minds as strenuous exercise to their bodies. Since women were prevented from receiving an education, they remained ignorant, which reinforced the stereotype that they could not, or should not, be educated.

Women's supposedly inverted anatomy also became a metaphor for their secretiveness and "dissimulation," a frequently used word. Randle Cotgrave defines the verb "*dissimuler*" as "to dissemble, counterfeit, disguise, play the hypocrite, pretend one thing and doe another," and he equates "dissimulation" with "hypocrisie" and "cloaking." Works on women's sexual nature started a type of literature referred to as the "secrets of women," like pseudo-Albertus's *De secretis mulierum* discussed above. In literary works, even the dresses women wore became metaphors for their hidden and deceitful nature. Dresses were thought to hide their limbs or true form, just as the "vagina," Latin for "sheath" or "scabbard," hid their sex organs.

However, not all medical and moral literature pointed out women's failings. According to Aristotle's *De animalibus*, women were more devout and full of pity than men. The "devout feminine sex" (devot sexe feminin) became a cliché in the Middle Ages and Renaissance.[39] Women were praised in doctrinals of the time for giving assiduously to charity and attending sermons. Their shame or extreme modesty, well reinforced by societal norms, was also considered a positive attribute in most cases. A common story of women's virtue was the Roman matron Lucretia, who, after having been raped by the king's son, called on her male relatives to avenge her shame and committed suicide. Pity, yet another "natural" female characteristic, was also praised, but it worked against women when lovesick men begged them to have "mercy" or "pity" on them and give in to their sexual advances, to award them the "don de mercy" (gift of mercy/pity). Chartier's *Belle dame sans mercy* (Beautiful lady without mercy) would play an important role in the medico–literary debate on fatal lovesickness.

MOLINET, CHAMPIER, LEMAIRE, AND
MARGUERITE DE NAVARRE

Jean Molinet (1435–1507), Symphorien Champier (1472–1538), Jean Lemaire de Belges (1473–1525), and Marguerite de Navarre (1492–1549) composed their works against the backdrop of these received medical ideas in the first half of the sixteenth century. They were contemporaries, and all participated in medical debates within the querelle des femmes. Each lived and worked either in the French or Burgundian courts; Lemaire worked in both. The patrons or would-be patrons of Molinet, Champier, and Lemaire—Anne of France (1460–1522), Anne of Brittany (1477–1514), and Margaret of Austria (1480–1530)—had strong political and familial ties with one another as well as with Marguerite de Navarre (1492–1549) and her mother, Louise de Savoie (1476–1531).

All knew one another or had mutual friends. Molinet and Lemaire were related by blood or kinship: Molinet was reportedly Lemaire's uncle or godfather. The young poet and chronicler followed in the elder Rhétoriqueur's footsteps as historian and secretary at the court of Margaret of Austria. Lemaire writes admiringly of his kinsman's literary production, and he was no doubt familiar with most, if not all, of Molinet's writings. In *La plainte du désiré* (1504), Lemaire praises him: "My Molinet (Mill) milling flowers and greenery, / Whose high renown will never perish" (Mon Molinet moulant fleur et verdure, / Dont le haut bruit jamais ne perira).[40] Lemaire also described his predecessor in an epitaph written after Molinet's death in 1507.[41]

Lemaire also knew and corresponded with the young Lyonnais physician Symphorien Champier. As financial clerk (clerc de finances) to Pierre de Bourbon (1438–1503), husband of Anne of France, from 1498 to 1503—and later as secretary and then historian for Margaret of Austria from 1503 to 1512—Lemaire made several trips to Lyon, especially as Margaret's special envoy to nearby Brou (Bourg-en-Bresse), where he oversaw the construction of the church dedicated to her late husband, Philibert le Beau, Duke of Savoy. According to Lemaire biographer and editor Jean Stecher, the young poet "was enthusiastically welcomed there by Champier on his first trip to Lyon."[42] Later, in a letter to Margaret's physician and astrologer, Pierre Picot, Lemaire describes Champier as "this very eloquent philosopher, orator, historian and physician, M. Symphorien Champier, Lyonnais" (ce très élégant philosophe, orateur, histoire [sic] et physicien, messire Symphorien Champier, lyonnois) and speaks of his "praiseworthy works, printed in Latin as in our Gallic tongue" (louables labeurs, imprimez tant en latin, comme en nostre langue gallicane).[43] Lemaire also wrote a poem in praise of Champier, playing on the physician's name in true Rhétoriqueur fashion.[44] According to Stecher, Champier was proud of the Rhétoriqueur's effusive praise and placed the compliment at the end of three of his published works: *De claris medicine scriptoribus, Ordre de la chevalerie*, and *Recueil des histoires des royaulmes d'Austrasie*.[45]

Marguerite, of course, was well known in the early Renaissance, and she and François Rabelais were acquainted.[46] Rabelais certainly knew Champier and knew of Lemaire, at least. In "Les Alibantes of Rabelais," James Wadsworth posits that the illustrious doctor and celebrated author was familiar with Champier's works. Both had studied in Montpellier and were doctors in Lyon in the 1530s. Several historians attest to their biographical and professional links.[47] In chapter 7 of *Pantagruel*, Rabelais includes Champier's *Campi clysteriorum*, published in 1532, in his list of the books contained in the Saint Victor library in Paris.[48] In chapter 30 of the same work, Rabelais includes "maistre Jean le Maire" in the underworld.[49] Some critics have also seen Raminagrobis as Lemaire in the *Tiers livre*.[50]

Rabelais's dedication of this misogynistic work to Marguerite de Navarre has created consternation for centuries. According to one critic, he could not have done so without her permission and full support.[51] Champier and Marguerite may have also known each other personally; he no doubt met her when he attended Francis I's coronation at Reims on 24 January 1515, as primary physician (primarius medicus) and adviser to Antoine de Calabre, Duke of Lorraine, one of Francis I's childhood friends.[52]

Molinet, Champier, Lemaire, and Marguerite also read and responded to many of the same authors. Molinet praises several fellow Rhétoriqueurs, and he cites Jean de Meun as a valuable literary predecessor. The third part of Champier's *Nef des dames vertueuses* (1503) contains a translation of sibylline prophecies by Jean Robertet, a writer whom Lemaire frequently praised. Lemaire also extols the virtues and talents of several of his contemporaries and predecessors in *La plainte du désiré*,[53] *Le temple d'honneur et de vertus*,[54] *La concorde des deux langages*,[55] *Les illustrations de Gaule et singularitez de Troye*,[56] and even his posthumous *Couronne margaritique*.[57] He compares Jean de Meun to Dante in his *Concorde des deux langages* and cites Martin Le Franc; both played an important role in the querelle de la rose and the querelle des femmes. While Marguerite de Navarre never mentions Lemaire, Champier, or Molinet, she cites Jean de Meun and Alain Chartier, and she may have also read Rabelais.[58]

All these writers not only knew or knew of one another—and also read and responded to the same works—but also dealt with lovesickness or pathologies of love: that is, the physical or medical aspects of love within the debate on women. For example, Christine de Pizan started the debate that became the querelle des femmes by attacking the misogyny in the *Roman de la rose*, but as the daughter of a physician, she also attacked the "Secrets of Women" medical tradition, which held that women were not only physically but also morally inferior to men. She also critiqued courtly love discourse, wherein male suitors used the threat of fatal lovesickness to seduce women. Molinet defended the *Roman de la rose* in his moralized version as an allegory of spiritual love, in which spiritually lovesick suitors or would-be crusaders dare not face death to reclaim the Holy Land. In his plea for a spiritual love quest, Molinet characterized Muslims as oversexed, aggressive cholerics and Christians as ideally sanguine in their treatment of women. The Lyonnais physician Champier defended women from their detractors in his *Nef des dames* while warning against the adverse effects of sexual excess, another form of fatal lovesickness, and offering remedies for infertility. Borrowing liberally from Marsilio Ficino, Champier offered an alternative view of and remedy for fatal lovesickness as an imperative to love one another spiritually rather than carnally, in his "Livre de vraye amour." Lemaire, who befriended and admired Champier, wrote on two pathological conditions: excessive grief, an extreme form of lovesickness that could lead to a wasting death or suicide, and the Great Pox, a new and deadly sexually transmitted disease. In the former, he praises Margaret of Austria as a virago capable of overcoming her "feminine weakness" (imbecilité féminine), and in the latter he appears to view women as a locus of contamination and depicts the disease as a loss of sexual difference, perhaps an irrational fear of the consequences of gender equality. Finally, Marguerite de Navarre, who nursed her husband, her brother the king, and several other family members through every type of illness, described lovesickness as a feigned illness but one with potentially fatal consequences, both physically and spiritually, in two of her works: *Les quatre dames et les quatre gentilzhommes* and the *Heptaméron.*

LOVE, MEDICINE, AND THE QUERELLE DES FEMMES

Chapter 1 demonstrates how the querelle des femmes grew out of a literary debate known as the querelle de la rose and examines the role Christine de Pizan played—or did not play—in both. Christine objected especially to Jean de Meun's misogynistic sequel to Guillaume de Lorris's thirteenth-century allegory of courtly love. While she instigated a debate that merged with, or grew into, the querelle des femmes, her role in it was overlooked in the first half of the sixteenth century. In fact, Martin Le Franc, citing her briefly in his *Champion des dames*, may have been one of a very small number of debaters to actually have read her works. After Le Franc, both male and female writers either failed to mention her or cited her as a sort of mythical character. Even though several manuscripts of her works were available in the libraries of noble families, few appeared in print in France in the sixteenth century.[59] However, her arguments appear and reappear throughout the sixteenth century, such as her advice to women to protect their reputations and spurn suitors who claim to be dying of lovesickness. The second chapter examines Jean Molinet's "translation" and defense of the *Roman de la rose*, titled *Le romant de la rose moralisé* (1500). Molinet attempts to control the reception of the romance and refute accusations made against it by slanderers or "evil tongues," among whom he counts certain "notable ladies," which no doubt included Christine, although her name never appears here or anywhere in his works. He declares slandering, "murmuring," or gossiping, personified by the allegorical figure Malebouche, a childlike or feminine trait. To refute the accusation that the *Roman de la rose* promotes "folle amour," he interprets the work anagogically as an allegory of spiritual love and a call for a crusade against the Turks that he hoped his dedicatee, Philippe de Clèves, would lead. In moralities that follow short, easily digestible chapter translations, Molinet apparently hoped to provide material for sermons to clerics so that they could "write" on the impressionable minds of women and provide an oral gloss for the written text. The *Romant de la rose moralisé* is one of the last attempts to translate and defend the romance. A few years later a translation, attributed to Clément Marot, would characterize the romance as less morally defensible.

Symphorien Champier purportedly wrote on both sides of the querelle des femmes; chapter 3 examines his *Nef des princes* (1502), which includes misogynistic passages, and his *Nef des dames vertueuses* (1503), considered a defense of women. Textual evidence indicates that he may have conceived of sections of both works, *Le gouvernement des princes* in the *Nef des princes* and *Le gouvernement de mariage* in the *Nef des dames*, as a single work. A syncretist, Champier gives consistent medical advice on infertility and sexual difference in the *Nefs* and his Latin works, such as the *Practica nova in medicina* (1517) and the *Periarchon* (1533), but he appears more interested in defending the medical profession from pharmacist interlopers and practitioners who could not read Latin and protecting males from a potentially fatal sexual excess than defending women. His treatment of Platonic love in the fourth book of the *Nef des dames*, titled "Le livre de vraye amour," has often been praised as the first introduction of Marsilio Ficino's

Renaissance Platonism in the vernacular but also roundly criticized for its poorly disguised misogyny. Yet this chapter demonstrates that Champier's philosophical and medical stance on women is not so easily categorized. Champier urges both women and men to love each other within marriage and urges men to treat women as equals, even though they were not. In his "Livre de vraye amour," he is consistently prowoman and promarriage for those who cannot remain celibate. The divine Platonic love he espouses in this fourth book comes from Marsilio Ficino and offers Champier a spiritual response to fatal lovesickness as a mandate to love one another spiritually rather than carnally.

Chapter 4 discusses Lemaire's participation in the medico–literary debates of the querelle des femmes in two works, both published posthumously. In the *Couronne margaritique*, written in 1504–5 but published in 1549, he praises Margaret of Austria as a virago but chastises her for a momentary lapse into "imbecillité feminine" as she grieves the death of her second husband. In this *complainte*, he offers her a therapeutic "crown" for her excessive grief, an extreme form of melancholy at the loss of a loved one and, purportedly, a common psychological weakness in women. In another posthumously published work, *Trois contes de Cupido et d'Atropos* (1526), Lemaire and two other authors present an allegory of the Great Pox. The work plays on sexual difference and portrays the illness as a loss of that difference, with a female Death, Atropos, playing a dominant "male" role and an emasculated Cupid losing both verbal and sexual power. Only Mercury, both the god of eloquence and a favored treatment for syphilis, can reestablish sexual difference and provide a remedy.

Finally, chapter 5 looks at Marguerite de Navarre's *Heptaméron*, in which five female and five male *devisants* offer different interpretations of tales that foreground sexual difference. In this work and her earlier *Les quatre dames et les quatre gentilzhommes*, Marguerite, the "family nurse," clearly portrays lovesickness as a feigned illness used to overcome women's honor in a society that treats women differently from men. In this game of sexual politics, Marguerite demonstrates through an untrustworthy male *devisant* in the *Heptaméron* how men play on women's natural pity to achieve an end that dishonors them. Although Marguerite provides a gender balance in discourse on sexual difference in these two multivoiced narratives, she nonetheless reflects the double bind that women experience in dealing with lovesick suitors.

The study of these four authors yields important insights into literary reception and views about gender identity and sexual difference in early modern France. The querelle des femmes was a debate not merely about women but also about various forms of interpretation, especially how men and women differ in their interpretations. In the first five decades of the sixteenth century, the world was changing from an oral to a written culture as printed books became more available and affordable, the literacy and book ownership of women increased, and vernacular French began to replace Latin. The medical profession was also changing: more and more doctors received university educations and distinguished themselves from "empirical" doctors, surgeons, and pharmacists—especially female practitioners—and more works on obstetrics and gynecology began to replace the "secrets of women" tradition and challenge long-held beliefs about the anatomy of women, as well as their role in both society and matters of love.[60]

1

Love or Seduction?

Christine de Pizan's Legacy from the Querelle de la Rose to the Querelle des Femmes

As previously noted, women's biological difference and its supposed connection to inferior moral character and intelligence were at the heart of the querelle des femmes. Many critics trace the querelle to misogynistic writings by such Greek and Roman authors as Aristotle, Plautus, and Ovid, while others believe it originated and grew in intensity in France after the querelle de la rose (1401–2), a literary dispute over the thirteenth-century *Roman de la rose*.[1] Christine de Pizan (1365–1434) started the debate by writing a poem in defense of women, "L'epistre au dieu d'amours" (1399), in which she accuses men of trying to seduce women and attacks Ovid and others—especially Jean de Meun's continuation of Guillaume de Lorris's romance. Why, she asks, does de Meun need to use such formidable weapons against such a supposedly weak-minded and morally compromised foe?[2]

In the poem, Christine asks for Cupid's help in defending women from men who defame them, such as Jean de Meun, and she takes to task the courtly love convention that women should surrender to men who claim that they are suffering from the ill effects of love or unrequited passion:

The loyal lovers' pose they strike is false.
Hiding behind their myriad deceits,

They go declaring that a woman's love
Inflames them sorely, keeps their hearts locked up;
The first laments, the second's heart is wrenched,
The next pretends to fill with tears, and sighs;
Another claims to sicken horribly:
Because of love's travail he's grown quite pale,
Now perishing, now very nearly dead.
Swearing their fervent oaths, they lie and vow
To be discreet and true, and then they crow.[3]

Christine thus describes men's attempts to seduce women by feigning ills or claiming that they might die from unrequited love. Here she alludes to lovesickness, an extreme form of courtly love that medical writers, like Jacques Ferrand, would later call a potentially fatal illness. The querelle de la rose started shortly after as an exchange of letters.

THE QUERELLE DE LA ROSE

In this literary and epistolary debate Christine de Pizan and Jean Gerson (1363–1429), French theologian and chancellor of the University of Paris, attacked Jean de Meun's continuation of Guillaume de Lorris's allegorical romance for its vulgarity, questionable advice on love, and ill treatment of women.[4] Their critiques as well as Jean de Montreuil and Gontier and Pierre Col's defenses of de Meun have been well documented in recent years.[5] In one letter, Jean Gerson cites eight articles, or objections, to the romance:[6] in the first, he asserts that the Old Woman teaches all young girls to sell their bodies and to deceive and lie; in the second, he objects to the Jealous Man who blames all women without exception; in the third, he attacks de Meun's assertion that celibacy among priests runs counter to Nature; in the fourth, sixth, and eighth articles, he accuses de Meun of using "extremely lustful, dirty, and forbidden words" and naming "shameful parts of the body and ugly, evil sins with holy and saintly words"; and in the fifth and seventh, he accuses the author of waging war on all virtues and encouraging carnal acts outside of marriage.[7] Christine, who, according to Earl Jeffrey Richards, shared an "intellectual friendship" with

Jean Gerson and owed much to his humanism, agreed with and expanded upon his articles.[8] In various letters to the defenders of the romance, she objects to de Meun's too-candid naming of the "secret" parts of the body (Raison . . . nomme les secrés membres plainement par non), the dubious teachings of the Old Woman, lust portrayed as morally superior to virtue, and the "shameful conclusion" (honteuse conclusion) in which the lover gains the rose.[9] She also criticizes de Meun's description of married ladies who deceive their husbands and his recording of evil deeds performed by women in the chapter on jealousy, even though, she adds, some excuse it as the words of the Jealous Man and not those of the author (Et la laidure qui la est recordee des femmes, dient plusseurs en luy excusant que ce fait le Jaloux qui parle).[10] She asserts that "he dared to defame and blame a whole sex without exception" (osa diffamer et blasmer tout ung sexe sans exepcion), and while she admits that the romance has some good parts, she states that since human nature tends toward evil, the other parts could cause people to opt for a dissolute and shameful life.[11]

Some modern critics insist that the debate was simply an exercise in rhetoric, but critics like Joan Kelly do not agree:

> The repetitiveness of the misogynist tradition nonetheless affected the responses of the prowomen side. Called again and again to rebut a flood of arguments that women were excluded from the concept of man in scripture, were not truly human, and were subject to man by the authority of religion and history, the feminists reiterated their ideas, which in themselves were novel, but did not develop them further. The static quality of the genre should not mislead us into accepting the commonly held notion that the *querelle* was a kind of literary game, however. Both its misogyny and its feminism expressed passionately held views and tell, as well, of a historically changing gender construction that was being imposed and resisted.[12]

Indeed, the defenders of the romance appeared outraged and did not stop at personal attacks on both Gerson and Christine—especially Christine. Jean de Montreuil, provost of Lille, defends the romance by citing "the excellence of De Meun's admirable art, his intelligence and knowledge" (de ammirabili artificio, ingenio ac doctrina), accusing those who attack it of having read it only superficially, if at all. He compares them to "drunks discussing at the dinner table" (instar eorum qui mense inter crapulas omnia) who too quickly attack such an "important [work] that was conceived and written with the sweat and hard work of many days and nights" (opus tantum, tot diebus ac noctibus tantoque cum sudore et attentione digesta elaboratum et editum).[13] He refers to the "respectable, satiric master Jean de Meun" (satiricum illum perseverum magistrum Johannem de Magduno) and calls him a "philosopher and poet of genius" (philosophum et poetam ingeniosissimum), while referring to Christine as "some woman, named Christine" (mulier quedam, nomine Cristina) and comparing her to the "Greek whore, who, according to Cicero, dared to write against the great philosopher Theophrastus" (grecam meretricem, ut refert Cicero, que 'contra Theofrastum, philosophum tantum, scribere ausa fuit').[14] Montreuil reminds Christine and other "presumptuous" writers that they are attacking a dead man who could, with one small wave of his hand, crush them if he were alive.[15] It is obvious to Montreuil that they do not understand the satiric task of de Meun, which allowed him to touch on subjects forbidden to others.[16] He also repeatedly questions whether they have indeed read the work at all or, if so, if they read just parts of it.

Pierre Col, canon of Paris, responds, in French, to de Meun's critics in a less volatile manner. He counters that the author created characters who speak accordingly and that their words do not express the author's opinions ("Jehan de Meung . . . fait chascun personnaige parler selonc qui lui appartient"); if there are vulgar words or some that offend women, de Meun is simply citing his characters. When Christine asks why he cites them at all, Col responds that de Meun wishes to teach the guardians of the castle how to guard it better.[17] To Christine's assertion that reading the romance would embarrass women readers, Col responds that it would only if these readers themselves were guilty of similar vices.[18] Gerson claims the contrary: all good women should blush at such things. In her final letter, Christine concludes,

And if I do not like the *Romance of the Rose*, it is simply because it incites evil and is a dishonest text, which encourages evil more than good deeds; and can be, in my opinion, the cause of the damnation and downfall of those who hear it and delight in it, and because it leads to bad morals. I swear to you on my soul and my faith that no other reason motivates me. And what you said afterwards, that perhaps we condemn it in order to entice others to read it, and thus our opinion of it is good, you can be certain that that is not our goal![19]

She, like Gerson, eventually decided to abandon the debate, which, they feared, was calling more attention to and interest in the work.

In *Debate and Dialogue*, Emily Cayley finds that while Christine's male contemporaries may have been indulging in a form of "jeu," or "play," Christine's participation in the querelle de la rose was far from playful.[20] As proof, Cayley cites Christine's first manuscript dossier of correspondence on the subject, which omits Jean de Montreuil's letters of February 1402.[21] She posits that when Christine circulated her version of the querelle, Montreuil withdrew from this unusual public display of what he considered a private debate.[22] In this "thwarted dialogue," Cayley points out, Montreuil never responded directly to Christine because she "refused to play the game by his rules."[23] Cayley also finds that Christine's choice of French, rather than the Latin in which Montreuil wrote, placed her at a disadvantage.[24]

Christine may have abandoned the epistolary debate, but she persisted in her vernacular defense of women. In *Le livre de la cité des dames* (1405), she takes not only de Meun but also Ovid and other ancient authorities who attacked women, as well as medieval misogynistic works like the *Lamentations de Mathéole*, to task.[25] This physician's daughter also attacks a popular medical work known as *De secretis mulierum*:[26]

"I know another small book in Latin, my lady, called the *Secreta mulierum*, *The Secrets of Women*, which discusses the constitution of their [women's] natural bodies and their great defects." She [Reason] replied, "You can see for yourself without further proof, this book was written carelessly and colored by hypocrisy, for if you have looked at it, you know that it is obviously a treatise composed of lies. Although some say that it was written by Aristotle, it is not believable that such a great philosopher could be charged with such contrived lies. For since women can clearly know with proof that certain things which he treats are not at all true, but pure fabrications, they can also conclude that the other details which he handles are outright lies. But don't you remember that he says in the beginning that some pope—I don't know which one— excommunicated every man who read the work to a woman or gave it to a woman to read?" [. . .] "It was done so that women would not know about the book and its contents, because the man who wrote it knew that if women read it or heard it read aloud, would know it was lies, would contradict it, and make fun of it. With this pretense the author wanted to trick and deceive the men who read it."[27]

Here, Reason lists three major critiques against *De secretis mulierum*. First, she finds it hard to believe that Aristotle wrote the work. While the work had been attributed, falsely, to the prolific thirteenth-century natural philosopher Albertus Magnus, Reason mentions only Aristotle, whom Lemay calls pseudo-Albertus's "favorite choice" of authorities, even when Aristotle was "peripheral to [the] discussion."[28] Perhaps she wished to avoid questioning a Christian authority like Albertus Magnus, finding it easier to attack his pagan source. Second, Reason contrasts natural philosophy and its theories with women's personal experience. Third, even though the work was written in Latin, a language that most women did not read, Reason claims that the author wished to ensure that it would not fall into the hands of women readers, who would find its claims laughable. Indeed, in the preface, pseudo-Albertus asks his male readers to keep the work confidential: "This is a serious work, therefore I beg you not to permit any child to peruse it, *nor anyone of childlike disposition*. If you keep this book to yourself, I promise to show you many things about different subjects as well as the art of medicine which, God willing, I shall discuss at some length."[29] Although women are not specifically mentioned, the message is clear: women were considered perpetual children and thought to possess a "childlike disposition." Christine appears to understand that this warning is not to protect children and women from harmful ideas or a too-explicit text but rather to keep women from reading this questionable "secret knowledge" of their own bodies and defending themselves from the misogyny in the text.

Later in the *Cité* Reason assures Christine that women are as intelligent as many men, but Christine responds that because of women's physical fragility, men think women are immoral: "Everyone knows that women have weak bodies, delicate and lacking in strength, and that they are naturally fearful. That is what terribly diminishes the reputation and authority of the female sex among men, for men claim that the body's imperfection brings about a diminished and poor moral character. Consequently, women are thought less worthy of praise."[30] Reason concedes that women are physically weaker than men, but she adds that women's souls are not only as good as those that God placed in men but also identical.[31] She then ends the work with advice to women not to fall prey to seducers who feign a potentially fatal lovesickness:

In brief, all women—whether noble, bourgeois, or lower-class—be well-informed in all things and cautious in defending your honor and chastity against your enemies! My ladies, see how these men accuse you of so many vices in everything. Make liars of them all by showing forth your virtue, and prove their attacks false by acting well, so that you can say with the Psalmist, "the vices of the evil will fall on their heads." Repel the deceptive flatterers who, using different charms, seek with various tricks to steal that which you must consummately guard, that is, your honor and the beauty of your praise. Oh, my ladies, flee, flee the foolish love they urge on you! Flee it, for God's sake, flee! For no good can come to you from it. Rather, rest assured that however deceptive their lures, their end is always to your detriment. And do not believe the contrary, for it cannot be otherwise. Remember, dear ladies, how these men call you frail, unserious, and easily influenced but yet try hard, using all kinds of strange and deceptive tricks, to catch you, just as one lays traps for wild animals. Flee, flee, my ladies, and avoid their company—under these smiles are hidden deadly and painful poisons. And so may it please you, my most respected ladies, to cultivate virtue, to flee vice, to increase and multiply our City, and to rejoice and act well.[32]

Several points are worth noting here. Christine not only advises women to preserve their virtue under attack by certain men but also cites several aspects that echo well into the fifteenth and sixteenth centuries: the dangers of persuasive eloquence, the folly of passion, the courtly love "game," and women's fragile reputations.

ALAIN CHARTIER

Even though Alain Chartier never mentions Christine in his works,[33] Charity Cannon Willard claims that he took up some of her ideas in his *Belle dame sans mercy*. Chartier's fair lady, she states, is one "whose ancestry is assuredly to be found in the pages of Christine's poetry."[34] The beautiful lady without mercy or pity turns aside her lover's pleas in the same way that Christine suggests in the *Livre de la cité des dames* as well as in "L'epistre au dieu d'amours," written twenty-five years earlier.[35] This second debate, which began around 1424 with *Belle dame*'s publication, is often referred to as the querelle de la *Belle dame sans mercy*, while some see it as the beginning of the querelle des femmes. Cayley cites forty manuscripts penned by participants in the querelle de la *Belle dame sans mercy*.[36] She posits that Chartier intended his ending to be read as ironic, with one moral for women and another for men, to elicit further debate:[37]

> Thus I beseech you, men in love, flee
> these braggarts and scandalmongers,
> and call them traitors,
> because they will impede your progress.
> Refusal has built a fortress against them
> so that their words will not be taken as truth,
> for they have had too much control
> over the land of love in recent times.
> As for you, ladies and young maidens,
> in whom honor is born and collected,
> be not so cruel as this one,
> neither individually nor collectively.
> Would that none of you resemble
> this lady whom you will now hear me name,
> and who should be called, it seems to me,
> The Belle Dame Sans Mercy.[38]

Cayley finds this "deferred judgment" and "closural ambiguity" characteristic of debate poetry of the time.[39]

Indeed, the "satiric" flavor of the work apparently offended some of
Chartier's female readers from the very beginning, forcing him to write a
poetic "Excusasion aux dames" (Apology to the ladies), in which he states
that mercy or pity is indeed a natural attribute of women:

Pity is fixed in the heart of a lady
just as diamond is set in gold,
but her virtue does not always serve
the pleasure of the lover.[40]

Cayley places him definitively on the prowoman side of the querelle des
femmes. The debate on women's pity or lack thereof for their lovesick
suitors would extend well into the sixteenth century.[41]

MARTIN LE FRANC

After Christine several other writers took up the cause of women, but few
more enthusiastically than Martin Le Franc, whose *Champion des dames* may
have been intended as satirical as well. Le Franc completed it as early as 1440
and dedicated it in his prologue to Philip of Burgundy, who, according to Le
Franc, had always revered the name of Love and been "singularly" interested
in the querelle des dames.[42] In this lengthy work, with the aid of the allegorical figure Franc Vouloir (Free Will), the Champion of Ladies confronts his
adversaries, Malebouche (Evil Tongue) and Villain Penser (Vile Thought).
In the first of five books, the Champion describes the attack by Malebouche
(Jean de Meun) against women and love, and the defense mounted by Franc
Vouloir; in the second, Vile Thought and Free Will engage in combat; in the
third, the Champion argues that men are more villainous than women in the
matter of love; in the fourth, he elevates women above men; and in the fifth
and final book, Le Franc deals primarily with the doctrine of Immaculate
Conception as the ultimate triumph of the female sex.[43] To misogynistic
comments such as "Woman is a damaged man / That is, an imperfect man"
(Femme est masle occasionné, / C'est-à-dire, ung homme imparfait) and
"Woman was made only to do evil" (Femme n'est faitte qu'à mal faire), the

Champion counters by attacking de Meun, "who did not resemble Master Alain in speaking courteously" (Qui en parlant courtoisement / N'a pas ressemblé maistre Alain), and by counseling marriage.[44]

Although Le Franc was obviously aware of Christine de Pizan's *Cité des dames,* her appearance in his *Champion des dames* is less impressive than Willard claims. First, the Champion of Ladies praises her as an eloquent love poet:

> But, finally, of things long past,
> Let's judge by what we now can see
> That the ladies who have passed
> Had of learning a treasury
> More precious far than gold can be,
> As did Lady Christine the late,
> Whose fame on horn and trumpet free
> Everywhere spreads and does not abate.
> I cannot her enough commend
> Without sorrow and sighing clamorous,
> Nor could those who to Love's court wend
> To serve the Prince of Love so joyous
> For truly all the flowers wondrous
> Had she in her garden fragrant,
> From which long or short verse gracious
> One makes in language elegant.
> To foreigners we can with zest
> Honor the worthy wise Christine,
> Whose mastery is manifest
> In letters and Latin language keen;
> We must not under drapes unseen
> Her many works and verses hide,
> So if death drapes in gabardine
> Her flesh, her fame will still abide.[45]

Even though Le Franc praises her knowledge of Latin, it remains somewhat controversial how well Christine read or wrote in Latin[46] and how well Le Franc knew her work. Next, the Champion praises her eloquence and wisdom, a literary ideal of the period, and compares her to Cicero (Tully) and Cato:

> But she was at once both Cato and Tully:
> Tully, for like him of eloquence
> Both rose and bud she gathered fully,
> And she had Cato's sapience.[47]

Was Le Franc in fact aware of Christine's role in the querelle de la rose? He might be alluding to it when he refers to her possession of the "rose and the bud." Finally, the Champion's adversary Slow Wit (Lourt Entendement) agrees that Christine is worthy of praise, but he adds a slur that would be repeated several times in the sixteenth century; he claims that her son Jean Castel wrote the works and gave her the credit:[48]

> "For all women, truly, it may happen
> As for Christine," Slow Wit said in slur,
> "All of whose books and verses were written,
> By her son Castel their actual author,"
> Then the seigneurs without demur,
> For then awarded her the praise,
> For freely one does not demur,
> At women's claims or challenge raise.[49]

Neither the "Champion," Free Will, nor his opponent, Slow Wit, mentions Christine's controversial role in the querelle de la rose, and unfortunately, Slow Wit has the last word on her; she is not mentioned again. That her son wrote the works attributed to her is not challenged; it would appear that the lords praise her simply because it would be unchivalrous not to accept her claim.

While Christine's appearance in the *Champion des dames* leaves much to be desired, Le Franc does counter accusations about women's inferior physical nature. For example, to the comment that woman is an imperfect male, the Champion retorts: "Is man more perfect in body / does he possess a unique beauty?" (Est homme plus parfait en corps, / A il singuliere beauté?).[50] Yet to the claim that women are full of "decaying matter" (pour-riture), the Champion simply cites their monthly "cleansing." To claims about their physical weakness, he posits that it may be more a reflection of their lack of physical activity than any innate condition.[51]

As the debate known as the querelle de la rose grew into the early modern cultural debate known as the querelle des femmes, it did not lose its literary aspects. As other writers joined the debate, some claimed that women were not only virtuous but should be considered equal and even superior to men.[52] These two debates provide us with a greater understanding of the cultural bias against women at the time and ideas about love and sex both within and outside of marriage, but they also offer a unique window into the history of literary reception and the changing status of women and writing in the early Renaissance. Male writers and doctors continued to link women's supposedly inferior biological nature to a greater susceptibility to immorality and even disease. Women, like Christine, were excluded from both debates. Yet, as more women became patrons, readers, and writers, Christine would become somewhat rehabilitated in France, and more women, like Marguerite de Navarre, would participate in the querelle des femmes. But until then, the querelle would remain largely a debate about women among men.

CHRISTINE DE PIZAN'S RECEPTION IN
THE QUERELLE DES FEMMES

Male writers continued to cite the *Roman de la rose* as a work of art and defend Jean de Meun from attacks by literary critics well into the sixteenth century,[53] but Christine de Pizan largely disappeared. Critics have greatly exaggerated her role in the querelle des femmes, and misinformation on her reception in the early Renaissance persists despite recent attempts to correct claims about her continued and consistent influence throughout the centuries, and to depict realistically her place in the literary canon.

Charity Cannon Willard "discovered" Christine in 1935 and purportedly saved her from obscurity. At the time, few of Christine's works were available in modern editions. In the preface to her book on Christine's life and works, Willard describes how it was not until the early 1980s that a larger readership finally began to examine Christine's works as modern editions started to appear.[54] Two decades later, in a collection of essays in 2003, an exuberant Margarete Zimmermann begins her article on Christine in the following manner:

No other author has inscribed herself so successfully and so endur-ingly into cultural memory as Christine de Pizan has done, and no one has been continuously present from the early modern period up to the debates in the twentieth and twenty-first centuries in the way that she has been. And which other woman writer commands such a *longue durée* in the memory of succeeding generations of readers, such a presence in two of the most important storage media, namely texts and images? Evocations of Christine de Pizan abound in early texts from the *Querelle des femmes* and in artwork owned by female rulers such as Margaret of Austria. The works of different women writers of the sixteenth century—e.g., Anne de Beaujeu, Gabrielle de Bourbon, Marguerite de Navarre, or Georgette de Montenay—acknowledge their familiarity with the great late medieval *écrivaine* and express their claim to power by referring to the *Cité des dames*.[55]

Zimmermann goes on to describe Christine's continuing popularity from the eighteenth through the twentieth century. However, until then, Chris-tine had drifted into relative obscurity long before the end of the fifteenth century. While the *Roman de la rose* continued to appear in print, with twenty-one editions in France from 1481–1538, very few of Christine's works appeared in print in the early sixteenth century, and Christine's name rarely appears in the works of male or female writers of the time.[56]

Although works on Christine's reception have proliferated in recent years, findings have been both scarce and disappointing. In her fine intro-duction to a collection titled *The Reception of Christine de Pizan from the Fifteenth through the Nineteenth Centuries*, published in 1991, Glenda McLeod offers a more balanced view of the history of Christine's reception. Noting how many times Christine has disappeared only to be "rediscovered," she blames Christine's periodic disappearances on her gender, the literary genres she chose, and even the polemical nature of her writings. She observes that Christine was largely ignored during the seventeenth, eighteenth, and most of the nineteenth centuries. McLeod decries the lack of a modern critical edition of Christine's *Livre de la cité des dames* in Middle French, a situation that has since been rectified.[57] Ironically, many of her works appeared in English before they did in French due to the political situation in England, where a woman would later rule the kingdom—a possibility denied women in France.[58]

Did Anne de Beaujeu, Gabrielle de Bourbon, Marguerite de Navarre, Georgette de Montenay, and other women writers, in Zimmerman's words, "acknowledge their familiarity with the great late medieval *écrivaine*" in their works or "express their claim to power by referring to the *Cité des dames*"? Willard claims that Anne of France owned copies of Christine's works but can only add that she "probably" read them when she was very young.[59] She finds that Anne's *Enseignements à sa fille, Suzanne de Bourbon* were "inspired" by Christine's *Le livre des trois vertus* but offers few textual proofs of that claim.[60] Anne de Beaujeu neither mentions Christine nor "acknowledges familiarity" with Christine's writings in the *Enseignements*; Willard bases her contention on the fact that they share some more-or-less conventional ideas on women's education while acknowledging significant differences.[61]

In her excellent edition of Gabrielle de Bourbon's *Œuvres spirituelles, 1510–1516*, which includes *Les doulleurs de la passion, Le voyage espirituel*, and *Le fort Chasteau*, Berriot-Salvadore points out that Gabrielle's library had a beautiful manuscript copy of Christine's *Le livre des trois vertus* and "imagines" the young girl reading it; yet Berriot-Salvadore finds only common themes in their works.[62] In Régine Reynolds-Cornell's *Witnessing an Era: Georgette de Montenay and the Emblèmes ou Devises Chrétiennes* and Alison Adams's *Webs of Allusion: French Protestant Emblem Books of the Sixteenth Century*, neither Christine nor her influence on de Montenay (ca. 1540–1607) is mentioned. In the 1537 collection of *Epistres familières et invectives de ma dame Hélisenne*, Hélisenne de Crenne praises Marguerite de Navarre but does not mention Christine even though she, like Christine, warns women not to give in to "folle amour."[63]

In her essay "Marguerite de Navarre as Reader of Christine de Pizan," Paula Sommers states categorically that Marguerite "never specifically mentions" Christine in her writings.[64] While "Christine was certainly known and respected by Marguerite's contemporaries," she adds, Marguerite's chosen themes in the *Heptaméron* and her other writings only "suggest affinities with Christine de Pizan."[65] Like Willard, Sommers sees "signs of Christine's influence" and some common themes in the queen's writings but can only speculate in her conclusion that "Marguerite de Navarre *may have read* a broad selection of works by Christine de Pizan."[66] Why would Marguerite remain silent on Christine? She mentions Jean de Meun twice in the *Heptaméron* and cites Alain Chartier's *Belle dame sans mercy* in novellas 12 and 56 to refute lovesick men's claims that women are without pity if they do not give in to men who attempt to seduce them.[67] In novella 12, Parlamente, often referred to as Marguerite's spokesperson, states that despite men's claims, lovesickness does not lead to death.[68]

While Christine's influence on early modern female writers in France has been exaggerated, her absence as an authority within vernacular works by male authors has been largely ignored.[69] Her first published works in France effectively erased her as the author by simply omitting her name or attributing her works to one of her sources.[70] By the first two decades of the sixteenth century, she had almost disappeared. Yet McLeod states that Christine enjoyed "a wide reputation in her own lifetime and during the Renaissance."[71] Willard claims "*The Book of the City of Ladies* continued to be read as part of the vogue for the lives of illustrious men and women inspired by the translations of Boccaccio" and specifies, "Evidence of this is to be found in Symphorien Champier's *Nef des dames (Ship of ladies)* printed in Lyon in 1503."[72] While Willard implies but does not directly state that Champier had read Christine and imitated her in his *Nef des dames*, Sommers goes a step further, claiming that the Lyonnais physician and author Symphorien Champier "acknowledges Christine in his *Nef des Dames (Ship of ladies;* 1503)."[73] However, Champier acknowledges neither *Le livre de la cité des dames* (1405) nor any of Christine's works in his *Nef des dames*.[74] *La cité des dames* and Champier's *Nef des dames* do have much in common: both are allegorical, defend women against their detractors—thus playing an important role in the querelle des femmes—depend heavily on Boccaccio's *De claris mulieribus*, and contain only favorable portraits of famous women. Nonetheless, while they share a common goal and even a common source, Champier's "ship" owes no debt, acknowledged or unacknowledged, to Christine's "city." Indeed, Champier modeled his "ship" on Sebastian Brant's immensely popular *Ship of Fools* (*Das Narrenschiff*), at least for its title, and borrowed heavily but not indiscriminately from Boccaccio.

Although both Champier and Christine wrote a profemale catalogue reminiscent of Boccaccio's *De claris mulieribus*, defended women, and claimed a certain measure of moral equality for women, Champier was apparently unfamiliar with Christine's *Cité*. Anne de France, to whom Champier dedicated the *Nef des dames*, may have owned copies of Christine's works,[75] but at the time that Champier wrote both *Nefs*, he was only just seeking patronage in the Bourbon court; his attempt would prove unsuccessful.[76] Whether because she wrote in genres that fell out of favor and subsequently out of the literary canon, was merely another vernacular writer seen to copy Boccaccio and add little to her "source," or was left out of male literary discourse due to her sex, Christine clearly did not enjoy the status of an authority in the *Nef des dames*, a work that was written in the vernacular, belonged to the same genre, and appeared in print less than one hundred years after her *Cité des dames*.[77]

A year after the *Nef des dames* appeared in Lyon, Alain Dufour published *Les vies des femmes célèbres* (1504), another catalogue of famous women, in the same city. Dufour does not mention Christine de Pizan, and according to G. Jeanneau, who published the critical edition in 1970, he owes nothing to Champier; he "perhaps" borrowed some details from Christine but very few, if so.[78] Though his greatest debt is to Boccaccio, Dufour, like Champier, treats women more kindly. Jeanneau asserts that Dufour seems to value nontraditional virtues in women, such as courage, physical endurance, and political acumen, while downplaying the more feminine attributes of delicacy, sweetness, and tenderness. Jeanneau concludes, "Sans doute la connaissance du cœur féminin était-elle incomplète chez Dufour" (Dufour's knowledge of the feminine heart was no doubt incomplete), and he finds Dufour a little misogynistic (quelque peu misogyne).[79]

In yet another catalogue of women, *La louenge de mariage* (The praise of marriage), published in 1523, Pierre de Lesnauderie (1450?–1522?), cites

Christine de Pizan in his third chapter on "De la litterature, clergie et science des femmes" (On the literature, learning and science of women): "Of Christiane of Pisa. Now Lady Christiane of Pisa comes to mind, she was very expert in the art of rhetoric and composed several beautiful doctrinals and volumes. And among them she composed the City of Ladies, in which city she brought to light and to memory many virtuous and well-known Ladies. The book is very beautiful and good to see and study for Ladies since it was composed by a woman."[80] Lesnauderie recommends the book especially to women readers, and he groups Christine with other women writers like Sappho, Proba, and Hildegard of Bingen. He seems more familiar with Christine than most writers of the time and had no doubt consulted a manuscript of *Le livre de la cité des dames*. But just a few years later, Jehan du Pré would omit Christine from his 1534 *Palais des nobles dames*, also published in Lyon.

The Rhétoriqueurs, a group of poets that bridges a sizeable critical gap in the querelle des femmes from Christine de Pizan to Marguerite de Navarre, would either ignore or mythologize Christine.[81] Their works, often written for female patrons, provide insight into the evolving attitudes of male writers toward women's bodies and their moral character in the early modern period as well as their place in the literary canon. The Rhétoriqueurs worked in the French and Burgundian courts for two generations of powerful female patrons, including Anne of France, Margaret of Austria, Anne of Brittany, and Marguerite de Navarre. Far from a homogeneous group, these poets nonetheless shared two major characteristics: they heaped praise on their fellow poet–chroniclers and cited Jean de Meun as an important literary predecessor.[82] However, most were either unaware of Christine de Pizan's criticism of de Meun's continuation of the *Romance of the Rose* or, if they knew of it, maintained an odd silence.

While Champier, a practicing physician, ignored Christine in his *Nef des dames*, it is perhaps more surprising that Jean Molinet, a prominent Rhétoriqueur, did as well. He worked as historian and librarian for Margaret of Austria from 1475 to his death in 1507. Sources indicate that Margaret owned a manuscript copy of the *Cité des dames*,[83] but there is no evidence that Molinet read it. However, according to Noël Dupire, editor of the

Rhétoriqueur poetry collection titled *Les faictz et ditz* (Acts and sayings), Molinet borrowed an anecdote about Marguerite de La Rivière (ca. 1330–90) from *Le livre de la cité des dames*.[84] Molinet's version of the anecdote is brief: "Marguerite de La Rivière, a very honest lady, flourishing in the park of nobility, proved worthy, through her great generosity, of opening the rich buds of these pleasant flowers, when she removed her golden crown that she had on her head, and pawned it for the sum of 500 florins and paid the ransom of a very old knight, very renowned in arms, prisoner of war by chance [par fortune] in the Chastellet prison in Paris."[85] Compare this to Christine's longer and more detailed version:

How many generous women of your time can I recall, without having to search in history books? It suffices to recall the great generosity of Marguerite, lady of La Rivière, who is still living. She was married to the late M. Bureau de La Rivière, who was the first chamberlain of the wise King Charles. This lady whose wisdom, virtue, and good morals were always recognized, one day attended a brilliant party given in Paris by the Duke of Anjou, the one who became King of Sicily; there was a great crowd of noble ladies, knights, and gentlemen in fine dress. This lady, who was young and beautiful, looked around her at the brilliant assemblage and realized that an eminent knight of excellent reputation, called Amanion de Pommiers, who has since died, was missing. She remembered this Amanion de Pommiers, despite his advanced age, because his worth and courage remained present in her memory, and she thought that there is no more beautiful ornament for a noble court than men of valor and great reputation, even when they are old. She also asked what this knight was doing that he was not present at the party. Someone answered that he was in the prison of Châtelet because of a debt of 500 francs that he had contracted while participating in tournaments. "Oh! what a shame for the kingdom, said this noble lady, that such a man should be imprisoned for debts, even for one hour!" She took off her splendid diadem that she was wearing, which was solid gold, and put on her long blond hair an ornament of periwinkles; then she gave the diadem to a page and told him: "Go give this diadem as security for what this lord owes so that they will immediately liberate him and he may come here." This was done, to the great praise of this lady.[86]

Evidence of direct borrowing is scarce indeed. In Molinet's version, the knight is a prisoner of war; in Christine's, he is in prison for his debts. Molinet probably found his version of the anecdote in an intermediary written or oral source.

Although few would expect Molinet to mention Christine in his poetry, whether she was the source of the anecdote in his *Chappelet des dames* or not, it is more extraordinary that he fails to mention her in his *Romant de la rose moralisé* (1500), written almost a century after the original querelle de la rose. Molinet attacks Gerson's misreading of the romance, but he never mentions Christine. Instead, he refers to "some notable ladies" (aucunes notables dames) and, as a possible counterpoint to Le Franc's women-slandering Malebouche, he equates these women and others who slander de Meun's romance with that same allegorical figure.[87] Molinet's "notable ladies" is also reminiscent of Montreuil's earlier-cited dismissive phrase "some woman" (quedam mulieram), used to refer to Christine in the querelle de la rose.

Molinet's nephew or godson, Jean Lemaire de Belges, never names Christine either even in his *Couronne margaritique*, written in praise of Margaret of Austria. Margaret may have been an admirer of Christine de Pizan, but Lemaire, a staunch admirer of Jean de Meun, apparently did not share her interest.[88] In a letter addressed to Margaret that includes his works in progress, Lemaire lists a *Palais d'honneur féminin*, but the work, if it ever existed, is no longer extant.[89] In the same letter, he mentions *La couronne margaritique* as a separate work. In that work, he cites several women worthy of praise but no women writers. In fact, the only female writer Lemaire praises in any of his works is Margaret herself.[90] Although the *Couronne*, published posthumously, is generally viewed as profemale, Lemaire refrained from actively engaging in the querelle himself.

Two other Rhétoriqueurs, Jean Marot and Jean Bouchet, only briefly mention Christine. Unlike Lemaire, Marot directly participated in the debate and wrote on both sides. While Marot briefly refers to Christine's "great wisdom" (grande sagesse) in his *La vraye disant advocate des dames* (ca. 1506),[91] he praises de Meun and draws two moral lessons from the *Roman de la rose* in his *Le doctrinal des princesses et nobles dames* (1506–14), one on female idleness and the other on chastity.[92] Marot's general advice for women, as in most doctrinals, is to control their tongues and sexuality. For example, he likens a woman's disloyal mouth to "bitterness covered in honey" (fiel couvert de miel), condemns women who slander or speak ill of others, and chides women who speak too much or too little: "For speaking too much lowers one's gravitas / And too little demonstrates simplicity / [A Princess] should be master of her own tongue." (Car trop parler sa gravité abaisse: / Et le trop peu, monstre simplicité / [Princesse] Estre doit de sa langue maistresse.)[93] He also advises the princess to avoid False Seeming's (Faulx Semblant's) school, a direct reference to de Meun.[94]

Changing genre and gender, Marot adopts a female narrative voice in his forensic monologue *La vraye disant advocate des dames* and turns the tables on those who attack women. In the prologue, the Advocate clearly indicates that there are "serpentine and venomous tongues" that have impugned women's honor.[95] She characterizes slanderers as misogynists and compares them to poisonous snakes: "You, villains with serpentine tongues / who wound your own origin" (vous villains à langue serpentine / Qui murtrissez vostre propre origine); "Asps and venomous vipers / You vomit out insults with your mouths / and vituperations, wounding our kind" (… aspics et venimeux viperes / De voz gueulles vomissez improperes / Et vituperes, murtrissant nostre gerre [genre]); and "Because when you poison our honor / You offend God, law and nature / By blaming us" (Car quant l'honneur de nous envenimez / Vous offencez dieu, la loy et nature / En nous blasmant).[96] Here, Marot has turned the Virgilian passage that de Meun cites in the romance, "to flee the serpent in the grass" (women), into an attack on those who slander women.

While Marot praises de Meun in the *Doctrinal des princesses*, the Advocate in this text compares the romance to Matheolus's *Lamentations* and contrasts it with the *Champion des dames*.[97] The Advocate claims that "Men and women are the same creature; / Defaming one, both are blamed" (L'homme et la femme est mesme(s) creature; / Diffamant l'ung, tous les deux sont blasmez).[98] Through what Helen Swift calls "the male appropriation of the feminine voice," the author attacks "slandering men" (malz embouchez) and defends women's intelligence and moral strength.[99] The Advocate clearly states that men see women as fragile, but like Christine de Pizan, she claims that women possess compensatory virtues like great eloquence, characterized as "honey" in their mouths (in contrast to the "bitterness in honey" stated in the doctrinal), and a cold nature that does not poison or destroy but rather tempers men's anger and excessively hot nature.[100] These virtues more than make up for women's relative physical weakness; moreover, women are well able to defend themselves verbally.[101] The biting tongues of slanderers (mesdisans) wound, and the Advocate refers to *their* venom and equates them with "mallebouche."[102] Malebouche, according to the Advocate,

Leaves an uglier track
than any venomous serpent or toad
Don't doubt at all that the furious thrust
Of a dagger or lance is less dangerous
Than a thrust of the tongue, which erases all honor
With its false report.[103]

Using Evil Tongue, or Male Bouche, in both works to attack and then defend women, as well as attacking and defending de Meun in both works, Marot demonstrates his rhetorical versatility and appears to treat the querelle as a rather sophisticated joke.

While Jean Marot turns Molinet's words (which echo de Meun's) against those who attack women and contrasts Martin Le Franc to de Meun, Jean Bouchet (1476–1550) embraces both in the *Jugement poetic de l'honneur feminin* (1538)—they are both "full of good things" (plains de bonne chose).[104] In the "Apologie" of the *Jugement*, addressed to a noblewoman, Anne de Laval (1505–54), Bouchet finds it absurd that men slander women and claims, as Christine and others do, that although women's bodies are more fragile than men's, their souls are identical.[105] And, he interprets women's supposedly colder nature in a different way: because women are colder, they are more chaste. He also finds women more devout—writers of the time constantly mention "le devot sexe feminin"—and full of pity.[106] The advice to men here, as in Champier's *Nef des dames*, is not to beat women or treat them like servants; sweet persuasions work better due to women's fragile nature.[107]

The most striking difference in Bouchet's work, though, is his praise of women's eloquence and writing. While many Rhétoriqueurs portrayed writing as a predominantly, or even uniquely, male endeavor, Bouchet cites several women writers, including Christine.[108] He had already praised Christine's work in his 1516 *Temple de bonne renommée*:

And they followed Christine of old
Who was once a great poet,
And mother of the orator Castel,
Who did so well that never was there such a case.[109]

In his *Jugement*, he also cites her command of Latin and Greek: "I could never forget the epistles, rondeaux and ballads in the French language . . . of Christine, who knew the Greek and Latin languages, and was mother of Castel, a man of perfect eloquence.[110] In both instances, though, he seems to value Christine more as the mother of fellow Rhétoriqueur Jean Castel than as a writer in her own right. Clearly, Christine was not versed in Greek; here, she becomes more humanist myth than late medieval writer, perhaps indicating she was more often cited than read.

In addition to praising women writers, Bouchet appears more accepting of women readers. He chastises contemporary men who try to prevent women from reading books in French; he sees no such prohibition in the Bible. Jean Gerson himself, he adds, wrote books in the vernacular. He agrees that reading parts of the Bible translated into French may be dangerous for women and that listening to a sermon poses fewer threats.[111] In fact, in the prefatory "Epistre aus lecteurs" (Letter to his Readers) of his three-part doctrinal, *Les triumphes de la noble et amoureuse dame* (1531), Bouchet claims he wrote it especially for those who could not read Latin and to distract women and girls who might otherwise spend their time reading dangerous French translations of the Bible or treatises by German heretics.[112] We can speculate that Bouchet's promotion of female readers and his two works written in praise of women for women patrons might be related, though this also bears witness to an increasing female readership. Clément Marot (1496–1544), Jean Marot's son, clearly knew various Rhétoriqueurs. For example, he knew or knew of Jean Lemaire de Belges: in the preface to his *Adolescence Clémentine* (1532–38), he thanks Lemaire for tutoring him in poetry.[113] And although we have no proof that he was personally acquainted with Molinet, Clément undoubtedly knew of Molinet and had read at least some of his works. Clément refers to both Lemaire and "Molinet aux vers fleuris" in his "Complaincte de monsieur le général Guillaume Preudhomme."[114] He also groups Molinet with Lemaire and Georges Chastellain as "Those from Hainaut [who] sing in full voice" (Ceulx de Haynaut [qui] chantent à pleines gorges) in "Des poëtes françois, à Salel."[115]

Clément was also undoubtedly familiar with the querelle de la rose and Christine's role in the dispute, if not firsthand then through Molinet or his father. Yet he mentions Christine only once in a letter to a Lyonnais writer, Jeanne Gaillarde:

> To my Lady Jeanne Gaillarde of Lyon,
> A woman of great knowledge:
> To win the prize in science and doctrine
> Christine de Pizan was well worthy
> In her time: but your golden Pen
> Would be adored by her today
> If, by divine will, she still lived.
> For just as fire refines Gold,
> Time has refined our language,
> And because of it, your eloquence is sure
> To win the prize.[116]

Christine had clearly acquired the reputation of a learned writer, but few still read her. The French language had changed, and, as Marot indicates, Christine's reputed eloquence was no longer accessible to early modern readers.

Molinet and Lemaire referred to women as fragile and weak while possessing the virtues of piety and pity, but both excluded most, if not all, women writers from the literary canon. Champier took up the defense of women, who, as he claimed in his prologue to the *Nef des dames,* could not read or take up a pen to defend themselves.[117] However, Bouchet's praise of women's writing and eloquence indicates that by the 1530s male writers had become more aware of female writers and readers, even if Christine was still largely absent from the sixteenth-century querelle des femmes.[118] While her works appear in some library collections, like Margaret of Austria's, they were no longer widely read by male or female authors or the reading public. However, a growing female readership increasingly vocal about misogynistic works, especially in the vernacular, no doubt influenced Rhétoriqueurs like Jean Marot, Bouchet, and Marot's son Clément to praise Christine, even if obliquely.

CONCLUSION

Though it has yet to appear, a complete history of the literary reception of Christine's works will hopefully include not only those authors, male and female, who praised and emulated her but also those who either were ignorant of her writings or chose to ignore them. Writing about authors who ignored Christine's accomplishments no more endorses their position than writing about misogyny endorses misogyny.[119] Even though Christine and her role in the querelle may largely have disappeared for various reasons stated earlier, an increasing number of "resisting readers" of medieval romances like the *Roman de la rose* challenged male authors who defended the work or attempted to control its reception. The next chapter will focus on one of the more absurd attempts to control the reception of the *Roman de la rose* and the counterattacks from its readers. Molinet's moralized version reveals much about how a typical Rhétoriqueur viewed women readers, interpreted the courtly love tradition, and used humoral medical theories to advance a "spiritual" love quest that had little to do with women's social status in early modern France.

2

From Physical to Spiritual Love

Molinet's *Romant de la rose moralisé* (1500)
and the Querelle des Femmes

Although much has been written about the *Roman de la rose* and the debate
it generated known as the querelle de la rose, *Le romant de la rose moralisé*, composed by the Rhétoriqueur poet and Burgundian chronicler Jean
Molinet (1435–1507) and published around 1500,[1] has received little critical
attention until recently.[2] The rather copious work (153 folios in the Balsarin
edition), was deemed unworthy of study by various critics for several decades
and has not yet appeared in a modern edition except for an unpublished
dissertation completed by Raymond Andes in 1948.[3] In the introduction
to his edition, Andes asserts that Molinet's moralities in his *Romant de la
rose moralisé* "lack cohesion, are absurd and deserve the vicious criticism
they have received" from such critics as Henry Guy and Pierre Champion.[4] The work, he adds, would only interest linguists, who might find
in it evidence of changes in Middle French, or those who might wish to
study it for "archaeological" reasons in order to gain "psychological insight
[into] the heart and mind of a typical Rhétoriqueur."[5] Some twenty years
later, Rosemond Tuve would also strongly criticize Molinet's "unsuccessful
translation" of the romance, his "bad allegory," and his "dreadful flaw" of
"shattering into fragments the unified work being allegorized."[6] She further
accuses Molinet of "allegorizing a startling but moral work, mak[ing] of it a

grossly immoral book."[7] Jean Dupire, Molinet's biographer and a much more sympathetic reader, could not deny the allegorical mess; most of Molinet's comparisons, he writes, are "disconcerting and even extravagant."[8] Michael Randall, too, has referred to Molinet's lack of "structural coherence" and his "often confusing . . . imagery."[9] However, more recently, Jean Devaux has defended the romance as a work well worth studying.[10]

It is not the aim of this chapter to rehabilitate Molinet's moralization of the romance or declare it a masterpiece of interpretive strategies; his allegories are indeed inconsistent and contradictory. However, his reworking of the romance is still well worth further study because it not only reveals insight into the mind of a typical Rhétoriqueur, as Andes claims, but also provides us an early sixteenth-century reading and attempted defense of a work that was coming under increasing attack for its vulgarity, questionable moral lessons, and unflattering portrayal of women. Molinet's moralized version constitutes an important chapter in both the querelle de la rose and the querelle des femmes.[11] The Rhétoriqueur clearly viewed women as inferior beings who needed help understanding the deeper moral lessons of the romance and who were prone to criticizing what they failed to understand. In his moralization, he demonstrates his gendered views on religion, women's inferior place in society, and the correct process of literary interpretation in his attempts to transform what he considered a misreading of the work as an allegory of physical love, or "amour fatuelle," into a correct reading of it as an allegory of spiritual love, or "amour espirituel." His primary goals then were to defend the romance from accusations that it promoted an illicit type of physical love and to promote a spiritual love quest, a crusade against the Turks to reclaim the Holy Land, a crusade that Molinet hoped Philippe de Clèves, Duke of Ravenstein, would lead.

In the prologue, Molinet tells us that he agreed to write a moralized version of the Roman de la rose for a "very awe-inspiring lord," (tresredoubté seigneur), whom he calls a "champion des dames" and who, he claims, was launching an amorous campaign of his own at the time. In chapter 86, we discover that the "lord" is Philippe de Clèves, Lord of Ravenstein (1459–1528), future author of a treatise on the art of war and military commander for Maximilian I as well as, later, Louis XII.[12] Molinet explains that the

poem had become increasingly difficult to read in the original. To facili-
tate his task, Molinet divided the romance into 107 chapters, to which he
tacked on "moralities" where he attempted to prove that the romance had
hidden meanings and that it was an allegory of spiritual love—not merely
a pornographic manual for seducing young women. Several critics have
already pointed out the general accuracy of Molinet's translation.[13] In this
section I attempt to explain why Molinet does not mention Philippe by
name in the prologue, why the work's publication in 1500 was so timely, and
what Molinet meant by Philippe's "queste amoureuse." In the moralized
version, Molinet uses a pathology of religions in his propagandistic goal
to promote peace among Christian nations that, he hoped, would unite
in a crusade to take back the Holy Land from the Turks, a crusade that he
hoped Philippe de Clèves would, and actually did, lead.

Although Dupire, Devaux, and others have refuted earlier critics who
claimed that the moralized romance was completed around 1483,[14] they do
not explain why Molinet refers to Philippe's "amorous quest" in the 1500
prologue, when Philippe had been married to Françoise de Luxembourg
for several years by then; they married in 1485. Nor do they explain why
Molinet praises the two treaties of Arras in chapter 85 (one in 1435 and
another in 1482)[15] yet maintains an odd silence regarding Margaret's subsequent repudiation by Charles VIII in 1491 and her marriage to Juan of
Castille in 1497.[16] Did Molinet simply begin the work in 1483 and publish
it without revisions several years later? Molinet apparently began his moralizing translation with a future crusade in mind, in the hope that France
and Burgundy would again unite, as they had done in 1435 and 1482. His
"queste amoureuse" described in the prologue refers undoubtedly to a
spiritual love quest, or crusade, rather than a physical one.

In 1483, Maximilian's goal of uniting Christian nations in a crusade
against the Turks seemed within reach. The future Holy Roman Emperor
had just made peace with France by the Treaty of Arras, and his military
leader, Duke Philippe de Clèves, was poised to lead the crusade. But, aided
by France, Flanders immediately rebelled against their new sovereign, and
Maximilian found himself embroiled in ongoing skirmishes with Flemish
forces that lasted until 1492. Instead of leading a crusade against the Turks,

Philippe, his lieutenant general, found himself charged with putting down the Flemish rebellion. In 1488, the Flemish captured Maximilian and forced him to sign a treaty. Philippe, his faithful commander, took Maximilian's place in prison, but the sovereign, now free, failed to keep to the treaty's terms, leaving Philippe in an untenable position. The duke consequently rebelled against Maximilian and joined the Flemish forces. Jean Devaux has demonstrated that throughout his *Chroniques*, Molinet sympathizes more with Philippe than Maximilian in this matter.[17] But as chronicler to Maximilian and his children—Philippe le Beau and Margaret of Austria—he could hardly have published a work that praised Philippe de Clèves while the latter was out of favor with the emperor. In his *Chroniques*, Molinet writes that the duke sought Maximilian out while the latter was on a hunting trip near Malines (Mechelen), Anvers (Antwerp), and Brussels in 1494, but that it was the first time they had met since Philippe's imprisonment. According to Molinet, the duke received a full pardon from the emperor.[18] Nonetheless, relations between the two remained tense, but Philippe was able to offer his services to his own cousin, Louis XII, who ascended the French throne in 1498 and needed Philippe's aid in the Italian Wars. It is perhaps this event that led Molinet to hope again for a future crusade and revise his romance's prologue. In fact, in 1501, Louis placed Philippe in charge of a large fleet of ships to lead just such a crusade against the Turks. In October of that year, Philippe arrived at Mytilene on the Greek island of Lesbos, which the Ottoman sultan Mehmed II had captured in 1462. He laid siege there to the Turks, but the mission failed. In his *Chroniques*, a disappointed Molinet attributes Philippe's defeat to lack of promised reinforcements.[19]

Before the ill-fated "crusade" of 1501, Molinet was apparently confident that the Turks would be pushed back. That explains much of the battle imagery in the prologue, in which Molinet praises Philippe's military prowess and compares love to a battle. Even though this might appear a simple metaphor, it has greater significance in the prologue. From the very first sentence, the author addresses his "lord" and compares Mars and Venus, war and love: "It did not suffice for your very high lordship prospering in the flower of youth to fight under the triumphant banner of Mars, the great god of battles, whose exploits you have seen more than any prince of your time, if with this, burning with amorous sparks, you desire to be champion of ladies following the very pleasant standard of Venus, goddess of Love."[20] Here, it should be noted again that Philippe married Françoise de Luxembourg in 1485 when he was approximately twenty-six and in the "flower of youth." Yet in 1500, at forty-one years of age, he could no longer be considered youthful. The chronicler also speaks of an "amorous artillery" (amoureuse artillerie) more tenderly tempered than the war artillery being forged at that time in Milan. The reference to war in Milan no doubt refers to Louis XII's invasion of Milan in 1499, a campaign in which Philippe played a leading role.

A SPIRITUAL LOVE QUEST OR CRUSADE AGAINST THE TURKS

Molinet states his intent to describe the dangers of love but pauses to define love. First, he cites Augustine's definition of love, "a kind of life which binds or seeks to bind some two together, namely, the lover and the beloved," from a passage where Augustine primarily discusses brotherly love.[21] Then he cites Rabanus Maurus: "In true love, nothing is too hard, nothing too bitter, nothing more grievous, nothing more mortal—and since love is so strong, what iron, what wound, what pain or what death will overcome it."[22] In his *Divine Names*, Denis the Aeropagite finds that "love lowers superiors to inferiors, raises inferiors to superiors, and links equals to equals."[23] In the same paragraph, the loving couples that Molinet names are not male–female, as one would expect, but male companions in arms. For example, he names Theseus and Pirothous (also Perotheus or Piritheus) from Ovid's *Tristia* and Damon and Phinteas from Valerius Maximus's *Factorum et dictorum memorabilium*.[24] Theseus and Pirothous were companions in arms who descended to hell; Theseus tries unsuccessfully to free Pirothous.[25] Damon is willing to die for Phinteas in service to Dionysius of Syracuse. Already, brotherly love and death permeate the prologue.

Molinet then cites passages from Cicero's *De amicitia* (7.23), where the dead live in the memories of their friends; Seneca the Younger's *Epistulae morales ad lucilium* (*Letters on Ethics: To Lucilius*), letter 9 on friendship—"If you wish to be loved, love" (Si vis amari, ama), and Solomon 8:6: "For love is strong like death" (Dilection est forte comme la mort). Molinet adds,

"Love is the impenetrable coat of mail that repels arrows, that sharpens swords/lances, anticipates dangers, cheats death" (Amour est hauberion impenetrable qui les dars rejecte, qui les glaives aguise, qui les perilz actend, qui de la mort se gabe).[26] He also quotes from Virgil's *Eclogues*, "Love conquers all," which Aeneas Sylvius, or Pope Pius II (1405–65), quotes in his love tragedy that ends in death, titled the *Tale of Two Lovers*.[27] Molinet quotes again from the work: "There is not a heart made of flesh but feels the pricks of love" (Il n'est cueur nul s'il est charnel qu'il ne sente les esguillons d'Amours).[28] Then, he adds a proverb: "Whoever loves always dies and is never dead" (Quiconques ayme tousjours meurt et jamais n'est mort).[29] So in this short paragraph, Molinet starts with the love between companions in arms who faced death for love of each other, briefly refers to a recent pope's tragic tale about a forbidden love that led to death, and ends with a proverb about a love that conquers death.

Molinet then outlines three "branches" or types of love: "amour divine," "amour naturelle," and "amour fatuelle."[30] The first and highest is of course "amour divine" (spiritual love), which leads to eternal life; the second, "amour naturelle," is a love that perpetuates the species and promotes harmony and peace among people and nations. He reserves his most strident condemnation for the third kind of love, "amour fatuelle" (foolish love), which leads to death, discord, and eternal damnation.[31] As examples of the latter, Molinet cites the tragic love stories of Jupiter and Callisto, Orpheus and Eurydice, and Pyramus and Thisbe, all cited in Ovid's *Metamorphoses*. Molinet was familiar, of course, with Ovid's *Metamorphoses* as well as its moralized version, *Ovide moralisé*.[32] He also adds a more recent tale of a Florentine who cuts out his eyes and sends them to his lover, who, wishing to send him hers, is prevented from doing so by her parents. She later marries him. In the next tale, which resembles Boccaccio's tale of the eaten heart in the *Decameron*, a Castilian in love with a French woman "par faulte de jouyssance," which can be translated as "for lack of sexual pleasure," goes abroad and dies, requesting that his heart be sent to his beloved after his death.[33] The woman places it in a box, but her husband finds it and feeds it to her in a soup. Shortly afterward, the woman dies. Yet another tale of self-destructive love is included in the manuscript of the *Romant de la rose moralisé* at the Hague:

A young girl from Boulenois was in love with a young man, who, to hold her in perpetual love, placed on her finger a gold ring and promised never to love another. A short time later, the young man entered into an agreement with another girl, to whom he became engaged with the help of his friends; he sent a letter to the first lady asking her, for love of him, to send back his ring. The girl, horribly shocked by this news, took great pains to pull the ring off her finger, but was unable to do so. And, like one touched by the branch of jealousy, half crazed, took a large knife with which one minces meat, put her finger on a block, and in this manner cut it off, and with great anger, she sent to her lover both the ring and the finger.[34]

All three tales demonstrate to what unnecessary extremes "amour fatuelle" can lead. In a long Rhétoriqueur-like definition of "amour fatuelle" that follows these tales, Molinet claims that this kind of love causes a "perturbation of the mind, drying-out of the limbs, shortening of life, perdition of the body, and damnation of the soul."[35] Even philosophers, kings, princes, and dukes suffer from this type of love, and he claims that he could give many more examples of such tales.

Molinet then shifts to those who suffered death for a higher love, martyrs of spiritual and natural love. Among the "champions of our faith," no doubt an allusion to Le Franc's *Champion des dames*, the chronicler cites several who sacrificed themselves for "natural love"—wives for husbands, husbands for wives, parents for children, children for parents, subjects for lord, and lord for subjects; he adds that even infidels have sacrificed themselves for their idols. Yet, Christians today, he laments, are reluctant to embrace martyrdom for God. "No one wants to die for the people, no one kills himself for ladies" (Nul ne veult mourir pour le peuple; nul ne se tue pour les dames).[36] Here, Molinet conflates "amour naturelle" and "amour divine," equating lovesickness that leads to death to abject devotion that leads to death in a holy war: "And even though their sufferers (patients) often say that they are very sick for the love of these women, yet they never die. The most painful wound and the most grievous torment that they have to bear after feigned sighs and tears are the trembling of white fevers."[37] According to Cotgrave, "blanches fièvres" (white fevers) refers to the pallor of lovesickness ("mal d'amour"). Molinet claims that lovesickness is more often feigned than fatal, just as true religious duty is more often talked about than acted upon.

Molinet claims that the believer professes love but is unwilling to die for Christ. In the next sentence, he addresses Philippe (without naming him) as "my very awe-inspiring prince who desires to be a student in the superb university of Love," and then refers to his lord's love quest (queste amoureuse).[38] As noted above, many have remarked that this would be strange in 1500, since Philippe had been happily married for 15 years. The "love quest" here, though, is a spiritual one—the crusade that Philippe pursued in 1501 to reconquer the Holy Land and other territories lost to the Turks, a goal that Molinet had already promoted in several earlier works, such as in his *Chronicles* and "La complainte de Grece."

MOLINET'S HUMORAL THEORY OF RELIGION

In several parts of his "moralized" version of the *Romance of the Rose*, Molinet attacks Turks, as he does repeatedly throughout his chronicles.[39] He sees Islam as a religion of hypermasculinity and unbridled sexuality and Muslims as polygamists and practitioners of "folle amour." In the ninety-sixth chapter, he interprets Jean de Meun's "reign of Jupiter" as a "reign of Mohammed," whom he describes as a "false prophet and destroyer of our faith" (faulx prophete, dislapideur de nostre foy), the "devil incarnate" (dyable incarné), and an "execrable deceiver" (prevaricateur execrable).[40] According to the Rhétoriqueur, the prophet practiced deception and magic and inflicted a horrible "wound" on the Church of God. He characterizes Mohammed as a sly imposter who, to convert Jews, required his followers to be circumcised, and who accepted—or pretended to accept—Christ's virgin birth in order to "pervert" Christians. Yet, Molinet adds, no doubt to scandalize his women readers, that Mohammed wrote in his Koran that a man can have up to four "legitimate" wives and can divorce them at will.[41] According to Molinet, Mohammed bragged that he could sleep with as many women as he liked because the angel Gabriel had revealed to him that, in so doing, he would father future prophets. Molinet describes the people taken in by Mohammed as simple and idiotic, and he offers as evidence Mohammed's "ridiculous exaggeration" that the angels in paradise "are so big that one can measure a league between their eyes."[42] He further describes the "reign of Mohammed" as a time when complete, shameless, ignominious, and detestable carnality began, a carnality that even savage beasts would refuse to practice. Mohammed, this "super-stitious and profane devil incarnate," he writes, converted "Alitia" and some Jews as well as "bad Christians," who had abandoned themselves to sloth and lust. "Alitia" is no doubt "Aïsha," Mohammed's child bride, whom he supposedly married when she was six or seven; the marriage was purportedly consummated when she was nine. Molinet typifies Jews as "cowardly, effeminate, and lily livered" (lasches et effeminez et trespu-sillanimes) and "bad Christians" as "lecherous and carnal, given over to sloth and miserable lasciviousness" (lubriques et carneux, habandonnez a fetardie et a lascivité miserable).[43] Molinet tells us that a third of the world, including Greece, Turkey, Syria, and "Barbarie," is "intoxicated" with Mohammed's "poison," and the wound has yet to heal.

After a lengthy, "literal," and confusing—or confused—interpretation of Jupiter's reign, where Jupiter names the stars and teaches both men and animals to hunt, Molinet reserves his most impressive interpretive strategy for the part where Jupiter puts an end to the long primal spring or golden age during which, according to Molinet, Christianity reigned supreme before he (Jupiter/Mohammed) divided the year into four seasons or the world into four types of people: Jews, Christians, Sarrasins (Muslims), and pagans. Molinet then compares the four seasons to the four major religions and the four humors (see table 2). In his system, Muslims are choleric; Jews, phlegmatic; pagans, melancholic; and Christians, sanguine.

To my knowledge, no one else has defined religious groups quite so systematically by humoral personality types. Molinet sees Muslims as choleric—that is, dominated by yellow bile, which was considered hot and dry; they are consequently overly aggressive, prone to anger, jealous, and lustful.[44] He sees Islam as an age of "virility" or puberty, a dangerous time of unbridled passion. While he criticizes Muslims for their unbridled sexual passion and aggressive personalities, frightening his female readers with

TABLE 2. Molinet's humoral theory of religions

Religion	Age	Season	Time of day	Element	Complexion
Christianity	Youth	Spring	Morning	Air	Sanguine (hot & moist)
Islam	Virility	Summer	Midday	Fire	Choleric (hot & dry)
Pagan	Maturity	Fall	Evening	Earth	Melancholic (cold & dry)
Judaism	Old age	Winter	Night	Water	Phlegmatic (cold & moist)

stories about Muslims' multiple wives, he reserves his greatest criticism for Jews, whom he typifies as phlegmatic: cold and humid. Women were also considered cold and humid. And like women, who were seen traditionally as gossips, he typifies Jews as *mesdisans*, or slanderers. Christ, he says, was crucified because he revealed his secrets to Jewish slanderers who betrayed him.[45] Medieval and early modern medical authorities, like Albertus Magnus, agreed that Jews were weak and effeminate, but they associated Jews more often with the melancholic temperament than the phlegmatic. Some even claimed Jews suffered from hemorrhoids, a debilitating loss of blood comparable to the female menses.[46] According to Molinet, phlegmatic Jews were linked to old age, a time when men are both feeble and impotent.

Through gendered language and nonnormative sexuality, Molinet demonstrates here his view that Christians were "sanguine," the ideal humoral type, but criticizes bad Christians for their feigned devotion and reluctance to die in a spiritual love quest or crusade; he compares them to fainthearted or false lovers unwilling to die for their beloved. Good, sanguine Christians keep to a happy medium between the choleric Arabs, who are hot and dry and motivated by lust, and phlegmatic Jews, who, like women, are cold and moist and, consequently, weak, fainthearted slanderers. Molinet often attacks slanderers throughout his moralized romance and pairs virile male sexuality with effective rhetorical performance.

While Molinet promoted a spiritual love quest, a crusade against the Turks, in the *Romant de la rose moralisé*, he also attempted to counter criticism against de Meun by offering moral interpretations and excuses for the misogynistic passages in the romance that slanderers, especially women, had attacked.[47] In doing so, he actively participated in the querelle des femmes on the side of the misogynists. Although Molinet authored the profemale *Chappelet des dames* in praise of Mary of Burgundy, the aging chronicler also wrote several crude and misogynistic works.[48] Even the moralities in the romance are peppered with misogynistic proverbs like "All women have their eyes on money" (Toutes femmes ont l'œil a l'argent) and "Women are inclined to cry and weep at will" (Femmes sont enclines a plourer et ont larmes a commandement).[49] He also speaks of the "subtlety and the malice of women" (subtilité et malice des femmes) and the "fragility of human nature more fickle than women's minds" (fragilité de nature humaine, plus variable que pensee de femme).[50] Yet, like others, he claims that he means only to defend men from "bad" women.

However, in the *Romant de la rose moralisé*, Molinet often ignores, excuses, or tempers de Meun's misogyny in his *moralités*. Here is just one example: "The author wants to justify some words inserted in his book to the displeasure of the feminine sex . . . And because his excuse seems valid and honest, I will refrain from offering any gloss" (Se veult justiffier l'acteur d'aucunes parolles qui semblent estre couchees en son livre au desplaisir du femenin sexe . . . Et pour ce que son excuse semble estre licite et honneste, je me deporte d'en faire quelque place).[51] Only once does he find that de Meun has gone too far in his attacks on women, when the poet states that good women are scarcer than phoenixes:

> Oh terrible opinion too hotly interjected with neither measure nor discretion, so quickly that it rings in the ears of women making their hearts tremble more than leaves on a tree. And if today women hearing these words were to tear at their clothing like the princes of old in Judea tore their robes when they heard blasphemies, not even a hat would

remain on their heads, because all [their clothing] would be torn to pieces. It seems to me that these words are harsh enough to destroy the honor of ladies. It seems to me that for God's Pleasure one could find a way to retract, soften, or modify them. . . . Good women, if there were any at that time, were through the corruption of gifts fallen, without holding firm like the women of today, who are very self-assured, just, and firm. *And if, as they say, Master Jehan de Meung was a Christian and good Catholic when he wrote this romance, he should never have written these words which must weigh heavily on his conscience.*[52]

Molinet appears to doubt the author's intent, and he clearly admits that there is room for a morally reprehensible interpretation of the text; however, he again equivocates, asserting that good women (preudefemmes) must have been scarce in those days unlike in the present day; or perhaps the author was suggesting a hypothetical future in which good women might become scarce. He adds that if there were ever a shortage of good women in the future, God would surely provide.[53] Tuve refers to Molinet's "playful humor" in this passage and posits that he abandoned himself to gaiety amid the ridiculousness of his task.[54] More likely, it appears to be the Rhétoriqueur's somewhat awkward attempt to make light of a passage that female readers might find offensive, while providing a comic touch for his male readers.

However, Molinet clearly did not consider women equal to men. In the following passage, Molinet moralizes and contradicts the Old Woman's claim that women were once free, leaving no doubt that he considered them inferior:

Women, who from their earliest beginnings, as the Old Lady says, were free without being subject to men, no more to one than to another, are compared to creatures newly born in the world, who are indifferent about obeying one law or another. But when, through the advice or good care of their parents and friends, they are baptized, they are bound to obey the Christian law on pain of damnation. Women should recognize that Eve, our first mother, from the day of her creation, was, by divine command, subject to the first man. What prerogative of freedom do they want to have when so many creatures are subject to others? We see that water extinguishes fire, fire corrects the earth, earth stops water, and water masters the air when a small rain stops great winds. Horses are tamed by the bridle, the bear by the muzzle, and the monkey by the leash [brayere]. And woman, to acquire honor and salvation, will be restrained by shame; shame will be the mirror where she will cast her eyes. Shame will be the mirror [grommette] that will save her from carnal concupiscence, and if Helen, as well as other miserable ladies, had first seen themselves in the light of shame and regret, so many high and great personnages would never have been killed, gobbled up in the jaws of Cerberus.[55]

Like many early modern authors, Molinet believed that women's baser and more animal nature is mainly controlled and even redeemed by their natural shame. And although Molinet blames Adam for eating the apple in the garden of Eden, for him, Eve remains the "cause of the mortal sin" (cause de ce mortel delict).[56] In fact, Molinet imagined women as constantly tempted to sin through their close association with the world of the senses. In moralizing the story of Zeuxis and the five beautiful women whom he painted to portray Nature in the *Roman de la rose*, Molinet reveals his attitude toward the female body:

His brush would have failed him, and his hand would have trembled, because five ladies who will be named after this were imperfect regarding the beauty of Nature's five sense organs. Eve, our first mother, was created in a state of innocence by our supreme Maker, the unequaled in the world; but she widened her throat, swallowing the forbidden fruit. Rebecca was very wise, but she deceived her husband by using the odor of Esau's clothing to please her son Jacob. Rachel exceeded the beauty of her era, but her evil hands stole her father's idols. Dinah, daughter of the good patriarch Jacob, was a good sort, but her roaming eyes were so curious to see new things that she was seized and raped by the son of the lord of Shechem. Marie, sister of Moses and Aaron, had the gift of prophecy but she did not know how to hold her tongue back from spreading rumors, so she suffered from leprosy [mesellerie] for seven days.[57]

All five senses are represented here by their respective organs: taste (throat), smell (the husband's nose), touch (hands), sight (eyes), and hearing (ear and tongue). Thus the parts of a woman's body lead to sins of the senses. A woman's body is thus transformed from an object of physical beauty and perfection to a means of spiritual pollution and imperfection. Molinet apparently shared de Meun's low opinion of women and was willing to alter his sources, even biblical passages, to cast a moral lesson that demonstrated women's inferior nature. Although Eve's "widened throat," which allows her to eat the forbidden fruit, demonstrating the sense of taste, is odd,[58] Rebecca's act of deceiving her husband by the "odor of Esau's clothing" conflicts with biblical accounts. In fact, Jacob's false hairiness, orchestrated by his mother Rebecca, allowed him to deceive his father and receive the hairier Esau's blessing, which indicates that the sense of touch is more appropriate here than the sense of smell.[59] If Molinet had claimed that Rebecca's story involved the sense of touch, he would not have been able to accuse Rachel, whose "mauvaises mains" (evil hands), representing the sense of touch, stole her father's idols.[60] As for the sense of sight, Molinet blames Dunah, or Dinah, the victim, for her own rape by Shechem because her curious eyes sought out novelties.[61] Even in biblical accounts Dinah is an innocent victim, and her brothers avenge the disgrace. Finally, the prophet Marie, or rather Miriam, sister of Moses and Aaron, represents the sense of hearing. Unable to keep her mouth from "murmuring," her punishment was to be afflicted with leprosy, an obvious outward manifestation of an inner corruption. Yet Aaron, also guilty of "murmuring" against Moses, did not suffer the same fate. How this relates to hearing is also odd—evidently Miriam repeated what she had heard. Through a heavy-handed manipulation of the allegory, Molinet even adds to the misogyny in his moralized version with his claim that "murmuring" is a feminine, or at least effeminate, trait.

As Ian Maclean has noted, Renaissance women were considered gossips and as unable to control their tongues as much as their sexuality. Molinet equates gossips and slanderers with "murmurers," who share that trait with two groups of men unable to perform sexually: one by nature and the other due to its members' religious vows. For instance, in chapter 19 Molinet cites Philippians 2:14 on murmuring: "Omnia agite sine murmuratione" (Do all things without murmuring), adding, "Murmuring is strongly prohibited in religion and just as the ravishing wolf takes the fat sheep, not by the feet, by the ear or by the lip, but by the throat, thus the enemy takes the murmuring cleric by his lying mouth."[62] Like clerics, old men too are prone to murmur or gripe: "And because man in his old age has lost the strength of his members and the ability *to raise his staff*, he endeavors to gossip and threaten, because there is nothing more cutting than the tongue" (Et pour ce que l'homme en son senecte aage a perdu la force de ses membres et le poix de *lever le baston*, il s'efforce lors de mesdire et menacer, car il n'a riens plus trenchant que la langue).[63] Clerics and old men, unable to perform sexually—that is, "raise their staffs"—exercise their tongues instead.

In fact it was a cleric—Jean Gerson—and Christine de Pizan who first attacked the romance orally (in Gerson's sermons) and in writing with their tongues and pens. From the prologue, Molinet fears that he will be attacked by "sharp, serpentine tongues (langues serpentines affillees).[64] The sharp tongues of critics appear often in Molinet's moralizations.[65] In a direct reference to the querelle de la rose, he characterizes critics of de Meun as "disciples of Murmuring," who grumble, complain, and hold the short swords of their tongues ready to attack:

> Several grumblers, disciples of Murmuring, have often drawn out halfway the short swords of their mouths to attack the author of this book saying that he has outrageously dishonored the female sex with his *biting writings*, but they should be pardoned since they are poor innocents, ignorant of the double meaning in the text of the said book. Some foolish and terrestrial lovers, given over to lewdness and full of lasciviousness, interpret it to their advantage and according to their own desire. "Whoever is of the earth speaks of the earth," but those who love spiritual pleasure, "which comes from heaven," they find good fruit, good happiness, and the honor of salvation. And it cannot be assumed that such a spiritual man as master Jean de Meun, more angelic than human, would want to besmear [touiller] the tail of his old age in the sewage of infamy, and dirty his renown, without extracting a profitable lesson.[66]

"Biting writings" (mordans ecritures) combines the mouth and the pen, the oral and the written word. Again, Molinet contrasts foolish, carnal love, "amour fatuelle," with spiritual love. Women and other victims of such love were incapable of understanding the "double meaning" (double exposicion) of the text. Only those who loved "spiritual pleasure" over the pleasures of the flesh could interpret the work correctly.

Yet Molinet only refers to one misreading critic by name in the text— Jean Gerson (1363–1429), Chancellor of the University of Paris, who a century earlier had sided with Christine de Pizan in the querelle de la rose.[67] Here the Rhétoriqueur attacks Gerson's critique of de Meun's dénouement, the plucking of the rose:

> Master Jean Gerson, a great authority in theology and possessing an excellent reputation, composed a book titled the "Condemnation of the Romance of the Rose" at the request and in support of *some notable ladies*, but in so doing he stopped at the literal meaning *without unraveling the spool* [*destouiller la fusée*]. He reacted like a small child to whom one has given a large green walnut, who, as soon as he has it in his hand, puts it in his mouth, acting as though it were an apple, and when it tastes bitter, he throws it down. But if he had the wisdom to remove the rind and the shell and to peel it, he would find the kernel of the nut very good and delicious. This venerable doctor, master Jean Gerson, who was not a child, but one of the great scholars of the world, stopped at disapproving of the greenness of this romance, which is *amour folle* that lasts just a short time, while detesting the lechery for the bitterness that one finds in the end, and [he] preferred to apply the subtlety of his mind to difficult matters and high speculation rather than to search for the very sweet and savory fruit in this hard and bitter shell.[68]

Jean de Montreuil had earlier accused those who attacked the romance of having read the great work only superficially, if at all, and he compared them to "drunks discussing at the dinner table" who too quickly attack such an "important [romance] conceived and written with the sweat and hard work of many days and nights."[69] Here, Molinet offers a detailed and metaphorical portrayal of the correct reading process with several comic elements typifying Gerson's misreading of the romance as a superficial, literal, and childlike perusal. This type of misreading was considered female, sensory, and pagan, while a more sophisticated reading was held by Molinet and his contemporaries as male, intellectual, and Christian.[70] "To unravel the spool" (destouiller la fusée), a particularly feminine metaphor, was no doubt intended to portray the chancellor's misreading as effeminate also. But then, somewhat paradoxically, Molinet excuses Gerson's misreading as the hasty judgment of a doctor and cleric with more theoretical and abstract matters on his subtle mind (engin); Gerson was undoubtedly distracted from these weighty matters by "some notable ladies" (aucunes notables dames), whom Molinet neither notes nor names.[71] No doubt Christine de Pizan numbered among them, but Molinet never mentions her anywhere in this work or elsewhere.[72] Molinet does not dare place Gerson among the group of critics whom he characterizes as motivated by lust; rather, he refers to such misreaders as slanderers, and he often equates them with Malebouche (also Male Bouche and Malle Bouche), the allegorical figure in the Roman de la rose. He calls Malebouche a murmurer several times in the text,[73] and murmuring (from the Latin murmurare, already negative in Roman historiogaphy) is also clearly declared an evil in Molinet's moralizations.

Molinet's view of the dangerous aspect of tongues as well as their close relationship to sexual performance is evident in the following long passage, where he refers to both tongues and penises as "staffs" or rods" (bastons) and compares them to swords and daggers. Here, the chronicler attempts to defend de Meun's use of the words couilles (balls or testicles) and vit (penis), which often scandalized medieval critics of the work:

In the preceding chapter Reason mentioned two, even three human members, which are the tongue, the testicles, and the penis . . . By what member can our Lord be better served, adored, praised, honored, admired, sought after [requis], blessed, and thanked than by the precious member of the tongue in whose form the Holy Spirit descended on the apostles? By what member can Nature be better served, increased, sustained, continued in its human species, than by the above-mentioned genital members, who are the hammers, anvils, tongs, furnace, bellows, and instruments by which nature forges [husque] and hammers constantly in order to have new vassals? There are no other comparable instruments by which so many noble and content personages have been fabricated on earth, worthy of being known, named, admired, and exalted above all others. I don't know how the Lover, who could not pluck the Rose without these [instruments], would want to reject them so villainously, unless it is because innumerable evils have come into this world through the misdeeds [mesus] of those who did not control them. I cannot ignore that the tongue is like a deadly *staff* that is large, cutting, and sharp on both sides like a *sword*, whose mouth is the scabbard and whose teeth are the guards, by whom a thousand men have received death through its cutting and serpentine venom; *but this pitiful case does not arise under its own power but by the indiscretion of those who have not known how to hold, lead, and unleash it.* In like manner I am not saying that male genitals are not marvelous *rods* in the manner of Flemish *daggers*, and [I know] that through the energetic pace of those who put them into service, cities are crushed [fondues], kingdoms destroyed and spoiled, and virgins deflowered; and yet it is not the fault of the balls nor of the penises, by which some women would much rather be struck and lanced ten times over than from a single blow from a sharp tongue.[74]

He compares the tongue to the Holy Ghost that praised, honored, and adored "our Lord," signifying divine love. Testicles and penises are the tools that Nature uses to reproduce the human species, signifying natural love. Tongues and penises are like swords and daggers that cause harm to others only when their owners cannot control them. Uncontrolled tongues have caused men's deaths through their venom, while uncontrolled male genitals have destroyed cities and kingdoms and raped virgins. Yet, Molinet cannot resist a measure of levity here as he claims that some women would rather be "struck" by a penis ten times than once by a sharp tongue.

According to Carla Mazzio, the word "tongue" in English (like *langue* in French, *glossa* in Greek, and *lingua* in Italian) is both a synecdoche for the body and a metonym for language, a "slippery" organ that is both subject and object, active and passive.[75] An "unruly organ," Mazzio adds, it seems to have a mind of its own, which often leads to isomorphic relations between the tongue and penis, "that other bodily member with an apparent will of its own."[76] She writes, "[As] associations between tongue and penis became more explicit in the sixteenth and seventeenth centuries, so too did the imagined relationship between rhetorical and sexual performance."[77]

Molinet also demonstrates his ambivalence toward tongues, which he considered good when controlled and evil when out of control, and the connection in his thought between the tongue and penis—representing rhetorical and sexual performance, respectively—in two of his extended metaphors or allegories: the story of Judith and Holophernes and de Meun's penis–plow metaphor. In the former, which follows chapter 54 of the *Romant de la rose moralisé*, "Comparison of False Seeming and Abstinence, Who Cut the Throat of Evil Tongue, to Judith and Abra, Who Cut Off the Head of Holophernes," Judith overcomes the evil-tongued Holophernes not just with her sensual power but, more important, with her eloquence:

False Seeming and Abstinence, who, under the cover of disguises, destroyed Evil Tongue, continually *murmuring* about the deeds of lovers, can be compared to Judith and Abra, her servant, who in order to vanquish the unfortunate, serpentine tongue of Holophernes, reviling the children of Israel, took up the cloth of happiness to accomplish a work of sadness, a language made up of soft laughter to engender horrible outcries, a hardy and *virile courage* in a *frail and feminine breast*, and so perfumed, saturated, and adorned [was she] with joyous words that, by means of the aid of the supreme Ruler, who directed the blow, Judith with her own knife cut the throat of the cruel Holophernes, so that never again would he mutter [bourbeta] a single word. Jesus Christ, in a similar manner, and his very humble Virgin Mother, wanting to silence the lies of the prince of darkness, who with false and *deceiving cacklings and gurglings* discouraged true and loyal lovers of the high, divine essence, disguised themselves in order to wander in the world, because Nature did not recognize the Mother nor understand that She was a pure virgin. And the Enemy devoted himself to the great wonder of the Son, who was dressed in humanity and in the clothing of true lovers, all-powerful God, eternal Creator. Nonetheless both the Mother and Son through holy works, lively words and virtuous sermons worked so well that infernal Evil Tongue, who was biting, obstructing, and devouring everyone, had his own *cursed tongue cut out*. And they did so not with a mere razor but with a sharp and pointed lance. And when Evil Tongue had been silenced, the door of heaven was opened to all who wish to see the very sweet and fair welcome of the divine countenance.[78]

Here, Molinet juxtaposes Judith's verbal eloquence (*joyeuses paroles*) with the slanders, or animallike babblings or gurglings, of the serpent-tongued Holophernes; however, there is no mention of Holophernes's slanders of the Jewish people in the Apocryphal Judith 7–16 or in *Le mystère de Judith et Holofernés*, a work also published around 1500 and recently attributed to Molinet.[79] The Rhétoriqueur strays far afield from the biblical passage in order to preach about the bad effects of slander: in a description bearing a striking resemblance to a castration scene, Judith, with the aid of Abra[80]— whom Molinet then equates with Jesus and Mary, respectively—wields both a sharp tongue and a sword to silence and cut the throat of Holophernes, whom Molinet compares to the devil: an infernal Malebouche. Molinet is careful to specify that the virago Judith uses a lance, a warlike weapon, rather than a razor, a domestic item. It is also noteworthy that although Judith and Abra cut off the Assyrian general's head, Jesus and Mary sever the devil's *tongue*, demonstrating that in Molinet's thought Malebouche is synonymous with "mauvaise langue" (evil tongue) and an out-of-control sexuality. He thus places emphasis on the tongue's intractability and the need to control it. Here, the sexual roles are reversed: Judith is on the side of the intellect while Holophernes represents the body; the Jewess plays the masculine and dominant role (viril couraige), and her eloquence is virtuous and powerful, while Holophernes's words are described as ineffectual, animal sounds, "cacklings," an expression more often used to describe women's discourse, as in hens' cackling. Molinet's rewriting of the story definitely bears both sexual and rhetorical overtones as Judith seduces, controls, and then conquers the serpent-tongued Holophernes through her superior eloquence, while he lacks both linguistic and sexual control.

In a second allegory, Molinet again pairs sexual and rhetorical performance by moralizing the de Meun passage where Genius preaches that all men should plow the field of nature or employ their styluses to write their names in posterity, both thinly veiled metaphors for the sex act. Here Molinet, who earlier had accused clerics of exercising their tongues because they could not perform sexually, now transforms the metaphor of the stylus/plow (penis) writing on tablets or fallow fields (women's wombs) into a stylus/tongue, writing on the tablets of women's minds or souls, thus transforming a carnal act into a spiritual one. Molinet interprets the metaphor to designate rhetorical rather than sexual performance. He urges clerics to use their tongues to write on the minds of the "rational creatures" before them, thus providing an oral gloss to the written text:

The state of the clergy is shown to us through the tablets that Genius mentions. The styluses [pens] of writers are like the pointed and sharp tongues of lettered people, like sermon givers, orators, and extractors of vices, used to insert virtues. And the precious tablets are the souls of reasonable creatures who come before them. For Aristotle says that the soul in the newness of creating is a type of blank slate desiring to be imprinted and painted with good morals and science. But today our writers are so hesitant [pausiers?] and our printers so faint-hearted that they use the blunt end of the stylus and do not dare heat the wax to write a good *exemplum*; and if they print some letter it will disappear the next day. The others, on the other hand, are so crude and outrageous, great braggarts and troublemakers that they penetrate and break the wax and the tablets with their very heavy points and the poor souls are so frightened, sad, and scared that they begin to despair. Whatever good subject matter they have at hand, if they do not maintain the proper form and tone and if they do not know how to follow a straight line, then they convert praise to reproach, honor to horror, and felicity to ferocity. With such styluses and venomous tongues was our Savior vilified on earth when by the claws [griffes] and hooks/writings [graffes] of scribes and pharisees he was chopped into pieces and undone [degraffez]. "Their tongues were sharpened." Such disheveled [eschemelés or eschevelés?] writers should consider the quantity and quality of their tablets as they drive on their styluses without disfiguring and follow the model and imitate the tablets of Moses which God wrote with his hand; they should follow the middle path without smearing or hacking.[81]

Molinet has transformed de Meun's extended metaphor on sexual practices that lead to procreation into an extended metaphor on effective writing/oratory; this is the only place where Molinet directly comments on the responsibility of "lettered people" to provide a correct, moral interpretation. He describes writers (greffiers) of the time, whom we might call commentators or literary critics, as either too heavy-handed or too fainthearted with their moralizing; they therefore either break the tablet or leave no lasting impression. In like manner, orators use their "sharp and piercing tongues" to insert virtues and extract vices, but too often they either frighten their audiences with their heavy-handed moralizing or leave no lasting moral lesson on the tabulae rasae of innocent souls. No doubt Molinet is speaking here of women. According to Ian Maclean, women were thought to have better memories than men; he states that "a combination of cold and moist [humors] produces a retentive memory because, like wax, impressions can be registered easily and remain fixed on cold and moist substances."[82] Molinet suggests that such writers/orators consider the makeup of their audience: "Such ... writers should consider the quantity and quality of their tablets before they apply their styluses" (Telz ... escrivains doyvent considerer les quantitez et qualitez des tables ains qu'ilz y fischent leurs greffes).[83]

Molinet appears to consider the diversity of his audience when dividing his moralized version of the *Roman de la rose* into easily digestible chapters with accompanying moral interpretations, thus providing written *exempla* for these orators, who would then provide a correct oral interpretation of the written word, too often misunderstood or purposely misinterpreted, with the spoken word, thus shaping the reception of the text for both sophisticated and unsophisticated readers/hearers. Thus, Tuve's criticism of Molinet's "dreadful flaw" of "shattering into fragments the unified work being allegorized" can be countered if one considers that Molinet did not write his moralized version to be read as a unified whole or as a substitute for the *Roman de la rose* but instead to serve as a supplement to the written text and as material for homilies.[84] By encouraging clerics to put their tongues, or substitute penises, to work in order to guide readers/hearers to a correct, moral interpretation, Molinet also posits that exegesis is primarily a male domain and that oral discourse can be used to control reception of the static printed text. According to Mazzio, many "early modern writers and grammarians took pains to assert the absolute primacy of the spoken over the written [word] . . . The imposition of orality onto textuality in many ways constitutes a resistance to the graphic, the decontextualized word."[85] With the *intentio auctoris* in doubt, or at least no longer easily discernible, it becomes the duty of the writer/orator, the experienced and well-intentioned male reader, to serve as intermediary and thus provide a moral context, especially for inexperienced women readers such as Christine de Pizan and the other "notable ladies" who had criticized de Meun's text.

Since Molinet apparently believed that both tongues and penises were unruly organs to be used for both good and evil, and that there were at least two separate groups that misread the romance (a group of the evil-minded and evil-tongued and another group of innocents—no doubt primarily female), his apparent contradiction in allegorizing *Malebouche* as *Sinderesis*, or Conscience, in chapters 37 and 82 can also be explained.[86] In chapter 37, titled "Male Bouche Compared to Sinderesis," Molinet likens *Malebouche* to a *bad* conscience: "One means by Evil Tongue, who day and night pricks and bites, Remorse of Conscience or Sinderesis, which awakens the poor sinner and is never content. It is the superior part of Reason which, like a brightly burning spark, can never be extinguished . . . to accomplish and satisfy the penances so that Evil Tongue, Remorseful Conscience, has no cause to murmur."[87] Sinderesis comes from the Greek συντήρησις, meaning "careful guarding or watching." The *Oxford Universal Dictionary* defines it as "that function or department of conscience which serves as a guide for conduct." This apparent contradiction has bothered most critics of the work, because it seems to depart from Molinet's earlier and sustained characterization of Malebouche as evil.

However, chapter 82, which bears the title "The Woman Who Does Not Cease Disgracing and Accusing Her Husband Conforms to Sinderesis, which Often Remorselessly Causes Remorse in Man's Conscience" (La femme qui ne cesse de obprobrier et accuser son mary se conforme a Sinderesis, qui souvent mort et remort la conscience de l'homme), offers a possible explanation for the contradiction. In this chapter, obviously intended to appease women readers, Molinet counters de Meun's widely criticized interpretation of a Virgilian passage—that man should flee the serpent, that is, woman, and not reveal his secrets to her—by stating that this admonition is both untrue and unacceptable.[88] Too circumspect to call de Meun a liar or even a slanderer, Molinet instead assures his readers that times no doubt have changed. Finally, he compares a wife to a man's conscience in that she is neither bad nor good but simply reflects the man's own conduct, a common argument used in the querelle des femmes:

> I imagine that the literal meaning of the above can be construed in a completely different way, *not to the detriment of ladies, but greatly to the benefit of men.* If I say that a woman who sees her husband sad and does not cease to ask him his thoughts is properly compared to sinderesis, a very excellent, diligent, and subtle virtue. And as the theologians say, Synderesis is the motivating force of the soul, stimulating the senses of man to cling to the good and reject evil. It is like the refined woman who seeks the source of the trouble, pricks, needles, and scolds like the spark of man's conscience; thus she ceases not to encircle from top to bottom in such a way that she pulls from his heart cruel vices, in order to so purge him by confession that he might be at peace with his conscience. And in doing this, nothing must be hidden; all must be discovered; all must be revealed in order for him to be returned [reduit] to a sure state of grace.[89]

Departing from his usual anagogical interpretation of passages from de Meun, Molinet adopts a "literal" mode of analysis here—perhaps as a direct appeal to his female readers—asserting that it depends on a man's actions whether his conscience is good or bad. He thus changes the moral lesson from one that slanders or harms women (au detriment des femmes) to one that "helps" men (a l'avance des hommes), and he also changes a negative portrayal of women to a positive one. Rather than slandering her husband and telling his secrets to all, a refined woman (fine femme) should be privy to all her husband's secrets and serve as the man's conscience, and a man should watch his own conduct and give her no cause to "murmur."

The *Romant de la rose moralisé* demonstrates that at least this Rhétoriqueur still found it necessary to defend de Meun from critics' attacks, especially from those who accused the poet of misogyny and vulgarity.[90] However, in his frequently half-hearted defense of de Meun, Molinet discloses as much information about his own theory of reading and his own misogyny as he does about the text he moralizes. Through the allegorical figure Malebouche, he characterizes critics of the romance as evil-tongued misreaders, but he nonetheless delineates different sets of misreaders: experienced, primarily male misreaders, motivated by lust, who interpret it to their advantage; old men who can no longer "lever le baston" and exercise their tongues instead; and women who have nothing but their tongues to wag. The Rhétoriqueur shows much sympathy for the latter, who were largely illiterate or, if literate, inexperienced in literary exegesis; he urges clerics not to use their tongues to criticize works like the *Roman de la rose*, even though Gerson had attacked the latter in his sermons, but rather to offer sermons that interpret the text as an allegory of divine love.[91] Molinet places all responsibility on the experienced, male readers or clerics to use their tongues to write on the retentive, cold, and moist wax tablets of female minds. By offering chapter moralities in his *Romant de la rose moralisé*, Molinet provides *exempla* for such sermons in his attempt to control the reception of a static and misunderstood written text and put an end to the literary debate on the *Roman de la rose*.

CLÉMENT MAROT'S "RECENSION"

But the debate did not end there. In 1526, five years after the last edition of Molinet's moralized version, a new translation of the *Romant de la rose* in verse surfaced without the author's name.[92] It would later be attributed to Clément Marot.[93] Raymond Andes, editor of the unpublished critical edition of Molinet's *Romant de la rose moralisé*, states that "the obvious similarity of the prologue of "Marot's Recension" with the prologue and other parts of Molinet's version invites close comparison."[94] He further asserts that Marot had read Molinet's prose translation, but a close examination reveals that Marot fashioned his prologue as a response to rather than an emulation of Molinet's somewhat awkward defense of de Meun. Both authors/translators mention its importance in providing material for sayings and moral precepts as a reason for publishing a new translation of the work. Marot calls them "good maxims, natural and moral sayings" (bonnes sentences propos et ditz naturelz et moraulx); while Molinet blames readers' misinterpretation of the work on the passage of time and the work's antiquated language, Marot, the good humanist, blames primarily printers' errors.[95] While Marot's modesty topos seems somewhat pro forma, perhaps because he published the work anonymously, Molinet clearly anticipates a bad reaction and fears he will be targeted by critics and misreaders.

Marot admits that there have been misreadings of the text in the past, and he refers to the double meaning of the text, the literal and a more "mystical reading":

> And even though one could say, as several others have said, that this book speaks in vain about the state of love, and can cause minds to turn to evil and lead them to perform dissolute acts because of the persuasive content therein concerning foolish love, for a foolish, sensual appetite or sensuality nourishes every evil and perverted [marastre] virtue. This is my motive (all honor preserved and put forward) [tout honneur sauvé et premis], that I answer that the author's intent was not simply and in itself poorly founded nor evil, because it may very well be that the said author did not set his thought and fantasy on the literal meaning, but rather his mind was drawn to the allegorical and moral meaning, like one saying one thing and meaning another.[96]

Marot adds a disclaimer by suggesting that de Meun may have said one thing and meant another. He then offers four possible allegorical interpretations for the Rose: the papal Rose, the state of grace, the virgin Mary, and the "glory of eternal happiness" (gloire d'éternelle béatitude), or God.[97]

Marot's treatment of Malle Bouche is also quite different from Molinet's. Instead of condemning those who read only the literal meaning of the text, Marot indicates that they will find therein "recreation for the mind and a delectable pleasure" (récréation d'esprit et plaisir délectable), and he interprets Malle Bouche allegorically as those who attack the Virgin Mary and decline to call her "mother of pity and mercy."[98] He thus sidesteps any discussion of the misogynistic content of the work. Marot concludes his brief "exposition moralle" by claiming that the *Roman de la rose* contains useful information for natural and moral philosophers, theologians, astrologers, mathematicians, alchemists, mirror makers, painters, and others born under the right stars who might wish to know all manner of arts and sciences.

According to Jennifer Monahan, the 1526 text attributed to Marot (perhaps in error) is not a moralization of the *Roman de la rose*:

In contrast to works like the fourteenth-century *Ovide Moralisé* or Jean Molinet's 1500 moralization of the *Roman de la Rose*, both of which contain almost as much gloss as text, the interpretive apparatus of the 1526 edition is quite scant. The marginal glosses are so timid that they would be more accurately characterized as rubrics. Hardly ever do they offer an interpretation of the text; instead they call attention to events in the plot, to mentions of *auctores*, and to well-known passages. Only very rarely do the glosses propose an interpretation; when they do, the author could hardly be said to be going out on an interpretive limb . . . The Exposition moralle, not the glosses, provides the only real interpretative apparatus, but the range of interpretations it proposes is quite limited.[99]

She discusses the ongoing attribution debate and adds further fuel to the side that casts doubt on Marot as the work's author.[100] By examining Marot's interpretation of the *Roman de la rose* in the *Temple de cupido* (1515) and comparing it to the *Exposition moralle* (1526), she finds inconsistencies that do not resolve the debate but still "further tip the scales away from a plausible attribution" to Marot.[101]

Clearly, the text of *Roman de la rose* was proving increasingly difficult to read as the language underwent vast changes, requiring a prose translation with moralizations, Molinet's version (1500–1521), and Marot's verse translation (1526–38) in the first few decades of the sixteenth century. After "Marot's" last edition of 1538, the work would wait until the seventeenth century for a new edition. As Monahan puts it, it was becoming more of a "cultural artifact" than a literary model. No further attempts were made to defend the work's misogynistic content in the late sixteenth century, since the romance no doubt also suffered from increasing objections among female readers. The querelle des femmes would replace the querelle de la rose but retain its literary character.

CONCLUSION

Molinet penned his moralized version of the Romance of the Rose to pursue two interrelated goals: first, he wished to defend the romance from its detractors, who claimed it was little more than a vulgar manual for seducing young women; second, he wished to demonstrate a higher, anagogical meaning that promoted a spiritual, rather than physical, love quest for sanguine Christians, who, like true lovers, would go on to reclaim the Holy Land taken by Muslims. Both failed. Only a few years later, writers and readers no longer claimed the work was morally defensible. And the crusades ended as European nations fought more among themselves than against a common foe, the Ottoman Turks.

Molinet saw the Christian man as virile, virtuous, and sanguine; that is, in possession of the ideal balance of hot and moist humors. Old men, Jews, and women were phlegmatic (cold and moist): effeminate, weak, and prone to slander. In his thought, a lack of a penis resulted in a weak intellect and an out-of-control tongue. For Molinet, writing was a male-dominated profession and closely related to male sexual performance. His work is full of interdictions against murmuring and slander and full of sexual metaphors for writing and speaking. Women writers are completely absent from Molinet's writings, as they were in the works of his successor, Jean Lemaire de Belges, whose only mention of a female writer is of his patron, Margaret of Austria. Although Lemaire wrote for women patrons such as Margaret, he did not consider them his intellectual equals. The same can be said for Symphorien Champier, the subject of the next chapter, who purportedly wrote on both sides of the querelle in his *Nef des princes* (1502) and *Nef des dames vertueuses* (1503). Champier would also introduce the Renaissance Platonism of Marsilio Ficino to France in the vernacular in his "Livre de vraye amour."

3

Platonic Love, Marriage, and Infertility in Symphorien Champier's *Nef des princes* (1502) and *Nef des dames* (1503)

The critical debate on Symphorien Champier's role in the querelle des femmes has centered around his two *Nefs*, the *Nef des princes* (1502) and the *Nef des dames vertueuses* (1503).[1] Published one year apart and no doubt written simultaneously, the two appear to present opposing views of women. While the Lyonnais physician, medical humanist, and author defends women against their detractors in the *Nef des dames*—dedicated to Anne of France and her daughter Suzanne de Bourbon—he inserts two misogynistic works in the *Nef des princes*.[2] The profemale passages of the *Nef des dames* have received critical attention recently, but most critics have ignored, downplayed, or explained away Champier's misogyny in the *Nef des princes*.[3] Studying the advice he offered in his two *Nefs* reveals that Champier's apparent "misogyny" in the *Nef des princes* and feminism in the *Nef des dames* are consistent, and that Champier not only wrote them at the same time but no doubt envisioned them as one work. In both, he contributed to the querelle des femmes and also engaged in such medical debates as how a medical doctor's profession differs from the professions of pharmacists, surgeons, and midwives; how "simple" medicines are superior to "compounds,"; what causes infertility in couples and how to remedy it; and when and how to use the vernacular in medical writings.[4]

As stated at the end of the previous chapter, Champier was also the first to introduce the Renaissance Platonism of Ficino into France in the vernacular with his "Livre de vraye amour," the fourth part of the *Nef des dames*. Yet, like most of his contemporaries, Champier saw marriage as inferior to celibacy and largely as a way to avoid sin and produce progeny. Indeed, Champier talks as much about producing healthy male heirs as creating a loving relationship within marriage, and he advocates Neoplatonic love more as a moralist and physician than a philosopher or feminist. Champier's views of sex, love, and marriage are remarkably consistent in his two *Nefs* as well as his later medical writings. In his *Practica nova* (1509), *Speculum Galeni* (1517), and *Periarchon* (1533), he avoids the more strident antifemale passages of his sources, such as Albertus Magnus, but emphasizes again and again how dangerous frequent coitus is to men's health. He seems more concerned with safeguarding men's fertility and the health of future progeny than exploiting women's supposedly physical inferiority or corrupting moral influence.

MISOGYNY IN THE *NEF DES PRINCES*

A close examination of Champier's *Nefs* reveals that he was as cautious a misogynist in the *Nef des princes* as he was a qualified feminist in the *Nef des dames*. The *Nef des princes*, a compendium of fifteen works in both French and Latin, purportedly offers an educational treatise aimed at young princes.[5] Two of the works warn young men away from evil women: the first a short letter in Latin written to Jacques Robertet on the occasion of his upcoming marriage,[6] the second a collection of misogynistic quotations in Latin; both describe various forms of feminine deceit. A third contains a French translation, supposedly Champier's own, of Matheolus's infamous and misogynistic *Liber lamentionum*, written around 1295, to which he gave the title "La malice des femmes." Critics have judged these works unworthy of serious study as well as an embarrassing chapter in the early Renaissance. A few have simply declared Champier a misogynist who wrote the *Nef des dames* as an apology addressed to offended female readers, who, they assumed, were more bothered by the Matheolus translation than by the collected Latin sayings. Not surprisingly, "La malice des femmes" is not included in either of the modern editions of the *Nef des princes*.[7]

In the letter to Jacques Robertet in Latin, Champier cites as examples of worthy wives Portia, wife of Marcus Brutus, and Artemisia, wife of Mausolus.[8] Portia swallowed burning coals in order to follow her husband in death. Inconsolable at her husband's death, Artemisia built a huge tomb, or "mausoleum," mixed his ashes in liquid, and drank it in order to remain a living monument to her husband in perpetual and faithful widowhood. Champier also recounts the legend of the self-sacrificing Menian women who visited their husbands in prison to switch clothes with them, allowing the men to escape and dying in their place.[9] It is this kind of woman, self-sacrificing and loyal until death, that Champier wishes as a worthy spouse for his correspondent—but, he adds, such women are rare.

The second work in Latin warns of the more common type of woman.[10] The complete title reads: "A work completely revised recounting to all the corrupt morals of women, selected and published by the very erudite Symphorien, distinguished authority in the art of poetry."[11] Here, Champier has compiled a humanist handbook on misogyny and a warning against marriage similar in tone and content to the popular fifteenth-century *Quinze joyes de mariage*. He quotes liberally, in Latin, from such classical authors as Plautus,[12] Cicero,[13] Ovid,[14] Seneca,[15] Valerius Maximus,[16] and Juvenal;[17] such patristic authors as Lactantius[18] and Saint Jerome;[19] and near contemporaries like Petrarch;[20] as well as numerous proverbs. He cites them one author at a time, without commentary and without regard to chronology or theme. At first glance the handbook appears an uninspired diatribe against women. For instance, it contains Secundus's oft-quoted definition of woman: "Woman is a confounding of man, an insane beast, a continual uneasiness of mind, an incessant fight, a daily hell, an impediment to solitude, the shipwreck of the incontinent man, a vessel of adultery, a pernicious battle, the worst animal, a very heavy burden, an insane viper, human property."[21] He also offers such biting quotes from Petrarch's misogynistic *Remediae fortunae* as, "Now you have a wife to rule over you—a tormentor of her stepchildren, envious of her mother-in-law, a yoke for your family, trouble in the kitchen, waste in your storehouse, expense to your coffer, an ornament to your hall, and display for your window in the day, and blinding radiance in your chamber at night. A heavy burden. Cruel chains to oppress your free shoulders and shackle your once free feet."[22] The faults common to women include garrulity—much discussed in Howard Bloch's *Medieval Misogyny*—but also bossiness, deceit, greed, infidelity, and promiscuity. Not surprisingly, most quotations warn of women's lack of control over both their tongues and their sexuality.

Yet in the table of contents at the end of the *Nef des princes*, Champier, or the editor, indicates that the work is more equivocal than a first impression would suggest: "On page 42 there are numerous notable sayings of philosophers against vice-ridden women *and in favor of the good.*"[23] Some do indeed refer to women as either good or bad, a stance in keeping with Champier's profemale prologue to the *Nef des dames*. Examples include, "There is nothing better than a kind wife . . . nothing worse than a cruel one."[24] Still others are surprisingly profemale[25] or gender neutral, like the following proverb: "Love grows through use, it shrinks with abuse."[26] Others reflect what Bloch refers to as "coincident contradiction," the prevailing Christian view of the dual nature of woman as simultaneously seducer and redeemer,[27] like the following quotation from Petrarch: Woman is "an invisible fire, a welcome wound, a savory poison, sweet bitterness, delectable affliction, delightful torment, alluring death. But you, madman, you must never believe a wanton woman. Her sex, heedlessness, levity, habitual lying, desire to deceive, and the guile of her crafty tricks, each of these alone and much more so, all of them combined, should render suspect whatever comes out of her mouth . . ."[28] Bloch states that during the Middle Ages, "woman was aligned . . . with the senses, the body, and the material, portrayed as pure appetite (economic, gastronomic, sexual)."[29] Her abundant orality and sexual lack of control were linked, as in the *Romant de la rose moralisé*.

Champier seems to delight in quoting misogynistic oxymorons like the one above regarding the nature of women, but he does so in Latin, a language that he knew most women could not read or understand. For example, in *Le myrouel des appothiquaires* (1532–33), a translation and summary of his *Castigationes seu emendationes pharmacopolarum* (1532), Champier aims his pharmacological advice at certain pharmacists and surgeons who could only read French or "kitchen Latin" (latin de cuysine).³⁰ Throughout the work he makes reference to chapters in the *Castigationes*, indicating that the pharmacists and surgeons might use the *Myrouel* as a simplified reference to prevent the worst abuses, while the *Castigationes* was for trained physicians. Most of the possible errors he points out stem from similar words in Latin and French for different pharmaceutical remedies. Later, he adds that these men who "cannot read Latin or rather [only] the Latin of women and of the kitchen" (Ne sçavent entendre latin ou bien que latin des femmes et de cuisine) risk killing their patients through their ignorance.³¹ In *Les lunectes des cirurgiens*, a work included in the 1532 edition of *Le myrouel*, Champier refers to "barbaric Latin where women, cunning of mind, understand the gist, for it is crude and rough [materiel], and easy to understand by people who have studied little and have a weak brain" (latin barbaresque dont les femmes subtiles d'esperit entendent la substance, car il est gros et materiel et facile d'entendre aux gens de petite estude et debille cervelle).³² Clearly, he did not think that women were the intellectual equals of men.

The third misogynistic work in the *Nef des princes* is a much-condensed version of Jehan Le Fèvre de Resson's fourteenth-century verse translation of Matheolus's *Lamentations* (346 verses vs. almost 10,000 verses in the original).³³ Champier's "Malice des femmes" begins with a commentary in the narrative voice of the "translator," who apologizes for the misogynistic content, professes no hatred toward women, and wishes to warn men against "bad" women but do no harm to the "good." Although Champier never claims to have personally translated the Matheolus text, he does not mention Resson and merely notes that the work was gathered (recueilly) from "Matheolus et *aultres.*" Champier seldom departs from the Resson translation, but in a few places, he summarizes and even censors it. Curiously, in these few verses we find many of the heroines that Champier praises in the pages of the *Nef des dames*—Dido, Lucretia, Medea, and Semiramis. The advice Champier gleans here mainly targets "bad" women's loquacity and lustfulness.

Champier claims that he includes the "Malice des femmes" "not to slander women [mesdire], but simply to warn [men] about the dangers that can come from women"; he adds that if there are any unpleasant or biting words therein on the subject of women, let the "bigamist" Matheolus be blamed, not himself.[34] More than two hundred rhyming octosyllabic couplets follow, most attributed to Matheolus, while others are in the author's narrative voice. In the first forty or so, Champier excuses himself twice more:

> I would like to excuse myself in these sayings
> For I do not slander the good [women]
> I have no desire to slander [them]
> Or to be hated for my foolish words
> God knows it and I promise you
> That towards woman I have no hatred.[35]

Again, Champier distinguishes between good and bad women and adds that he himself does not hate women. In the third apology, he adds that these "biting" and misogynistic words are from histories and other "ancient memoirs." Clearly, Champier knew that the poem would offend women readers:

> Some words might be biting
> But they do not come from me
> Not one word nor even half
> which may not be found in histories
> and in ancient memoirs.[36]

In fact, according to at least one critic, the Matheolus translation's inclusion in the *Nef des princes* so offended women readers that Champier was compelled to write the *Nef des dames* as an apology.[37]

FEMINISM IN THE *NEF DES DAMES*

In the prologue to the *Nef des dames*, Champier admits that there were indeed evil women in history, but he gallantly blames their husbands for setting a bad example. He takes up the defense of women against "slanderers" (mesdisans) because women are "like sheep before the wolf, and normally do not read the scriptures to know how to defend themselves, and because of this they do not say a word."[38] Later in the text, although he does not endorse the view that men and women are equal,[39] Champier nonetheless establishes a qualified equality—they are equal in "some" things and "sometimes."[40] He does not specify which things or when, but he takes the rather unusual position of urging men to treat women as equals,[41] which goes far beyond what many other profemale querelle writers recommended in the early years of the sixteenth century. Champier speaks out against infidelity in both sexes, divorce under any circumstances—especially for infertility—requiring dowries, wife beating, treating women like servants or children, and young women marrying old men.[42]

It is possible that Champier's style betrays a kind of rhetorical irony in the *Nef des dames*. The second *Nef* is highly rhetorical, especially in the prologue, where Champier takes to task detractors of women. Referring to the "feminization of the esthetic," Bloch posits that highly rhetorical texts were considered suspect by male readers since they were thought to appeal to the senses and considered an attempt to seduce the reader with, as Bloch puts it, "that which is defined as the essence of the feminine, the ruses of rhetoric."[43] Indeed, texts that were written from a profemale stance in the High Middle Ages often opted for the loquacity that was generally criticized as a female trait, perhaps clueing the male reader in to an ironic text. Curiously, although rhetorical devices are almost completely absent in the *Nef des princes*, Champier uses several throughout the *Nef des dames*: metaphor, simile, hyperbole, antithesis, asyndeton, anastrophe, chiasmus, apostrophe, and anaphora abound. Anaphora is especially favored, as in the following example: "*Look* at the idolatry . . . *Look* at the cruelties . . . *Look* to find . . ."[44] The most striking example of anaphora occurs when Champier harangues his fellow physicians, who, unlike himself, neglect the seven liberal arts: "*How* will you recognize the illness by the artery or pulse without knowing the figures and consonances of music like dyapason, dyapente, dyatesseron and others? *How* will you know the time to give the required medicine if you don't know the disposition of the sky . . . ? *How* will you know how to behave towards your patient if you haven't read moral philosophy . . . ? *How* will you speak Latin without grammar . . . ? *How* will you understand the truth of a proposition without logic? *How* will you persuade your patient to be healthy without rhetoric?"[45] Champier shows himself a master of invective in these and other passages. In another invective, he uses apostrophe and *exclamatio* to attack women's detractors and slanderers: "Oh, evil person full of all felicity"; in another, he chides old men who marry young women: "*Oh*, cursed lust. *Oh*, unworthy bestiality. *Oh*, unfortunate old age."[46] Like most of his contemporaries, Champier was well versed in classical rhetoric and knew the pseudo-Ciceronian *Rhetorica ad herennium*, which suggests the use of *exclamatio* in invectives to arouse the audience's indignation and elicit an emotional reaction.

Yet it is doubtful that Champier intended the *Nef des dames* to be read ironically. For years critics have struggled to explain why Champier apparently wrote on both sides of the querelle—perhaps to apologize to offended female readers, to convey a newly discovered Renaissance Platonism, or to gain patronage from Anne of France, an attempt that ultimately failed.[47] A comparison of the medical content of both *Nefs* reveals no inconsistencies in the advice he offers both men and women. Champier may have been much more profemale than his contemporaries, but he shared the traditional medical view that women possessed a baser nature than and were physically and intellectually inferior to their male counterparts.

MEDICAL ADVICE IN THE *NEFS*

Champier is as consistent in his attitude toward women in both *Nefs* as he is in the medical advice he offers in each. The titles of the respective chapters that contain most of that advice, "Le regime et *gouvernement* d'ung prince" and "Le *gouvernement* de mariage," reveal their close relationship. In fact, they appear to have come from one work, the material of which was later divided between the two *Nefs*—no doubt to take advantage of the popularity of Sebastian Brant's *Das Narrenschiff* (1494), also known as *Nef des fous*, and Josse Bade's *Stultiferae naves* (1499), or *Nef des folles*. Champier's *Nefs* share not only similar medical advice but also often the same wording on how to choose the ideal mate (especially for the purposes of producing progeny), when men and women should marry in order to ensure healthy children, how to avoid the dangers of excessive sexual activity to preserve one's health and produce healthy children, and how to choose the ideal doctor (Champier himself?) who will aid the couple in their reproductive efforts. Like most of his contemporaries who delved into gynecology and obstetrics—which, as Monica Green notes in *Making Women's Medicine Masculine*, were previously female-dominated endeavors—Champier's main goal was to aid his patrons in producing a male heir. To this end he offers fertility and prenatal advice in the *Nef des dames* and postnatal advice in the *Nef des princes*, a division of labor (no pun intended) in keeping with the woman's important reproductive role prior to birth and the man's subsequent role as educator of the princely heir. That might also explain why there is more medical advice in the *Nef des dames* and more educational precepts in the *Nef des princes*.[48]

For example, in the *Nef des princes*, Champier's medical advice includes how to cut the umbilical cord, how to choose a wet nurse, and when the child should be allowed to eat solid food, exercise, and drink wine. All the advice here is rather typical and conforms to that offered by Simon de Vallambert and others decades later.[49] Occasionally, the division of material seems somewhat clumsy since the advice on how to find a good wife appears in both *Nefs*, while how to find a good husband is only included in the *Nef des dames*.[50] Other advice, such as when to marry, overlaps the two *Nefs*. In both, Champier often refers to the other work, providing further proof that he composed them at approximately the same time and quite possibly as one work.[51]

From the very beginning of the *Nef des princes*, Champier offers indications of how he organized the material. For example, he states that he will first speak of the body, then of the mind: "Two types of training are necessary for a prince when he comes into this world. One is of the body, the other is of the soul; first we will speak of the body, because we believe that the body is formed before God gives it a reasoning soul. And we will sometimes speak of this formation, not like Hippocrates or Galen or Rhazes, but as fits our purpose, which is unlike theirs, for they taught through an occasionally demonstrative way what we intend to say through recitation and example, as the subject matter requires."[52] A few lines later, he adds, "As for the formation of the body, we will speak no more at present: because the subject matter is not pertinent"; that part, the advice on how to propagate and avoid infertility, was relegated to the *Nef des dames*.[53] Then again, Champier states, "Since in the earlier parts, we spoke of the manner and governing of a prince as relates to the body, now it is suitable to speak of the teaching and morals that he should be taught in his youth."[54] It is only in chapter 19 of the second book of the *Nef des dames* that Champier outlines how a woman should teach her children good morals, but he refers back to the *Nef des princes*—"And I spoke more fully and in detail in the *Nef des princes* on how the father should instruct his young child"—another indication that he may have envisaged the two works as one.[55] Here he simply states that the father should "correct [his children] early" (corrigés les de bonne heure) and that the mother should not be too loving or tender.[56]

As Christine Hill has pointed out, the educational advice in the *Nef des princes*, largely borrowed from *De liberorum* by Aeneas Sylvius Piccolomini, is centered on the young male child.[57] After the male child or prince is born—actually, from the moment of his birth—the man takes charge of him. The educational advice in the first book of the *Nef des princes* deals with the needs of the prince's body from birth to fourteen years of age: what he should eat, what he should avoid (wine), the choice of a wet nurse, the choice of a tutor, the company he should keep, and the physical exercise he should do. In book 2, Champier deals with the moral and intellectual instruction of the adolescent prince and his choice of a wife at between twenty to twenty-five years of age.

The limited educational advice for women in the *Nef des dames* appears only at the end of the "Gouvernement de mariage"[58] Champier advises ladies to refrain from talking too much—referring quite clearly to women's tendency toward loquacity—and to monitor their daughters, who are too easily influenced by the eloquence of potential suitors:

> Princess or renowned lady, do your best to prevent your daughters and young girls from being designated [affaitees] as talkative. And keep watch at all times. And especially when you speak with lords or with others, like at the table or elsewhere. For, most often, when they see that their lady is in counsel with someone, they cackle and chat with young men or gentlemen. And sometimes you will find them lying down or on their knees on the ground or sometimes in some chimney corner. For light is repugnant to them as they chat about this and that. Not about Saint John

or Saint Luke, but about illicit things. And sometimes together they play their game [font leur tripot] from whence come many evils, for what the devil cannot do by himself, he does through these flatterers and young men. And he recognizes very well every countenance, every opportunity, every virgin. It happens many times, and is, most often, a *poisonous and bitter sweetness. An infected eloquence.* And thus where there should be true sweetness, honest purity of body and soul, kindness, humility, innocence, and grace adorned with wisdom, you will find false tales, dishonest words, lies, disparaging comments, jealousy, bitterness, bad taste, infamy, lack of grace, and kindness. And often due to the carelessness of their mistress. Think, Lady, about accounting for yourself before the one from whom you hold mastery and domination over your sheep. May your daughters be always before you where you can see them. And if you speak to someone, have your eyes always on them. If not both eyes, then at least the right eye. By doing this, you will prosper.[59]

Thus, a woman's only educational task is to watch over her female child's virtue at all times. Champier also directly appeals to the mother, princess, or lady to fight her own tendency to gossip in order to do the job, adopting the familar "tu" form in his appeals. He only uses the third person ("A prince should . . .") in the *Nef des princes*, demonstrating a higher regard for the prince than for his lady.

Champier follows this advice with a dire warning designed to ensure that the princess or lady heeds his message. He describes hell, a fate that awaits the unwary mother if she fails in her diligence:

Dark and shadowy hell, according to the philosophers, is in the center and the middle of earth and is the world's latrine. For all the excrement and filth of the world is distilled therein, and in there is darkness and afflictions. And if all the philosophers who ever existed had always spoken of this place and of the penalties of this place, they would never have known how to count the afflictions, torments and infamies which are therein. There is every filth, fire, obscurity, putrid and rotten smoke and stinking odor and hateful shadow, inestimable affliction without end and frightening frigidity, horrible cries and lamentations, and innumerable maledictions. Unimaginable deepness, enormous forms, perpetual torments without the ability to die, pains which one could not endure in this world, a mirror of all vices perpetrated in this world, no hope, lack of grace, rivers hot like fire and cold as ice. And so many others that it would be impossible for any human man to count.[60]

Since, like most of his contemporaries, he considered women naturally more fearful than men, Champier apparently intended to scare them into good behavior. In a chapter titled "La filozomie de la femme" (The physiognomy of woman), Champier offers a description of women's anatomy and their characteristic fear:

> According to Rhazes in the second book of the *Almansor*, woman among all living genders [sic] has a weaker heart than the male. And she cannot stand as much pain or exercise as a man. And she is more in danger [dangereuse] and frail and more easily moved and more easily appeased, and she has a smaller head than the male, a thinner and frailer face and neck and narrower shoulders and smaller and shorter ribs and fleshier thighs and buttocks, and she has thinner hands and she is by nature *more fearful and timorous* than the male.[61]

Yet, in this passage, Champier hides behind Rhazes, a medical authority, to convey a statement about women's physical, intellectual, and moral inferiority to men.

Although his tone differs in the *Nef des princes*, Champier offers consistent medical advice in both *Nefs*. For example, in both writings he urges the prince to marry a tall woman, since the children of tall women live longer.[62] In the *Nef des princes*, he advises a man to marry at twenty or twenty-five, and in the *Nef des dames* he states a woman should not marry until she is twenty-one, especially if she is short.[63] Citing Aristotle's *De animalibus* or *Historia animalium* on the dangers of precocious sexual activity and pregnancy among young women, Champier declares emphatically that no man should marry a girl under sixteen, because the couple's children may die at birth or at a very young age.[64] In a marginal note, Aristotle warns parents to protect their very young daughters for health reasons (they might give birth to deformed children or die themselves) and for moral reasons (they might become sexually insatiable); "For the females who are sexually active while quite young become more intemperate, and so do the males if they are unguarded either in one direction or both. For the channels become dilated and make an easy passage for fluids in this part of the body; and at the same time their old memory of the accompanying pleasure creates desire for the intercourse that then took place. At the same time, the memory that one had of the pleasure experienced makes one desire coitus."[65] Champier does not translate the note into French; he "refrains from doing so in order to speak modestly" (desquelles me deporte pour honestement parler). Here, "honestement" means "modestly" or "correctly"; he apparently wished to protect his female readers from the too-salacious details in the passage.

In the first Latin quotation in what has been called his "misogynistic handbook" in the *Nef des princes*, Champier quotes Theophrastus's *Liber de nuptiis* from Saint Jerome's misogynistic *Epistola adversus Jovinianum*. The passage warns his male readers what might happen if they marry a very young girl.[66] In the *Nef des dames*, Champier includes a more female-friendly version in French:

At this time [between the ages of sixteen and twenty] one knows the woman's health. And this is why a man should wait to marry until this time. Because when one takes a young woman [as wife] one does not know what one has chosen. And often in youth, before their flowers or natural purgations [menstrual periods] they are healthy and afterwards sick the rest of their lives. And instead of being served, one has to serve. And thus women's illnesses often come from having married too early. And bad is the pleasure that leaves in its wake a long penance.[67]

Champier omits all references to women's possible moral and physical flaws to make the passage more palatable for his women readers. The emphasis here is on preserving the woman's health, but he cannot refrain from adding that the potential groom need not be burdened with a sickly bride.

Although he expresses concern here for women's health, Champier seems unusually preoccupied in both *Nefs* with sexual overindulgence in men. In the *Nef des princes*, he warns that a man risks not only his own health but also his future progeny by such excess.[68] In the *Nef des dames*, he discusses those dangers at great length in two consecutive chapters, chapter 11 on "How women and men should avoid too many carnal pleasures" (Comment la femme et l'omme se doivent garder de trop user de leur plaisances charnelles) and chapter 12 on "At what time and at what age the work of the flesh is harfmul" (En quel temps et aage l'oeuvre de la chair est nuysible).[69] Although chapter 11 supposedly pertains to both men and women, man is clearly its focus. Champier cites and quotes several medical authorities on male sexual excess throughout the work. Excessive sexual activity can affect the eyes and weaken the body, according to Aristotle.[70] Avicenna agrees that sexual excess has an adverse effect on the eyes and is contraindicated for the thin, the elderly, and the weak.[71] Averroes discusses seminal superfluity, or excess, which can be tolerated more by those with hot and humid complexions than the cold and dry.[72] Rhazes describes the sunken eyes of those who indulge in too much sexual activity.[73] Champier quotes Haly Abbas, who also states that sex is for the young and vigorous, not for the old.[74] Haly Rodoam agrees that old men, who are cold and dry, are at greater risk than others.[75] Finding multiple sources who all cited each other or the same sources (mostly Galen and Aristotle) gave Champier solid ground for claims that sexual excess affected men adversely. In both *Nefs*, Champier favors winter and, especially, spring for conception, and he is very clear about what time of day and under what conditions one can safely engage in sexual activity (vacquer à generation) with desired results.[76] Citing both Haly Abbas[77] and Avicenna,[78] he notes that a *man* who has sex on a full stomach weakens his body and nerves, causes pain in his knees and legs, creates blockages (opilations) and excess humours (grosses humeurs) throughout his body, and risks dropsy, asthma, gout, tremblings in his arms and legs, and even death. He concludes that the most propitious time to produce progeny with the least risk is in the morning upon waking.[79] He clearly indicates that man runs a greater risk than woman by his use of "l'homme" and the single pronoun "il." In humoral medicine, women were imagined as not only cold and humid but also passive during sex; they therefore risked little or nothing from a loss of heat. In fact, they were thought to benefit from the man's heat. Champier seems particularly concerned with the effects of sexual overindulgence on the man's health and continued fertility. In the French text, he claims that it damages a man's nerves and stomach and weakens his extremities; it can lead to illnesses like gout, even death, and, as stated above, it is especially harmful to the eyes. Those most at risk are the naturally thin, melancholics, clerics who have abstained from sex for many years, and the elderly, mainly due to their excessive dryness. At moderate risk are the phlegmatics, and those least threatened are the sanguine, who are hot and humid. Consequently, Champier appeals directly to his female readers, who were thought to benefit from sexual intercourse—if they love their husbands and want them to live a long time, they should bridle *their* superfluous lust and think of the dangers that can ensue. It is not clear here whether Champier is speaking of women's lust or their husbands'—the possessive adjective could apply to either, and it was no doubt purposely ambiguous so as to offend neither men nor women.

The medical advice that Champier offers in the *Nef des dames* is unusual in that he wrote in the vernacular. Infertility and obstetrics were the almost-exclusive domains of midwives in the Middle Ages, but, as Katharine Park notes, "by the middle of the fifteenth century male medical writers had developed enough confidence in their mastery of the subject that they began to present themselves as equal or even superior to female experts, notably midwives."[80] Champier participated in that newfound confidence at the beginning of the sixteenth century.

In "On the Sterile Woman" (De la femme sterile), perhaps the most important and, medically speaking, daring chapter in the work, Champier places equal blame for infertility on both sexes—a minority opinion among his contemporaries—and even states that the problem may lie with the couple's sexual incompatibility. He departs further from established practice and the prevailing Christian view by reassuring his noble patients that their infertility is not due to their immorality. In this chapter he cites Rhazes[81] and Avenzoar[82] apparently in order to refute them. According to Champier, they mistakenly call infertile men eunuchs and claim that eunuchs have bad morals. Again, the focus is on male infertility, and Champier couches his rather unorthodox position as an attack on the misguided theories of the infidel Arabs, not those of most of his Christian colleagues.

By listing—in the vernacular—several of the possible causes of sterility in the woman, in the man, and in the couple, Champier offers valuable fertility advice for the time. For instance, he advises the woman who wishes to avoid infertility to refrain from drinking too much cold water and eating bitter meats or vinegar, to avoid strong emotions like anger and sadness, and also to remain inactive and sexually docile in bed. He advises the man to refrain from eating and drinking too much and the couple to work together on their sexual incompatibility to increase their chances of conceiving. However, Champier also cites excessive lust in a man and mental defect in a woman as possible causes of the condition, thus not entirely avoiding the issue of a causal immorality.

A little further, he brags that he has cured at least three infertile couples through diet and medicine. Here he pauses, though, to state that he would have included other medical remedies for infertility if it were not a matter subject to the noble science of medicine: "I will refrain at present and will leave it to the prudent physicians who have turned their understanding to the things of nature."[83] However, that reticence only pertains to the vernacular; he offers two remedies in the marginal notes in Latin, drawn from Avenzoar.[84] Both are clearly treatments for men and advice on how to produce a male child.

While both *Nefs* were written mostly in the vernacular, there are numerous marginal notes in Latin throughout—approximately 150 in the *Nef des princes* and 300 in the *Nef des dames*—that serve various functions. A few appear in both works. The author refers to most of these briefly or translates them into French, and he provides still others as supplementary authorities. Most of what might be considered misogynistic in both works remains in Latin, with one notable exception. In the *Nef des princes*, Champier warns men to stay away from women during their menstrual flow or suffer the consequences: their wives might give birth to deformed children—while this was a common belief in early modern Europe, it does not appear often in Champier's other works.[85]

In both *Nefs*, Champier also gives self-serving advice on how to choose a doctor and outlines the superiority of the medical profession over that of lawyers and pharmacists. Pharmacists sometimes overstep the bounds of their profession and invade the domain of doctors to the detriment of their patients, he chides. Medicine, he states, is the most noble and useful of human sciences when it is well practiced but not when it is abused. Doctors—he uses the term "medicins"—should be devoid of vice and well educated in the liberal arts, such as grammar. He even asks the rhetorical question, "Comment parleras tu Latin sans grammaire?" (How will you speak Latin without grammar?) He thus takes to task ignorant, "empirical" doctors who did not study formally and did not read Latin. He later published, in Lyon, a diatribe against pharmacists first in Latin and then in French, the latter titled *Le myrouel des appothiquaires et pharmacopoles* (The mirror of apothecaries and pharmacists; ca. 1532). He pursued the goal of raising the medical profession above the lesser professions of pharmacy and surgery in several Latin works as well.[86] The physician–author dedicated the *Nef des dames* to Anne of France, or Anne de Beaujeu, and her daughter Suzanne de Bourbon (1491–1521) in a failed bid for patronage. Anne had suffered for many years from infertility, finally producing her only daughter.[87] She also owned at least three medical books and was one of few women of the early modern period known to do so.[88] She stands alone among women of her time as the dedicatee of a Latin text on fertility and gynecology at the end of the fifteenth century.[89] After Champier's attempt to gain patronage from Anne failed, his patrons were all male.[90] With the exception of the one French work on the apothecary profession mentioned above, his later volumes written in the vernacular (five in all) were all historical and celebrated the war exploits of his male patrons and friends (such as his relative by marriage, the nobleman Bayard) or his own grievances during the riots in Lyon.[91] Champier would go on to pen approximately thirty-five medical works in Latin during his lifetime, most devoted to his favorite authority, Galen.

MEDICAL ADVICE IN CHAMPIER'S LATIN WORKS

In at least three of these works—*Practica nova in medicina* (1517),[92] *Speculum Galeni* (1517),[93] and *Periarchon* (1533)[94]—Champier deals with sex organs and pathological conditions that affect fertility. All three reveal Champier's growing obsession with, or perhaps his developing specialization in, curing infertility and male sexual dysfunction. They also provide evidence that the physician and author was often less stridently misogynistic than his sources, even when Champier was writing in Latin.

Practica Nova (1517)

In the *Practica nova*, Champier displays his medical erudition and pharmaceutical knowledge. A *practica* was an encyclopedic reference work that dealt with particular diseases and remedies, usually classifying them by organ and ordering them from head to foot. This type of literature reflected a growing market for medical learning among both physicians and lay readers, usually *male* lay readers who could read Latin. Champier's *Practica* contains a prologue, five books, and a treatise on fevers. In the first book, he defines medicine and outlines the four humors; in the second, he lists illnesses thought to originate in the head, such as headaches, epilepsy, madness, and even the "new" disease *morbus neapolitanus* or *morbus gallicus*, known as syphilis today—no doubt because its symptoms first appeared on the face.[95] Illnesses like a sore throat (synanche), asthma, and coughs appear in the third book. The fourth contains indications for stomach, liver, and spleen problems; and disorders of the kidneys, bladder, and genitals fill the fifth. After a brief description of each medical condition, he prescribes various pharmaceutical remedies.

In book 5 of the *Practica*, Champier deals with various impediments to reproductive health. In chapter 2, "On the Illnesses of the Generative Members" (De egritudines membrorum generativorum), he appears preoccupied with men's sexual dysfunction, especially with such pathological conditions—thought to cause or be caused by male sexual "excess"—as satyriasis, priapism, and "gomorrea," "incontinent sperm," (spermatis incontinentiam) or involuntary emissions. All three, he says, can lead to a man's sudden and premature death (unde celeriter moriuntur homines). He cites, in turn, Greek and Latin medical authorities such as Galen; Arab and Carthaginian (or Phoenician) authors such as Rhazes, Isaac,[96] and Serapion,[97] and "recent" authors such as Avicenna. Yet Champier does not always maintain these separations; for example, Avicenna often appears in the latter two categories.

In book 5, chapter 3, "On Illnesses of the Matrix (Womb)" (De egritudines matricis) Champier examines such gynecological conditions as menstrual retention, uterine or womb suffocation (suffocationem matricis), vaginal constriction, postpartum hemorroids, and even "testiculos mulierum," a possible reference to prolapse, uterine displacement, or the common belief that in some women excessive heat caused their genitals to protrude and could even provoke a sex change late in life.[98] From the very beginning of the chapter, where Champier summarizes ancient Greek and Latin authorities, he embraces the idea of the movable uterus that, like an animal, descends in the woman's body when it desires coitus. Citing Aristotle, he refers to menstrual blood as *semen incoctum*, or "uncooked semen." He also finds that most of women's illnesses come from the matrix (Ex vulva quoque feminis vehemens malum nascitur); in early modern medical literature, terms like "vulva," "matrix," and "womb" were fairly interchangeable.[99] From "Arab" authorities, he adds information about when menstruation in women starts (at fourteen years old) and stops (at about fifty), defines it as a purging of excess humors, and notes that women who exercise strenuously may not menstruate; all common beliefs. He cites Galen, Avicenna, and Rhazes, but appears to add little to them. Yet, his choice of sources and what he includes and excludes reveal much about his attitude toward women.

Speculum Galeni (1517)

For example, in the *Speculum Galeni*, which appeared in print at approximately the same time, Champier presents Galen's views on women. He does this especially in the chapter "On Women's Sufferings" (De passionibus mulierum), which is based on Galen's "Gynecology" and translated from Greek into Latin by "Nicolao de Rhegyo de Calabria," or Niccolò da Reggio.[100] He writes about the dangers of uterine suffocation and its cures, especially the practice of suffumigation: restoring the moving uterus/womb to its proper place by holding sweet-smelling items below a woman's vaginal opening and foul-smelling ones, like sulphur, at her nostrils. He also discusses various symptoms that emanate from the matrix/womb such as excessive bleeding, as well as tumors, ulcers, dropsy, and hemorrhoids, along with their cures, most of which make use of a pessary. He also adds advice on determining the sex of a pregnant woman's child, but this content covers barely three folios (236v–38r). Clearly, pathological female conditions were not his main interest here.

Periarchon (1533)

In a later work, the *Periarchon* (ΠΣΡΙ ΑΡΚΟΝ),[101] which means "On Principles," Champier gathers authorities on reproduction and infertility but again pays little attention to women.[102] In this treatise, Champier sets aside his favorite authority, Galen, to concentrate on Aristotle as interpreted by Albertus Magnus. Champier's *Periarchon* contains an odd assortment of topics, such as a chapter on giants and centaurs (chapter 26), but the last half of the book (chapters 21 through 42) deals mostly with desire, sperm, sexual intercourse, and reproductive health. For example, chapter 24 bears the title "De spermate titillatione & septo traverso" (On sperm, tickling and the diaphragm [defense wall]). Champier begins here with the claim that "Human semen, that is, sperm . . . is moved by four forces: nature, soul, heat, and spirit"; sperm, he adds, is the product of the fourth digestion, an idea repeated multiple times in his main source, Albertus Magnus's *De animalibus.* Then, Champier appears to digress to a discussion about the importance of the diaphragm and laughter. He writes about "tickling" (titillatione) and then cites book 13 of Albertus Magnus's *De animalibus* on laughter and the diaphragm (in Latin, *saeptum transversum* refers to a barrier to crossing or a defense wall).[103] In this chapter, Champier seems particularly interested in proving man's superiority over other animals by his ability to laugh, a possible forerunner of Rabelais's "Rire est le propre de l'homme" (Laughter is peculiar to mankind), but he also seems to focus on the "spirit" that is released during a pleasurable experience.

Chapter 25, "The Cause of Pleasure in Coitus" (Causa suavitatis in coitu) may explain the link between coitus and laughter. According to Champier in this rather brief chapter, pleasure in coitus is necessary for humans to perpetuate the species. What do tickling and laughter have to do with sperm, then? According to Cadden, "Notions about the causes and sites of pleasure were closely tied to notions about the origins and pathways of desire or semen"; she offers Gilbertus Anglicus as an example of the physiology of pleasure:

> The idea or memory of pleasure was widely held to be the motive cause of arousal, seed production, and ultimately, pleasure itself... The appetite for intercourse arises from thought, which produces a motion toward sexual pleasure. This, in turn, effects an excitation of spirit in the heart, which passes to the penis, where, made subtle by a virtue there, it enters the hollow nerves of the penis, filling and extending it. Gilbert goes on to say that the brain is the organ which ultimately sends the semen to the penis, and the liver is the origin of the appetite and pleasure.[104]

For Albertus and Champier too, "spirit" and pleasure arose in the brain and descended into the generative members.

In chapter 35, titled "De semine genitali" (On semen of the genitals), Champier focuses on the production of male semen and its superiority to other superfluities, not only due to its origin in the brain but also to its highly "digested" or "cooked" state. Citing book 3 of Albertus Magnus's *De animalibus*, where the thirteenth-century author repeats the earlier claim that sperm is "the humor . . . that is the superfluity separated off in the fourth digestion," Albertus adds that after the third digestion semen "is not yet coagulated, assimilated, and joined to a particular member."[105] Male sperm was well digested, unlike menstrual blood, which, as Albertus writes elsewhere, "is nothing but undigested sperm."[106] Albertus even balks at calling menses "sperm" but accepts Galen's terminology, if not his theory, since the thirteenth-century doctor believed that menstrual blood was inferior and did not deserve the term. Champier later adds a quotation from Albertus's "fifth book," actually the third book of *De animalibus*:

> Hippocrates of Cos said that sperm descends from the head through two veins which he called spermatic. They are behind the ears and are connected with the *nucha* at the upper part of the joining of the head and neck. They then come to the kidneys and this is why the pleasure of intercourse is felt in the kidneys. The veins next come to the channel of the penis. He said that an indication of this is that certain men,

wounded in battle in such a way that involved the cutting away of these veins became sterile and, moreover, did not produce sperm. Galen, however, said that he did not know whether what Hippocrates said was true. The most likely statement that can be made on this opinion is that the sperm, which is the superfluity of the fourth digestion, is exuded by all the members but especially by the head. It might also be that it undergoes decoction and fermentation in order to be completed more quickly since the nobler powers of the soul lie in the head. It then descends through the porousness of the uniform members and is drawn into the testicles, just as blood is drawn by a cupping glass. It turns white in the testicle and undergoes digestion with the formative power, which is from the heart. It is then complete for generation . . .[107]

To back up the claim that sperm originates in the head, where the nobler powers of the soul lie, Champier cites yet another authority, John Chrysostom (ca. 354–407), bishop of Constantinople, who wrote a commentary on the book of Matthew. All this contributed to the debate on sperm's superiority to other "superfluities" produced by the human body such as urine, mucous, and menstrual blood, and was intended to claim that men's heat was needed to digest or "cook" the sperm in order to produce healthy offspring.

Champier again quotes Albertus to claim that a young man does not produce good, well-digested sperm until he is approximately twenty-one years old: sperm "is suitable and is good, however, at the fulfillment of the third seven year period. For it is then most frequently that the longitudinal diameter comes to a stop or almost does so and the body begins to thicken according to the diameters of width and depth. Therefore, the sperm too is then rendered thicker and more globular and its heat is rendered hotter by the superfluous moisture that has dried up in it. For this reason it is more suitable for generation."[108] A little further in the text, Champier again quotes Albertus, who confirms that "a male human, at around twenty years, has semen that has perfectly matured."[109] However, a possible editorial error in Champier's text pushes the age back to thirty years of age.[110] In the *Nef des princes* though, he cites twenty-one to twenty-five as the age for young men to marry.[111] Champier again cites Albertus, who offers a detailed description of good, baby-producing sperm: "Sperm is a watery, buttery, fatty substance, in many ways like the substance of oil. There is in it the fine earthiness that is in the fats, yet in those that are like this, it is the spiritual, moist air that is dominant. In those which have a substance of this sort, the thickening is not caused only by the earthiness getting up in them but also by the very fine, spiritual, windy air which lies shut up within them by the heat and motion."[112] Champier's focus on sperm continues even into chapter 37: "Mulierum secreta," or "Secrets of women."

Here, the Lyonnais physician might be expected to contribute to the "Secrets of Women" tradition that Monica Green typifies as a male-to-male conversation about the deficiencies of the female body.[113] Instead, Champier returns to his and Albertus's obsession with high quality sperm, as he cites two more passages from De animalibus: "Sperm should be glandular and hail-like when it is touched as if it were made up of little acorns [glandula] and soft pieces of hail. For then, a large amount of strong spirit can be held in its thickness also with the power that forms a perfect and vigorous young. This spirit, along with its power, is not found in thin sperm, and if it were it would evaporate. Such hail-like sperm is only in a man's body."[114] The focus here is on men's health and producing a male child. In book 18 of De animalibus, not cited by Champier, Albertus indicates that "moist, phlegmatic [men] . . . whose complexion is feminine generate females, more often than those whose semen is globular and granular, congealed as it were."[115] This helps to explain Champier's obsession with thick versus thin semen: one produces males while the other produces females. And then, citing Albertus again, Champier describes the kind of man that produces the most sperm: "The men who produce the most sperm are those who are neither very fleshy nor fat, for in these the sperm passes over into bodily nourishment. Those who are light in color have the material for sperm because of their moisture, but they might have little of the power that produces the sperm and pushes it along. Therefore it is not improbable that dark men who are not very fleshy or very thin have a great deal of sperm."[116] Dark (virile) men produce the most sperm while pale (passive) women produce the best environment for babies. In this chapter, supposedly on women, Champier describes the ideal baby-producing woman, again taking his text from *De animalibus*: "Likewise, women who are somewhat pale draw more and absorb more sperm with their vulvas than do other women and they thus almost empty and dry out males. The reason for this is the suitability of such women for pregnancy, for the whiteness signifies softness in them and the pallor a depletion from superfluous menstrual blood. The womb is then cleaned out and draws the sperm from the penis like a cupping glass."[117] Pallor thus indicates cleanliness and a lack of residual menstrual blood that might damage the sperm and foetus.

Albertus Magnus's *De animalibus* is a lengthy and digressive work on animals, with several comparisons between animals and humans scattered throughout. Champier quotes seven separate passages to prove the superiority of sperm to other "superfluities" in books 3, 5, 9, and 16, which indicates a careful and far-from-disinterested reading. In his quest to gain noble male patrons, Champier's ability to aid in producing male heirs and preserving men's health could only be advantageous.

While he focuses on men, Champier does finally deal with women, but only briefly in chapter 37, "Mulierum secreta." He cites two short passages from Albertus's *De animalibus* on women's anatomy, both from book 1. In the first he claims, "In many ways the womb is similar to the male penis"; again, he embraces the commonplace about women's inverted (and inferior) anatomy.[118] In the second he claims, "Pythagoras says that the womb is an animal in its own right"; Champier endorses the idea that a woman's womb is simply "an animal within an animal."[119] Pythagoras was not the only one who held such beliefs; Hippocrates and Galen did as well. By citing Albertus Magnus, who in turn cites Pythagoras, Champier perhaps removes himself further from such an unenlightened view of women's anatomy, one that was slowly changing in some medical circles by 1533.

Finally, Champier describes one female ailment—"vulva impedita," or obstruction of the womb—but again his focus is on men. The womb obstruction is simply an impediment to intercourse or to a woman's "deflowering" (deflorari). Champier pauses to refer to legal decrees about frigidity, evil deeds, and impotence, but he offers little medical advice—only patience and acceptance. Then he cites Celsus's *Medicinae feminarum*, which is in fact *De medicina* and not a specifically gynecological work: "Occasionally [women's] genitals do not allow for coitus, the orifices having coalesced. And this sometimes happens even in the mother's womb; and sometimes when ulceration has occurred in those parts, and through bad treatment there the margins have become united during healing."[120] Celsus concentrates on women's anatomy in the seventh book of his *De medicina*, but it would seem that Champier calls it *De medicina feminarum* so that it appears a work on gynecology.

The next line is unattributed but does not appear to come from Albertus Magnus or Celsus: "For generation, these things are necessary, that one perceive female menses, and that the man's semen not be less congealed or liquid; this is called genital food and is suitable for generation."[121] Then, after the long disquisition on healthy sperm quoted above, followed by a comment on the rarity of multiple births, Champier adds a moral admonition to his readers. There is a maximum number of possible conceptions, he writes, and if one exceeds that number, there may be monstrous births and other complications. It should be noted, he adds, that if a man exceeds that number, he will exhaust the *spiritus* (in the semen), corrupt his stomach, and weaken his heart and brain. Nothing could be worse for his natural constitution (ingenium). In a succeeding chapter titled "Venus diminishes men, and males who copulate frequently become old quickly" (Venus diminuit vires, et mares multum coeuntes citius senescunt), Champier returns to his oft-repeated warnings in the *Nef des dames*, the *Practica*, and other works. Frequent coitus ages men, making them humid, cold, and vulnerable to blindness and other maladies. Here he could have cited Albertus, who repeatedly warns about the adverse effects of sexual excess for men, yet this time Champier cites Avicenna and Constantine instead.[122]

Although Champier cites generous passages from Albertus Magnus's *De animalibus* in the *Periarchon*, he avoids the more misogynistic passages like, "One must hold the opinion that the female sex is a sort of natural flaw with which a fetation is stricken."[123] Nor does he cite Albertus's more misogynistic *Quaestiones* or pseudo-Albertus's *De secretis mulierum*. Rather than concentrate on women's deficiencies in the *Periarchon*, Champier appears more interested in proving male superiority over other animals and ensuring the production of healthy sperm, a hospitable womb, and male offspring rather than attacking women as inferior beings. His relative silence on the harmful effects of menstrual blood, an obsession of Albertus Magnus's and of the author of De secretis mulierum, was rare among his contemporaries.[124] Yet, women's health only concerned Champier when it interfered with successful intercourse and reproduction.

From the very beginning of his medical and writing careers, Champier viewed the field of medicine as a male-dominated profession where a liberal arts education, especially a firm grounding in Latin, separated doctors (medecins) from pharmacists (apothicaires) and surgeons, who often overstepped the bounds of their lesser professions.[125] In both Nefs, but especially in the Nef des dames, Champier takes to task "empiricists" who could not read Latin. Women also belonged to that category, and Champier apparently thought of them more as patients than potential colleagues. For instance, he mentions a midwife (obstetrix) only once in the Practica nova, and he only lists two women "healers" among the praiseworthy women in the Nef des dames: Cibele, who confined her cures to children and animals (no adults), and Sainte Geneviève, who healed all manner of illnesses not by means of her skill but through her "prophetic spirit."[126] Champier would seem more a medical elitist than medical misogynist. Women were simply uneducated, like so many others, and could not read Latin, a professional necessity. Like many of his contemporaries, it never occurred to Champier to challenge the prevailing Galenic attitude toward women. As Green notes, "Deliberate misogyny was unnecessary . . . there was no question of suppressing women's authority since no one imagined they had any authority to suppress."[127] She characterizes the field of gynecology in medieval and early Renaissance Europe as "a territory of interplay, a contest between men and women for access to and control over medical knowledge of the female body."[128] Champier did not attack women practitioners; he simply ignored them.

PLATONIC LOVE AND MARRIAGE

In both Nefs, Champier urges men and women repeatedly to love one other with "true and perfect love" within the bonds of marriage,[129] but it is only in "Le livre de vraye amour," the fourth book of the *Nef des dames*, that he deals exclusively with love. Probably due to its historical contribution to the spread of Neoplatonism in France in the vernacular, this fourth book has received the most critical scrutiny of all. Nevertheless, certain aspects—most notably the prefatory letter, the three stories that Champier uses to demonstrate different kinds of divine love, and his Phoebus and Lucilia allegory—have puzzled critics who have found in them a misogynistic departure from the rest of the work. Only one critic, Tracconaglia, has praised Champier's feminism unequivocally in his approach to Ficinian Neoplatonism. In fact, as stated earlier, Tracconaglia credits Champier's reading of Ficino's *De amore* for transforming the Lyonnais physician from a misogynist in the *Nef des princes* to a feminist in the *Nef des dames*.[130]

James Wadsworth published the first edition of the "Livre de vraye amour" in 1962 but declined to edit the other three because he thought they "probably [did] not merit the honor"; he calls the fourth book the "first, or at least the first lengthy expression in French of Ficinian Neo-Platonism," and he found it "charming in its own right to those who seek in it a quaint freshness, but also an interesting and telling witness of the encounter of the new Italian learning with traditional French moralistic attitudes."[131] He also chose to include the prefatory letter that Champier addressed to his fellow physician André Briau and appended to the presentation copy of the first edition. Wadsworth called it an excellent example of the genre of epistolary friendship, "a *virtuous friendship* between two men whom Platonic love inspires," as well as a good introduction to the book.[132] In his introduction to the edition, Wadsworth refers to Champier's feminism but finds it "imbued with medieval misogyny."[133]

Champier's *Nef des dames* does indeed bear traces of misogyny, but his position in the fourth book does not break with his profemale and promarriage stance in the rest of the work as some have recently claimed. Accusations aimed at the fourth book include: the author discards his position on gender equality presented in the first two books;[134] Champier's prefatory letter to André Briau is homoerotic and consequently misogamist;[135] Champier's three stories included in the book are largely misogynistic; and the final allegory is aimed as the principal moral message to women, whom the author views as more lascivious than men.[136] How to respond to these charges? First of all, in the *Nef des dames* Champier neither endorses full gender equality nor focuses on women's physical and moral inferiority. Champier was prowoman, if one considers what that meant in early modern France. As previously stated, although he did not think that women were equal to men, he urged men to treat women as equals. And he was promarriage for those who could not remain celibate. He believed and stated that sex within marriage was for procreation only, and he considered sexual overindulgence potentially fatal, especially for men. In the *Nef des dames*, he clearly distinguishes between sex and love. The love between men he advocates in the fourth book is of a divine and not sexual nature, while the love he encourages between men and women can be both human—directed at producing progeny within marriage—and divine.

Second, Champier's letter to Briau bears no traces of homoeroticism but could perhaps be called homosocial.[137] In the letter, Champier distinguishes three kinds of love: divine, human, and bestial. The first two, he claims, are "stripped of all lasciviousness," while the last is "lascivious and wanton."[138] It is the first of these that Champier offers Briau. In it, Champier describes how he and Briau have both been shot by Cupid's arrows and share the "love by which men of the same profession are bound together as by the strongest bonds."[139] Although Katherine Crawford refers to the "intense desire circulating around the figure of Briau" in this letter and claims that "Champier's language about Briau resonates with intense physical desire," she offers no textual proof other than Cupid's arrows, which she terms "phallic."[140] Indeed, after Briau's body receives the arrow in his breast (pectus), the rest of the letter is a history of and encomium to the medical profession that Champier defined and defended all his life. He urges Briau and all those who follow the profession to embrace virtue and avoid vices such as envy. In the final sentence, he addresses Briau as the "perfect lover" (l'amant parfait), but he is clearly referring to a spiritual friendship between fellow physicians rather than a carnal relationship.

Third, the three stories recounted in the fourth book were no doubt read quite differently in the sixteenth century than today. In the first, intended to demonstrate a woman's love for a man, Champier cites as his sources

Herodotus, Cicero, and Aulus Gellius, and recounts how Artemisia mourned the loss of her husband, Mausolus, by mixing his ashes in liquid and drinking them and by building a lasting monument to him, a mausoleum, "one of the wonders of the world" (ung des spectacles du monde).[141] Champier recounts the same story in the *Nef des princes* in his letter to Jacques Robertet and in the first book of the *Nef des dames* to demonstrate a woman's love for her husband.[142] Yet Crawford faults Champier for recounting Artemesia's "postmortem cannibalism" and for omitting Artemesia's "unsettlingly masculine" role in the story as ruler of her people.[143] By drinking Mausolus's ashes, Artemesia becomes a living monument to her husband and rules in his stead. Indeed, Champier does not omit her martial role in the story: "After the death of her husband, this woman took Rhodes by force and wisdom and held the kingdom of Syria [Caria] and of Cos in peace and subjection."[144] The physician–author also displays no such reticence in the first book of the *Nef des dames*, where he cites several heroines who took up arms and ruled in various countries.[145] Others have also found fault with the relative brevity of this story in comparison to the two others that recount a man's love for a woman and a man's love for a man. Champier's brevity may be due to the fact that the story was indeed well known in the late Middle Ages and early Renaissance; by citing three classical sources, Champier demonstrates the story's importance.

Champier bases his second story, intended to demonstrate a man's love for a woman, on Boccaccio's *Decameron* 5.1 and, as Wadsworth notes, through the intermediary of Filippo Beroaldo.[146] However, in this case, he does not cite either source. In all three versions, Cymon falls in love with Iphigenia—whose beauty, both physical and moral, has a major civilizing influence on him—but she is betrothed to Passimonde. After acquiring a civilizing education inspired by his love for Iphigenia, Cymon abducts her, but his ship is blown off course. He ends up in the prison of the governor of the land, Lysimachus, who has fallen in love with Cassandra, who, in turn, is betrothed to Passimonde's brother, Hormisdas. The two men, Cymon and Lysimachus, show up at the wedding, murder the two bridegrooms, and abduct their brides. According to Champier, the story illustrates "how much strength and vigor Nature gives to beauty in which resides love."[147]

Champier assures the reader that Cymon loves Iphigenia "honestly" and not in a carnal way. He ends with an invective, urging men to love their wives in a similar manner and choose love of the soul over physical beauty.[148]

While critics have found these two stories puzzling, they were probably not viewed as such at the time.[149] Before telling the three tales, Champier informs his female audience that they will find the tales "useful" (utiles) in discovering the virtue and power of love; Boccaccio offers his women readers similar assurances.[150] Early modern women no doubt enjoyed tales of how their beauty (of body and soul) could inspire heroic abductions and how men's powerful desire could move them to acts of daredevil prowess yet stop them short of rape out of deference for the virtuous loved one. Or perhaps men simply assumed women enjoyed these tales? But can modern readers assume that early modern women read "against the grain," that they were what Judith Fetterley calls "resisting readers"? In this second story, Champier insists that Cymon's love is of a higher and more transcendent nature since he used his higher senses of sight, hearing, and soul, which, according to Ficino, are superior to the lower senses of smell, touch, and taste. Cymon loves Iphigenia for the beauty of her body, for the "colors of her voice through speaking prudently" (par couleurs de voix par prudamment parler), and for her "living well and justly" (bien vivant et justement)— perceived through the eyes, ears, and soul, respectively. He thus urges men to love with all three types of love—soul, sight, and sound—but of the three, he claims, love of the soul is the highest.[151]

It is the third story, based on *Decameron* 10.8 and intended to show a man's love for a man, that has caused the most critical consternation.[152] Here, the Greek Gisippus recognizes the cause of his good friend Titus's malady. Unable to drink, eat, or sleep, the young Roman suffers from lovesickness for Sophronia, Gisippus's fiancée.[153] Consequently, Gisippus offers him a self-sacrificing gift: Gisippus "loved his [Titus's] life better than anyone else and he preferred to lose a wife than a friend, because one can more easily find another wife than a friend."[154] The two friends conspire to fool Gisippus's new bride by having Titus consummate the union. When she learns of their deceit, Sophronia and her relatives are angry but begrudgingly accept the situation. Later, Titus returns the favor by saving Gisippus's life and gives his sister as wife to his friend. While this story appears misogynistic today, it is faithful to Boccaccio's account, although much shortened, and it probably did not strike early modern readers as unusual or overtly misogynistic. Champier shows no indication that the friendship between the two males was erotic or corporeal, regardless of claims that the two men (couples?) lived happily ever after. It may appear that Champier endorses here the view that "brotherly" friendships between equals are superior to heterosexual unions since only males can be equals. However, he also endorses the view that heterosexual unions can be both corporeal and soulful, partaking of both human love (for procreation) and divine love.[155]

Although these three stories appear misogynistic to a modern audience, it is in the final allegory of Lucilia's fall into carnal desire and its moral that critics claim to have found evidence of Champier's break with his earlier feminism. In this allegory, Phoebus represents God, the "author of life-giving medicine" (aucteur de medicine vitale), and Lucilia "the reasoning soul" (l'ame raisonnable).[156] Champier describes Lucilia's fall into lasciviousness as a result of indulging her lower senses of smell, touch, and taste: she succumbs to the softness of the grass (doulceur de l'erbe), the sweet odors (doulces senteurs et odeurs) of flowers, and the taste of sweet fruits (pommes doulces poyres, cerises prunes et aultres doulx fruitaiges) that only serve to increase her carnal appetite.[157] Again, borrowing from Ficino, these are the carnal senses that Champier warned against at the beginning of the "Livre de vraye amour":

> Love is nothing but desire of a thing beautiful and honest. And there are three types of beauty, that is beauty of the soul, beauty of the body, and beauty of the voice. Beauty of the soul is perceived by reason [or understanding]. Beauty of the body through the eyes. Beauty of the voice by the ears. And because Love is nothing but the desire for beauty, Love is content with understanding, the eyes, and the ears. *Love does not desire but rather avoids the senses of taste, fragrance, and touch. Thus Love seeks neither touch, taste nor odors but contents herself with the three stated above. An appetite which demands other senses than understanding, voice or sight is not Love but voluptuousness and madness.*[158]

Lucilia's senses of touch, taste, and smell lead to a physical and moral malady: fatal lovesickness. Champier adds certain pathological features to Ficino's account: Lucilia succumbs to a fever and suffers from "a terrible thirst and diarrhea [flux de ventre] and a contraction of the diaphragm with chest pain, shortness of breath, and a terrible cough, which are signs of death" (une merveilleuse soifz et flux de ventre et une singulte avec pleuresie et alaine estroicte et toux terrible, qui sont signes de mort), all symptoms of fatal lovesickness as it was understood in early modern medicine.[159] He then adds that God, the divine doctor, cures those who suffer from illness and moral failures.

Right before recounting this allegory, Champier quotes from Ficino and warns about the ill effects of lovesickness in those who love carnally:

> Socrates, Plato, Aristotle, Dyogenes and other philosophers have said that carnal love and concupiscence is a type of anger and fury by which false lovers are in a state of desire [en sollicitude] night and day and as long as their anger burns leading them to fire and then this anger through a burning up (heating to dryness) [adustion] converts to melancholy and like blind men without thinking they fall into fire and misery and like beasts living in the world they fall into the pit of hell. On this subject, Lysias the Theban, and Socrates in *Phaedrus* demonstrate the disadvantages of this love which all should flee like a snake or bitterness covered in honey. And do not be fooled by it [her]. For under the grass lies the venom and the serpent leading to the pit of hell.[160]

The story is intended to provide a model of "false love." Nevertheless, Crawford refers to this allegory as offering "gendered expectations" because Lucilia is styled as female and Phoebus as male. She and Reeser both see women as Champier's target audience for the moral of the story. Indeed, Crawford claims that here Champier "warns that women especially are prone to 'false love' (faulse amor)."[161] Yet, here Lucilia represents the "reasoning soul" and Phoebus God, the "author of life-giving medicine" (aucteur de medicine vitale)—this does not represent a typical father–daughter relationship.[162] Reeser makes much of Lucilia's shedding of her lascivious clothing after she has fallen into carnal love as a sign of "Lucilia's sexual mutability, dependent on an idea of the uncontrollable nature of female sexuality."[163] Most early modern readers would read this allegorically as Lucilia, the soul, shedding her carnal appetite (body) to free herself of sin rather than an indication that Champier thought women were more lacking in sexual control than men. In fact, such a reading is inconsistent with not only Champier's other three books but also his Latin works examined in this chapter.

According to Champier and Ficino, the "reasoning soul" falls victim to the lower senses of touch, smell, and taste, which leads to "several maladies," but if one repents, as Lucilia does in this allegory, one is forgiven and healed by God the physician. For Champier, Plato's divine love was beyond physical desire. Although Champier addresses women specifically after the Lucilia allegory, he then immediately appeals to both women and men to love spiritually rather than carnally.[164] In this passage of the "Livre de vraye amour," Champier cites Ficino, who substitutes spiritual lovesickness for the fatal lovesickness of carnal love:

> Thus, according to Orpheus, the man who loves dies. And in love there is a death and two resurrections: the man who loves dies in loving when he leaves himself to love another and is resurrected in the one loved when he is loved ardently. And he is resurrected another time when he knows that he is loved by the one he loves without pretending. Oh, the good death that comes out of two lives. Oh, the good transformation when one gives his love to another as his own and keeps his own. Oh, the marvelous gain when a man is made two by love.[165]

A man who loves dies only to be resurrected as part of another. Here Champier offers a Ficinian counterargument to the *Belle dame sans mercy* by claiming that both men and women who are loved spiritually kill those who do not reciprocate:

> He who does not love the one who loves him is considered a murderer and not only a murderer but also a sacreligious person and thief. Because he possesses the riches of the one who loves him. That is why he is a thief. He is a murderer, because he retains his soul by which he is loved. And whoever holds back his soul from another by which the

body and wealth are possessed [is a sacreligious person] because he is a murderer, a sacreligious person and thief and merits death three times over. And he should be sent away to die unless he loves the one who loves him[166]

Not only do those who do not reciprocate love kill the lover, their refusal is considered a sacrilege. In Ficino, Champier finds a response to querelle authors who claimed that women who refused their lovesick suitors were guilty of murder. He sanitizes that message by changing it from bestial love or carnal love outside of marriage—a sin—to spiritual love, a Christian obligation to love one another or face the consequences of spiritual death.

CONCLUSION

What then was Champier's role in the querelle des femmes and his view of love and marriage? While Champier introduced Ficinian Neoplatonism into the vernacular in his *Nef des dames* and saw friendships between male equals as noncarnal and divine, he also believed that divine love was possible and even necessary within marriage. He adhered to the religious doctrine that celibacy was superior to marriage, but marriage was necessary for those who could not embrace celibacy, a path he eschewed himself. Unlike Molinet and Lemaire, Champier married, fathered children, and did not take clerical vows. Champier's misogyny in the *Nef des princes* was largely borrowed, and most of it remained in Latin. He no doubt knew that his vernacular translation of Matheolus would offend women, but he took care to apologize repeatedly in the work and place blame on the author. In the *Nef des dames*, while he claimed male superiority, Champier adopted a profemale stance by declaring that men and women were equal in some ways, without specifying how, and by urging men to treat women as equals.

In fact, Champier's views on treating women well (but not as equals) gained him some popularity among the women of Lyon according to his friend, correspondent, and fellow physician Gonsalvo of Toledo.[167] In one of Gonsalvo's letters to Champier, quoted in the latter's *Libelli duo* (1506), the fellow physician congratulates Champier on his newfound popularity, observing that women were mobbing the young physician in the streets of Lyon and that he even owed his favorable marriage to Marguerite de Terrail, a first cousin of the renowned chevalier Pierre de Terrail de Bayard (1475–1524), to the profemale work.[168] Although this may be just another example of Champier's shameless self-promotion, it cannot be overlooked that while the *Nef des princes* saw two editions,[169] the *Nef des dames* appeared in three.[170] The 1515 Paris edition was a popular one that omitted the Latin marginalia of the other two editions, and the 1531 edition appeared in an octavo format more suited to a female reading public.

Despite what Brian P. Copenhaver calls Champier's "disputatious character" and "fondness for controversy," the Lyonnais physician declined to take part in debates about women's inferiority, maintaining a relative silence on the subject for the rest of his long career and refraining from actively participating in both the misogynistic "Secrets of Women" tradition and the debate on women's role in procreation.[171] Yet he railed against Arab and Jewish medical authorities, astrology, and the occult arts, as well as surgeons, pharmacists, and other "empiricists" who challenged the authority of trained doctors like himself, encroached on their territory, or killed their patients with their ignorance and lack of linguistic and medical knowledge. Indeed, during and after the *Nef des dames*, gynecology and obstetrics only occasionally occupied Champier's thoughts and pen. He held mainly to the middle ground in the querelle des femmes by offering advice on how to deal with "bad women" in his *Nef des princes* and advocating useful medical advice and better treatment of women in the vernacular in the *Nef des dames*, while focusing on men in both his medical works in Latin and his later writings in French.

Champier embraced Ficino's Neoplatonism, albeit without giving him credit, because he viewed Ficino as a champion of the medical profession—which Champier praised and defended throughout his career—as well as a moralist who railed against the evils of carnality and "venereal madness" in particular. As Reeser has pointed out, this madness was thought to lead to disharmony in the body, but it also threatened the soul.[172] If we allow for a Jaussian "horizon of expectations"—what the reader expects from a text depends on the time and place of the reader—Champier's women readers no doubt viewed Champier's feminism quite differently than we do today.

Even Christine de Pizan did not preach full equality of the sexes—only that men's and women's souls were identical. Indeed, early modern works professing sexual equality and even female superiority that were written by men were rare and sometimes satirical. Early modern readers no doubt viewed Champier as prowoman despite his expression of a qualified gender equality and persistent traces of medieval misogyny. They would no doubt have applauded his Christian interpretation of Plato and endorsement of a desexualized, spiritual form of Neoplatonic love.

4

Love and Death in Lemaire's *Couronne Margaritique* and the *Trois contes de Cupido et d'Atropos*

Excessive Grief and the Great Pox

Jean Lemaire de Belges wrote a large number of *complaintes*, or laments, for his patrons in his early years; these include *Le temple d'honneur et de vertus* (1504) at the death of Pierre de Bourbon in late 1503 and *La plainte du désiré* (1504) at the death of Louis de Luxembourg, Count of Ligny, in 1504. In fact, Lemaire may well have feared that he was cursed, since two of his first noble patrons died from illness in quick succession early in his career. Later, after an unsuccessful attempt to gain patronage from Anne of France, Pierre de Bourbon's widow, Lemaire would work for several more years in the service of Margaret of Austria, whose device, "Fortune infortune fort une" (Fortune mistreats strongly a woman), bears witness to the fact that the chronicler's fortunes did not improve. He later penned the *Couronne margaritique* (1504–5), at the death of Margaret's beloved husband Philibert le Beau of Savoy, who died on September 10, 1504, and *Les regretz de la dame infortunee* (1506), at the death of Margaret's brother, Philippe le Beau.[1] *Les regretz* appeared in print for the first time in 1509. Around 1511–12, Lemaire moved to the French court to work for Anne of Brittany and, after the deaths of Anne and her second husband, Louis XII, in 1514 and 1515 respectively, Lemaire disappeared. Some reported that he died from the new scourge known as the Great Pox.[2] After his death, *Les trois contes de Cupido et d'Atropos*, a three-poem allegory of the Great Pox purportedly completed in 1520, was published in 1526 under his name.[3] *La couronne* did not appear in print until 1549.[4] Together, they constitute chapters in the querelle des femmes and comment on received medical ideas of the time: the former on excessive grief, a supposedly common feminine malady, and the latter on the Great Pox. The former has been declared profemale and the latter misogynistic. In both, Lemaire reveals his views on love and death, the fragility of the female sex, the therapeutic role of literature, and the power of language.

DEATH IN LEMAIRE'S *COMPLAINTES*

In Lemaire's early career, circumstances forced him to write several laments, a genre he apparently disliked and wished to abandon in order to devote his time to writing his magnum opus, the three-volume *Illustrations de Gaule et singularitez de Troye* (1511–13).[5] With each *complainte*, his portrayal of Death as an allegorical, female figure began to take form. In the *Couronne* and the *Trois contes*, Lemaire portrays Death as a bow-and-arrow-wielding Atropos. Yet, in his first lament, *Le temple d'honneur et de vertus* (1504), there is no mention of Atropos or her arrows. Lemaire writes only of portents and astrological signs foretelling Pierre de Bourbon's tragic death.

A few weeks later, in *La plainte du désiré* (1504), Lemaire castigates Death but does not yet call her Atropos.[6] He describes her as proud (fiere, orguilleuse) as well as arrogant and boastful (venteuse; 83) several times, but he also calls her horrible, hideous, sad, perverse, outrageous, malevolent, obscure, dark (brune; 89), black, and bloody (sanguinolente; 84). Described as "soporific" (soporifere; 70), Atropos possesses a "sleep-inducing power" (force somnolente; 84), but she is also "pestilent" (pestifere; 70) and full of poison (venins; 69). Yet Lemaire seems confused as to how she inflicts her sleep-inducing power or poison on victims. In one part, he refers to Death's "pincers" (espinces or tenailles; 86, 79); in another she "bites" (mort mordant and mort qui mort; 68, 77), and in yet another; she shoots "strong, rigid arrows" (ses dartz fors et roidz; 74). He claims that Death killed the Count of Ligny with a single strike of her pickax (du seul bout de son pic; 83), with a shower of sparks (a fait voler les estincelles; 74), and finally with her deadly "Gorgon stare" (regart gorgonicque; 89). His portrait of Death, while passionate, is inconsistent.

In the *Regretz* (1506), Lemaire adopts Margaret's narrative voice and again castigates Death (Mort), but he does not refer to her as Atropos:

Death detestable and unworldly [immonde]
O biting Death, cruel and raging
Your great disarray strongly grows and abounds
On an almost despairing woman
That there is no eloquence in the world
That might draw from its fertile source to describe
All the crimes that you have committed against me.[7]

Margaret calls Death bitter, cruel, infamous, horrible, and black, and she refers to Death "biting with her proud pincers" (mordant de ses fieres espinces).[8] It seems odd that Lemaire would have abandoned the allegorical figure of Atropos in order to sound more like Margaret, which raises doubts as to whether he wrote the poem.[9]

EXCESSIVE GRIEF IN THE *COURONNE MARGARITIQUE*

Yet in the *Couronne* and the *Trois contes de Cupido et d'Atropos*, Death clearly takes on the form of Atropos, and her characterization is more consistently female. In the short first part of the *Couronne*, devoted to the account of Philibert's death, Lemaire identifies Death as Atropos: "And the other was [Misfortune's] wife, too well-known by the whole world, called Death, one of the three sisters, who spare no one: the one that the Ancients called Atropos, that is, without return."[10] Here Atropos is the "Huntress of men" (Veneresse des hommes) and the wife and companion of the allegorical figure Misfortune (Infortune), and it is Atropos who strikes Philibert le Beau with one of her deadly arrows.[11] The etymology of her name, "sans retour," was no doubt drawn from Boccaccio's *Genealogia deorum*, one of Lemaire's sources for the *Illustrations*, and Boccaccio also presents an oration in the *Couronne*.[12] Misfortune (Infortune) refers to Atropos's "bloody hand" (main sanguinolente), asks her to "prepare her sharp arrow" (Apreste ton dard affiné), and then urges her, "Bend your bow" (Bende ton arc).[13] The author later calls her the "female exterminator of human lineage" (l'exterminéresse dhumain lignage), perhaps alluding to Philibert and Margaret's childless state.[14] Finally, Death "opens her pestilent quiver and then strikes a blow with one of her sharpest and most inevitable arrows" (ouvrit son carquois pestifere: Si en tira promptement une flesche des plus agues et des plus inevitables).[15] After a rugged hunt, the exhausted and overheated Philibert sits down in the shade, and Lemaire tells us that by doing so, the young prince added "venom" to other poisons.[16] In humoral medicine, cooling oneself in the shade after intense physical exertion and drinking cold water were thought to cause a potentially lethal humoral imbalance. Lemaire describes Atropos's actions vividly: "Atropos . . . pulled so hard on her Turkish bow that she almost made it round" (Atropos . . . enfonça parfondement son arc Turquois jusques à l'amener presques en rondesse), and "The mortal iron penetrating the live entrails hid itself in his blood up to the feathers [of the arrow]" (Le fer mortifer penetrant les vives entrailles se mussa dedens son sang jusques aux empenons).[17] The wound appears invisible and leaves no scar, yet the mortal arrowhead (vireton mortel) pierces nerves and veins.[18] He chastises Philibert for not remembering to search for the herb "Dictamus," which could have cured him. Lemaire may be referring to *Origanum dictamnus*, or "dittany," a magic herb that was thought capable of expelling arrows.[19] Margaret crushes her pearls into a powder and makes a potion that Philibert drinks, but to no effect. Lemaire describes how the poison spreads to all his members. The only thing that will ease the boiling blood in his veins is phlebotomy, but Phebe, the "goddess of all humidity," opposes it.[20] According to Boccaccio's *Genealogia deorum*, Phebe was one of several names for the moon.[21] He adds, "It was said that she [the Moon] favored Jupiter against the Titans, that is, against the gods, on account of her cool and humid complexion which often inhibits the vapors of men."[22] Lemaire may have used the name "Phebe" due to its resemblance to "phlebotomy." In any case, refused a lifesaving bloodletting, Philibert dies, overcome by the poison in his blood and too much corrupting humidity, associated with a female moon. Lemaire associates women's cool and humid complexion with the moon, which regulates menstrual cycles; in fact, later in the text, he will describe Margaret, who has triumphed over her weak female nature, as a moon that has merely undergone a brief eclipse.[23]

The description of Philibert's death clearly indicates that Lemaire had an interest in medicine. In the *complaintes*, Lemaire also endorses the received medical idea that women are more emotionally susceptible to the deleterious effects of excessive grief, a form of melancholy. One of the genre conventions of *complaintes* is to urge listeners to dry their tears. For example, in his dedication to Anne of France, Pierre de Bourbon's widow, in *Le temple d'honneur et de vertus*, Lemaire tells her, "Dry your tears and wipe your face, bathed in tears" (Seiche tes larmes & torche ta face, arrousée de pleurs) and "Leave off feminine tenderness, and show your princess's heart and constance! Banish sadness from your heart and take up again laughter, even though it may be difficult now!" (Laisse donc tendreur feminine et monstre cueur & constance de princesse! Baniz tristesse de ton cueur et reprens hylarité combien que ce te soit chose presentement difficille!).[24] Lemaire often refers to women's natural inclination toward pity and compassion; for example, Entendement (Understanding) tells Anne, "Through your *feminine pity* and *womanly compassion*, you have mourned the death of your late lord and husband, cried over his passing and lamented the separation of you two with a great outpouring of tears and regrets emanating from your loving breast." (Tu . . . as par *pitié feminine* et *compassion muliebre* plaingt le decez de ton feu seigneur & espoux, plouré son trespas et lamenté la separation de vous deux par une grande effusion de larmes et de regretz, partans de la source de ton amoureuse poictrine.)[25] However, he does not fear that Anne, an exceptionally strong woman, will fall prey to excessive grief. In the dedication, he describes her ability to avoid "shipwreck" in a passage that undoubtedly reflects Champier's *Nef des dames vertueuses*, dedicated to Anne and published the previous year:[26]

Grief upon grief reinforced by bitterness might have furnished enough impetuous winds and storms to trouble the sea of prudence in which you navigate tranquilly with a full sail, very high and noble princess.

Your precious ship of constancy, well-equipped with all other virtues might have suffered shipwreck against the rock of impatience. For, by the strength of several mortal waves, these past six years you lost three glorious patrons ruling your ship, one of whom was king, another, a duke, and the third, a count. The first your beloved brother. The second your very dear husband. And the last your well-loved first cousin. The sovereign ruler of this worldly sea wished to draw these to him to demonstrate that He alone suffices to guide [them] to the port of salvation without the aid of any other human pilot. Thus you risk no peril under such a pilot since you yourself help at the rudder by pointing your prow clearly toward the very bright virginal North Star [transmontaine] above, wearing a crown of twelve stars, dressed with rays from the sun and with the moon under her feet.[27]

He reminds her that she has recently guided her "ship" through the perilous waters of grief three times: at the death of her brother, Charles VIII; her husband, Pierre de Bourbon; and, more recently, her cousin, Louis de Luxembourg.

Unlike Anne of France, Margaret of Austria seems overcome with excessive grief (dueil excessif) at the death of her brother in the *Regretz*:

Before my eyes appears an abyss
Confusing, strange, and without a clear outcome [sort unanime]
Of future events, which I dreadfully fear:
All is mixed up, there is no rhyme or reason,
All is in flux and considered dangerous [dangereux estime]
All will be put outside of law and rule [roye].[28]

Even though the poem ends with Margaret's device, "Fort, Infortune, Fort Une," most critics name Lemaire as its author, although the proof of this appears scant and, in my opinion, substantial doubt remains.[29] If Lemaire did indeed write this poem, he avoided mythological allusions, as I noted previously, perhaps because he considered them too sophisticated for his patron's writing style. He also seems singularly adept at conveying the psychology of female grief as a mixture of fear and mental confusion.

Following the vogue of works in praise of women, such as Boccaccio's *De
claris mulieribus*, Christine's *Cité des dames*, Molinet's *Chappelet des dames*,
and Champier's *Nef des dames vertueuses*, among many others, the much
longer second part of the *Couronne margaritique* praises Philibert's widow,
Margaret of Austria. In the *Couronne*, Lemaire describes Margaret as suicidal
at the sudden death of her young and vigorous husband. She let her "noble
courage formerly more than virile . . . be vanquished by feminine imbecility/
weakness" (noble courage jadis plus que virile . . . être vaincu par imbecilité
feminine).[30] "Imbecillité" referred to weakness in both body and mind.
Lemaire describes Margaret as on the edge of insanity and describes her
attempt to throw herself from a window to a certain death: "At that time it
was too miserably piteous to see the very disconsolate princess, with her
fears affirmed, to begin a despairing and inconsolable grief, scratching her
beautiful face, pulling out her golden hair, and giving voice to the great number of cries and shouts that emanated from her very amorous stomach. And
even more so, due to the furious ardor of her true conjugal love, to want to
irrevocably throw herself to her death."[31] She is kept from harm by her loyal
servants, but the narrator asks, "Oh, ardant and inextinguishable flame of
marital affection, burning in the chaste breast of this very unfortunate lady!
How do you dare approach the dangerous straits of your insanity? Certainly
through your overabundant excess, you thought to add an instance whose
memory would be worthy of tears to other stories of pitiful remembrance."[32]
He refers to her temporary insanity as a fall, perhaps an allusion to original
sin or an echo of her attempted suicide: "That is, [Misfortune] firmly wished
that this very excellent lady, without any regard for the dignity of her person,
and without being mindful of her customary virtues, might go beyond the
limits of reason and let herself fall into some great extremity of desolation
and impatience" (Cestadire, il cuida fermement que icelle tresexcellente
dame, sans avoir regard à la dignité de sa personne, et sans estre memorative
de ses coutumieres vertus, deust oultrepasser les limites de raison, et se

laisser cheoir en quelque grande extremité dimpatience desolatoire).[33] A little further, Lemaire describes her mental state as "teetering on the edge of a pitiful mishap, almost on the edge of a future, dangerous peril, from a great affliction, devoid of joy" (branlant en un piteux accident presque sur le bort de periclitation dangereuse prochaine dun grand encombrier destituee de joye) and refers to her "perilous fall" (perilleuse decadence), referring no doubt to her temporary insanity.[34] Still later, Margaret is ashamed of "sliding" (glisser).[35] Lemaire repeatedly refers to her near suicide: "The death ... of her lord ... that almost led her to take a fatal step (le trespas ... de son seigneur ... qui presques l'a menee au pas mortel) and to "her sadness/ grief [that] more than redoubled in time, and she began to suffer and tried desperately to throw herself from a high window to the ground, without hope of avoiding death (son malheur plus que redoublé en continuation, se mit en peine et s'efforça desesperement de se jetter d'une haute fenestre à terre, sans espoir d'evasion de mort).[36] Whether Lemaire intended to arouse the pity of his reading public or chastise Margaret for her temporary fall or weakness is not clear.[37]

In early modern medicine, madness was also explained as an imbalance of the four humors. Excessive grief, a form of melancholy caused by an excess of black bile, was thought to affect women more than men.[38] Lemaire describes Margaret's condition as an "extreme passion": "When a high and noble heart is pressed by such extreme passions, the senses take over, blinding the eyes of understanding in such a way that reason can only remedy it with great difficulty (quand un haut et noble coeur est pressé de passions si extremes, sensualité survenant, bende les yeux de lentendement de telle sorte que raison ny peult donner remede sinon à grand difficulté).[39] A "passion," from the Latin noun "passio," was another word for "suffering" and "illness" as well as an intense emotion. Excessive grief was considered a mental illness and even a type of love melancholy or lovesickness due to the loss of a desired object.[40] Lemaire attempts to help Margaret overcome her grief and regain her emotional and physical balance by recalling events from her own past—a sort of therapeutic *ars memoriae*—by offering her portraits of famous women who exemplify her own virtues and, especially, by offering her healing gems to comfort her by chasing away bad thoughts, nightmares, and the "venom" of misfortune.

In Lemaire's *Couronne*, ten authorities/orators present a famous woman and the corresponding jewel of an allegorical "crown." They include, in chronological order, Isidore of Seville (560–636), Albertus Magnus (1193–1280), Arnaud de Villeneuve (1235–1311), Vincent de Beauvais (d. ca. 1264), Giovanni Boccaccio (1313–75), Georges Chastellain, Martin Le Franc, Marsilio Ficino (1433–99), Jean Robertet, and Robert Gaguin. As Pierre Jodogne has noted, all the orators died before 1503 and were Christian authorities in three major areas: scientific, moral, and historical.[41] Four also bore significant feminist credentials in the querelle des femmes: Boccaccio had written the ambiguously profemale *De claris mulieribus*, Martin Le Franc the less ambiguous *Champion des dames*, Robertet a work on the sibyls that was later "borrowed" by Champier for his *Nef des dames vertueuses*, and Robert Gaguin a *Compendium* in praise of Margaret herself.[42] Three were medical authorities: Marsilio Ficino, Albertus Magnus, and Arnaud de Villeneuve.[43] Lemaire no doubt became familiar with Ficino and early modern medicine through his friendship with Champier, who was credited with first introducing Ficino's Neoplatonism into the vernacular in France in the fourth book of the *Nef des dames* (1503).[44] As early as 1506, Lemaire's correspondence bears witness to his familiarity with Champier's works in both Latin and French.[45] So, seven of the ten were either doctors, feminists, or men who wrote works in praise of women.

Several, though, could also be considered misogynists. Albertus Magnus included attacks against women, whom he characterized in *De animalibus* and *Quaestiones* as "imperfect men" and creatures to be avoided; Lemaire, like several others, no doubt attributed to him the virulently misogynistic *De secretis mulierum*, a medical work on women that divulged their secret weaknesses and inferior anatomy. Yet another, Boccaccio, viewed exceptional women as viragos in his *De claris mulieribus*—women with masculine virtues who had risen above their anatomy to do great works. Lemaire may also have been familiar with Boccaccio's virulently misogynistic *Il corbaccio* (1355), but he never mentions it elsewhere, even in his *Illustrations*. Vincent de Beauvais, an encyclopedist, also included Secundus's widely cited definition of woman in his *Speculum historiale*.[46]

A few of the orator authorities also served as sources for the *Couronne*. Lemaire used works by Albertus Magnus (*De mineralibus* and *De virtutibus lapidem*), Isidore (*Etymologies*), and Vincent de Beauvais (*Speculum morale* and *De lapidibus pretiosis*) for the medical/magical properties of the gems.[47] For portraits of the famous women, Lemaire used mostly passages from Boccaccio, and for virtues, he drew from Vincent de Beauvais's *Speculum morale*, Boccaccio's *Genealogia deorum*, and Robert Gaguin's *Compendium*, as well as the Bible and a few classical sources.[48]

There are two other narrative voices in the *Couronne*—the Acteur and the allegorical figure Virtue (Vertu). Apart from these two, who demonstrate some individual qualities, the narrative voices of the authorities are undifferentiated. Indeed, Lemaire appears to have adopted the authorities to offer Margaret medical and psychological advice that he could not offer himself, as he would subsequently adopt the narrative voice of a parrot, the "green lover," in *Les epîtres de l'amant vert* to encourage her to stem her grief at the death of her brother (1506). The allegorical figure Virtue calls upon these moral and medical authorities, deceased Christians, to judge different parts of the celestial crown, a product of *her* (Virtue's) imagination.[49] Despite Michael F. O. Jenkins's claim to the contrary, there is no real "oratorical contest" here.[50] The "judges" do not invent: they simply judge, deduce, conclude, explain, demonstrate, and narrate the crown's "concordance" or harmony.[51]

The word "concorde" is rich in connotation for Lemaire, as in the *Concorde du genre humain* and the enigmatic *Concorde des deux langages*. Virtue refers to the "mutual harmony" (concorde si mutuelle) among the different virtues of the crown and "the harmony they have with each other (la concordance qu'elles ont l'une avec l'autre).[52] She seems particularly interested in how the different parts of the crown go together—in addition to "concordance," Virtue refers to things that "conform" and to the "concatenation" of the virtues, and adds that all virtuous practices are "conjoined" (conjointes) in a perfect way.[53] Cotgrave defines "concorde" as "concord, accord, harmonie" but also "peace, agreement, quietnesse," and even a "composition." "Concorder" means to pacify or quiet. He defines "concath-enation" as a "chaining of things together." Likewise, a "conformation" or act of conforming is a "framing, fashioning, or a disposition of things to a likeness between themselves, and a fitness altogether." The result is what Lemaire calls a "magical" harmony.

In Lemaire's Neoplatonic philosophy, harmony and peace in Margaret's spiritual crown (macrocosm) will reflect—or here, actually restore—harmony and peace in her body and mind (microcosm). Evelien Chayes notes that in Renaissance lapidaries, jewels were thought to have a tempering effect on an imbalance or disequilibrium of humors.[54] Lemaire mentions temperance several times in the *Couronne*. The work begins with the virtue moderation, a virtue, he states, that belongs to the family of the cardinal virtue temperance.[55] Moderation also tempers "passions of courage." Lemaire adds, "It's a virtue that moderates all emotions, and a true *tranquility of the heart*, the opposite of pride and the enemy of *intemperance and superfluity*."[56] "Superfluity" is often used in medieval and Renaissance medicine to refer to an excess of harmful humors or any excess of passion.

The crown's gems, then, cure both physical and psychological ailments. Critics have long compared Lemaire's *Couronne* with his uncle Jean Molinet's *Chappelet des dames* (1478). Both are dedicated to women patrons—the *Chappelet* to Marie de Bourgogne and the *Couronne* to her daughter Margaret of Austria—and both are a sort of crown or garland written in praise of women.[57] Both also refer to their own tributes as memorials, or a sort of art of memory, and play on each woman's name. For example, in the *Chappelet*, the allegorical figure Experience refers to the chappelet as a "memorial" and explains to the narrator,

Then I began with complete diligence
To remember, by heart and by rote [rolle?],
the effect and redolence of the noble flowers.[58]

The authors also refer to a mystery contained in both works.[59]

However, in *Le chappellet des dames*, Molinet does little more than list the usual women of classical antiquity as well as the Bible, saints, and some near-contemporary noblewomen whose names correspond to the five letters of the name "Marie." The corresponding flowers (Marguerite, Ancollye, Rose, Iennette, Englantier) that spell out her name not only enhance beauty but also comfort the mind, cure melancholy, improve eyesight and appetite, and promote overall health. Their salutary properties promote both corporeal and spiritual well-being, ward off evil spirits, and cure the bites of poisonous creatures. They also clearly spell out therapeutic virtues like "Recovery of great happiness" (Recouvrance de grand leesse) and "Hope" (Esperance). This work, like Molinet's *Trosne d'honneur* (after 1467), aims at stopping the flow of feminine tears and excessive grief, a common malady among noblewomen at the loss of a loved one. In the *Trosne*, the allegorical figure Virtue speaks to Nobility: "I am your mother Virtue; have you forgotten the praiseworthy continence and the temperate morals that you learned in my school? O, failing heart, fragile nature, tender feminine will of very poor resistance, do you not know how to limit [amesuré] your tears through a controlling reason?"[60]

Critics have neglected one other aspect that makes them even more alike—both also insist on the works' medicinal and restorative properties.[61] At the beginning of the *Chappelet*, Molinet refers to the medicinal qualities of the five flowers in the garland—the daisy (marguerite), the columbine (ancollye), the rose, the narcissus (jennette), and the dog flower (englantier). He attributes the garland to Asclepius, an ancient Greek god of medicine: "If the garland for which Asclepius, our very expert doctor, was held in great esteem, because it destroyed basilisks (basiliques) and cured the shepherds through the strength of the herbs from which it was wisely composed, this one should not be held in less esteem, because it not only cures the sick, but also resuscitates the dead and leads their souls to the highest blessedness."[62] He also speaks of the medicinal properties of the columbine:

> Your fruit, your flower, and your root
> are medicine,
> which gives us health and life.[63]

The columbine also eases the pain of recent childbirth and destroys melancholy.[64] He describes the rose in the following manner: "The rose is the brain's just comfort . . . the eye's clarity, the tongue's appetite, the nose's solace, the hand's softness, the desire of the heart, the breast's health, the stomach's aid, and there is nothing more stimulating to help human nature, through the art of medicine, than the rose, be it through waters, oils, syrups, conserves, ointments (electuaires), cough remedies (chucades), plasters and poultices (cataplasmes)."[65] He claims that the properties of the narcissus (jennette) are salutary "for one's corporeal as well as spiritual wellbeing, because it expels and drives away bad spirits behind the one who through good devotion gathers and wears it" (tant pour le bien corporel que pour l'espirituel, car elle expulse et deboutte les mauvais espris arriere de celluy qui par bonne devotion le coeulle et porte), and, through it, "the one who wears its noble and angelic name can drive away bad spirits (poeut rebouter les mauvais esperis arriere de celluy qui en son coeur porte son hault nom angelicque).[66] The eglantine, or dog rose, "comforts the stomach, mitigates daily fevers and cures venomous bites (conforte l'estomac, mitigue la fiebvre cotidienne et sy garit morsure venimeuse).[67] The emphasis here is on driving away bad spirits and curing venomous bites and melancholy. Lemaire targets the same major problems in the *Couronne*.

In the *Couronne*, Lemaire insists repeatedly on the therapeutic effects of the gems that appear in the crown; not surprisingly, most offer protection from and cures for grief. For instance, the margarite, or pearl, comforts or brings strength to all grieving hearts (conforte tous coeurs desolez; 69), the emerald keeps away sadness (garde l'homme de tristesse; 114), and the jasper makes the wearer joyous (rend joyeux; 125).[68] There are also several that keep away bad dreams and bad thoughts: diamonds chase away nocturnal phantoms (chasse . . . fantosmes nocturnes; 76–77), amethysts keep away bad spirits and bad thoughts (reboute les mauvais esprits [et] les mauvaises cogitations . . . [fait] fuyr tout mauvais pensement; 98, 108), coral chases away Plutonic shadows and nocturnal spirits, and keeps away bad dreams (chasse les ombres Plutoniques, et les esprits nocturnes, et garde de mauvais songes; 85), the jasper stone chases away all nocturnal phantoms (chasse toutes manieres de fantosmes nocturnes; 125), and garnets do not allow any nocturnal shadow to obscure their beauty (pour nulle tenebrosité nocturne ne laisse obscurcir sa propre beauté; 142). And, since Margaret has proven effective in resisting the "venom" of Infortune in the past and is again suffering from it, the gems are also capable of curing poisons and guarding against poisonous animals. Diamonds guard against all poisons and poisonous animals, while amethysts and jaspers guard against venom. They also guard against madness or lunacy and various passions: pearls cure all passions (68–69), diamonds help "lunatics" and do not tolerate bad spirits in the body (Elle proufite aux lunatiques, et à ceux qui ont quelque esprit malin dedens le corps; 76), and topazes mitigate "lunatic passions" (passion lunatique; 140).

Several critics have also noted that the crown resembles an art of memory (Moderation = Margarite = Marguerite de Danemark). Two of the gems, the emerald (57, 114) and the garnet (escarboucle; 57, 151), even increase memory. Lemaire implies that Margaret can recover from this latest misfortune if she remembers that she has survived much worse in the past. One event mentioned several times and in at least half of the orations is her repudiation by Charles VIII.[69] Other lesser but still impressive misfortunes include the perilous trip to Spain in which she married the Infant of Spain, his tragic death when she was pregnant, and her subsequent loss of their child. The last virtue of the crown is experience, which includes "memories." Through the crown, she will profit from her experience and regain her wholeness, her once-virile courage, and thus her mental health.

Lemaire also seems preoccupied with female virility, which is often accompanied by courage in the Couronne.[70] Margaret's once-virile courage is matched by the famous women she is compared to, such as Dido, whom Lemaire declares a "virago."[71] Although Dido, who killed herself, may be a questionable example for calming a suicidal woman, there are several reasons why Lemaire chose her. After dispensing with Virgil's "lying account" (fiction menteresse) that Aeneas had offered to marry Dido but then abandoned her, Lemaire chooses instead Boccaccio's account that Dido—or Elissa, the founder of Carthage—killed herself rather than accede to a forced marriage with a foreign king so that she would not violate her promise to remain chaste and faithful to her deceased husband Acerbus, or Sychaeus. Boccaccio's Dido is a "model of unsullied widowhood."[72] Lemaire's Elissa, a chaste widow who, "not wishing to be polluted by the lustful embraces of a very cruel African King, a Moor and a barbarian, gave herself up courageously to a marvelous death" (pour non estre pollue, par les luxurieux embrasemens dun Roy African trescruel More et Barbare, se donna courageusement elle mesmes la merveilleuse mort).[73] Lemaire may have momentarily forgotten Margaret's attempted suicide, but he then refers to Elissa's experience and Dido's "virilité de courage." He also chose Dido, the virago, because she did a man's work, following the definition of "virago" offered by Isidore of Seville.[74] Margaret, he hoped, would do the man's work of making peace between the Burgundians and the French, even though she had been gravely offended by her repudiation at the hands of Charles VIII.

Lemaire praises Margaret's former eloquence and her role as peacemaker. He offers several examples of Margaret's eloquence in times of stress, such as her play on words (sarments/serments) at Charles's abandonment[75] and her witty poem when she faced shipwreck: "Ci-git Margot la gentill' demoiselle / Qui ha deux maris et encore est pucelle."[76] He also praises the eloquent poems she wrote about her life and misfortunes. In this work, as in Lemaire's Concorde des deux langages, harmony—internal and external—is inextricably linked to eloquence, which is in turn linked to Venus and the feminine. Through the magical/medical properties of the crown's gems, Margaret will not only vanquish her temporary, "feminine" insanity but also regain a sexual balance and her former talents as orator and peace-maker like those of a virago or androgyne in the Concorde, who "from a noble, virile and masculine heart, pronounced many noble terms . . . through feminine eloquence" (d'un haut cœur viril et masculin, prononce maints nobles termes . . . par elegance [éloquence] feminine).[77]

So, is the Couronne a "grand triomphe honnorable pour le sexe feminin" or a cure for temporary female insanity? Probably both, but definitely the latter. Through his narrative authorities, Lemaire offers Margaret a crown with stones that will temper her passions and cure nocturnal phantasies (bad dreams), with famous women (mostly widows who overcame their grief) and virtues that emphasize moderation and memories of the past misfortunes Margaret herself had overcome. Finally, he hopes that the crown will restore her once-virile courage, which, combined with her natural feminine eloquence, will aid in her work as ideal peacemaker.

Several critical works have appeared in the past thirty years on Jean Lemaire de Belges's poetry and prose, especially his enigmatic *Concorde des deux langages*.[78] But despite the current interest in sexual rhetoric and early modern medicine, the *Trois contes de Cupido et d'Atropos*, a three-part allegorical poem on the "Great Pox," or syphilis,[79] remains largely untouched. For decades, scholars claimed it unworthy of critical attention,[80] and a recent article confirmed old suspicions about the work's obscenity and deemed it misogynistic as well.[81] Yet the most serious critical reservation remains the doubtful provenance of two of the three poems. Many critics have avoided analyzing the poems due to this problem. For example, after a short summary of the poems in *Artful Eloquence*, Jenkins states, "But as Lemaire's authorship of this (third)—and the first—piece is disputed, I shall do no more than mention it in passing."[82] More recently, Elisabeth Caron set aside the question of provenance and treated all three as either translated or composed by Lemaire: "Since I won't resolve the question of attribution, and since there was a clear effort for coherence among these three jokes (facéties), I will hold to the opinion of the first printer."[83] In fact, much of her analysis depends upon reading into the first two poems the misogyny evident in the third.

The first poem consists of a hundred verses composed in terza rima and is purportedly based on an Italian original "invented" by Serafino Ciminelli dall'Aquila (ca. 1446–1500) that left no trace except this poem. For many years, scholars have disagreed over Lemaire's "translation" of a poem, or poems, by Ciminelli. Lemaire clearly admired the Italian poet and placed him in the company of "renowned and authoritative authors" (acteurs renommés et auctoriséz) like Dante, Petrarch, and Boccaccio in the *Concorde des deux langages*.[84] The title of the 1526 edition of the *Trois contes* indicates that the first of the three poems was merely "invented" by Ciminelli (*Les trois comptes intitulez de Cupido et de Atropos dont le premier fut inventé par Seraphin poete Italien*), while the 1549 edition added that it was "translated" by Lemaire (*Les trois contes intitulez de Cupido et d'Atropos dont*

le premier fut inventé par Seraphin poëte italien, et traduit par Jean le Maire).
So far, critics and literary scholars have not found the poem, so for many
years several preferred to believe the work a free adaptation, rather than
a translation, of an Italian original. In *Jean Lemaire, der erste humanistische
Dichter Frankreichs* (1893), Philipp August Becker identified two Ciminelli
sonnets as the sources of the *Trois contes*.[85] Henry Guy, Jean Frappier, and
Marcel Françon, among others, followed his lead.[86] More recently, however,
Jodogne agreed with the conclusion of literary critics Ferdinando Neri and
Carlo Dionisotti, who found it highly unlikely that the two sonnets cited
by Becker provided Lemaire's model for the first poem. In the sonnets, the
poet's Lady, not Atropos, appropriates Cupid's arrows.[87] Both cite several
late fifteenth- and early sixteenth-century Neo-Latin emblems and Italian
poems that more closely resemble the first poem's subject matter and that
point to an anterior source, but the work's origins remain unresolved.

The two other poems are much longer—402 and 351 verses
respectively—written in decasyllabic couplets, and attributed to Lemaire.
The third poem, though, bears interior evidence that places its composition
in 1520, approximately five years after Lemaire had left public life. In the third
poem, or conte, the author indicates the date and place of composition:
"Mil cinq cens vingt, le premier de Septembre, / Ses grans estats desquelz
je vous remembre / Furent à Tours assignez, puis tenus."[88] The first known
edition was published by Galliot du Pré in Paris in 1526 and included works
by other Rhetoriqueur poets. The three poems then appeared, in whole or
in part, in three other sixteenth-century editions: a 1539 Lyon edition by
François Juste; a 1540 Paris edition published by Alain Lotrian, titled *Le
triumphe de très haulte Dame Verolle, royne du Puy d'Amours, nouvellement
composé par l'inventeur de menus plaisirs honestes* and containing a poem on
syphilis, universally judged as spuriously attributed to Lemaire; and a 1549
Lyon edition, published by Jean de Tournes and prepared by Antoine du
Moulin, that contained several other Lemaire works.[89] Lemaire disappeared
from the French and Burgundian courts around 1514–15, shortly after the
deaths of Anne of Brittany and Louis XII, and many place his death at or
near that date.[90]

In *Jean Lemaire de Belges: Écrivain franco-bourguignon*, Pierre Jodogne offers the following conclusions gleaned from more than a century of critical debate on the work's problematic attribution: the first of the three poems is no doubt Lemaire's translation of an original Italian poem no longer extant, probably the work of Ciminelli or at least attributed to him;[91] the second is most likely a Lemaire original; and the third bears the marks of another, inferior hand, perhaps that of a younger poet steeped in forensic rhetoric, who added a conclusion to the work after Lemaire's death.[92] The second poem thus remains the only one that most critics attribute to Lemaire with few, if any, reservations.

An examination of Lemaire's use of rhetorical devices in this disjointed, much-maligned, and many-authored work within the context of Lemaire's corpus and early modern medical debate on the Great Pox reveals a play on sameness and difference that points to an overall structure, no doubt largely of Lemaire's design albeit not entirely by his hand. It mirrors his *Concorde des deux langages* and conveys a humanistic message about the power of language to lead to a medical cure for this as-yet-unnamed disease. In his study on the *Concorde*, Robert Cottrell sees "every major Renaissance text . . . [as] a point of convergence, a locus of sameness and difference," and adds that Lemaire's *Concorde* begins with a "discorde," or difference, between two languages: French and Italian. It looks back to an idyllic sameness or "primal undifferentiation," since both come from a common source (Latin), then attempts to find a *concorde*, or re-created sameness, between them—which the allegorical figure Labeur Historien reveals is an "unattainable goal."[93] The *Concorde* thus moves from a structured sameness to difference (discorde) to a deferred sameness (concorde). Cottrell calls it an "allegory of desire," defining "desire" as that which seeks but never attains the "restitution of a prior state."[94] In the allegory of disease of the *Trois contes*, or, as one critic puts it, Lemaire's "second *Concorde*,"[95] the poet takes the opposite path. He progresses from a "primal differentiation" between Cupid and Atropos to a sameness—or a discordant and monstrous undifferentiation—between love and death (syphilis), then returns to a delayed difference or provisional cure for the disease (the element mercury) brought about through the power of language, personified by Mercury, the god of eloquence.

After an introductory tercet, the fictional narrator opens the first poem in medias res, with the male Cupid and the female Atropos literally colliding in midair. He points out two resemblances right away: both are blind and capable of flight.[96] Although Atropos wants to be on her way, Cupid invites her to stop her evildoing for a time and join him for a drink. A debate ensues in which both claim their individual superiority, playing on the life–death dichotomy. Atropos plays on the love-as-a-living-death metaphor of courtly literature to insist on their similarities, claiming that her victims meet a quick death while Cupid's languish.[97] Cupid then insists on the differences between them, retorting that his victims live joyously and opposing her "grand douleur" with his "joyeux desir."[98] Before entering the tavern, he further distances himself from Atropos with a series of antitheses:

[Cupid:] Each one adores me, and I am the triumphant God:
[Atropos:] But every one flees from you like the devil
[Cupid:] You are cold and I am hot-blooded.[99]

In medieval humoral medicine, the female (Atropos) is cold and the male (Cupid) is hot, but they depart from the traditional "sexed" roles of language. According to Howard Bloch, medieval women were often associated with poetic eloquence, persuasive rhetoric, and deception, while men were deemed more prosaic, literal, and truthful.[100] Even in the *Concorde*, Lemaire describes the idealized defender of the French language as a kind of virago or androygyne: "She who from a high, *virile, and masculine* heart was uttering many noble, amorous, and *prudent* terms with *feminine eloquence*" (celle qui d'un hault *cueur virille et masculin* pronunçoit maintz nobles termes amoureux et *prudentz*, par *elegance feminine*).[101] However, here, at the poem's midpoint, Atropos interprets the love-as-death metaphor literally, while Cupid rejects it and continues to insist on their differences and separate identities.[102] The narrator intervenes to agree with Death and point out, yet again, their similarities: "One makes us languish, the other takes away life." (L'un fait languir [Cupid], l'autre nous tolt le vivre [Atropos]). Love's "danger," he adds, is far worse than Death's; setting up a time ellipsis, the narrator poses the rhetorical question: "But what finally happened to him and her?[103]

The poem resumes as the two, now drunk, leave the tavern to the relief of the owner: "Ils s'en vont hors *puis* d'un lez, *puis* de l'autre; / *Sans* dire adieu, *sans* tenir bonne voye" (They go away outside now on one side, now on the other; / Without saying goodbye, without holding to the right path).[104] The repetition of "puis" and the anaphora in "sans" create a halting rhythm that imitates their drunken gait. Clumsy and confused, they pick each other's arrows up and aim them at their traditional victims. With the antithetical verse, "Death gives us light, Cupido gives us shadow" (Mort fait *lumiere*, et Cupido fait *ombre*), the role reversal is complete.[105] In the following two tercets, the narrator describes the results:

> And with every arrow that false Cupid lets fly
> She made men and women amorous,
> Burning with a flame, subject to Cupid
> Many a beau, lively and full of vigor,
> I saw fall, struck by a deadly arrow
> And many an old man languishing from love.[106]

The author of the first conte thus alternates between the false Atropos (Cupid) and the false Cupid (Atropos) and ends by grouping them together as an undifferentiated couple, a sort of monstrous "androgyna."[107] He demonstrates that *both* share the same attributes in the two tercets by repeating the word "tous" three times in six verses and applying the same adjectives to both. In his *Poetics*, Aristotle describes a good metaphor as an "intuitive perception of the similarity of dissimilars," but here the dissimilars (love and death) have become indistinguishable as the metaphor takes on a literal reality.[108] The narrator insists, for the third time, on the pair's mutual blindness and ends with two antithetical verses: "One threatens me, the other tricks me: / One puts in the ground, and the other in bed" (L'un me menasse, à moy l'autre ne conte: / L'un met en terre, et l'autre met en couche).[109] Which, then, is Atropos, and which, Cupid?

This first poem's mythographic treatment of a medical condition no doubt appealed to Lemaire. Carlo Dionisotti and Jodogne claim that it could not have possibly emanated from a purely Italian source but offer no further explanation.[110] If Lemaire freely adapted his source, what did he inherit from the French tradition and what did he borrow from Italian sources? One French element may be the name "Atropos"; Atropos does not appear in any of the Neo-Latin emblems and Italian poems that Ferdinando Neri and Dionisotti cite as the poem's literary antecedents. The characterization of Death as Atropos was already a part of the medieval French literary and iconographic tradition; Karl Guthke, in *The Gender of Death*, cites Jean de Meun and Christine de Pizan as just two examples of French writers who equated Death with Atropos, and in an early fifteenth-century illumination for Christine's *Epître d'Othéa*, Atropos appears as an arrow- or spear-throwing, winged female.[111] The Italian or Neo-Latin tradition no doubt provided the novel initiating event, a collision between Death and Cupid that leads to an exchange of both bow and arrows. As we have already seen, a rather unconventional, bow-and-arrow-wielding Atropos already appears in the *Couronne margaritique*, written in 1504. Lemaire was probably already familiar with the Serafino poem around 1504–5, when he composed the *Couronne*, and he may have composed this "translation" as early as 1504 but not completed it until much later.

Whether Lemaire invented, freely adapted, or simply translated the first poem, it establishes the theme of linguistic confusion before this monstrous disease that the Franco-Burgundian poet will exploit to humanistic ends in the second. Lemaire picks up the narrative with a drunken Cupid, who returns home and wreaks havoc. Mentioned only once in the first conte, Venus plays a much larger role in the second. Introduced as "formerly sweet and then bitter" (or' douce et puis amere), she lies sleeping in a "poesle," a heated room or bed with hanging curtains, in her castle, garnished with jewels.[112] The description, though similar to the ekphrasis of the Temple of Venus in the *Concorde*, is much less developed. In both, Venus is surrounded by nymphs, precious gems, music, and pleasant odors, but the narrator only pauses briefly here before continuing the narrative.

The drunken Cupid falls asleep and carelessly discards one of Atropos's arrows, now in his possession, inadvertently wounding his daughter Volupté (Sensual Pleasure). Her grandmother Venus quickly heals her with a heavenly "balm." When Venus discovers that Cupid has exchanged his ivory bow for Atropos's "hideous, black" one, she warns her nymphs not to touch it, chastises the still unconscious Cupid, and demands that he be carried outside the castle.[113] She clearly blames Cupid for Volupté's near death: "I know truly that he did something bad." (Je scay de vray qu'il en ha fait du mal.)[114] A nymph wraps the offending arrow in a rug and throws it in the moat, where its "poison" pollutes the water; kills fish, swans, and ducks; and causes four of the nymphs to take to their beds. Nymphs then carry the still-sleeping Cupid outside the castle walls and place him in the courtyard. Venus calls them all together and makes them swear not to let Cupid reenter the castle until he has regained his own bow and arrows.

All then hear a horrible noise outside the castle. At first not alarmed by the crowd she sees through the window, or "verrière," Venus orders the drawbridge raised and joins her nymphs as they put on their finery and prepare to meet the young men.[115] The narrator informs us that they intend to make their suitors suffer the pangs of love before "giving in" to them (ains que rendre se veullent). Rather than evidence of the poet's attempt to blame women for the spread of syphilis, which is definitely out of character for Lemaire, this passage is yet another instance of his rather unenlightened but far from overtly misogynistic view of the psychology of female love.[116] Indeed, throughout this second poem Lemaire depicts Venus and her nymphs sympathetically. For example, the women recoil in horror at the eerie sight of Atropos, who reaches the castle driving before her old men carrying dead young men on their horses: "Et chacun d'eux porte un jeune homme mort; / Dessus sa croupe, et s'approchent bien fort."[117] The narrator tells us that the "natural order of things" (droit de naturelle usance) has been disturbed; "old men" (viellars) have replaced the youthful, "virile men" (gaillars).

Atropos orders the old men to lay down the dead youths like "swine" on the ground; she then peppers the elderly suitors with Cupid's arrows. When they cry out in pain, Cupid awakens, and Venus again chides him for his drunkenness. Filled with remorse, he confesses that it is *his* fault that Atropos has his bow and he has hers. He wants to return it but learns that Venus has already thrown it into the moat. Overjoyed with the role reversal, Atropos taunts Venus, contrasting Cupid before and after, first as a "fancy man" (fringereau) and then as an executioner (bourreau).[118] Atropos's speech, both eloquent and well constructed, constitutes twenty-six of the ninety-eight lines of direct speech in the poem.[119] She demands entry into the castle to take Cupid's place and, now unable to kill those who refuse, threatens to make them amorous or have Cupid kill them. Unlike the eloquent and persuasive Venus of the Judgment of Paris in Lemaire's *Illustrations*, this Venus now remains silent; during the exchange between Cupid and Atropos, the poet tells us twice that Venus is deeply grieved and hates Cupid for having placed her in an untenable position.

Cupid, who had addressed Atropos as "belle dame" in the first conte, resorts to name-calling; she is now an "ugly corpse" (orde charogne) with "stinking breath" (haleine puante).[120] Having lost his sharp tongue along with his bow and arrows, he demands that Atropos return his bow in an alliterative and childlike phrase with repeated possessive forms: "R̲ens m̲oy m̲on a̲r̲c que tu m̲'as de̲r̲obé" (Give me back my bow that you took from me).[121]

After Cupid's short and ineffectual speech of only nine verses, Atropos continues as eloquently as before. Since Cupid cannot return her bow, she will retain his, and then she suggests triumphantly that they exchange names as well:

I also want us to exchange names,
And that each of us take the other's:
For from now on in every cry and clamor,
Death you will be called, and I Love:
Love I will be, and you proclaimed Death,
By every one hated, feared, and blamed.[122]

Atropos insists on the name exchange four times in two tercets, the latter two in yet another chiasmus. The ambiguity and confusion created by the frequent parallel constructions in this and the first conte now result in a loss of sexual difference and consequent onomastic confusion as the love-as-death metaphor becomes literal.

Night falls, and the first-person narrator tells us that he does not know the outcome of the dispute. He only knows that to cure the waters poisoned by Atropos's bow and arrows, Venus threw in flowers, which eventually cleared and sweetened them. But although these "sweetened waters" (l'eaue emmiellée) from "venereal streams" (fossez veneriques) may appear clear, they retain their poison. The valley flowers again, and "several society people" (plusieurs mondains d'une et d'autre nature)—both male and female—gather the sweet fruits of their love and think it safe again to drink the "silvery liquid" (liqueur argentine) that runs through the "plain of lust" (plaine de luxure).[123] This passage is reminiscent of what critics have called the "fleshiness," or overt sexuality, of the Temple of Venus in the *Concorde*, where Lemaire describes similar couplings amid "silvery fountains" (fontaines argentines) and "grassy shores" (rives herbues).[124] Yet, here, those who drink the waters begin to manifest the classic signs of venereal disease, vividly described in the following passage:

> When the *venom* was ripe,
> Big buds without flowers grew on them,
> So very hideous, so ugly, and so enormous,
> That no one had ever seen such deformed faces,
> Nature had never before received
> Such a mortal injury on Her beautiful face,
> On forehead, neck, chin, and nose:
> Never had one seen so many people full of buds/pustules.
> And what is worse, this so harmful venom,
> Through its hidden and invisible malice
> Searched out the arteries,
> And caused such strange mysteries,
> Danger, the pain of passion and gout
> That one could find no remedy at all
> Other than to cry out, sigh, lament,
> Weep and complain, and wish for death.[125]

The ulcerous skin lesions of the first and second stages of syphilis are likened to "buds without flowers" (boutons sans fleur); in the third stage, the central nervous system degenerates as the patient nears death. The narrator adds that some, cured like Volupté, seem to recover but remain carriers of an "invisible poison."

Lemaire now describes a sort of medical Tower of Babel and the fruitless efforts to find the "proper name" for the disease, echoing the debate between Cupid and Atropos over their "proper names" and attributes. Here his use of "propre" can mean not only "fitting" or "proper" but also literal, as opposed to figurative, and original, former, or "anterior to others," a name that indicates the disease's origin, essence and, possible cure. In the early years of the sixteenth century, some named the disease according to its symptoms or its supposed geographical origin, others likened it to known illnesses like elephantiasis and leprosy (two that Lemaire does not explicitly mention), and still others sought a religious precedent or moralistic name. Among the attempts to name it according to its symptoms, a form of metonymy, Lemaire cites "mentagra" (Latin), "lesbones" or "las buas" (Spanish), and "groisse blatre" ("grosse Blätter" in German), all of which refer to the skin eruptions characteristic of the disease.[126] "Le mal françois" (from the Lombards) or "souvenir" of Naples (from the French) placed blame on a foreigner or the "other." Names invited comparison with existing illnesses like "verole grosse" (French) and "Pocken" (Flemish and Picard), both references to smallpox; "clavela" or "la clavelée" (from the inhabitants of the Savoy region), a sheep illness characterized by similar pustules; and "sahaphati," or asaphati, a skin disease named by Persians and called "tinia" in Latin.[127] Finally, Lemaire refers to "the disease of Job," named after the Old Testament patriarch who became the patron saint of leprosy, pox, and other illnesses in the Middle Ages,[128] and to "Sainte Reine"—or as Stecher identifies her, "Sainte Rogne"—who was thought to cure "la rogne," a common skin ailment also known as "la gale," or scabies, which mostly afflicted sheep.[129] A Sainte Reine was born in Autun and martyred in 252 in Alésia (Côte d'Or); her connection to the skin ailment cannot be confirmed, but her hagiographic attributes seem to have been borrowed from Saint Margaret of Antioch, the third-century patron saint of pregnant women and safe childbirth deliveries, as well as those suffering from disfiguring illnesses or wounds of the face.[130]

Morbus gallicus, the "French disease," was the name that often persisted, even after Fracastoro published his very popular poem in 1531 naming the disease after Syphulus, his main character—the term "syphilis" would not be universally adopted for many years.[131] Brian P. Copenhaver claims that

Champier abhorred the appellation "French disease" but used it himself on occasion.[132] The disease remained officially unnamed, since there was no medical agreement on the right one. According to the authors of *The Great Pox*, "The giving of names [in medicine] was a significant business"; medical authorities like Niccolò Leoniceno "could not accept the most popular, vernacular denomination ('French Disease') of the disease, because it meant little more than the accidents of geography surrounding its recent appearance."[133] As early as 1497, Leoniceno noted that "the 'true name' of the disease had not yet been given to it by contemporary physicians. The true name, for Leoniceno, would have been either that given by the ancients, or one that carried some greater degree of meaning. Most of the contemporary physicians identified it with *elephantiasis*, deceived (says Leoniceno) by the similarity between the diseases. But Leoniceno did not give a new name to *Morbus Gallicus*."[134] He, like many other medical authorities, restricted himself to describing the disease's symptoms. Debates centered on whether the disease was new or old; if old, as Leoniceno believed, finding the right name among the works of ancient authorities, like Galen or Hippocrates, would be sufficient to find a cure. The narrator of the second poem evidently agrees to leave the disease unnamed—not because it is "unnameable," as Caron offers, but because it would be tantamount to offering a cure. Instead, the narrator ends the poem ironically: Although no one knows what to call this new disease, one thing is certain—Venus and Cupid's names have been forever muddied, and chastity, for so long unpopular, is now back in fashion.

The third *conte*, heavily marked by a forensic rhetoric unlike Lemaire's own, contains four long speeches, each approximately fifty to sixty verses long and interspersed with narrative passages.[135] The first, Venus's appeal to Jupiter, consists of an *exordium* and a *narratio*. The author has Venus blame herself and her son for the spread of the disease and even refers to original sin; this misogynistic passage departs from Lemaire's more sympathetic treatment of Venus in the second *conte*. In fact, the author of the third *conte* mentions Venus's role in the spread of the disease four times: the narrator mentions it first, then Venus, then Megara, and finally Mercury. The narrator also uses similar alliterative adjectives to place blame on both

Venus and Atropos and to draw a parallel between them: Venus's actions cause "a thousand miserable misfortunes" (mille *malheures meschans*), while Atropos's arrows are "miserable arrows, unfortunate and accursed" (traictz *meschans, malheureux* et maulditz).[136]

The two longest and most developed speeches that follow, Volupté's and Megara's, constitute the *exordium*, often aimed at winning the good will of the judge or jury; here, it is characterized by *vituperatio*, as the two trade insults and question each other's motives and legal rights. Both speeches are well balanced yet uninspired, and again both reflect the earlier similarities and differences between Cupid and Atropos with still more chiasmic constructions such as Megara's characterization of Volupté: "Venom of honor, poison of virtue" (Venin d'honneur, de vertu la poison).[137] Volupté insists on the differences between Death and Cupid by stating ironically: "They are as alike as death and life" (Qu'ilz sont pareilz, ainsi que mort et vie).[138] Like Atropos in the first conte, Megara points out their metaphorical similarities, playing on the same life–death dichotomy:

If Death's bow is sad and painful,
Love's is grievous and languorous:
One sends at once from this world to the next.
The other, a living death makes the features fade.
. . . .
Better from death to lose suddenly life's vigor
Than to live in love, and languish away.[139]

The poet of the third conte thus imitates the two preceding poems by playing with the rhetorical symmetry and parallel structures of these two speeches to demonstrate the linguistic confusion caused by the disease and the impossibility of finding a resolution or cure without divine intervention.

Finally, the poet imitates the deus ex machina ending of the *Concorde des deux langages*. In the *Concorde*, the allegorical figure Labeur Historien shows the two languages kissing in a mirror as the actual *concorde*, original union, or primal undifferentiation—but this is a deferred *concorde*: the narrator will only experience it after his death (après le decours de ma vie, et non devant).[140] In this third conte, Jupiter, described as "hating false Discord" and as the god "[who] transforms disharmony into good harmony" ([qui] met tout discord en bonne concordance), sends Mercury, god of eloquence, to resolve the forensic stalemate between Volupté and Megara.[141] Mercury restores the bows and arrows to their rightful owners and thus reestablishes their difference, but the resolution is only provisional. The real *concorde* will come with the fullness of time: "Water must run its course" (Il faut que l'eaue ayt cours).[142] To agree, at least in part, with Caron's thesis, the water here may very well refer to women's watery or wet humors. Mercury works here on two levels, metaphorical and literal, that reflect the wordplay in the poem. Mercury as god of eloquence represents the power of language, while the element mercury was used externally to cure syphilis in the late fifteenth and early sixteenth centuries.[143]

The *Trois contes* describes a linguistic *discorde* that only Mercury, the god of eloquence—and, by extension, language—can resolve. Through the use of parallel and antithetical structures, Ciminelli, Lemaire, and his imitator or third author portray a linguistic confusion between Cupid and Atropos, which results in an onomastic confusion and unthinkable gender role reversal that mirrors the early modern medical debate on the disease, its origin, and its cure. Unlike the *Concorde des deux langages*, here the *discorde* is based on sameness and looks back to a primal differentiation, when the male Cupid and female Death were separate. The *Trois contes* thus conveys a message about the power of language to create an original and literal differentiation between love and death and to lead to a "proper name" and cure for this as-yet-unnamed disease. Like the *Concorde des deux langages*, these three poems constitute an allegory of desire and, ironically, an antidote to desire,[144] in which the authors look back with nostalgia to a differentiated past when love as death was merely a metaphor.

CONCLUSION

In both the *Couronne* and the *Trois contes de Cupido et d'Atropos*, Lemaire demonstrates an intense interest in medicine, one perhaps arising from his close friendship with Symphorien Champier, whom he met in Lyon. Lemaire also discovered other humanist writings in Lyon, such as the letters of Ficino, one of his sources for the second book of his *Illustrations de Gaule et singularitez de Troye* (1511–13).[145] At the same time, Lemaire cannot refrain from displaying his view of the author's role and the power of language in both works. A writer typically confers glory on his patrons, but, in the case of the *Couronne*, the male author Lemaire apparently felt free to chastise his female patron for displaying "imbecillité feminine," or excessive grief, a form of erotomania, or love melancholy—however short-lived—at the unexpected, tragic death of her husband. For this woman, who supposedly had a cold and humid nature and therefore a retentive memory, an art of memory served to remind her of past victories over multiple misfortunes and a Christian reward in heaven. But, more important, this spiritual crown replete with gems possessing therapeutic powers served to heal her tempo-rary humoral imbalance and allow her to transcend corporeality in order to resume her historic and atypically female role of peacemaker.

Like the *Couronne*, the *Trois contes* is yet another work on love and death, and it too only appeared in print after the death of the author. Cimi-nelli, Lemaire, and the third poet depict the Great Pox as not only another imbalance of humours but also a breakdown in male and female roles. A male Cupid and a female Atropos exchange roles and even names to depict the sexual chaos of this new, or perhaps old, scourge. Only language—in the figure of Mercury, the god of language and the favored cure for the disease—can re-create a provisional sexual difference until a cure is found. An original sexual difference, a clear separation of male and female, and by extension a provisional pause in male–female sexual unions, is the only answer to this new form of lovesickness.

5

Fatal Lovesickness in Marguerite de Navarre's *Quatre dames et quatre gentilzhommes* and the *Heptaméron*

In an article on Marguerite's play *Le mallade* (ca. 1535), Colette Winn makes a strong case for the queen's critical attitude toward abuses in the medical profession and her lifelong interest in medicine.[1] In *Marguerite de Navarre, Mother of the Renaissance*, Patricia and Rouben Cholakian point out Marguerite's charitable work in founding hospitals and reforming existing ones. They describe how many times Marguerite rushed to the bedside of a sick relative, calling her the "family nurse" and an "early heroine of medical history."[2] Contemporaries like Brantôme also praised Marguerite's nursing skills: he credited her with "curing" Francis I of a life-threatening illness when the king was held hostage in Spain in 1525.[3] But in "Marguerite de Navarre's *Heptaméron* and the Received Idea: The Problematics of Lovesickness," Donald A. Beecher offers novellas 26 and 50 as examples of tales in which Marguerite uses lovesickness "merely [as] a factual auxiliary barely extending into the realm of theme."[4] He contends that close scrutiny of the malady's clinical aspects in the novellas, a largely fruitless endeavor, would be tantamount to "literary archaeology."[5] However, Marguerite was steeped in the medical knowledge of her time, and in two of her works, *Les quatre dames et les quatre gentilzhommes* and the *Heptaméron*, Marguerite focuses on lovesickness and portrays it as a feigned illness intended to win over women's resistance to male sexual advances. In the sixteenth century, lovesickness was not only a Petrarchan poetic convention but also a medical condition thought to be caused by unrequited passion; it was also known as erotomania or erotic melancholy.[6] Examining lovesickness and other received medical ideas in *Les quatre dames* and the *Heptaméron* leads to a better understanding of these works, their author, and one of the major points of contention in the querelle des femmes. Indeed, Marguerite's complex narrative strategies and skillful use of the controversial medico–moral debate on lovesickness in both works conveyed a richly textured message about literary interpretation and sexual difference to her contemporary, active readers.

Lovesickness figures prominently in the *Quatre dames*, a work in verse first published in 1547.[7] Even though critics have judged the work severely over the years,[8] it is nonetheless worthy of study. It prefigures the *Heptaméron* in gender parity—four women and four men speak or write the letters—treats lovesickness as a potentially fatal illness, and reveals much about Marguerite's role in the querelle des femmes.[9]

LOVESICKNESS IN *LES QUATRE DAMES ET LES QUATRE GENTILZHOMMES*

In *Les quatre dames et les quatre gentilzhommes*, Marguerite uses poetic conventions of love to respond to Alain Chartier's *La belle dame sans mercy*, in which women are accused of lacking natural pity when they refuse men who use "lovesickness" as a ruse and threat to gain women's "gift of pity" (don de mercy), or sexual surrender.[10] Here, she adopts the narrative voices of four ladies and four gentlemen; according to André Gendre, five of the eight parts (pièces) are letters; the first lady's and first gentlemen's are "single-voiced dialogues" (dialogues à une voix), and the second lady's resembles a last will and testament.[11] The second and fourth ladies as well as all four gentlemen describe their lovesick sufferings. All profess to prefer death to their endless sufferings—all except the first gentleman, who has already died from them and speaks from beyond the grave. Marguerite's lovesick ladies and gentlemen describe the condition as an illness,[12] a form of madness,[13] a type of melancholy,[14] and even a living death.[15] The sufferers change appearance,[16] sigh, cry out, and complain;[17] or, in later manifestations, remain completely mute. They use various metaphors to describe love or personify it: love is a Cupid who shoots fatal arrows,[18] a sweet nourishment that becomes a dangerous meal,[19] and a sweetness transformed into a poison.[20] The male lovers' preferred methods for ending their suffering include hanging themselves, setting themselves on fire, drowning in the sea, or dying in battle. The two lovesick women simply pray for death as deliverance from an intolerable situation, although the second lady briefly entertains committing suicide by hanging or by fire.

While critics have compared various parts of the *Quatre dames* to novellas in the *Heptaméron*, the first lady's and the first gentleman's monologues, or "dialogues à une voix," at the start of each section have been the two most closely associated with Marguerite's *Heptaméron*. Pierre Jourda compares the first lady to three characters—Marguerite herself, the heroine of novella 4, and Floride in novella 10—and the first gentleman to the milord of novella 57.[21] But the novellas most commonly linked to the first gentleman's are novellas 9 and 26, which center around lovesickness.[22] These two novellas will be the subject of the second part of this chapter. In the *Quatre dames*, Marguerite focuses on lovers who threaten suicide or claim to be suffering from a languishing melancholy, but the reader can already detect traces of her future indictment against fatal lovesickness in the *Heptaméron*. Lovesickness was a hotly debated topic in the sixteenth century. Physicians, natural philosophers, and moralists argued over whether lovesickness was a real illness, whether it was potentially fatal, whether it affected men or women more, and whether therapeutic intercourse or making love to another, a commonly prescribed cure thought quite efficacious, was morally defensible.

The first of the four ladies does not suffer from lovesickness; rather, she is not lovesick. She starts her account proclaiming, "I do not wish to love, yet too loved I am / I am hunted by the one that I flee" (Aymer ne veux, et trop aymée suis / Cerchée suis de celuy, que je fuys).[23] In fact, it is not because she is loved but because she is "loved too much" (trop aymée; 9, 106, 255) that she suffers. She even addresses her suitor as "Too loving" (trop aymant; 13) and later characterizes his love as "extreme" (135) and as "a love without measure" (un amour sans moyen; 222). She finds it no laughing matter to suffer from the unwanted advances of a man who haunts her home and incessantly declares his love. She compliments him by touting his physical and moral virtues, but she resolutely refuses to swim in such a dangerous sea: "I do not wish to swim in a Sea / So perilous, and where there is so much bitterness, / and nothing sweet" (Je ne veux point nager en la Mer / Tant perilleuse, et où tant a d'amer, / et rien de doulx; 34–36). She has seen too many swimmers who were once "wise" (sages) "become more than foolish" (devenir . . . pis que foulz; 39). She refers to her extreme lover as "unwise" (peu sage; 57) and to his "foolish love" (Fol Amour; 118) and his "foolish intention" (fole intention; 237). "Fol" and "fole" carry the connotation of "crazy" as well, and she hopes that her clear rejection will restore his sanity and cure him of the foolish love that is making him rave (Ce fol Amour, qui vous fait insenser; 114–17). She encourages him to find another (94, 161–63) and suggests a "very wise woman" (une bien sage; 186) who will return his love.[24] In novella 26 of the *Heptaméron*, Marguerite's *devisant* will use "sage" and "folle" to describe the two women, one of whom dies of lovesickness.

The first lady hopes to cure her suitor's "illness," which she describes in detail. His appearance and behavior have changed:

> You are losing countenance and speech
> Your grace and conversation
> And I too all pleasure and peace
> When I see that life, complexion, and pulse,
> Joy and health are failing in you because of me.[25]

She sees the pain written on his face and chides him for allowing himself to waste away:

> It would be better, completely nude or in a doublet
> To die of hunger
> Than to languish, so handsome, so strong, so *healthy*.[26]

The message is clear: her suitor is healthy and strong but is allowing himself to languish. She speaks of his sighs and complaints (134), his "extreme" pain (203), and the poison in his heart (244–45). She also warns him of the dangerous outcome (dangereuse fin; 101) to which his "foolish Love" will lead him and tells him she already sees the combat with Death on his face (55). She warns him repeatedly that his love will end in his death and adds that it is not only his health and sanity that he risks but hers as well. That is no doubt why she refers five times to her own death: she would rather die than give in to him (107–23); his sighs and extreme love are killing her (132–36); if she could cure him by her death, she would willingly do so (137–38); she would rather die than be seduced (164–71); and he will die as well as cause her death if he does not cease his advances:

> You will die from it;
> And you will be the cause of my death
> Go away; for you will gain nothing.[27]

Her message could not be clearer as she urges him to "go elsewhere" (Allez ailleurs).[28] She regrets ever having made his acquaintance and wishes to cut off all contact. Finally, the lady challenges him to change his attitude or commit suicide, no doubt something he had threatened to do before:

> If this cannot be
> As I say, and if you are not master
> Of your heart, then let it now find pasture
> Where it will; or with a cord or rope [chevestre]
> Make a noose [licol],
> And hang yourself high by the neck
> Demonstrating that a soft and effeminate heart
> By loving too much constrains you to be crazy.[29]

Here she also calls his bluff by questioning his masculinity. Rather than a courageous heart, he possesses a soft, feminine heart, and she accuses him of playing at the suffering lover, a clear indication that she believes his illness may simply be a ruse to seduce her.

Finally, the lady claims that she will love no one else either. Jourda characterizes the first lady's monologue as an example of "coquetterie and indifference," which no doubt arises from a misreading of the last line: "I will never love anyone but you" (Qu'autre que vous je n'aymeray jamais).[30] André Gendre corrects the seeming contradiction by adding the unstated but understood "non plus": "I will never love anyone else *either*."[31] Indeed, Marguerite has fashioned here a positive model for female readers who might find themselves in similar circumstances, that is, threatened by a lovesick suitor who sighs and languishes or threatens to commit suicide if they do not give in to his sexual advances.

While the second, third, and fourth gentlemen also threaten suicide to end their lovesickness, the first gentleman's monologue offers us the only account of lovesickness that has already led to death. From paradise, he says, God allows him, like all dead lovers, to declare his love:

> Their love, it is permitted by God,
> That after Death has put to sleep their bodies,
> Quite clearly,
> That they might show to their Ladies, how
> For them they died in pain and torment.[32]

In this example of what he calls "pure love," he praises his loved one's refusal to accept even "wise" suitors or listen to their declarations. In life, he served as her confidant, kept silent, never wanting to displease her by declaring his love. He repeatedly describes his fear of displeasing her, using words like "crainte," "craingnant," "avoir peur," and "paoureux." In the medical and moral literature of the time, fear was considered an especially female failing, but here, Marguerite sees his fear in a different light; his selfless love led him to keep silent. The gentleman then gives a metaphorical account of his death. He trapped Love in his heart, and when it could not be declared or released, Love ruptured the man's heart.[33] Marguerite offers a more feasible physiological explanation for the death of the lovesick lady of Pamplona in novella 26.

Fear and dissimulation play a large role in both novella 26 and in the *Quatre dames*. The first gentleman emphasizes the hidden nature of his love; he uses the verbs "to dissimulate" (dissimuler), "to conceal" (celer), "to cover up" (couvrir), "to swallow" (avaller), and "to hide" (cacher). Yet, he claims that his secret love for his lady nonetheless shone through his eyes, and he lightly chides her for not noticing. Here Marguerite gives us a portrait of true "perfect love," (parfaite amour) a self-sacrificing and pious love where the sufferer remains silent rather than lead another into a possibly tempting sin. But she also alludes to other outcomes of lovesickness, as the gentleman claims that others who have tried to seduce his beloved died, went insane, or found themselves in constant pain.[34]

In these eight poems, Marguerite not only examines various cases of unhappy lovers but also begins to examine lovesickness as well. She focuses on "foolish" or "extreme" love and warns that it can lead to death through lingering illness or suicide. At the same time, she hints that lovesickness may be a simple ploy to win over a lady's defenses in order to seduce her and gain the "don de mercy." If there is any doubt that Marguerite is questioning whether lovesickness is real or feigned, she alludes to Chartier's *Belle dame sans mercy* in the third gentleman's letter, in which he addresses his beloved as his "Dame sans pitié" and calls her cruel for refusing his love. Marguerite also cites *La belle dame sans mercy* in novella 12 of the *Heptaméron*, where Parlamente, speaking of lovesickness, says: "*The Beautiful Lady without Pity* teaches us that such a gentle love hardly kills people."[35] Yet the first gentleman apparently died of lovesickness. In the first gentleman's speech, Marguerite emphasizes the dissimulation that causes the kind of lovesickness that can lead to a premature death. She indicates here and in the *Heptaméron* that when outward appearance and inward truth do not coincide, the result can be illness and even death. In these two letters and in the *Heptaméron*, she demonstrates that lovesickness is more often a feigned than real illness and potentially but unnecessarily fatal.

FATAL LOVESICKNESS IN THE *HEPTAMÉRON*

Illness plays an important role in the *Heptaméron* from the very beginning.[36] In the prologue, the *devisants* have all traveled to the waters of Cauterets to cure various maladies. Before their arrival there, many, we are told, had been "abandoned by doctors" but are on the point of returning home completely healed. We are not informed of who was ill—we only discover that Dagoucin and Saffredent were not. In their refuge at Notre Dame de Sarrance, Parlamente, whom we are told is neither "lazy nor melancholic," asks that Oisille offer a pastime and notes, "Because if we have no pleasant or virtuous activity, we are in danger of *remaining sick.*"[37] The newly widowed Longarine adds, "But what is worse, we'll become troublesome [or annoying], which is an *incurable illness,* because there is no one, male or female, among us, who doesn't have a reason for *extreme sadness*" (Mais, qui pis est, nous deviendrons fascheuses, qui est *une maladie incurable*; car il n'y a nul ni nulle de nous, s'ilz regardent leur perte, qu'il n'ayt occasion d'*extresme tristesse*).[38] Oisille replies that she has searched for a "remedy" all her life and found it in Holy Scripture, where one finds "the true and perfect joy of the soul, whence proceeds the tranquility and *health* of the body" (la vraye et parfaicte joye de l'esprit, dont procedde le repos et *la santé* du corps).[39] It has kept her healthy in her old age; she finds food (pâture) for her soul, which protects her from various illnesses/ evils (maux). Ennasuitte adds that if they don't have a pleasant activity, they will be dead the next day. Marguerite's *devisants* clearly indicate that melancholy—extreme sadness—can lead to serious illness and even death.

While the deaths in the prologue to Boccaccio's *Decameron* are caused by illness, in the *Heptaméron*'s prologue all deaths occur in other ways, such as bandits, bears, and floodwaters. In fact, a survey of Marguerite's seventy-two tales reveals that there are approximately 128 deaths and that they take place in only twenty-three of the seventy-two novellas. If we subtract the 84 deaths that occur in battle (novellas 10 and 13), 2 suicides, 17 murders, 4 executions, 1 accidental death, and then further reduce the number by 6 "natural deaths"—where the cause of death is indeterminate but suggestive of old age—only 16 occur from illness. Of those, there are approximately 7 "sudden deaths" from indeterminate causes—most appear, however, to be the result of a bad conscience or sudden emotional shock. For example, in novella 21, Rolandine's brother dies suddenly after refusing to grant her an inheritance, the possible result of a bad conscience or divine wrath. In novella 22 a priest dies shortly after he confesses to an attempted rape, and in novella 70 the duke's niece collapses from the shock of her revealed love affair and dies.

Of the nine remaining deaths from illness, Marguerite names only two potentially fatal ones—a "catarrhe," or bad cold (in one of the tales a woman recovers from a potentially fatal cold when she sees her husband in the arms of a chambermaid) and lovesickness, or "mal d'amour." Lovesickness is named only once in the *Heptaméron* as a "mal d'amour" in novella 20. Marguerite differentiates between love and lovesickness by defining sufferers of the latter as ill or fearful of dying. Feigned lovesickness is more prevalent than "real" lovesickness. In fact, there are almost as many feigned illnesses, eight in all, as real ones mentioned in the *Heptaméron*. A man feigns illness to hide scratches on his face (novella 4); a woman uses her brother's supposed illness as a pretext to leave a door open for her lover (novella 14); a young woman claims to be suffering from a migraine, and then a pain in her leg, to be alone with her lover or secret husband (novella 21); a woman fakes an illness to hide the traces of a beating she received from her husband, disguised as her beloved (novella 35); a woman feigns illness to leave her lawful husband and join a lover (novellas 60 and 61); and a woman claims to be sick and pregnant to get her husband to reveal a secret that she passes on to others (novella 70). In every one of these, the feigned illness hides a particular sin. In only two cases, novellas 42 and 63, do people feign illness to *avoid* sin.

Real and potentially fatal illnesses such as smallpox, measles, malaria, scarlet fever, chicken pox, and plague, so prevalent in the day, are completely absent from the *Heptaméron*. The absence of real illnesses with long-lasting effects in the novellas can be explained as conforming to the *devisants'* wish to avoid melancholic tales. In novella 40, Nomerfide explains that since death is inevitable, a quick death is preferable: "And as for death, that you call cruel, it seems to me that, since it is necessary, the shortest [death] is the best, because one knows only too well that the passage is inevitable; but I hold those who remain only a short while in the suburbs of death "happy," because from "happiness," such as it is in this world, they fly to an eternal happiness in the other."[40] When Simontaut asks her, "What do you call the suburbs of death?" (Que appellez vous les faulx bourgs de la mort?), she answers,

> Those who have tribulations in their souls . . . those who have been ill a long time, and who because of extreme corporeal or *spiritual* pain, have

come to devalue death and find the hour [of their death] too long in coming, I say that those persons have passed through the suburbs and will tell you of the hostels where they have cried out more than rested. This woman [Rolandine's aunt] could not help but lose her husband through death, but she was exempt, through her brother's anger, to see her husband ill or troubled for a long time.⁴¹

Marguerite, twice widowed, witnessed the deaths of many family members and, in later years, suffered from a debilitating condition. But here she cites both spiritual and physical pain and suggests that the former is as dangerous as the latter. Suffering in the mind is often worse than death.

On several occasions, the *devisants* refer to a person's heart and soul exercising power over the body and leading to physical illnesses. For instance, in novella 63, Oisille talks about the heart's control over the body. If one has really given one's heart to something, such as the perfection of sciences, God, or a woman, one can overcome the body's need for sex, even for food and drink: "When the body is subject to the mind, it is almost insensitive to the imperfections of the flesh" (Quant le corps est subject à l'esprit, il est quasi incensible aux imperfections de la chair).⁴² To illustrate her point, she describes a man who, while looking at his wife, was able to hold a candle in his bare hand until it was burned to the bone.⁴³ In novella 67, Simontaut tells a tale of a man who betrayed captain Roberval and was stranded with his wife on an island inhabited only by beasts. The woman brought the "food" of the New Testament with her and read it incessantly. Marguerite refers to the woman as her husband's spiritual guide and "doctor" (medecin). The two fight off and even eat the wild beasts on the island. Their bread runs out, water makes the man swell up, and he dies. The woman survives, no doubt because her soul was stronger than her husband's and paradoxically sustained her weaker body: "God is able to nourish his servants in a desert, like at the greatest feast in the world" (Dieu est puissant de nourrir en ung desert ses serviteurs, comme au plus grand festin du monde).⁴⁴

There are so few real illnesses and so many "feigned" ones in the *Heptaméron*, no doubt to prove that lovesickness is often feigned and, if real, unnecessarily fatal. Novellas 3, 9, 10, 13, 20, 22, 26, and 50 describe lovesickness both real and feigned.[45] As in *Les quatre dames et les quatre gentilzhommes*, erotomania, or erotic melancholy, has many symptoms. In fact, in the *Heptaméron* Marguerite appears to have added a substantially larger number of symptoms to insist on the medical aspects of the debate. Here, the sufferer often complains of dying because of unrequited love, or is described as "melancholic" or extremely sad. The sufferer may also refuse to eat or drink, lose sleep, sweat profusely, or faint. A person struck by erotomania may suffer from a constant fever, cold extremities, an intestinal or liver obstruction, constant pain, or a rapid heart rate, turning deathly pale or yellow from jaundice and, in some extreme cases, changing appearance completely, becoming unrecognizable. Lovesickness is often not only described as a malady but also as temporary insanity or a blind passion or fury beyond the control of the sufferer. All complain of a fire burning from within, usually in the vicinity of their hearts.

Yet erotic melancholy leads directly to death only twice in the *Heptaméron*. A man dies of it in novella 9, a woman in novella 26. The former purports to show "a gentleman's virtuous love unto death" (l'amour vertueuse d'un gentilhomme jusques à la mort); the latter, "the difference between a foolish and wise lady, which demonstrates the different effects of love" (la différence d'une folle et saige dame, ausquelles se monstr<e>t les differendz effectz d'amour).[46] However, instead of meeting readers' expectations with an exemplary portrait of a woman's virtuous demise in novella 26,[47] Saffredent responds to and reconfigures Dagoucin's novella 9 as a didactic cautionary tale. He casts the man as the central figure, a Paris facing a Neoplatonic choice between two Venuses: a "wise," chaste lady and a "foolish," lascivious one.[48]

Marguerite apparently trusted her readers to recognize Saffredent's recasting of Dagoucin's earlier tale and to interpret it accordingly. According to Colette Winn, Marguerite's tales often echo each other.[49] A novella may refer back to an earlier one, or a "histoire-modèle," and propose an alternative view of the subject through repeated and altered scenes. By calling on the memory of the earlier tale, this *texte-écho* invites readers "to retrace their steps to discover links that are not explicitly described in the text" (revenir sur ses pas pour découvrir des liens qui ne sont pas explicitement décrits dans le texte).[50] In *Reading in the Renaissance,* Marian Rothstein adds that sixteenth-century readers, well versed in arts of memory, would have recognized narrative pairings in the *Heptaméron,* "bringing one situation to reflect on another, adding psychological and moral depth to the collection" through what Rothstein terms an active reading.[51]

Novellas 9 and 26 present one such narrative pair, as evidenced by Saffredent's metatextual comments before and after each, the novella he relates the day before, and his use of analogous intertextual episodes and intratextual doublings in novella 26. An active reading of novella 26 against the backdrop of received medical ideas on lovesickness reveals how Saffredent's refashioning or corrective reading of novella 9 and his play on literal and figurative meanings present two conflicting readings—one that appears to praise the wise lady as a model of virtue and another that censures her hypocrisy.

In both novellas, Dagoucin and Saffredent each accuse women of hypocrisy in a love affair that ends tragically. In Dagoucin's, a young man is not allowed to marry his beloved for social and economic reasons, even though he thinks she loves him. His face shows the ravages of his condition, and his weakened heart finally fails.[52] Dagoucin blames the young woman's silence for his death: "Absolute love leads to death when it is too hidden and unknown" (parfaicte amour mene les gens à la mort, par trop estre cellée et mescongneue).[53] If *she* had only revealed *her* inner feelings, *he* might not have died.

In Saffredent's *texte-écho,* however, a young woman hides her inner feelings and causes her own death. In this case study, two women are in love with the same young man, the lord of Avannes, who falls in love with one of them: the virtuous wife of his adoptive father. Knowing that revealing his love will end their friendship, he decides to cure his lovesickness by sleeping with the other, foolish woman. Therapeutic intercourse as medical cure for lovesickness originated in the first century AD and was popularized in the Middle Ages by such "Arab" medical authorities as Rhazes (d. 935) and Avicenna (d. 1087).[54] Although it "jarred with Christian morality," western Christian doctors began to recommend it as well, and by the sixteenth century it had become the predominant cure.[55] However, in this case the cure apparently failed, since Avannes, weary from sexual overindulgence with the foolish woman, returns to his adoptive father's home and proclaims his love for the wise woman. She remains silent, a fatal decision.

Saffredent's metatextual commentary before novella 9 already begins to contradict conceiving of novella 26 as an *exemplum* for women. Here, he expresses doubt that lovesickness can be fatal: "*Not by speaking but by dying did they confess their faith*. I have heard tell of those who die from love, but never have I seen one die from it! And since I have escaped, despite the vexations I have suffered from it, I don't think that anyone could ever die from it."[56] In the discussion after novella 9, he agrees with Hircan that the dead lover was singularly lacking in courage and boasts that any man can win over any woman if she loves him and if he is daring and wise enough in his pursuit:

Madame . . . to confirm Hircan's argument, with which I agree, I beg you to believe that Fortune aids the *audacious*, and that there is no man, if he is loved by a lady, and if he knows how to pursue her *wisely* and with affection, who, in the end, will not get everything he asks for, or in part. But *ignorance and foolish fear* lead men to lose out in many adventures, and they base their defeat on the virtue of their beloved [amye], whom they have never touched even with a finger: for no place well assaulted will ever remain untaken.[57]

Indeed, Saffredent demonstrates in both novellas 20 and 26 that their own fears are all that prevent men from attaining sexual favors from virtuous women.

In novella 20, Saffredent offers a partial response to novella 9 and a prelude to novella 26. The protagonist, "le seigneur de Ryant," hesitates to approach a seemingly virtuous woman because he fears he will lose her friendship: "He had long been the servant of a widowed lady, whom he loved and revered so much that, because he *feared* losing her good grace, he did not dare to approach what he desired the most."[58] Later he catches her in flagrante delicto with an unworthy muleteer; the sight immediately cures him of his "mal d'amour." The novella's language indicates a medical condition: the "poor martyr" (pouvre martir) is "cured and delivered from a continuous pain" (guary et delivré de la continuelle douleur).[59] Avicenna suggests that denigrating the beloved cures lovesickness and that the lovesick might hire an old woman (thought to be more efficacious than others) to say horrible things about her.[60] Here, the woman's own actions disgrace her, and, "in a moment" the seigneur de Ryant finds the strength to extinguish the "fire" that had burned so long for this woman; Saffredent tells us that the young woman covers her face in shame for her "dissimulation."[61] In the discussion afterward, Saffredent again points out the woman's hypocrisy, but Oisille, who challenges the tale's veracity, casts suspicion on his motives.[62] Through Oisille, Marguerite hints at Saffredent's preoccupation with responding to novella 9 and his willingness to stretch the truth to do so. By portraying the true nature of the idealized object of beauty and revealing the cause of the seigneur de Ryant's lovesickness as a carnal woman, Saffredent emphasizes the gentleman's needless fear in approaching her and prepares the reception of novella 26.

While the metatextual commentary that precedes novella 26 might lead readers to expect that Saffredent will be kind to women, the novella offers at best an ambivalent *exemplum* of a woman's ill-fated virtue. No doubt alluding to Saffredent's portrait of the immoral noblewoman in novella 20, Longarine asks him not to insult women but rather to show good where it exists and to tell the truth.[63] Saffredent simply invites his female listeners to follow "whichever example they find most pleasing."[64]

It seems unlikely that sixteenth-century readers would have ignored Saffredent's strong reaction to novella 9 and his intervening tale of a gentleman cured of lovesickness by his lady's choice of lover (novella 20). Even then, the analogous scenes he draws invite a more reflective reading of novella 26. Parallels include:

1. The male lover wears a "mask" in both.
2. The male lover impetuously jumps on or into bed.
3. The male lover requests a kiss that is first refused but eventually bestowed through the intervention of another.
4. The dying lover reveals the cause of his/her death to the beloved.
5. The surviving lover embraces the dead lover and makes known his/her love.
6. The survivor mourns the lover's death.

In each of these scenes, Saffredent skillfully reconfigures the earlier tale by echoing words and images, doubling the female characters, offering a commentary based on contemporary medicine, and playing on literal and figurative meanings of conventions of courtly love.

When the young man in novella 9 falls ill from unrequited love, Dagoucin tells us that "he covered his face's beauty with a death mask" (il couvrist la beauté de son visaige du masque de la mort).[65] In novella 26, Avannes's real mask, a false nose and beard, allows him to gain access to the "foolish" woman's household, but when he later falls ill, his illness makes him unrecognizable: "Without a mask, one could hardly recognize him" (Sans porter masque, on le pouvait bien déconnaître).[66] By doubling the mask metaphor, Saffredent plays on literal and figurative meanings to double and contrast two different maladies as well as the effects of the two women's affection and attraction on Avannes. As the young man sets out for the foolish woman's house, the wise woman guesses his destination and warns him to watch out for his health. After multiple amorous encounters with him, the foolish, lascivious woman, who possesses such "lust that reason, conscience, order, and measure no longer found a place in her" (telle volupté que raison, conscience, ordre ni mesure n'avoient plus de lieu en elle), callously sends Avannes home, since she "does not like him sick as much as she does healthy" ([elle] ne l'aymoit pas tant mallade que sain).[67] Avannes's "youth and delicate complexion" have suffered from the affair, and he is now pale, thin, and barely recognizable due to his "foolish love" (fol amor) and "dazed senses" (sens ebettez).[68] He is evidently suffering from the deleterious effects of excessive sexual activity rather than lovesickness. According to sixteenth-century medical beliefs, both extremes—sexual excess and sexual deprivation—were thought deadly. While a surfeit of semen could become corrupted and lead to excessive black bile (cholera nigra), lovesickness, its opposite, could cause a depletion of semen (supposedly fed by blood), which was thought to lead to anemia, pallor, sunken eyes, and eventual death. According to a pseudo-Aristotelian text well known in the early modern period, multiple sexual encounters caused weakness in men and other harmful conditions.[69] Avicenna claimed that coitus, unlike other bodily "evacuations," led to a general weakness among men.[70] Averroes too found that the depletion of sperm, produced by blood, could be extremely harmful since it is unlike other bodily "overabundances" (superfluitates) such as mucus, saliva, sweat, and urine.[71] These beliefs still held sway in the sixteenth century, as evidenced by the Lyonnais physician Symphorien Champier's advice to his readers on sexual overindulgence in the second book of his popular *Nef des dames* (published in 1503, 1515, and 1531).[72] Thus, the cure—therapeutic intercourse with another—was worse than the illness for Avannes, especially due to his tender age of approximately seventeen. According to the well-known medical authority Haly Abbas, young men were especially susceptible to illness from sexual overindulgence,[73] a malady from which women were held to be largely immune in early modern medical literature.[74] In his refashioning of novella 9, Saffredent draws attention to sexual excess as possibly fatal, at least for men, and thus offers a truly fatal malady to counterbalance lovesickness, which he earlier proclaimed unlikely to be fatal.

In novella 9, the young man dying from lovesickness is "two inches from death" (à deux doidz de la mort); yet, invigorated by his lover's unexpected appearance, he jumps on the bed and greets her (il se gecta en se seant sur son lict), leaving some doubt as to how near death he really is.[75] Saffredent echoes the scene in novella 26. However, when the recently recovered Avannes jumps on the wise woman's bed, his hope of "being treated as a husband" (estre traictez en mary) fails, mainly because he loses heart and fears the consequences of his action (craignant que la demonstracion qu'il avoit faicte de son desir lui feist perdre la privaulté qu'il avoit envers elle).[76] In an earlier analogous scene, Avannes audaciously lies down in the foolish woman's bed and is much better received: "*Not as a fearful stable boy* ... without asking his lady's permission, he *audaciously* lay down next to her" (*non comme pallefrenier craintif* ... sans demander congé à la dame, *audacieusement* se coucha auprès d'elle).[77] By doubling the scene within the novella, Saffredent points out that Avannes need not have feared the wise lady; had he been more audacious, he might well have succeeded. Indeed, throughout novella 26, Saffredent emphasizes the role that fear plays in Avannes's dealings with the wise lady and his consequent lack of amorous success.[78]

Two other paired scenes hinge on a kiss. Dagoucin's dying hero voices an audacious but too-tardy request that his beloved kiss him. She hesitates, but her mother allows her to kiss him because he no longer presents a sexual threat (voyant qu'il n'y avoit plus en luy sentement ne force d'homme vif).[79] In novella 26, the wise woman refuses to kiss Avannes, who *does* pose a sexual threat, but kisses him later at her husband's insistence. Her refusal paradoxically stokes an internal fire in Avannes's breast: "The fire that her words had started in the poor lord's heart began to grow due to the much-desired kiss, so strongly sought and so cruelly refused" (le feu que la parolle avoit commancé d'allumer au cueur du pouvre seigneur, commança à croistre par le baiser tant desiré, si fort requis et si cruellement refusé).[80] He outwardly demonstrates his inward passion or figurative fire by literally setting fire to his own house as a ploy to regain entry into the wise woman's household. And while his internal fire is externalized, preventing his lapse into a fatal lovesickness, the lovesick young woman continues to burn internally (au-dedans brusloit incessamment) with a "hidden flame" (flamme cachée) and with dire consequences.[81]

In yet another pair of analogous scenes, the dying lover cites the cause of the fatal malady. The young man in novella 9 unequivocally blames the young woman for his death: "What moved you, Madame, to come visit one who already has a foot in the grave and of whose death you are the cause?" (Quelle occasion vous esmeut, Madame, de venir visiter celluy qui a desja le pied en la fosse, et de la mort duquel vous estes l'occasion?).[82] After relating the man's tragic death, Dagoucin agrees: "And the *triumph* of the funeral were the tears, the weeping, and the laments of the poor damsel, who declared her love as much after his death as she had *dissimulated* it during his life, *as if satisfying the wrong that she had done him*" (Et la *triumphe* des obseques furent les lermes, les pleurs et les criz de ceste pouvre damoiselle, qui d'autant plus se declaira après la mort qu'elle s'estoit *dissimulée* durant la vye, quasy comme *satisfaisant du tort qu'elle lui avoit tenu*).[83] In novella 26, on the contrary, the dying woman exculpates the young Avannes by paradoxically blaming herself: "But know that *the 'no' that* so often *I said* to you did me so much harm to pronounce that it *is the cause of my death*, but I am happy because God granted me the grace not to have allowed the violence of my love to stain my conscience and reputation."[84] Although she insists on the virtue of her actions, she also expresses relief in her fortuitous death, indicating that she was beginning to relent and, given more time, might have succumbed to his advances. The wise "dame de Pampelonne" then offers Avannes some final words of advice:

> I have been able to declare my affection equal to yours, despite the fact that the honor of women and men is not similar. I ask you, sir, that from now on *you will not fear* to approach the greatest and most virtuous ladies that you can because in such hearts abide the greatest passions and *those more wisely conducted.* And the grace, beauty, and honesty in them will not permit your love *to till the ground without fruit.*[85]

Virtuous women experience equally great passion, but they control it more wisely, which can be understood to mean that they refrain from illicit love affairs. Alternatively, it can be read as a message that Avannes would risk much less physically by "addressing himself" to a wise rather than a foolish lady like the other "dame de Pampelonne." She also hints that he will one day meet with success with such ladies, but the passage bears a double meaning since she never mentions marriage. By placing these words in the mouth of the wise lady, Saffredent is no doubt advising young men like Avannes to try harder and fear not the consequences of seducing virtuous ladies if they do so wisely and with affection, as he indicates in the discussion after novella 9.

The differences between the two remarkably similar death scenes also reveal and reinforce Saffredent's refashioning of the earlier tale and his didactic intent. In novella 9, the young woman embraces her dead lover and finally declares her love: "The love that the damsel had always hidden declared itself immediately so strongly that the mother and servants of the dead man had trouble separating the union. *But with some effort they pulled the living woman,* worse off than dead, *from the arms of the dead man,* whom they buried honorably.[86] The wording of novella 26 echoes this passage: "And when he realized that she was dead, he ran to her body, which, when alive, he would have approached with *fear,* and embraced and kissed it in such a way that *only with great effort were they able to pull him from her arms.*"[87]

But while Dagoucin blames the woman's hypocrisy and dissimulation for the young man's death—he "triumphs" over the woman who "wronged" him—Saffredent places the focus on Avannes's fear.

The young lady of novella 9 and Avannes also bear quite different marks of their grief. The guilty young woman suffers for the rest of her life, never finding anyone equal to her dead lover (quelque mary que on luy donnast pour l'appaiser, n'a jamais eu joye en son cueur), while the seemingly innocent Avannes simply avoids women for several years and wears black for more than two years.[88] As further evidence of Avannes's blameless conduct, Saffredent characterizes the husband's reaction as "happier than ever" (plus contant que jamais) upon hearing about his wife's virtue unto death from Avannes's own lips, and he mourns the loss of his virtuous wife the more deeply.[89] In fact, the rich widower, whom Avannes had attempted to cuckold, paradoxically demonstrates his gratitude by serving the young man for the rest of his life. This extreme form of male bonding can be attributed to a classical intertext—the tale of Antiochus's secret love for his stepmother Stratonice, so often told and retold in medieval and Renaissance literature.[90] In it, Antiochus's father Seleucis discovers the cause of his son's near-fatal lovesickness and offers him "his dear wife" as a cure.[91] The outcome of novella 26 conforms more to Christian morality, but the story still bears marks of the young man's incestuous love for his stepmother and the father's extraordinary devotion to his son.

By presenting analogous intertextual and intratextual scenes and doubling the female characters in novella 26, Saffredent points out Avannes's deft handling of the affair with the foolish lady and his fearful mishandling of the wise one. To emphasize the sole difference between the wise and foolish ladies—the "different effects of love" on both—he describes them as remarkably similar, proving Parlamente's assertion at the end of novella 9 that Saffredent and Hircan think all women are alike (vous estimez toutes les femmes pareilles).[92] First, the two signifieds bear almost the same signifier: one is "une dame demeurant en la ville de Pampelonne" (a lady living in the city of Pampelonne) while the other is "a young gentlewoman near Pampelune, who had a house in the city" (une jeune gentilfemme près de Pampelune, qui avoit maison en la ville."[93] In fact, the reader learns that to go from one house to the other, the young man need only walk the length of a street (il n'avoit que à traverser la longueur d'une rue).[94] Later, Saffredent will differentiate between the two women by simply using the adjectives *sage* and *folle*.

Second, although both women are only about ten years older than Avannes, they are curiously figured as his "mother," no doubt to emphasize their role in his sex education but also perhaps to echo the Stratonice intertext. Avannes refers to the wise one as "my mother, your wife" (ma mère, vostre femme), and he is received in the bed of the foolish one as "the finest son ever" (le plus beau filz qui fust en son temps).[95]

Third, both women suffer from their husbands' frequent absences and unsatisfying, childless marriages. As Méniel has pointed out, both men have "external passions" (passions extérieures à l'amour) that exclude their wives and ironically place each in the path of the would-be lover.[96] Although the wise one admires her husband's goodness and virtue, he is much older than she and far from good looking, while the foolish one's husband is described as "fantasticque," which bears a distinctly pejorative meaning.[97]

Fourth, both women fall ill. While one dies of a hidden illness due to concealing her love, the other merely feigns illness, another form of dissimulation, to stay home and indulge in an extramarital affair. Finally, both dress as virtuous women. They both wear a "chamarre," a simple dress that hides their form, the body under the dress, and their sexual nature.[98] Throughout novella 26, Saffredent implies that in all but their different reactions to love, the two women are interchangeable. When the wise lady repels Avannes's sexual advances, she tells him that if she were to give in, she would be "other than [she] is" (autre que je ne suis): in effect, the other woman.[99] By emphasizing their similarities, Saffredent can place into relief their most salient difference—wisdom or lack thereof—and Avannes's audacity with one and fearful comportment with the other.

In concluding the tale, Saffredent announces: "Ladies, there you see the difference between a wise and foolish lady, from whence one sees the different effects of love, by which one received a glorious and praiseworthy death, and the other shameful and infamous renown that made her life too long."[100] But whose life was too long, and who enjoyed a glorious and praiseworthy death? According to Gisèle Mathieu-Castellani, the moral lesson is ambiguous since the foolish woman safeguarded her honor by dissimulating, while the wise one, by confessing her love, compromised hers.[101]

As several other critics have noted, the discussion that follows alternately praises and censures the wise woman, leaving the tale without a clear moral lesson.[102] It breaks down more or less along gender lines, with *devisants* Hircan and Géburon accusing the wise woman of hypocrisy in dissimulating her love, and *devisantes* Parlamente, Nomerfide, and Longarine defending her actions. Oisille, who had earlier questioned the veracity of novella 20, is a notable exception. She begins the discussion by praising Saffredent's account mainly because she knows and admires the lord of Avannes: "Truly . . . you have told us the finest story that ever was. And whoever has known the person as I have will find it even better, for I have never seen such a fine gentleman nor one with better grace than the lord of Avannes."[103] By having Oisille, the unimpeachable moral authority, judge the story at face value and refrain from passing judgment on the wise lady, Marguerite leaves the debate more balanced and ambivalent but also renders Saffredent's next pronouncement all the more provocative and seemingly contradictory.[104]

After Oisille's comment, Saffredent claims that the wise woman committed suicide or "let herself die," a verdict shared by at least one other male contemporary:[105] "To show herself more virtuous outwardly than she was in her heart, and *to dissimulate* a love that nature would demand that she bear for such a noble lord, *she let herself die* rather than give herself the enjoyment of what he desired *overtly* and she desired *covertly*!"[106] Méniel sees here the "counterpoint to the position [Saffredent] adopted in his narrative."[107] However, it is consistent with both Mathieu-Castellani's interpretation of the ambivalent moral of Saffredent's tale, as well as the active reading of novella 26 outlined in this study.[108] It also reflects the debate on lovesickness and its most controversial cure, therapeutic intercourse, with *devisants* voicing the concerns of doctors (who often recommended it to preserve the health of the body), and *devisantes* adopting the stance of theologians (who condemned it and preferred to save the soul). Here and within the novella, a sixteenth-century reader would have recognized received medical ideas about women's anatomy as well as women's and men's respective vulnerability to erotic melancholy and its symptoms. For example, Hircan uses a dress as a metaphor in the ensuing discussion to portray women's dissimulation, which, in turn, suggests a received scientific idea about women's bodies: "Also their dresses are so long and so well woven with *dissimulation* that one cannot know what lies beneath because, if their honor were not more susceptible to stain than ours, *you would find that Nature has forgotten no more in them than in us.*"[109] According to early sixteenth-century Galenists, women were biologically "imperfect" men with identical sex organs simply inverted and hidden within.[110] Medical authorities often saw women's hidden anatomy as evidence of their innate inferiority and dissimulating nature. Here, though, Hircan excuses their dissimulation by referring to the different strictures placed on women in society, a point of view shared by several of Marguerite's characters and *devisants*.[111] Later in the tales, Hircan and Saffredent depict dissimulation as a cultural construct that affects the rich more than the poor[112] and women more than men.[113] According to medieval and Renaissance medical authorities, lovesickness too was thought to affect nobles more than common people.[114] However, they disagreed on whether men or women were more susceptible. Most medieval authorities weighed in on the side of men's more intense and frequent suffering, while some early modern authors such as Jacques Ferrand (born 1575) viewed women as the primary victims.[115] No matter who suffered more from the illness, Marguerite makes it clear that therapeutic intercourse was not a socially acceptable option for women in the early modern period. The wise lady—or "dissimulatress," as Lawrence Kritzman calls her—clearly dies of lovesickness because, rightly or wrongly, she refuses the coital cure.[116]

Saffredent alludes to yet another received scientific idea within the novella by recommending that Avannes avoid fear in his amorous exploits. Medical authorities thought of lovesickness or erotic melancholy as a subcategory of melancholy. Galen and his followers considered fear, one of the characteristics or symptoms of melancholy, as both a typically female trait and one of the causes of excessive amounts of black bile (*cholera nigra*), or dangerous black humors that were thought to fog the patient's brain and eventually lead to death.[117] By refusing to succumb to fear, both the cause and symptom of lovesickness, Avannes might preserve his health from the humoral imbalance of erotic melancholy. He might also enjoy greater success by refusing to idealize his loved one in the courtly or Neoplatonic manner and refusing, thus, to abase himself and his masculinity.[118]

While to modern readers the moral of novella 26 may appear ambivalent—and lovesickness a quaintly antiquated medical notion and mere support for plot—sixteenth-century readers, well versed in arts of memory and commonly received medical ideas on lovesickness, would no doubt have recognized Saffredent's rewriting of novella 9 and interpreted it quite differently. Lovesickness provided Marguerite an opportunity to raise the moral dilemma of therapeutic intercourse, a medical cure prescribed for men and denied women, that not only offered a commentary on sexual difference and women's place in society but also opposed the needs of the body and the dictates of Christian sexual morality. Active readers would have noted that while Saffredent appears to praise the virtuous woman and censure the foolish, he skillfully reconfigures novella 9 into a tale that conveys a hidden and morally questionable message: men should fearlessly pursue virtuous women who will conduct love affairs in a wise manner that does not risk their own reputation or, perhaps more important, the man's health. Marguerite thus sets Saffredent up as an unreliable narrator who places his virtuous heroine in a double bind—if she gives in, she commits adultery; if she doesn't, she commits suicide—as she offers us the ironic portrait of a dissimulating male accusing women of dissimulation.

CONCLUSION

Marguerite showcases lovesickness in seven of the eight parts of *Les quatre dames et les quatre gentilzhommes* and in three novellas in the *Heptaméron* to examine the medico–literary debate on lovesickness in the querelle des femmes. She was well versed in both the received medical ideas about the ailment and the literary tradition and sociological conditions that created it. She takes a feminist stand in the querelle by pointing out that men's and women's honor are different and that women may suffer from socie-tal censure if they engage in the "coital cure," but she also points out that according to early modern medical beliefs, men also suffer physically from sexual excess. By portraying lovesickness as a feigned illness, she did not underestimate its potentially fatal consequences and clearly understood the power of the mind over the body. The multiple points of view in both works allowed Marguerite to explore the various literary and medical arguments surrounding the illness, and in doing so, she clearly demonstrates that the querelle des femmes was a debate not only about women's physical and moral nature but also about literary interpretation.

Conclusion

From Courtly Love to Fatal Lovesickness

According to the humoral theory of medicine, women's biological make-up justified their lesser roles in early modern society. Women were thought not only the weaker sex but prone to moral failings as well. Christine de Pizan, a physician's daughter, understood this and challenged one of the most revered literary texts of her time, the *Roman de la rose*. In what became known as the querelle de la rose, she characterized Jean de Meun's cynical continuation of Guillaume de Lorris's courtly love poem as a seduction manual, designed to overcome women's defenses and "pluck the Rose." Why, she asked, was such a literary arsenal needed to overcome a supposedly immoral and easy prey? Complaining to the god of love, she described the threat of fatal lovesickness as just another ruse to gain an unsuspecting woman's trust, and in her *Cité des dames* she praised women for their accomplishments and urged them not to give in to "fol amor." Although her male contemporaries refused to engage with Christine in letters, and later writers ignored her works or even attributed them to her son, many of her arguments surfaced and resurfaced in the querelle des femmes.

Some have characterized the querelle des femmes in a limited way, noting the presence or absence of certain "hallmark techniques" such as a polemical stance and a catalogue of famous women.[1] Others have concentrated on where its writers stood on women's equality. Were women declared inferior, equal, or superior in their writings? Some of the texts touting women's superiority betray a measure of irony, and as critics like Régine Reynolds-Cornell and Mireille Huchon have demonstrated, doubt exists as to whether some of the "liberated" female writers of the time, like Jeanne Flore and Louise Labé, actually existed. Still others have dismissed the debate on women as a mere rhetorical exercise. In this book, I have concentrated on the role of received medical ideas in the querelle des femmes and attempted to reconstruct an early modern reading of the texts to determine how these authors interpreted the courtly love commonplace of women's pity or mercy on a dying lover. In addition, I have explored where these texts stood in contemporary debates on women's supposed sexual insatiability, its biological effects on men's lives and fertility, and whether erotomania—erotic melancholy—was a fatal illness.

While the two women who frame this study defended women and based much of what they wrote on personal experience, the three male participants included here appealed to male authority and tradition in their writings. Molinet, Champier, and Lemaire used received medical ideas about women and the querelle des femmes as a popular literary forum not only to display their rhetorical skills and gain patronage—often from powerful female patrons—but also to advance personal, political, and professional agendas. For example, by defending and moralizing the Roman de la rose, Molinet hoped to accomplish two interrelated goals: to control reception of the work by countering attacks from women readers like Christine and to promote a future crusade against the Turks to reclaim the Holy Land. In his moralized version, he characterizes the "notable women" who attacked the romance as slanderers and "murmurers" who only understood the work's literal meaning; he also depicts Gerson's reading of the text as a childlike and overly sensual reading: a typical female reading. Molinet modernized the language of the Roman de la rose and divided it into easily digestible chapters with clear, moral lessons for "literal" women readers. Transforming de Meun's penis–plow metaphor to a tongue–mind one, he appealed to clerics to "write" on the extremely retentive, moist, and warm minds of their female parishioners with their tongues and offer a "correct" interpretation of the text: a call for a spiritual love quest, a crusade against the Turks to reclaim the lost Holy Land. The Rhétoriqueur also chastises men who, he claims, suffer from a type of fatal lovesickness—a desire to rid the Holy Land of Muslims—but refuse to participate in and die for the cause. He urges these "sanguine" Christians to take up arms against the "choleric" and sexually out-of-control Muslims. Philippe de Clèves—the Duke of Ravenstein and Molinet's dedicatee—did in fact lead this "queste amoreuse" with unfortunate results against the Turks in 1501, one year after the work's publication.

Champier's immediate goal in writing the *Nef des dames vertueuses* and dedicating it to Anne of France was to gain patronage as a physician in her court. While defending women and offering useful advice for infertility, a condition that Anne suffered from for many years, in the *Nef des dames*, Champier pursued two interrelated and self-serving goals. The first, as evidenced in the second book of the *Nef des dames*, was to advertise his skills as a physician to increase the royal couple's fertility. Excessive coitus was, to Champier, a literal form of potentially fatal lovesickness that caused men to become old before their time and interfered with the formation of vigorous sperm that produced healthy male progeny. In the *Nef des dames* and other works, Champier was apparently as little concerned with women's health as he was with their education. In addition to promoting his fertility services, the Lyonnais physician promoted the medical profession as markedly superior to the lesser professions of pharmacy, surgery, and midwifery. Indeed, he excluded all uneducated "empiricists," not just women. And although Champier defended marriage as a viable, albeit inferior, alternative to celibacy—an alternative with procreation as its main goal—the Platonic love he introduced in the vernacular in the work's fourth book, "Le livre de vraye amour," favors Platonic love in the form of a brotherhood among fellow physicians over heterosexual love.

Jean Lemaire de Belges participated in the querelle des femmes in two posthumous works, the *Couronne margaritique* and the *Trois contes de Cupido et d'Atropos*; the *Palais d'honneur féminin* that he promised Margaret of Austria in a letter dated 1510 is no longer extant—if, in fact, he ever wrote it. In the first two works, Lemaire, like Champier, seems more motivated to promote his profession than defend women. In the *Couronnne*, Lemaire flatters Margaret by comparing her to famous women and portraying her as a virago, an exceptionally virile woman, yet chastises her for what he calls her "imbecillité feminine": her excessive grief at the death of her husband, a state of mind that drove her to attempt to take her own life. He describes this "female weakness" as a form of fatal lovesickness that results from an excess of melancholy or black bile, and he places jewels with medicinal properties that cure grief and melancholy in her allegorical "crown." By recalling past misfortunes that she overcame with this art of memory, replete with therapeutic gems that cure grief and melancholy, he hoped to cure her through the therapeutic power of language and urge her to continue the "masculine" role of peacemaker in the future.

Lemaire offers another linguistic cure in the *Trois contes de Cupido et d'Atropos*, in which he describes syphilis, or the Great Pox, as another form of fatal lovesickness. In the second of the three poems, the only one that has been attributed unquestionably to Lemaire, the poet portrays the illness as a breakdown of sexual identity as well as of onomastic difference. When Cupid and Atropos exchange arrows by mistake, a male Cupid takes on the female role, becoming childlike and verbally ineffectual; the female Atropos becomes powerful, aggressive, and eloquent, even suggesting that they change names as well as roles. Lemaire indicates that a cure will arise from giving the disease a proper name that reflects its true origin as well as reestablishing sexual difference and a separation of the sexes so that the "water" eventually runs clean, undoubtedly an allusion to women's purportedly humid nature. In the final poem, thought to be by Lemaire's design if not his hand, Mercury—the god of eloquence and, by extension, language, but also the element that served as the favored cure for the illness—brings the debate to a close by reestablishing a provisional sexual separation and normative gender difference.

Marguerite de Navarre reintroduced real women's experiences into the debate in her *Quatre dames et quatre gentilzhommes* and *Heptaméron* but adopted a stance more equivocal than Christine's by offering an equilibrium between female and male narrative voices. In both works, Marguerite's female characters criticize courtly love as a game where women are often the losers as well as accused of hypocrisy and "dissimulation." In the *Hep-taméron*, Marguerite demonstrates the hypocrisy of Saffredent, a male devisant who criticizes women for dissimulation, by subtly pointing out his own dissimulation in recounting a tale of fatal lovesickness. In so doing, Marguerite demonstrates how lovesickness was a feigned or psychosomatic but still dangerous illness that could be fatal to both men and women by resulting in a wasting death or suicide. She contrasts it with sexual over-indulgence, a "real" disease that could lead not only to physical but also spiritual corruption and death.

Much has been written about Marguerite's silence on Christine even though the former and her literary predecessor shared many of the same views, such as how women should shun lovesick suitors and protect their reputations. But even more has been written on Marguerite's role in the querelle des femmes. While some see Marguerite as a feminist, others cite her evangelical fervor and evenhandedness in pointing out the sins of both sexes. Yet critics have repeatedly discerned Marguerite's profemale authorial voice in the pages of the *Heptaméron* and elsewhere.[2] Marguerite's desire to appear objective might have been influenced by the example of Jeanne Flore. If Jeanne Flore's *Contes amoureux* constituted an easily recognized literary hoax that promoted the message to have mercy on the lovesick and respond favorably to Venus's mandate of love, and if Marguerite participated in this hoax, as Régine Reynolds-Cornell suggests, this might explain why Marguerite was more circumspect in her works than Christine, who suf-fered from attacks on her reputation during her lifetime. Did Marguerite de Navarre adopt multivoiced narratives in her poetry and prose to avoid criticism about her views on women? As the king's sister, she was more immune to accusations and mockery than others but also recognized the limitations of that protection. And how does one explain François Rabelais's dedication to Marguerite in his *Tiers livre*? Was she flattered, repulsed, or simply amused? By dedicating this comically misogynistic work to her, did Rabelais recognize her participation in the querelle as well as her interest in received medical ideas such as fatal lovesickness?

From Christine de Pizan's questioning of *De secretis mulierum* in the *Livre de la cité des dames* to Marguerite de Navarre's attack on courtly love conventions as well as literary and medical lore on fatal lovesickness, misogynists based many of their arguments on women's weaker physiognomy, which supposedly affected both their minds and morals. This book covers only part of the debate on this in the fifteenth century and the first half of the sixteenth century, a period of change that transformed education and saw the invention of the printing press, increasing female literacy, the rise of the vernacular, and greater specialization in medical professions. During this time, more women began to participate as both readers and writers of the written word and challenge the "secrets of women" tradition, along with received medical ideas and courtly love conventions about fatal lovesickness. Yet the querelle des femmes remained largely a debate among men about women in the early decades of sixteenth-century France. The male-authored texts in this volume reveal an increasing fear of female power and authority as well as a desire to control not only the reception of literary works by this new reading public but also women's bodies and sexuality. They portray sexual relationships as dangerous and even potentially fatal to both sexes and advocate the separation of the sexes as both a moral and biological ideal. The querelle offered these writers opportunities to pursue self-serving goals (e.g., promote a crusade, gain female patronage, define and defend their professions as author or doctor) and maintain male authority. These male-authored querelle texts had little to do with promoting gender equality.

Works in the Querelle de la Rose and the
Querelle des Femmes (1240–1673)

Guillaume de Lorris (d. ca. 1240). *Le roman de la rose* [*The romance of the rose*]. 1240.

Jean de Meun (d. ca. 1305). *Le roman de la rose* [*The romance of the rose*]. 1275–80. Continuation of Guillaume de Lorris's *Roman de la rose*. 1236.

Anonymous. *Le blastogne des fames* and *Le blasme des fames* [*The praise of women* and *The blaming of women*]. 1300s.

Matheolus (Mathieu de Boulogne). *Liber lamentationum Matheoluli* [*Les lamentations de Mathéole; The lamentations of Matheolus*]. 1295.

Guillaume de Deguileville (1295–before 1358). *Le pèlerinage de vie humaine* [*The pilgrimage of human life*]. 1355.

Bocaccio, Giovanni (1313–75). *De claris mulieribus* [*On famous women*]. 1355–59. Translated into French in 1493.

———. *Il corbaccio* [*The corbaccio, or The labyrinth of love*]. 1355.

Chaucer, Geoffrey (d. 1400). *The Legend of Good Women*. 1372–86.

Ordre de l'escu vert à la Dame Blanche. Knightly order for the defense of women's interests and honor. Founded in France in 1399.

Christine de Pizan (1364–1430). "L'epistre au dieu d'amour" ["The epistle of the god of love"]. 1399.

Gerson, Jean (1363–1429). *Le traité contre le roman de la rose* [*Treatise against the romance of the rose*]. 1402.

Christine de Pizan. *Le livre de la cité des dames* [*The book of the city of ladies*]. 1404–5.

Chartier, Alain (ca. 1390–ca. 1440). *La belle dame sans mercy* [*The beautiful lady without pity*]. 1424.

Rodríguez de la Cámara, Juan. *Triunfo de las donas* [*The triumph of ladies*]. 1443.

Alvaro de Luna, Don. *El libro de las virtuosas et claras mugeres* [*The book of virtuous and famous ladies*]. 1446.

Martin Le Franc (ca. 1410–61). *Le champion des dames* [*The champion of ladies*]. Written 1440–42, published 1485.

Nogarola, Isotto. *De pari aut impari Evae atque Adae peccato* [*On the equal or unequal sin of Eve and Adam*]. 1451.

Philippe Bouton, *Le mirouer des dames*. 1477–82.

La Sale, Antoine de. *Les quinze joyes de mariage* [*The fifteen joys of marriage*]. Late 1400s.

Goggio, Bartolomeo. *De laudibus mulierum* [*In praise of women*]. 1487?

Foresti, Jacopo Filippo. *De plurimis claris selectisque mulieribus* [*Concerning many famous and select women*]. 1497.

Molinet, Jean (1435–1507). *Le roman de la rose moralisé* [*The moralized romance of the rose*]. 1500.

Equicola, Maria. *De mulieribus* [*On women*]. Written in 1500 or 1501, published in 1501.

Champier, Symphorien (1472–1539). *La nef des princes* [*The ship of princes*]. 1502.

———. *La nef des dames vertueuses* [*The ship of virtuous ladies*]. 1503.

Dufour, Antoine. *Les vies des femmes celebres* [*The lives of famous women*]. 1504.

Lemaire de Belges, Jean (1473–1515?). *La couronne margaritique* [*The Margaritic crown*]. Written after 1504, published in 1549.

Marot, Jean. *La vraye disant advocate des dames* [*The truth-talking advocate for ladies*]. 1506.

Catherine d'Amboise. *Livre des prudents et imprudents* [*Book of the prudent and imprudent*]. 1509.

Agrippa von Nettesheim (1486–1535). *De nobilitate et proecellentia feminei sexus declamatio* [*On the nobility and preeminence of the female sex*]. Written in 1509, published in 1529, and first translated into French in 1537 as *Declamation de la noblesse & preexcelle(n)ce du sexe feminine*.

Marot, Jean. *Le doctrinal des princesses* [*The education of princesses*]. 1506–15.

Bouchet, Jean. *Le temple de bonne renommée et repos des hommes et femmes illustres* [*The temple of good renown and rest for illustrious men and women*]. 1516.

Lesnauderie, Pierre de. *La louenge de mariage et recueil des hystoires des bonnes, vertueuses et illustres dames* [*The praise of marriage and collection of good, virtuous, and famous ladies*]. 1523.

Vives, Juan Luis (1492–1540). *De institutione fœminae Christianae* [*The instruction of a Christian woman*]. 1523.

Capra, Galeazzo Flavio. *Della eccellenza e dignità delle donne* [*On the excellence and dignity of women*]. 1525.

Castiglione, Baldassare (1478–1529). *Il cortegiano* [*Book of the courtier*]. 1528.

Bouchet, Jean (1476–1557). *Les triumphes de la noble et amoureuse dame et l'Art d'hon-nestement aimer* [*The triumphs of the noble and amorous lady and the art of loving honestly*]. 1531.

Du Pré, Jehan (14??–15??). *Le palais des nobles dames* [*The palace of noble ladies*]. 1532.

Gratien du Pont (14??–154?). *Les controverses des sexes masculin et femenin* [*The con-troversies of the masculine and feminine sexes*]. 1534.

Bouchet, Jean (1476–1557). *Jugement poetic de l'honnneur feminin* [*Poetic judgement of feminine honor*]. 1538.

Hélisenne de Crenne (1510–52). *Les epistres familières et invectives* [*Personal and invec-tive letters*]. 1539.

Elyot, Sir Thomas (ca. 1490–1546). *The Defense of Good Women*. 1540.

Sperone, Speroni (1500–1588). *Dialogo delle dignità delle donne* [*Dialogue on the dignity of women*]. 1542.

Vaughan, Robert [Robert Burdet?]. *A Dialogue Defensive for Women against Malicious Detractors*. 1542.

Grosynhill, Edward. *Mulierum paean* [*The praise of all women*]. 1542.

Landi, Ortensio (1512–ca. 1553). *Paradossi* [*Paradoxes*]. 1543.

Cristóbal de Castillego (1491–1556). *Diálogo de mujeres* [*A dialogue on women*]. 1544.

Giolito de' Ferrari, Gabriel (ca. 1508–78). *Della nobilità et eccelenza delle donne* [*On the dignity and excellence of women*]. 1545.

Rabelais, François (1494–1553). *Le tiers livre*. [*The third book*]. 1546.

Marguerite de Navarre (1492–1549). *Les quatre dames et les quatre gentilzhommes*. 1547.

Firenzuola, Angelo. *On the Beauty of Women*. 1548.

Domenichi, Lodovico. *La nobilità delle donne* [*The dignity of women*]. 1549.

Terracina, Laura. *Discorso sopra tutti li primi canti d'Orlando Furioso* [*Discourse on all the first cantos of the Orlando Furioso*]. 1550.

Sébillet, Thomas. *La louenge des femmes, invention extraite du commentaire de Panta-gruel, sur l'Androgyne de Platon* [*The praise of women, an invention taken from the commentary of Pantagruel on Plato's Androgyna*]. 1551.

Billon, François de. *Le fort inexpugnable de l'honneur du sexe féminin* [*The unassailable fort of the honor of the female sex*]. 1555.

Bruto, Giovanni Michele (1517–92). *La instituzione di una fanciulla nata nobilmente* [*The education of a young noble lady*]. 1555.

Marguerite de Navarre (1492–1549). *L'heptaméron* [*The Heptameron*]. 1558.

Knox, John (1513–72). *The First Blast of the Trumpet against the Monstrous Regiment of Women*. 1558.

Aylmer, John (1521–94). *An Harborowe for Faithfull and Trewe Subjects, agaynst the Late Blowne Blaste, Concerning the Government of Wemen*. 1559.

More, Edward (grandson of Sir Thomas More; 1537–620). *A Little and Brief Treatise Called the Defense of Women*. 1560.

Marconville, Jean de (1520–80). *De la bonté and mauvaiseté des femmes* [*On the good and evil of women*]. 1564.

Philippe Desportes (1546–1606). *Stances du mariage* [*Stances on marriage*]. 1578.

Nicole Liébault (née Estienne; 1542–89). *Les misères de la femme mariée* [*Woes of the married woman*]. ca. 1575–80.

Romieu, Marie de (1545–90). *Brief discours, que l'excellence de la femme surpasse celle de l'homme* [*Brief discourse that the excellence of women surpasses that of men*]. 1581.

León, Fray Luis de (1527–91). *La perfecta casada* [*The perfect married woman*]. 1583.

Sabuco, Oliva (1562–1622). *Nueva filosofia de la naturaleza del hombre.* [*New philosophy of human nature*]. 1587.

Anger, Jane [pseud.]. *Her Protection for Women*. 1589.

Breton, Nicholas (1555–1626). *The praise of virtuous ladies*. 1597

Pontaymeri, Alexandre de. *Paradoxe apologétique, où il est fidellement démonstré que la femme est beaucoup plus parfaicte que l'homme en toute action de vertu* [*Apologetic paradox, where it is faithfully demonstrated that woman is much more perfect than man in every virtuous action*]. 1594.

Passi, Giuseppe (1569–1620). *I donneschi difetti* [*The defects of women*]. 1599.

Fonte, Moderata (1555–92). *Il merito delle donne* [*Women's worth*]. 1600.

Marinelli, Lucrezia (1571–1653). *La nobiltà et l'eccellenza delle donne co' diffetti et man-camenti de gli uomini.* [*The nobility and excellence of women and the defects and vices of men*]. 1600.

Passi, Giuseppe (1569–1620). *I difetti degli uomini* [*The defects of men*]. 1603.

Baudot, François-Nicolas (1590–1652). *Traité de la perfection des femmes comparée à celle des hommes* [*Treatise on the perfection of women compared to men*]. 1617.

Olivier, Jacques (15??–16??). *Alphabet de l'imperfection et malice des femmes* [*The alphabet of the imperfection and malice of women*]. 1617.

L'Escale, Chevalier de. *Alphabet de l'excellence et perfection des femmes, contre l'infasme alphabet de leur imperfection et malice* [*Alphabet of the excellence and perfection of women, against the infamous alphabet of their imperfection and malice*]. 1617.

Gournay, Marie de (1565–1645). *Egalité des hommes et des femmes* [*The equality of men and women*]. 1622.

Les caquets de l'accouchée [*Gossipings around the woman who has just given birth*]. 1622.

Gournay, Marie de (1565–1645). *Le grief des dames* [*The ladies' grievance*]. 1626.

Schurman, Anna Maria van (1607–78). *Dissertatio de ingenii muliebris ad doctrinam, & meliores litteras aptitudine* [*The learned maid, or Whether a maid may be a scholar*]. 1638.

Poullain de la Barre, François (1647–1725). *De l'egalité des deux sexes* [*The equality of both sexes*]. 1673.

APPENDIX 2

Major Early Modern Medical Authorities, Translators, and Commentators

Hippocrates (ca. 460–377 BC). Born on the island of Cos, Hippocrates was the most famous physician of antiquity and one of the least known. He is often called the Father of Medicine. His works were known in the Middle Age but mainly through so-called "Arab" commentators. The entire *Hippocratic Corpus* did not appear in print in Latin until 1525. A separate edition of his work on women's diseases, *De foeminea natura*, translated into Latin by Marco Fabio Calvi, was published in Paris in 1526. The first complete Greek edition appeared in 1526 from Aldine Press in Venice.

Aristotle (384–322 BC). Author of *De animalibus* or *Historia animalium*, a work of natural philosophy that was considered an important medical source.

Galen of Pergamum (129–199/216). Author of *De usu partium* (*On The Usefulness of the Parts*), *De locis affectis* (*On the Affected Parts*), *Ars parva* (*Small Art*, or *Art of Medicine*), and several other works known throughout the Middle Ages. Galen also wrote several commentaries on works by Hippocrates.

Oribasius (325–403). Medical compiler and commentator who quoted his sources accurately and whose master authority was Galen. He dedicated his seventy-volume Greek encyclopedia to his benefactor Julianus Apostata (331–90); only about one third is extant. The encyclopedia has chapters on pregnancy, parturition, lactation, and the early education of children, as well as urinary and sexual diseases.

Paul of Aegina (ca. 625–ca. 690). The last great physician of Byzantine culture who practiced and taught in Alexandria just prior to the destruction of the great medical and cultural center. One of the last Greek compilers.

Isaac Israeli (ca. 832–ca. 932), or Isaac Judaeus. An Egyptian Jew who composed an important work on pharmacology, translated into Latin under the title *De gradibus simplicum*, that became the foundation for most subsequent medieval works on the subject. Avicenna (980–1037) was said to have drawn inspiration from his writings. Constantine Africanus translated some of his works into Latin in the eleventh century.

Rhazes (865–925/929), or Razi, or Rasis. A native Persian who wrote *Liber ad Almansorem* (*Book for al-Mansūr*), translated by Gerard of Cremona in the twelfth century, published in Bologna in 1489 and in Venice in 1497. It was one of the most widely read medieval medical manuals in Europe and was used as a textbook well into the sixteenth century (Pormann and Savage-Smith, Medieval Islamic Medicine, 163).

Albucasis (ca. 936–ca. 1013), or Abū 'l-Qāsim az-Zahrāwī Khalaf ibn al-'Abbas. An Arab Muslim physician who was considered a great surgeon. He wrote *Kitab al-Tasrif*, a thirty-volume encyclopedia of medical practices, translated into Latin by Gerard of Cremona in the twelfth century.

Haly Abbas (fl. ca. 983), or 'Alī ibn al-'Abbās al-Majūsī. A Persian physician whose magnum opus was titled *Kitāb kāmil aṣ-ṣina 'ah aṭ-ṭibbīyah* (*Complete Book of the Medical Art*), also known as *Al-kitāb al-malikī* (*The Royal Book*) and *Pantegni* (*Whole Art*) in Latin. The extant editions are *Omnium librorum Halyabatis*, published in Venice by Jehan le Noir in 1492 and translated by Stephen of Antioch, and a 1523 Lyons edition annotated by Michael of Capella. He also wrote *Theorice* (a commentary on Galen), and *Liber totius medicinae* (a medical survey). His work was the basis for the *Pantegni* of Constantinus Africanus (d. 1087).

Alī ibn Ridwān (d. 1068), or Ali-Ben-Rodhouan or Haly Rodoam. Egyptian physician and author of a commentary on Galen, *Antiqua thegni Galeni translatio cum commento Haly Rodoam*, or the *Thegni Galeni*, published in Venice by Jehan le Noir in 1492.

Avicenna (980–1037), or Ibn Sīnā. Arab scientist and mathematician who followed the teachings of Galen and Hippocrates, and author of *Canon of Medicine* (*Canon medicinae*, or *Kitāb al-qānūn fi 'ṭ-ṭibb*), a medical textbook accepted as an authoritative medical work that superseded the treatises of Rhazes, Haly Abbas, and Avenzoar. The *Canon* was translated into Latin by Gerard of Cremona prior to his death in 1187 and was used as a textbook in medical schools from the thirteenth to the sixteenth centuries. He discusses lovesickness ("ilisci" or "'ishq") in the third book of the *Canon*. Constantine and Avicenna were considered the standard authorities on lovesickness in the thirteenth and fourteenth centuries. Only the first of the *Canon*'s five books has been translated into English: *The Canon of Medicine* (*Kitāb al-qānūn fi 'l-ṭibb*), published in 1999.

Constantine the African (ca. 1020–87), or Constantinus Africanus. Born in Carthage, Constantine was an Arab scholar turned Christian monk, and the chief translator in Europe, during the Middle Ages and Renaissance, of medical works in Greek and Arabic, notably the works of Rhazes and Avicenna. He translated as many as forty Greek classics from Arabic into Latin. Among his Latin translations are the *Pantegni*, which was a portion of Haly Abbas's *Kitāb al-malakī*, and various writings of Hippocrates and Galen. Constantine also wrote *Viaticum*, an adaptation and translation of ibn al-Jazzār's popular medical handbook, *Zād al-musāfir wa-qūt al-hādir* (Provisions for the traveler and the nourishment of the sedentary). '*Ishq*, or passionate love, is the subject of chapter 20 of the *Viaticum*. See Wack, *Lovesickness* for a complete analysis of the *Viaticum*.

Hildegard of Bingen (1098–1179). A celebrated medieval monastic physician. Her medical writings consist primarily of two books, *Liber simplicis medicinae* and *Liber compositae medicinae*, written between the years 1151 and 1159.

Avenzoar (1113–62), or Abū Marwān ibn Zuhr. One of the most distinguished physicians of Arabic Spain, a great admirer of Galen, and contemporary or tutor of Averroes. From his writings it appears that the offices of physician, surgeon, and apothecary were already considered distinct professions. His *Kitāb al-taysir fi 'l-mudāwāh wa 't-tadbīr* (Easy guide to therapy and dietetics), or *Theisir*, and the *Liber theicrisi dahalmodana vahaltadabir* (Venice: Gregoriis, 1490) are one and the same work.

Gerard of Cremona (1114–87). Moved to Toledo in Spain to learn Arabic and subsequently translated many medical works from Arabic into Latin, including Avicenna's *Canon of Medicine* and Rhazes's *Liber ad Almansorem* (*Book for al-Mansur*).

Burgundio of Pisa (twelfth century). Published a Latin translation of Galen's *De complexionibus*, a commentary on Hippocrates' *Aphorisms*, and other Galenic works directly from Greek into Latin.

Averroes (1126–98), or Abu al-Walid ibn Rushd. Author of the *Kitāb al-Kulliyyāt fi 'ṭ-ṭibb* (The book of general principles), or *Colliget*. This compendium of the science of medicine was translated into Latin in 1255 by a Jewish physician, Banacasa of Padua. The *Colliget* is, in fact, a commentary on Avicenna's *Canon of Medicine*. Particularly concerned with reconciling Aristotle and Galen, Averroes nonetheless preferred Aristotle to Galen. His detailed commentaries on Aristotle earned him the title "The Commentator."

Trotula. According to Faith Wallis, this text was assembled at the end of the twelfth century and consists of three Salternitan tracts on health care for women: *On the Conditions of Women*, *Treatments for Women*, and *Women's Cosmetics*. *Treatments for Women* is attributed to Trota, a female physician of Salerno (McWebb, *Medieval Medicine*, 185). For a translation of the work, see Green, *Trotula*.

Serapion the Younger. Wrote the *Book of Simple Medicaments*, probably in Arabic, in the twelfth or thirteenth century. The work was translated into Latin in the late thirteenth century.

Maimonides (1135–204) or Mūsā ibn Maymūn. One of the most learned physicians of the Arabo–Spanish period. The most popular of his medical writings is the *Kitāb al-Fuṣūl fi 'ṭ-ṭibb* (Book of principles of medicine), a collection of 1500 aphorisms extracted from Galen's writings, together with forty-two critical remarks. The book contains twenty-five chapters; chapter 16 is devoted to gynecology. The treatise on sexual intercourse, written by Maimonides at the request of a nephew of Saladin, comprises nineteen chapters on the nature of man, the utility and harmfulness of sexual intercourse, remedies to create and inhibit the desire for sexual intercourse, and all kinds of cosmetics. It was translated into Latin as *De coitu* by John of Capua in the early fourteenth century (Jacquart and Thomasset, *Sexuality and Medicine*, 22).

Peter of Spain (d. 1277). A Portuguese logician, philosopher, and doctor who taught medicine in Siena from 1246 to 1250. His series of questions on *amor hereos* in *Questions on the Viaticum* were composed in Siena and are extant in two versions. He was elected Pope John XXI in 1276, the only contemporary pope whom Dante placed in paradise. He also compiled the earliest surviving Western commentaries on Aristotle's *De anima* and *De animalibus*, the latter forming the basis for Albertus Magnus's own *Quaestiones super De animalibus*.

Albertus Magnus (ca. 1200–1280), or Albert von Bollstädt. Born in Cologne but educated primarily in Padua, Albertus Magnus was the preeminent natural philosopher of the thirteenth century. His *De animalibus* and *Quaestiones super De animalibus*, expansive and digressive commentaries on Aristotle's *De animalibus*, were well known in the Renaissance. *De secretis mulierum* was spuriously attributed to him. See Albertus Magnus, *On Animals*.

William of Saliceto (ca. 1210–ca. 1277), or Guglielmo de Saliceto. Studied medicine and surgery at the University of Bologna, where he subsequently lectured on surgery. He also taught at the universities of Verona, Pavia, and Piacenza. His magnum opus, *Chyrurgia* (1271–75), served as a textbook on surgery. See William of Saliceto, *Surgery of William of Saliceto*.

John of Capua (late thirteenth to early fourteenth century). Translated Avenzoar's *Theisir* and Maimonides's *De coitu* into Latin (Jacquart and Thomasset, *Sexuality and Medicine*, 22).

Arnaud de Villeneuve (ca. 1235–1312), or Arnald of Villanova. One of the most extraordinary personalities among the scholastics of the Middle Ages. He received his medical education at Naples and practiced medicine in Paris, Montpellier, Barcelona, and Rome. Physician, alchemist, astrologer, diplomat, social reformer, and translator of medical works from Arabic into Latin, he possessed encyclopedic knowledge. A prolific writer, he purportedly authored approximately sixty works on various subjects such as surgery, gynecology, and poisons. Even his birthplace and the works written by, or simply attributed to, him remain subjects of debate. Champier wrote a biography of Arnaud that was included in his *Opera omnia*, published in Basel in 1585.

Bernard de Gordon (fl. 1285–1308), or Bernardus Gordonus. A professor at the prestigious medical school of the University of Montpellier. His *Lilium medicinae* (Lily of medicine; 1305) was printed in Sevilla in 1495 and in Venice in 1496. Eight editions appeared before 1500. According to Mary Frances Wack, Bernard of Gordon was "the most misogynistic of writers on lovesickness" in his exposition of *amor hereos* in the *Lilium medicinae* (*Lovesickness*, 88). See Bernard de Gordon, *Lilio de medicina*, the modern edition of the 1495 Sevilla edition, published in 1991.

Peter of Abano (1250–1316), also known as Pietro d'Abano and Petrus De Apono, or Aponensis. Italian physician and philosopher. After studying medicine and philosophy at Paris, where he also taught medicine for some time, he settled at Padua, where he gained a reputation as the most celebrated teacher and the most skillful physician of his time. His *Conciliator controversiam quae inter philosophos et medicos versantur* (published in Mantua in 1472 and Venice in 1476) covered the entire field of contemporary knowledge, including theoretical and practical medicine. He became known as the "conciliator." His true master in medicine was Avicenna. He translated some of Galen's and Aristotle's writings from Greek into Latin and was a firm believer in astrology as applied to medicine. Brian P. Copenhaver calls him a "notorious proponent of magical medicine" (*Symphorien Champier*, 213).

Niccolò da Reggio, or Niccolò di Theoprepos from Reggio in Calabria. Translated more than fifty works by Galen into Latin in the first half of the fourteenth century, from approximately 1308 to 1345.

Guy de Chauliac (ca. 1300–1368/70). A professor at the University of Padua and the most eminent surgeon of the Middle Ages. Born near Lyons, he received his medical degree at the University of Paris. He studied anatomy at the University of Bologna, the only place at that time where anatomy was studied directly from the human cadaver. His medical career began in 1345 in Avignon, where he was physician to the papal court. His famous work, *Chirurgia magna* (ca. 1363), is an exhaustive and critically inspired collection of surgical knowledge; it was used as a textbook centuries after his death. The *Chirurgia magna* passed through many editions: the first was published in Paris in 1478, and the Latin edition appeared in Venice in 1498. Symphorien Champier published a translation of and commentary on one of Guy de Chauliac's surgical treatises under the title *Le guidon en français*.

Jacopo da Forlì (ca. 1364–1414), also known as Giacomo della Torre and Iacobus Foroliviensis. Jacopo da Forlì "taught medicine, logic, and philosophy during his career at Padua and Bologna" at the end of the fourteenth century (Cadden, *Meanings of Sex Difference*, 112). According to Copenhaver, Jacopo da Forlì was best known among his contemporaries for his commentaries on Hippocrates, Galen, and Avicenna (*Symphorien Champier*, 219).

Ugo Benzi (1376–1479), also known as Hugo of Sienna. He wrote commentaries on Hippocrates, Galen, and Avicenna's *Canon*.

Jacques Despars (1380?–1458), also known by his Latin name Jacobus de Partibus. Author of an important commentary on Avicenna's *Canon*.

Niccolò Leoniceno (1428–1524), or Leonicenus. An Italian scholar of Greek who taught at the Universities of Padua and Bologna. He translated Hippocrates and Galen into Latin and praised the scholarship of Rhazes but frequently criticized Avicenna. In his *Libellus de epidemia quam vulgo morbum gallicum vocant* (Little book on the epidemic that they call the Gallic disease), published in 1497, Leoniceno provided the first clinical description of syphilis (Sournia, 148).

Sacchi, Bartolomeo, dit Platina (1421–81). Author of *De honesta voluptate et valetudine* (1473–75), in Latin; a French translation appeared in 1505. See Sacchi, *Le Platine en français*. In book 1, there is a chapter with the title "De habiter avec femme" (Sacchi, *Le Platine en français*, 8).

Marsilio Ficino (1433–99). Prominent Platonist and author of several works on Christian Platonism, such as *Commentarium in convivium Platonis, de amore* (*Commentary on the Symposium of Plato, on Love*), in which he describes the physiology of love. See Ficino, *Commentaire sur le banquet*.

Symphorien Champier (ca. 1472–ca. 1540). Lyonnais physician and author of several works in Latin on medical topics. These include *Practica nova* (1517) and *Periarchon* (1533). He also composed *Castigationes seu emendationes pharmacopolarum ac Arabum medicorum* (1532), which he later translated into French with the title *Le myrouel des appothiquaires* (1532–33), in which he attacks pharmacists for overstepping and encroaching on the rightful territory of better-trained physicians. His favorite authority was Galen; he published Latin commentaries and translations of Galen, such as *Rosa gallica* (1514), *Ars parva Galeni* (1516?) and *Speculum Galeni* (1517).

Girolamo Fracastoro (1483–1553), or Fracastorius. The first distinguished physician to advance a scientific understanding of contagion (syphilis). His prose essay *De contagione et contagionis morbis* (Contagion; 1546) is the first truly comprehensive statement that syphilis can be transmitted by sexual contact. His earlier poem, *Syphilis sive morbus gallicus* (Syphilis or the French disease; 1530), gave the name to the malady.

François Rabelais (1492–1553). A prominent humanist of the French Renaissance. Born in Chinon on the Vienne in the province of Touraine, Rabelais entered the faculty of medicine at Montpellier in 1530 and earned a bachelor's degree in a remarkably short time. By 1532 he had moved from Montpellier to Lyons, where he met and possibly worked with, if not for, Symphorien Champier. In 1537 he took his doctor's degree at Montpellier and was soon appointed lecturer on the Greek text of Hippocrates. Author of *Pantagruel, Gargantua, Le tiers livre, Le quart livre,* and at least part of *Le cinquième livre,* he participated in the querelle des femmes, especially in the *Tiers livre* dedicated to Marguerite de Navarre, as well as in debates on medical issues of the time.

Paracelsus (1493–1541), or Theophrastus Bombastus von Hohenheim. A Swiss-born physician–alchemist and controversial figure who wrote his works in German, he was one of the first to break away from the orthodox schools of Galen and Avicenna. According to Sournia, Paracelsus might have been known as the "father of pharmaceutical chemistry" had he not mixed in a large measure of astrology and occultism in his writings (*Histoire de la médecine,* 151–52). See Paracelsus, *Selected Writings.*

Ambroise Paré (ca. 1510–90). A French surgeon who obtained anatomical knowledge and adapted it for use in the army. He published a work on surgery, *Ten Books of Surgery with the Magazine of the Instruments Necessary for It* (1564), *Complete Works* (1575), and *Apologie and Treatise* (1585).

Gabriel Fallopius (1523–62), or Gabriele Falloppio. Professor at the University of Padua who studied the reproductive organs in both sexes and described the eponymous Fallopian tube, which leads from the ovaries to the uterus. He did so in *Observationes anatomicae* (Venice, 1561), a critical commentary on and addition to Vesalius's *De humani corporis fabrica* (1543).

Andreas Vesalius (1514–64), or Andries van Wesel. Anatomist, physician, and author of the 1543 *De humani corporis fabrica* (On the fabric of the human body), with its detailed illustrations of anatomy. He published a second edition of the work in 1553–55. For a modern edition of his "epitome" in French and in Latin (in facing pages), see Vésale, *Résumé de ses livres.*

Simon de Vallambert (d. after 1558). Author of *Cinq livres de la manière de nourrir et gouverner les enfans dès leur naissance* (Five books on the manner of feeding and raising children from birth; 1565), a work on the care of newborns and children. See Vallambert, *De la manière,* Colette Winn's recent critical edition of the work.

Laurent Joubert (1529–82). Chancellor of the Faculté de Médecine, the famous medical school in Montpellier. He denounced medical errors in his *Erreurs populaires* (*Popular Errors*), written in the vernacular. The work was a bestseller that saw at least twenty-one editions between 1578 and 1608, including two editions in

Italian and Latin (Worth-Stylianou, *Les traités d'obstétrique*, 193). The first edition was printed in Bordeaux by S. Millanges. For a modern English translation, see Joubert, *Popular Errors*.

Jean Liébault (1535–96). Doctor, agronomist, and author of a graphic gynecological treatise in French, titled *Trois livres appartenans aux infirmitez et maladies des femmes* (Three books on the infirmities and illnesses of women; 1582). Evelyne Berriot-Salvadore considers the work the "precursor of gynecology" (*Un corps, un destin*, 35n1), and Valérie Worth-Stylianou claims that the work is a translation and free adaptation of Giovanni Marinello's *Le medicine partenenti all'infermità delle donne*, first published in Venice in 1563 (*Les traités d'obstétrique*, 258). Yet Worth-Stylianou finds that Liébault greatly expanded on Marinello's skeleton (*Les traités d'obstétrique*, 260). Gianna Pomata calls Liébault's extremely popular three-volume gynecological text, reissued ten times between 1582 and 1674, a "hybrid" in that it "combines the treatment of women's health issues with an articulate and passionate defence of women from negative stereotypes" ("Was There a Querelle?," 336).

André du Laurens (1558–1609). Condemned Aristotle's description of woman as a monster of nature or incomplete man in his influential *Historia anatomica humani corporis* (Anatomical description of the human body; 1593).

Jacques Ferrand (1575–??). Known for his famous encyclopedic treatise on lovesickness, which first appeared in 1610 under the title *Traicté de l'essence et guerison de l'amour et de la melancholie erotique*. A much-expanded second edition appeared in 1623. For a modern English translation of the second edition, see Jacques Ferrand, *A Treatise on Lovesickness*.

Louis de Serres (15??–16??). Published *Discours de la nature, causes, signes et curation des empeschements de la conception et de la sterilité des femmes* (A discourse on the nature, causes, signs and treatment of the failures to conceive and sterility among women) in 1625 (Worth-Stylianou, *Les traités d'obstétrique*, 433–43).

NOTES

All translations are mine unless otherwise indicated.

INTRODUCTION

1. Christine, *Cité des dames*, 66–67.
2. Here are only a few of the recent additions to scholarship on the querelle des femmes: Brownlee and Francis, "Querelles des femmes"; Zegura, "Gender and Patriarchy"; Ferguson and McKinley, "*Heptaméron*: Word, Spirit, World"; Campbell, "The *Querelle des femmes*"; Gianni Pomata, "Was There a Querelle?"; Rezvani, "*Heptaméron*'s 67th Tale"; Swift, "Pourquoi appellerions"; Swift, *Gender, Writing, and Performance*; Mathieu-Castellani, *Quenouille et la lyre*.
3. Donald A. Beecher finds lovesickness in the Renaissance "a prime example of contagion from a distance" and claims that the theory of contamination combined the poetic and the scientific to bring "the darts of Cupid ever closer to the best scientific analyses of the physiology of vision." Frelick writes about "discourses of contagion," the theory that one could become infected with lovesickness simply by reading literary works about passionate love. Both refer to a literalizing of metaphor in early modern medical discourse. See Beecher, "Windows on Contagion," 32, 36; Frelick "Contagions of Love," 48, 54.
4. See Green, *Making Women's Medicine Masculine*; Park, *Secrets of Women*; Allen, *Wages of Sin*; Cadden, *Meanings of Sex Difference*; Berriot-Salvadore, *Un corps, un destin*; and Siraisi, *Medieval and Early Renaissance*. See also Helen Rodnite Lemay's introduction to her excellent translation of *De secretis mulierum* in *Women's Secrets*. I am also greatly indebted to Kenneth F. Kitchell and Irven Michael Resnick's monumental two-volume (1827 pages) translation of Albertus Magnus's *On Animals*.

5. Berriot-Salvadore, *Un corps, un destin*, 1.

6. According to Nancy Siraisi, *On Complexions* and other Galenic works in Latin translation were being taught by 1300 in Montpellier and elsewhere; *Medieval and Early Renaissance*, 84. See also Durling, *Burgundio of Pisa's Translation*.

7. Galen, *De usu partium*, 2:297; Galen, *On the Usefulness*, 628–29.

8. Galen, *De usu partium*, 2:299; Galen, *On the Usefulness*, 630.

9. Andreas Vesalius's *De humani corporis fabrica libri septem* (On the fabric of the human body in seven books) appeared in print in 1543 but did not end the speculation on women's inverted anatomy. Such cultural historians as Thomas Laqueur and Katharine Park have debated the prevalence of the one-sex model in early modern Europe. Park claims that the idea of genital homology maintained its popularity in the first half of the sixteenth century. See Laqueur, *Making Sex*, 63–113; Park, *Secrets of Women*, 186–88.

10. "Le sexe n'est autre chose que la difference du masle et de la femelle: en laquelle faut considerer que la femme a tousiours moins de chaleur que l'homme, *aussi qu'elle a quelques parties peu differentes, et situées en autre lieu que l'homme*: d'avantage que les parties spermatiques d'icelle sont plus froides, et plus molles et moins seiches que celles de l'homme, et que les actions naturelles ne sont tant parfaites en elle qu'en l'homme. A la nature de la femme faut rapporter les chastrés, car ils degenerent en tel sexe, et retiennent la nature d'iceluy, comme on voit par la voix feminine, et defaut de poil par l'imbecile chaleur: toutesfois, faut avoir esgard qu'aucunes femmes approchent grandement de la nature de l'homme, comme appert à la voix virile, et quelquesfois on les voit porter barbe au menton. Au contraire, aucuns hommes retiennent de la nature de la femme, pour autant on les appelle effeminés. L'hermaphrodite, a raison qu'il tient de la nature de l'homme et de la femme, il est moyen entre les deux, participant de l'un et de l'autre." Paré, *Œuvres complètes d'Ambroise Paré*, 11:60–61; emphasis added.

The work cited here is from Paré's "Introduction to Surgery" (Introduction à la chirurgie).

11. "As for [women's] testicles, they do not differ from men's hardly at all . . . they are smaller and flatter, because of a lack of heat which was unable to make them rise or grow . . . and they are simpler . . . if you look at the parts [sexual organs] of men and women, you will find no difference in the number of parts, but only in their placement and use. For what men have on the outside, women have on the inside, as much by Nature's providence as by weakness of woman, who, unlike man, was unable to expel and propel outside these parts." (Quant aux Testicules, ils ne different de ceux des hommes presque en rien . . . ils sont aussi plus petis & de figure plus platte, pour le défaut de chaleur, qui ne les a peu faire lever ny croistre: & de composition plus simple . . . si tu contemples les parties tant de l'homme que de

la femme, tu ne les trouveras differentes l'une de l'autre touchant le nombre des parties, ains en la diverse situation et usage d'icelles. Car ce que l'homme a au dehors, la femme l'a au dedans, tant par la providence de Nature, que de l'imbecilité d'icelle, qui n'a peu expeller & jetter dehors lesdites parties, comme à l'homme.) This text comes from chapters 33 and 34 of *De l'anatomie* in Paré, *Œuvres* (1575), 129–30. See also Paré, *Œuvres complètes d'Ambroise Paré*, 163–64.

12. Galen, *De usu partium*, 2:302–4.

13. Galen, *De usu partium*, 2:307.

14. Aristotle, *Generation of Animals*, 726a–29a, 774a. For a discussion of early modern views on menstruation, see McClive, *Menstruation and Procreation*; however, McClive deals mainly with a later period, roughly from the mid-sixteenth century to the eighteenth.

15. The pseudo–Albertus Magnus work *De secretis mulierum*, an extremely popular treatise on women's "secretive" anatomy and moral weakness, was written at about the same time that Jean de Meun was composing his misogynistic continuation of Guillaume de Lorris's *Roman de la rose*. In the introduction to her English translation, Lemay counts eighty-three manuscripts of the treatise, with fifty printed editions in the fifteenth century and over seventy more in the sixteenth. According to Cadden, by the fifteenth century *De secretis mulierum* was also available in French and German translations, but, although it was the subject of commentaries and discussed in university settings, it "never had an official place in a university curriculum." See Lemay, introduction to *Women's Secrets*, 1; Cadden, *Meanings*, 116.

16. "Mulier etiam est vir occasionatus et habet naturam defectus et privationis respectu maris, ideo naturaliter diffidit de se; et ideo quod non potest acquirere per se, nilitur acquiere per mendacia et diabolicas deceptiones. Unde, ut breviter dicam, ab omni muliere est cavendum tanquam a serpente venenosa et diabolo cornuto, et si fas esset dicere, quae scio de mulieribus, totus mundus stuperet." Albertus Magnus, *Quaestiones super "De animalibus,"* book 15, quaestio 11, 265–66.

17. Lemay, introduction to *Women's Secrets*, 52.

18. Lemay, *Women's Secrets*, 35, 16.

19. See Cadden, *Meanings*, 228–58; Berriot-Salvadore, *Un corps, un destin*, 25–26.

20. Cadden, *Meanings*, 231.

21. For a discussion of how the Salic law was applied in sixteenth-century France, see Adams and Rechtschaffen, "Isabeau of Bavaria," 119–20.

22. Plato, *Collected Dialogues*, 1210. Even though this end passage was missing from the twelfth-century version of the *Timaeus*, which was accompanied by the commentary of Chalcidius, the idea of a wandering womb, dissatisfied and troublesome if infertile, was widespread throughout the Middle Ages; it is difficult, if not

impossible, to determine its origin. Cadden, *Meanings*, 14n2, 14–15. In the latter part of the sixteenth century, several medical authorities abandoned the theory.

23. For a discussion of the longstanding myths of the poisonous woman (femme-vénimeuse,) see Berriot-Salvadore, *Un corps, un destin*, 23–25.

24. Berriot-Salvadore, *Un corps, un destin*, 47.

25. See Wack, *Lovesickness*; Wells, *Secret Wound*; Allen, *Wages of Sin*, 1–24; and Beecher and Ciavolella, "Jacques Ferrand."

26. See Ficino, *Commentaire sur le banquet*; Ferrand, *Treatise on Lovesickness*.

27. Allen, *Wages of Sin*, 15.

28. Aristotle, *History of Animals*, 582a.

29. Galen, *De usu partium*, 2:323.

30. Gerulaitis, "Incunabula," 85.

31. Oriel, *Scars of Venus*, 12–13.

32. "Pour un petit plaisir je Soufre mille maux / Je fais contre un Hyver deux esté ce me semble / Partout le corps je sue et ma machoir tremble / Je ne croy jamais voir la fin de mes travaux."

33. Albertus Magnus, *De secretis mulierum*, 51.

34. 1 Timothy 3:11; Titus 2:3.

35. James 3:6, 3:8.

36. 1 Timothy 2:11–12; Maclean, *Renaissance Notion*, 16, 18.

37. Maclean, *Renaissance Notion*, 41.

38. Cadden, *Meanings*, 184.

39. Maclean writes that "an early Marian prayer includes the phrase 'pray for the devout female sex.'" See *Renaissance Notion*, 20.

40. Lemaire, *Œuvres*, 3:172.

41. In true Rhétoriqueur fashion, Lemaire plays on Molinet's name: "He alone milled sweet words in his clean mill [molin net]" (C'est luy seul qui moulait doulx motz en molin net). Lemaire, *Œuvres*, 4:31.

42. Stecher writes, "The dreamer of Belges was welcomed with open arms by . . . Symphorien Champier, Bayard's vain relative." Stecher, "Notice," 4:xii.

43. Lemaire, *Œuvres*, 4:428.

44. Again, Lemaire's effusive praise concentrates on the name of the person praised: "Gentle Champier, rich, pure, and whole field [champ] . . . / You will be named a fertile ground / A field [champ] full of honor and glory [floriture] / Well cultivated, noble, gentle Champier." Stecher, "Notice," 4:xii–xiiin4.

45. Stecher, "Notice," 4:xiiin4.

46. See Huchon, *Rabelais*, 246.

47. For Rabelais's response in *Gargantua* and *Pantagruel* to Champier's role in the medical debates in Lyon in the 1530s, see Antonioli, *Rabelais et la médecine*, 104–13.

According to Alain Boucher, "Symphorien Champier, doctor and alderman of the city, Rector of the Hospital . . . having studied at Montpellier, had certainly heard of Rabelais, especially since his son Antoine was in the same class as he. He saw in him perhaps a collaborator able to help him in his literary works. Some thought that Rabelais had played the role of 'slave' [nègre] in his literary works: it is best not to endorse this theory without proof." Boucher, "Les années médicales," 198–99. He adds, "Symphorien Champier was one of the rectors, from 1533 to 1535 during Rabelais's stay, and he gave him his support. During the same period, he published five medical works, including the '*Mirror of Pharmacists*' [*Myrouel des appothicaires*] in 1532 and '*The Gallic Garden*' [*Hortus gallicus*] in 1533, perhaps with Rabelais's collaboration." Boucher, "Les années médicales," 201. In a later work, Boucher claims that Rabelais "was seduced by the untiring and prolific literary output of this turbulent and envied person [Champier], and that is perhaps why he chose Lyon. In any case, it was Champier who gave the author of *Pantagruel* the idea to focus on Hippocrates whose major principles he promoted"; Boucher adds that "Champier served as a kind of mentor among his Lyon colleagues. [Champier] introduced [Rabelais] to Sébastien Gryphe, who edited 'Some Books by Hippocrates and Galen, revised by François Rabelais, a perfectly accomplished physician.'" Boucher, "L'héritage lyonnais d'Hippocrate," 220–21.

48. Rabelais, *Pantagruel*, 255.

49. Rabelais, *Pantagruel*, 372.

50. Rabelais, *Tiers livre*, 489–91. See, for example, Lefranc, "L'identification de Raminagrobis."

51. Jean Céard, in Rabelais, *Tiers livre*, 4n1. For a convincing argument of "intertextual echoes" of Rabelais's *Pantagruel* in Marguerite's *Heptaméron*, see Blaylock, "International Echoes," 13.

52. Champier writes about witnessing the coronation in *Gestes ensemble la vie*, 157–58.

53. Here, he praises Alain Chartier (1385–1430), Jean Robertet (ca. 1402–ca. 1494), Georges Chastellain (1405–75), Arnould Gréban (ca. 1420–ca. 1485), Guillaume Crétin (1460–1525), and Mellin de Saint-Gelais (1491–1558). Lemaire, *Œuvres*, 3:172.

54. The list of famous French writers includes Jean Froissart (1347–1405), Alain Chartier, Jean Robertet, Georges Chastellain, Martin Le Franc (1410–61), Simon Greban (active in the 1450s), Jean Meschinot (1420–91), Robert Gaguin (1433–1501), and Octavien de Saint-Gelais (1468–1502). Lemaire, *Œuvres*, 3:231.

55. The famous orators include Jean de Meun (1250–1305), Jean Froissart, Alain Chartier, Georges Chastellain (1405–14), the two Grebans (Arnould and Simon), Jean Meschinot, Jacques Milet (1425–66), Jean Molinet (1435–1507), and Guillaume Crétin. Lemaire, *Œuvres*, 3:172.

56. In book 1 of the *Illustrations*, Lemaire cites Alain Chartier's "description de France," Robert Gaguin's "histoire françoise," and Jacques de Guise's (1340–99) "histoire de Belges" as his sources; Lemaire, *Œuvres*, 1:345. In book 2, he cites Jacques de Bergame again; Lemaire, *Œuvres*, 2:7. In book 3, he cites Robert Gaguin and Jacques de Guise; Lemaire, *Œuvres*, 2:253–54.

57. Among the orators who present the "crown" to Margaret are Martin Le Franc (1410–61), Robert Gaguin, Jean Robertet, and Georges Chastellain. Lemaire, *Œuvres* 4:62–69, 78–82, 97–108, 128–40.

58. In the *Heptaméron*, Marguerite cites de Meun in novellas 24 and 29 and Chartier in novellas 12 and 56. See also Bauschatz, "Rabelais and Marguerite," 398.

59. See Kennedy, *Christine de Pizan*.

60. According to Berriot-Salvadore, the 1550s saw a "decisive evolution in medical literature," with increasing numbers of works in obstetrics and "feminine pathology" offering "a didactic mirror where woman and man are invited to look at themselves." *Un corps, un destin*, 2.

1. LOVE OR SEDUCTION?

1. According to Evelyne Berriot-Salvadore, the querelle des femmes began in the sixteenth century and lasted until the early seventeenth; *Un corps, un destin*, 1. Emma Cayley traces it back to the fifteenth century and finds that Christine initiated it by participating in the literary debate on the *Roman de la Rose*, even though the male participants "merely tolerated" her; *Debate and Dialogue*, 68. Gisela Bock and Margarete Zimmermann find that the querelle des femmes began in the late Middle Ages and merely "gained momentum" with Christine's *Cité des dames*; "European *Querelle*," 93.

2. Christine, *Poems of Cupid*, 53.

3. Christine, *Poems of Cupid*, 34, 36; emphasis added.

4. All references to the querelle de la rose come from Eric Hicks's critical edition, *Débat*. The most recent anthology to date, *Debating the Roman de la rose*, edited by Christine McWebb and translated from the Latin by Earl Jeffrey Richards, focuses on the work's reception from 1340 to 1410 and includes works hitherto unconnected with it. For a discussion of the reception of the *Roman de la rose* in the century before Christine de Pizan and Jean Gerson began the querelle, see Badel, *Roman*. Guillaume de Lorris wrote the first four thousand lines of the *Roman de la rose* in the first half of the thirteenth century, and Jean de Meun composed the remainder (approximately eighteen thousand lines) between 1275 and 1280. The first part is an allegorical poem, an "Art of Love" after the model of Ovid, intended for an aristocratic audience. The second part continues the allegory but in a very different vein for a bourgeois audience.

5. See Desmond, "Ethics of Reading"; Hult, *"Roman de la rose"*; Brown-Grant, *Christine de Pizan*; Suranyi, "Fifteenth-Century Woman's Pathway"; Sullivan, "At the Limit"; Baird, "Pierre Col"; Baird and Kane, *La querelle*, and Baird and Kane, "Defense of the Opponents."

6. English translations of the querelle come from McWebb, *Debating the Roman*.

7. Hicks, *Débat*, 60–63.

8. See Richards, "Intellectual Friendship."

9. Hicks, *Débat*, 50, 26, 56.

10. Hicks, *Débat*, 52.

11. Hicks, *Débat*, 57.

12. Kelly, "Early Feminist Theory," 13.

13. Hicks, *Débat*, 32, 34.

14. Hicks, *Débat*, 38, 44.

15. Hicks, *Débat*, 42.

16. Hicks, *Débat*, 42–44.

17. Hicks, *Débat*, 100, 106.

18. Hicks, *Débat*, 103.

19. Hicks, *Débat*, 148.

20. Cayley, *Debate and Dialogue*, 55–56.

21. Cayley, *Debate and Dialogue*, 55.

22. Cayley, *Debate and Dialogue*, 73.

23. Cayley, *Debate and Dialogue*, 75.

24. Cayley, *Debate and Dialogue*, 77.

25. See Van Hamel, *Les Lamentations de Matheolus*.

26. Christine's father, Tommaso da Pizzano, served as personal physician and court astrologer for the French king Charles V. He had studied medicine at the University of Bologna in his early years. According to Willard, Charles V owned sixty volumes devoted to medicine and surgery; since many of these manuscripts came from the University of Bologna, Willard credits Tomasso with aiding Charles, as his "scientific adviser," in acquiring such an impressive library in the field. Willard, *Christine de Pizan*, 30. A knowledge of the seven liberal arts (arithmetic, geometry, music, astronomy, grammar, rhetoric, and logic) was thought necessary preparation for the study of medicine. Astrology and medicine were not considered separate disciplines. Indeed, constellations were thought to govern not only a person's destiny but also parts of the body at different times of the year.

27. Christine, *City of Ladies*, 22–23; Christine, *Cité des dames*, 53–54.

28. Lemay, introduction to *Women's Secrets*, 17.

29. Lemay, *Women's Secrets*, 59; emphasis added.

30. Christine, *Cité des dames*, 66–67.

31. "And this soul, God created it as good, as noble, identical in the body of the woman as in that of man." Christine, *Cité des dames*, 55.

32. Christine, *City of Ladies*, 256–57; Christine, *Cité des dames*, 277–78.

33. Cayley finds only a possible intertext of the *Livre de la cité des dames* in Chartier's *Livre des quatre dames*, completed between 1420 and 1422. Cayley, *Debate and Dialogue*, 125.

34. Willard, *Christine de Pizan*, 61.

35. Christine, *Poems of Cupid*, 34, 36; emphasis added.

36. Cayley, *Debate and Dialogue*, 162–63n106.

37. Cayley, *Debate and Dialogue*, 120–21.

38. McRae, *Alain Chartier*, 93; Chartier, *Poetical Works*, 359–60.

39. Cayley, *Debate and Dialogue*, 112–13.

40. McRae, *Alain Chartier*, 199; Chartier, *Poetical Works*, 367.

41. Nancy Frelick also places Chartier on the prowoman side and claims that Marguerite de Navarre refers directly to Chartier's *Belle dame sans mercy* twice in the *Heptaméron* "to bolster [her] critique of courtly love as antifeminist"; she mentions that "in Marguerite's text, Chartier is criticized by womanizing *devisants*, who see his doctrine as spoiling their game, and praised by women, who speak of his teachings as profitable to young ladies." Frelick, "Love, Mercy," 325. Frelick offers Anne de Graville's sixteenth-century version of Chartier's *Belle dame* that omitted the ambiguous parts of the text to provide an "idea of its reception by ladies at the court of François Ier." Frelick, "Love, Mercy," 326n2. For an analysis of de Graville's "rewriting" of Chartier's work into "a didactic text by a woman, and for the benefit of other women," see Delogu, "A Fair Lady," 471, 483.

42. Le Franc, *Champion*, 1:3.

43. See Deschaux, introduction to *Le champion des dames*, 1:xxx–xxliii.

44. Le Franc, *Champion*, 162, 163, 221.

45. Le Franc, *Trial of Womankind*, 135–36; Le Franc, *Champion*, 4:178.

46. In "'Perdre son latin,'" Thelma Fenster points out that Christine only wrote in French but possessed a good reading knowledge of Latin. Fenster adds that by writing in French, Christine made her role in the querelle de la rose more public, as writing in Latin was a more private form of discourse. She asserts that the querelle de la rose was the "first recorded literary debate in French" and finds Christine's French prose style Latinized and exaggeratedly so, even for the time: "The Debate of the *Rose* thus foreshadows Christine's later project by offering the spectacle of a confrontation of cultures, one learned and exclusivizing, the other in the language of the majority, but learned too." Fenster, "'Perdre son latin,'" 91–93, 96–97, 103–4.

47. Le Franc, *Trial of Womankind*, 136; Le Franc, *Champion* 4:179.

48. Jean Castel was a minor poet whose only extant work, a poem, is titled "Le pin." For a comparison of the son's poem and the mother's works, see Delsaux, "Le pin," 346–52.

49. Le Franc, *Trial of Womankind*, 136–37; Le Franc, *Champion*, 4:179.

50. Le Franc, *Champion*, 2:5417–18.

51. The champion may be referring to noblewomen rather than hardworking peasant women. Saffredent, one of Marguerite de Navarre's *devisants*, will claim that members of the nobility, both men and women, are less healthy due to their idle lifestyle. *Heptaméron*, 29:279–80.

52. Heinrich Cornelius Agrippa von Nettesheim's ironic *Declamation on the Nobility and Preeminence of the Female Sex* (*De nobilitate et praecellentia foeminei sexus*, written in 1509 and dedicated to Margaret of Austria, argued for women's superiority over men and was not taken seriously by his dedicatee or most readers of the time. See Rabil, "Agrippa and the Feminist," 3–37. Agrippa does not mention Christine, but he cites several female poets of antiquity. He adds, "If, in our time, education had not been prohibited to women, today also very well-educated women would be considered more talented than men." Agrippa, *Declamation on the Nobility*, 83.

53. The *Roman de la rose* was extremely popular in the first decades of the sixteenth century. It saw twenty-two editions between 1481 and 1538; seven were published during 1526–38. Glidden, "Marot's *Le Roman*," 143.

54. Willard, *Christine de Pizan*, 11.

55. Zimmermann, "Christine de Pizan," 57. As proof of the claim that Margaret of Austria possessed artwork based on Christine's *Cité des dames*, Zimmerman cites Bell, "Lost Tapestry"; and Bell, "New Approach." See Zimmermann, "Christine de Pizan," 74n2. Margaret owned a copy of *Le livre de la cité des dames* as early as 1482 and later acquired another copy; she also received a set of six tapestry panels depicting scenes from Christine's *Cité des dames* as a gift at Tournai in 1513. See Bell, *Lost Tapestries*, 87, 42. However, Zimmerman offers no proof that Anne de Beaujeu, Gabrielle de Bourbon, Marguerite de Navarre, and Georgette de Montenay referred to Christine or the *Cité des dames*.

56. Swift, *Gender, Writing, and Performance*, 24. The only sixteenth-century edition of *Le livre de la cité des dames* to appear in print was an English translation, *The Boke of the Cyte of Ladyes*, published in London by H. Pepwell in 1521. See Kennedy, *Christine de Pizan*, 94.

57. McLeod, *Reception*, ii–iv. Patricia Caraffi and Earl Jeffrey Richards published a bilingual critical edition of Christine's *Livre de la cité des dames* in 1997, with the Middle French and Italian translations on facing pages. See Kennedy, *Christine de Pizan*, 162–63. Kennedy also cites two previously unpublished critical editions

of the *Livre de la cité des dames*, one edited by Lange (1974) and the other by Curnow (1975). Kennedy, *Christine de Pizan*, 94.

58. Brian Anslay translated the work, which carries a verse preface by one of Christine's patrons: the third earl of Kent, Richard Grey. For a description of the two extant printed editions of the translation and the manuscript that the translation was based on, see Curnow, "*Boke of the Cyte*." Citing Campbell's "Christine de Pisan en Angleterre," she attests to Christine's popularity in England by noting that today the British Museum owns thirteen manuscripts of Christine's works and the Oxford Bodleian Library four, and that by the middle of the sixteenth century five of Christine's works had been translated into English. See Curnow, "*Boke of the Cyte*," 129, 137n18. According to Constance Jordan, "Ansley's printed *Boke* had . . . a polemical dimension that the French manuscript *Cité des dames* lacked," given that Anne Boleyn's daughter, the future Elizabeth I, was destined for the crown. Jordan, *Renaissance Feminism*, 106.

59. Willard, "Anne de France," 63.

60. Willard, "Anne de France," 59–60.

61. Willard, "Anne de France," 66–67.

62. Bourbon, *Œuvres spirituelles*, 21n14. See also the notes on pages 44, 56, 89, 90, 157, 159, 160, 191, 200.

63. Hélisenne de Crenne, *Epistres familières*, 130–31, 95.

64. Sommers, "Marguerite," 74.

65. Sommers, "Marguerite," 72.

66. Sommers, "Marguerite," 80; emphasis added.

67. One of Marguerite's *devisantes*, Longarine, talks about Jean de Meun's teachings (doctrine) in novella 24, which include deceit and lies. Marguerite, *Heptaméron*, 24:249. In novella 29, Saffredent quotes de Meun: "Whether frieze or lawn you wear / Love's fancies free do linger there" (Aussy bien sont amourettes / Soubz bureaux que soubz brunettes). Marguerite, *Heptaméron*, 29:279. Catharine Randall cites Paul A. Chilton's translation: according to Randall, "bureau," or "bure," refers to a rough fabric that monks wear, and "brunette" a "soft, high quality textile" worn by the very rich; *Earthly Treasures*, 224. See also Marguerite, *Heptaméron*, 12:117; 56:422.

68. In novella 12, Parlamente says that "such a gentle malady (love) / rarely kills people" (sy gracieuse malladye / ne mect gueres de gens à mort). Marguerite, *Heptaméron*, 12:117.

69. In an excellent article, "Reconstruction of an Author," Cynthia Jane Brown is one of the few to clearly demonstrate how Christine's fortunes dipped in the late fifteenth century and the first two decades of the sixteenth century. Brown's article focuses on Christine's *Livre des fais d'armes et de chevalerie*, first printed

by Antoine Vérard in 1488 but without Christine's name. As Brown states, later French publishers would reinstate Christine's name and image to appeal to an ever-increasing number of women readers, but she demonstrates that Christine was definitely not a "household name" by the end of the sixteenth century. She also lists French authors who cited or ignored Christine in their writings. See Brown, "Reconstruction of an Author," 215, 219, 237–38n37.

70. Antoine Vérard attributed L'art de chevalerie selon vegece (1488) to Vegetius, but, as Brown indicates, Christine's name had already disappeared from fifteen of the twenty-four extant manuscripts of the work. Brown, "Reconstruction," 215. Le trésor de la cité des dames appeared in two French editions in 1497 and 1503; both were attributed to "dame Cristine"; Brown doubts that readers of the time knew who she was and posits that Christine's "literary fame in France [seemed] to have diminished" already. Brown, "Reconstruction," 219. The sole printed copy of Le livre de la cité des dames appeared in print in English translation in 1521; it was not until 1536 and 1549 that printers published Le tresor de la cité des dames and Le chemin de long estude, under the names "Christine de la Cité de Pise" and "Christine de Pise." Brown, "Reconstruction," 217.

71. McLeod, Reception, ii.

72. Willard, Christine de Pizan, 220.

73. Sommers, "Marguerite," 73. The myth of Christine's influence on Champier is particularly persistent. Glenda McLeod also lists Champier's Nef des dames as one of the "later catalogs that acknowledged [Christine's] work." See McLeod, Virtue, 141. More recently, François Rigolot claimed that Christine was "quoted . . . approvingly" in Champier's Nef des dames (1503)." Rigolot, "Invention," 86.

74. All references to Champier's Nef des dames vertueuses come from the 2007 critical edition.

75. Anne owned and purportedly read the Livre des trois vertus, but there is no evidence that she owned a copy of the Livre de la cité des dames. See Willard, "Anne de France," 59–69.

76. Another especially stubborn myth surrounding the Nef des dames is that Anne of France commissioned the work. See Cholakian and Cholakian, Marguerite de Navarre, 11, 49; Clavier and Viennot, introduction to Les enseignements, 15.

77. For a closer comparison of the two works, see Kem, "Symphorien Champier and Christine."

78. Jeanneau, "Introduction" to Les vies des femmes celebres, xxxi–xxxvi.

79. Jeanneau, "Introduction" to Les vies des femmes celebres, liii–liv.

80. Lesnauderie, La louenge de mariage, 28.

81. The following authors are often referred to as "Rhétoriqueurs" (in chronological order): Georges Chastellain (1415–74), Henri Baude (act. 1460–95); Jean

Meschinot (ca. 1420–90), Jean Molinet (1435–1507), Jean Marot (1450–1526), Guillaume Crétin (1465–1525), Octavien de Saint-Gelais (1468–1502), André de la Vigne (act. 1485–1515), Jean Lemaire de Belges (1473–1515 and after), Jean Parmentier (act. 1515–30), Jean Robertet (act. 1460–1500), Jean d'Auton (act. 1499–1528), Pierre Gringore (act. 1500–1535), and Jean Bouchet (1476–1557). See Zumthor, *Le masque*, 12; Zumthor, *Anthologie*, 15. Jean Castel, Christine de Pizan's son, is also included in some lists. For a recent article comparing French and Burgundian Rhétoriqueurs, see Thiry, "Rhétoriqueurs de Bourgogne," 101–16.

82. For example, Lemaire praises Georges Chastellain, Jean Robertet, Jean Meschinot, Octavien de Saint-Gelais, and Guillaume Crétin in *Le temple d'honneur et de vertus* (1503); Chastellain, Robertet, Jean Molinet, Saint-Gelais, Crétin, and Jean d'Auton in *La plainte du désiré* (1504); Chastellain and Molinet in *La concorde du genre humain* (1508), and Chastellain, Meschinot, Molinet, and Saint-Gelais in *La concorde des deux langages* (1511). In his works, Guillaume Crétin names Jean Marot, Meschinot, Jean d'Auton, Molinet, Lemaire, Saint-Gelais, André de la Vigne, and Pierre Gringore. In his *Deploration dudit cretin sur le trespas de feu Okergan, tresorier de Sainct Martin de Tours*, Crétin calls upon Chastellain, Chartier, Meschinot, Jacques Milet, Pierre de Nesson, Molinet, and Saint-Gelais to help him mourn composer Johannes Ockeghem; in his *Plainte sur le trespas de . . . Guillaume de Byssipat*, Crétin summons his illustrious predecessors, Jean d'Auton, Lemaire, Jacques de Bigue, Macé de Villebresme, Jean de Paris, Jean Marot, and André De La Vigne to help him compose yet another lament. See Crétin, *Œuvres poétiques*, 68–69, 91.

All imitate de Meun or cite him as an important literary predecessor. For example, Meschinot cites the *Roman de la rose* in his *Lunettes des princes* and borrows de Meun's allegorical figures Raison, Faux Semblant, and Male Bouche. See Meschinot, *Lunettes*, 24, 17, 80, 84. Jean Molinet praises de Meun in his *Art de rhétorique vulgaire*; in his *Romant de la rose moralisé*, Molinet refers to the romance as a kind of literary "Lord's prayer" that he hesitates to "moralize," and he likens its two authors to Moses (Guillaume de Lorris) and John the Baptist (Jean de Meun). See Molinet in Andes, *Le romant*, §50. In his *Séjour d'honneur*, Octavien de Saint-Gelais speaks of "the great honor that De Meun won in France." Saint-Gelais, *Séjour*, 218. Jean Lemaire de Belges praises de Meun in his *Concorde du genre humain*, and in *La concorde des deux langages* he names de Meun the French equivalent, if not superior, of Dante. See Lemaire, *Concorde du genre humain*, 54; Lemaire, *Concorde des deux langages*, 4. Finally, Jean Bouchet praises him in several works, such as *Regnars traversant les perilleuses voyes des folles fiances du monde* (1504), *Le temple de bonne renommée* (1517), and *Les angoisses et remèdes d'amour du traverseur* (1536). See Badel, *Roman*, 507–11.

83. Margaret of Austria owned a copy of the *Livre de la cité des dames* and *Livre des trois vertus* in a large, illustrated volume, complete with traces of candle wax on the pages. See Willard, "Margaret of Austria," 355.

84. Molinet, *Faictz et dictz*, 937n108.

85. Molinet, *Faictz et dictz*, 108.

86. Christine, *Cité des dames*, 234–35.

87. Molinet, *Le romant de la rose moralisé*, §97:698.

88. Bell claims that Margaret of Austria received a set of six tapestry panels depicting scenes from Christine's *Cité des dames* as a gift at Tournai in 1513, but by that time Lemaire had left Marguerite's service for the French court. Bell, *Lost Tapestries*, 42.

89. Lemaire, *Œuvres*, 4:395.

90. Lemaire, *Œuvres* 4:111. There is one slight exception: in *La concorde des deux langages*, Lemaire mentions "sapphic" verses. Lemaire, *Concorde des deux langages*, 19.

91. Marot, *Deux recueils*, 110.

92. Jean Marot expresses his admiration for de Meun in a rondeau titled "To Avoid Idleness" (D'eviter Oisiveté) and in "To Be Chaste while Beautiful" (D'estre chaste en estant belle). Marot, *Deux recueils*, 17.

93. Marot, *Deux recueils*, 6–7, 8, 9.

94. The poem is titled "To Pray in Spirit and Truth" (De prier en esperit et verité). Marot, *Deux recueils*, 18.

95. Marot, *Deux recueils*, 94.

96. Marot, *Deux recueils*, 96–97.

97. Marot, *Deux recueils*, 100.

98. Marot, *Deux recueils*, 97.

99. Swift, *Gender, Writing, and Performance*, 179; Marot, *Deux recueils*, 101.

100. Marot, *Deux recueils*, 101–2.

101. Marot, *Deux receuils*, 102.

102. "Slanderers, please restrain / Your tongue, which stings and bites"; "Your lizard tongue / Please then restrain it"; "Jealousy with Evil Tongue / . . . struck . . . / Our honor, purer than genuine gold." Marot, *Deux recueils*, 107, 111, 116.

103. Marot, *Deux recueils*, 116.

104. Bouchet, *Œuvres*, 1:196.

105. Bouchet, *Œuvres*, 1:169–71.

106. Bouchet, *Œuvres*, 1:172, 171.

107. Bouchet, *Œuvres*, 1:188–89.

108. He also cites Hildegard of Bingen and her medical works. See Bouchet, *Œuvres*, 1:176–79.

109. "Et les suyvoit Christine l'ancienne, / Qui fut jadis grant rhetoricienne, / Et mere aussi de l'orateur Castel, / Qui fit si bien que onc ne viz ung cas tel." Bouchet,

Temple, 341. In true Rhétoriqueur fashion, Bouchet plays on the name Castel with "cas tel" (such a case), but Le Franc had used the same play on words earlier.

110. "Je ne sçauroye oublïer les epistres, rondeaux, et ballades en langue françoyse . . . de Christine, qui [s]avoit la langue Grecque et Latine, et fut mere de Castel, homme de parfaicte eloquence." Bouchet, *Œuvres*, 1:178.

111. Bouchet, *Œuvres*, 1:179.

112. *Les triumphes* probably appeared in print for the first time in 1531 and enjoyed considerable popularity and several Paris editions until 1555, when its popularity began to wane; its final edition appeared in Louvain in 1563. Britnell, *Jean Bouchet*, 221–22. Bouchet writes:

> My principal intention has always been, through fictions, poetry, and histories, to praise virtues and condemn vices, as one can see by reading them. And even more to distract women and girls from reading the French translation of the Old and New Testaments, which is a dangerous thing to read in several passages as translated [selong la seule lettre] and certain short treatises by some German heretics translated from Latin into French, which under the sweetness of the evangelical doctrine there are interposed several errors too scandalous and pernicious to Christianity. Bouchet, *Triumphes*, v.

113. Marot, *Œuvres*, 1:18.

114. Marot, *Œuvres*, 2:388.

115. Marot, *Œuvres*, 2:361.

116. Marot, *Œuvres*, 1:143.

117. Champier, *Nef des dames* (2007), 56–57.

118. Yet another author, François de Billon, defends women in *Fort inexpugnable du sexe feminin* (1555), which contains a section praising such women writers of the time as Marguerite de Navarre, Marguerite de Bourg, Claudine et Jeanne Scève, Jeanne Gaillarde, Pernette du Guillet, and Hélisenne de Crenne, but he does not mention Christine. Billon, *Fort*, 31–36.

119. On the topic of scholarly reaction to writing about misogyny, see Bloch, *Medieval Misogyny*, 1.

2. FROM PHYSICAL TO SPIRITUAL LOVE

1. *Le romant de la rose moralisé cler et net* was printed by Vérard between 1500 and 1503, in Lyon in 1503, and in Paris by Veuve Michel le Noir in 1521. Rosemond Tuve posits that it was probably composed much earlier, perhaps in 1482; *Allegorical Imagery*, 237. However, Noël Dupire makes a strong case for the work's composition after 1498 in *Jean Molinet*, 72–78.

2. Recent critical works on Molinet's moralized version of the romance include Schaefer, "Jean Molinet"; Devaux, "Tradition textuelle et techniques"; Devaux, "Pour plus fresche memoire"; and Croft, "Pygmalion and the Metamorphosis." See also Michael Randall's chapter "The Flamboyant Allegory of Jean Molinet's *Romant de la rose moralisé*" in *Building Resemblance*, 13–39. Jacqueline Schaefer sees the moralized version as worthy of critical attention: "In this rapid survey, we have had no other goal than to provide a little water from our own mill for the rehabilitation of this really fascinating work that merits the erudite attention that some of our colleagues are devoting to it." Schaefer, "Jean Molinet," 410.

3. See Andes, "*Le romant*." Subsequent page references to the *Romant de la rose moralisé* are taken from this edition and accompanied by chapter indications in Arabic numerals placed before colons. Andes bases his text on the first edition (Vérard) and provides ample proof that the Balsarin edition, printed in 1503 at Lyon, was copied from the earlier Vérard rendering. Andes, "*Le romant*," 18–19. Jean Devaux's modern edition, currently in preparation, is based on ms. 128 C5 in La Haye, Bibliothèque royale. See Devaux, "De l'amour profane," 19n34; Devaux, "Tradition textuelle," 379n8, and Schaefer, "Jean Molinet Rhétoriqueur," 393n1. All translations are mine.

4. Andes, "*Le romant*," xxxii.

5. Andes, "*Le romant*," xxxii–xxxiii.

6. Tuve, *Allegorical Imagery*, 265, 245. Tuve describes Molinet's moralized version as "a warning of how not to read." Tuve, *Allegorical Imagery*, 232. She also criticizes his "untenably contradictory meanings tossed about to alight where they can find a foothold in the text," his "shocking taste," his "disregard of responsible allegorical reading in favor of mere equations with what he would like to have the piece mean," and his "potpourri of images with Christological meanings." Tuve, *Allegorical Imagery*, 238, 263, 265.

7. Tuve, *Allegorical Imagery*, 245. Heather M. Arden endorses Tuve's interpretation and criticizes Molinet's "imposed allegory" as not "consistent with the spirit of the text." Arden, *Romance of the Rose*, 88.

8. Dupire, *Jean Molinet*, 101.

9. Randall, *Building Resemblance*, 13, 21.

10. See Devaux, "Tradition textuelle," (2006), "Pour plus fresche memoire," (2006), and "De l'amour profane à l'amour sacré:" (2004).

11. At least one critic, Noël Dupire, has referred to Molinet's role in the querelle de la rose but only cursorily: "On the other hand, Molinet cannot admit, with Jean de Meun, that there are fewer good women than phoenixes. He takes his turn defending female honor; he also finds that Jean Gerson did not know how to disentangle the secret meaning from the old poem (chapter 107). There he adds

an unexpected chapter to the debate on the *Romance of the Rose*." Dupire, *Jean Molinet*, 100.

12. Molinet writes: "It reminds us of monseigneur Philippe of Cleves, lord of Ravestain, upon whose request I have undertaken this work . . ." Molinet, *Romant de la rose moralisé*, 86:559. See Philippe de Clèves, *L'instruction de toutes*, written around 1516.

13. Andes, "*Le romant*," 25–27.

14. Bourdillon, *Early Editions*, 147, 160, 162; Dupire, *Jean Molinet*, 72–78; Devaux, *Jean Molinet*, 604; Devaux, "Pour plus fresche mémoire," 558.

15. The treaty of Arras of 1435 reconciled Charles VII and Philip the Good of Burgundy at the close of the Hundred Years' War. The treaty signed by Louis XI and Maximilian I in 1482 called for the marriage of Archduchess Margaret of Austria to Charles VIII, heir to the French throne.

16. Andes, "*Le romant*," 85:536, 539–44.

17. Devaux examines the "fierce struggle" (lutte acharnée) between Philippe and Maximilian from 1488 to 1492, and he points out passages in the *Chronicles* where Molinet sides with Philippe and paints Maximilian in subtly negative ways. Devaux, *Jean Molinet*, 561–81.

18. Molinet, *Chroniques*, 5:9–10.

19. Molinet, *Chroniques*, 5:183–91.

20. Prologue to Andes, "*Le romant*," 15.

21. Augustine, *The Trinity*, 266; Augustine, *De trinitate*, 8.10.

22. Prologue to Andes, "*Le romant*," 15; its source is unknown. Rabanus Maurus (ca. 780–856) was author of the encyclopedic *De rerum naturis* and *De institutione clericorum*.

23. Prologue to Andes, "*Le romant*," 16. According to Andes, the work mentioned here is generally attributed to Denis the Aeropagite, but there is considerable doubt about its authorship. Andes, "*Le romant*," 710n3.

24. Ovid, *Tristia*, 1.9.31–32; Valerius Maximus, *Factorum*, 4.7.

25. Prologue to Andes, "*Le romant*," 16. See Ovid, *Tristia*, 1.9.31–32.

26. Prologue to Andes, "*Le romant*," 16.

27. Prologue to Andes, "*Le romant*," 16. See also Virgil, *Eclogues*, 10.69; Piccolomini, *Tale of Two Lovers*, 23.

28. Piccolomini, *Tale of Two Lovers*, 53. In the preface to the work, Sylvius Piccolomini states the moral aim of his tale: "And this story teaches youths not to arm themselves for the warfare of love, which is more bitter than sweet; but, putting away passion, which drives men mad, to pursue the study of virtue, for she alone can make her possessor happy. While, if there is anyone that does not know

from other sources how many evils love conceals, he may learn from this." See Piccolomini, *Tale of Two Lovers*, 10.

29. "You knew love's empire: long pursuit, short laughter, few joys, many fears, always dying, never dead—that's the lover." See Piccolomini, *Tale of Two Lovers*, 22.

30. Prologue to Andes, "*Le romant*," 16–17.

31. Cotgrave defines "fatuité" as "foolishnesse, doltishnesse, blockishnesse, dulnesse, ideotisme, sottishnesse."

32. Andes, "*Le romant*," 15:101.

33. See Boccaccio, *Decameron*, 6:9.

34. "Une jeusne fille de Boulenois fut enamouree d'ung jeusne fils, lequel pour retenance de perpetuele amour, lui lança ou doy une verge d'or, promettant jamais avoir aultre. Peu de temps aprés, le jovencel enoeulla une autre fille, laquelle il fiancha par le gré de ses amis et manda a sa premiere dame par amours qu'elle lui renvoyast sa verge. La fille fort esbahie de ces nouvelles mist grand paine a tirer hors l'aneau de son doy, ce que faire ne poeult. Et comme touchie d'ung rain de jalousie a demi foursenée, print ung grant couteau dont on minche la paree, mit son doy sur le bloc, si le trencha et par grand couroux, renvoya a son ami et l'aneau et le doy." Cited in Dupire, *Jean Molinet*, 72–73. In Cotgrave, Dictionarie, "ennoüer" means "to make a knot or ty on a knot."

35. Prologue to Andes, "*Le romant*," 17.

36. Prologue to Andes, "*Le romant*," 19.

37. "Et combien que leurs paciens dient souvent qu'ilz sont fort malades pour l'amour d'elles, si ne meurent ilz jamais. La plus angoisseuse playe et le plus grief torment qu'ilz ayent a porter aprés souspirs et larmes faintes sont tremblement de blanches fievres." Prologue to Andes, "*Le romant*," 19–20.

38. Prologue to Andes, "*Le romant*," 20.

39. Throughout the *Chroniques*, Molinet expresses his disdain for Muslims, especially for the "grant Turcq," no doubt Bayezid II, sultan of the Ottoman Empire from 1482 to 1512. For example, in chapter 74, he quotes at length from Maximilian's speech against the Turks. See Molinet, *Chroniques*, 2:248–70.

40. Molinet, *Romant de la rose moralisé*, 96:630. See also Molinet, *Chroniques*, I:263.

41. Molinet, *Romant de la rose moralisé*, 96:629–30.

42. Molinet, *Romant de la rose moralisé*, 96:630.

43. Molinet, *Romant de la rose moralisé*, 96:630, 631. He also compares Islam, or "Mohammed's law," to the reign of Jupiter "completely given over to lasciviousness and lechery" (du tout adonné a lascivie et lubricité). Molinet, *Romant de la rose moralisé*, 96:624.

44. Molinet, *Romant de la rose moralisé*, 56:378.

45. Molinet, *Romant de la rose moralisé*, 56:378.

46. Resnick, *Marks of Distinction*, 181–84.

47. An earlier version of this part of chapter 2 appeared in *Fifteenth-Century Studies*. See Kem, "'Malebouche,' Metaphors of Misreadings."

48. See, for example, the "Sermon de Billouart" and the "Ballade de la Maladie de Naples." Molinet, *Faitz et dictz*, 2:508–9; 2:853–54.

49. Molinet, *Romant de la rose moralisé*, 41:263; 62:407.

50. Molinet, *Romant de la rose moralisé*, 44:277; 56:377.

51. Molinet, *Romant de la rose moralisé*, 75:457.

52. "O terrible sentence trop chauldement entregectée sans mesure et discrecion, si tost qu'elle ruit es oreilles des femmes, elle leur fait trembler le cueur au ventre plus dru que fueillettes sur l'arbre. Et se la mode estoit aux dames oyans ces mots de deschirer leurs achemens, comme c'estoit anciennement aux princes de Judée de derompre leurs robes quant ilz oioyent blasphemes, ne leur demourroit cueuvre chief sur teste. Car tout seroit debrisé par pieces et par morseaulx. Ja soit ce que ces mots soyent rigoreux assez pour terrer l'honneur des dames, il me semble qu'au Dieu Plaisir l'on trouvera façon de l'en retrencher, adoulcir, et modifier ... les preudefemmes, s'aucunes en y avoit en ce temps, estoient par corruption de dons legierement abatues sans tenir pied ferme comme celles de maintenant, qui sont fort asseurees, fort justes, et bien confirmées. *Et se l'on dit que maistre Jehan de Meun estoit christien et bon catholicque quant il compila ce romant, si ne devoient sortir les motz dessusditz hors de sa pleüme sans grandement grever sa conscience.*" Molinet, *Romant de la rose moralisé*, 40:257–58; emphasis added.

53. Molinet, *Romant de la rose moralisé*, 40:259.

54. Tuve, *Allegorical Imagery*, 239n8.

55. Molinet, *Romant de la rose moralisé*, 64:412.

56. Molinet, *Romant de la rose moralisé*, 83:517.

57. Molinet, *Romant de la rose moralisé*, 80:490–91.

58. Could this be a veiled allusion to the widened passages of a woman's sex organs after losing her virginity?

59. Genesis 27:21–28.

60. Genesis 31:19.

61. Genesis 34:1–31.

62. Molinet, *Romant de la rose moralisé*, 19:131. Several other writers of the period refer to "murmuring" as gossip and link it to Malebouche. See for example, Le Franc, *Champion*, 1:2426; 4:17193–94.

63. Molinet, *Romant de la rose moralisé*, 20:138; emphasis added.

64. Prologue to Molinet, *Romant de la rose moralisé*, 21. *Affilez* means both "sharp" and "glib." The Rhétoriqueur, fond of wordplay, no doubt chose the word for its double meaning.

65. Here are just two examples: "And what was worse is that short swords sharpened on both sides, very cutting and venomous like the tongues of naysayers, were drawn against him to touch his heart"; "Thus he gave him many a tongue lashing which is worse than ten blows of a sword." Molinet, *Romant de la rose moralisé*, 86:559; 102:667.

66. Molinet, *Romant de la rose moralisé*, 107:697–98; emphasis added.

67. For a listing of the chapters of Molinet's moralized version and their corresponding verses in the original *Roman de la rose*, see Dupire, 90–91. In his treatise on the romance, Jean Gerson cites eight articles or objections; see "Traictié d'une vision faite contre *Le ronmant de la rose*" in Hicks, *Débat*, 59–87. See also chapter 1 of this book.

68. "Maistre Jehan Jarson, fort auctorisé en theologie et de tresclere renommee, *a la requeste et faveur d'aucunes notables dames*, composa ung petit livre intitulé la *Reprobation du romant de la Rose*, mais en ce faisant il s'arresta sur le sens littéral *sans destouiller la fusée*. Et fit ainsi que le petit enfant auquel on donne une grosse, verde noix de geauge, si tost qu'il la tient dedans sa main il la porte en sa bouche cuydant que ce soit une pomme, et quant il la sent si amere il la rue à ses pieds. Mais se il avoit l'advisement de la mettre et oster hors de l'escorce et de la coquille et puis la peler, il trouveroit le cerneau moult bon et fort friant. Ce venerable docteur, maistre Jehan Jarson, qui n'estoit pas enfant, mais l'ung des plus grans clercs de tout le monde, s'arresta seulement a redarguer la verdure de ce romant, c'est amour folle, qui pou dure, en detestant paillardise pour l'amertume qui s'i trouve en fin, et ayma mieulx applicquer la subtillité de son engin en matieres ardues et de plus haulte speculation que chercher fruit fort doulx et savoureux en escaille dure et amere.] Molinet, *Romant de la rose moralisé*, 107:698; emphasis added.

69. Hicks, *Débat*, 35, 45.

70. R. Howard Bloch claims that during the Middle Ages the feminine was "synonymous with the realm of the senses":

> The contrast between the letter—on the side of the body, the senses, the temporal, and the worldly—as opposed to the spirit, which is on the side of mind, form, and divinity, is in the early centuries of Christianity a means of understanding the world and of constituting community. It functions to create an opposition between female and male that relegates the feminine, and ultimately woman, to the inferior side, and it also works as the ideological sign of identity of the Christian: to be on the side of the spirit is to understand without the aid of the senses. Bloch, *Medieval Misogyny*, 105, 31.

71. Michael Randall has pointed out Molinet's rather mixed criticism here: "Although Gerson is criticized for not having understood the real meaning of the *Rose*, the

terms Molinet uses to express his criticism are those of someone who would seem to agree rather than disagree with the author of the 'Contre le Roman de la Rose'. The terms that Molinet uses to express his admonishment perhaps show the real nature of the *Roman de la rose.*" It would appear from this context that Randall is referring to Molinet's agreement with Gerson's theological outlook rather than his defense of women. He states that Gerson's reason for siding with Christine de Pizan has more to do with the work's immorality than its misogyny. Randall, *Building Resemblance,* 24, 15.

72. Molinet shows no evidence here or anywhere else of having read Christine's writings. His silence on Christine, or perhaps even his ignorance of her writings and role in the querelle, was shared by other male authors like Lemaire, Champier, and Agrippa von Nettesheim, all of whom wrote querelle works for powerful female patrons.

73. Molinet attacks murmurers or equates them with Male Bouche throughout his *moralités* in the *Romant de la rose moralisé.* Here are just a few examples: "Male Bouche Murmurant" (16:109), "Craindre pareillement la male bouche des murmurans" (16:110), "Male Bouche ou Murmure" (19:130), "Malle Bouche et [sic] Murmure . . . car Murmure est fille d'Ire" (19:131), "Male Bouche Envieuse qui reveille le guet et ne cesse durant la nuyt de murmurer . . ." (20:138), "Male Bouche envyeuses qui ne cessent de murmurer" (20:139), "L'envieuse faulse et rioteuse Male Bouche . . . le vray amant craignant Murmure" (54:367).

74. Molinet, *Romant de la rose moralisé,* 35:219–20; emphasis added.

75. Mazzio, "Sins of the Tongue," 54–56.

76. Mazzio, "Sins of the Tongue," 58–59.

77. Mazzio, "Sins of the Tongue," 59.

78. "Faulx Semblant et Abstinence, qui soubz la couverture d'habis dissimulez, ont destruit Male Bouche, continuellement *murmurant* sur le fait des amoureux, pevent estre equiparez a Judich et Abra, sa chamberiere, qui pour suppediter la malheureuse et serpentine bouche de Holofernes, vilipendant les enfans d'Israel, prindrent vestement de leesse pour fournir oeuvre de tristesse, langaige confit en doulx riz pour engendrer horribles cris, hardement et *viril couraige* en *fresle et femenin corsaige*; et tellement fut embasmé, imbué, et achemmé de joyeuses parolles ce cruel Holofernes, que, moyennant l'ajutoire du supernel Gubernateur, qui le cop adressa, Judich de son trenchant mesmes *luy couppa la gorge,* si que oncques puis un tout seul mot ne bourbeta, Jesuchrist semblablement et sa treshumble Vierge Mere, vueillans accoiser les bourdes du prince de tenebres, qui par faulx *caquetz falacés et gargouillemens,* deprimoit les vrais et loyaulx amans de la haulte essence divine, se desguiserent pour peleriner au monde, car Nature ne sceüt congnoistre la Mere ne entendre qu'elle estoit pure vierge. Et l'Ennemy se donnoit grant merveille du Filz, lequel estoit d'humanité avestu et tenu des vrais

amoureux, Dieu tout puissant, Createur eternel. Toutesvoyes et la Mere et le Filz par sainctes œuvres, vives paroles, et vertueux sermons besongnerent tellement que la Male Bouche infernale, qui chascun mordoit, engorgoit, et engloutissoit, eüt par iceulx la *mauldicte langue coupee*, non point d'ung rasoir proprement, mais d'ung trenchant et fort agu fer de lance. Et quant Male bouche fut close, la porte du ciel fut ouverte a tous ceulx qui de la divine face desirent veoir le tresdoulx bel acueil." Molinet, *Romant de la rose moralisé*, 54:366–67; emphasis added.

79. Graham A. Runnalls makes a strong case for Molinet's authorship of this portion of the anonymous work *Le mystere du viel testament*. See "L'Auteur: Jean Molinet," in Runnalls, introduction to *Le mystère de Judith*, 59–78. According to the British scholar, the work was first published in 1500 and therefore would have been written at about the same time as the *Romant de la rose moralisé*. In the mystery play, Judith is described as verbally adept, but Holophernes, a man of action rather than words, is far from eloquent.

80. According to Runnalls, the name "Abra" comes from a Latin substantive signifying "servant," used in the Vulgate. See *Judith* 10:10; [Molinet?], *Mystère*, 250.

81. Molinet, *Romant de la rose moralisé*, 91:601–2. "Their tongues were sharpened" comes from Psalm 140:3: "They make their tongues sharp as serpents; the poisons of vipers are on their lips" (Acuerunt linguas suas sicut serpentis: Venenum aspidum sub labiis eorum). In Dictionarie, Cotgrave defines "eschevelé" as "discheveled, ruffled, whole hair falls loose, or in disorder, about the eares," and it was, revealingly, "a word most proper, and most used in the feminine." He offers another meaning, which seems less likely, but that could also refer to clerics: "Also, bared, as of haire, made bare or bald." Molinet could also have chosen the word because of its double meaning. He is clearly playing with the words "graffes," "griffes," and "greffes" to demonstrate how writing can defame and disfigure.

82. Maclean, *Renaissance Notion*, 42.

83. James J. Murphy cites an oft-quoted passage from Gregory the Great's *Cura pastoralis* on the diversity of hearers in an orator's audience: "One and the same exhortation does not suit all, insasmuch as neither are all bound together by similarity of character . . . Therefore according to the quality of hearers ought the discourse of teachers be fashioned, so as to suit all and each in their several needs, and yet never deviate from the art of common edification." Murphy, *Rhetoric in the Middle*, 293.

84. Tuve, *Allegorical Imagery*, 285.

85. Mazzio, "Sins of the Tongue," 70.

86. Randall has previously pointed out this contradiction and attributes it to Molinet's attempt to describe both the spiritual—or ineffable—and the secular. See Randall, *Building Resemblance*, 36.

87. Molinet, *Romant de la rose moralisé*, 37:242.

88. De Meun, *Roman de la rose*, v. 16347–706. See also Christine de Pizan's letter to Jehan Johannez in Hicks, *Débat*, 17.

89. Molinet, *Romant de la rose moralisé*, 82: 507–8; emphasis added.

90. According to Sylvia Huot, "the allegorization of the *Rose* as developed by both Molinet and Marot shows that the interpretation of the poem remained problematic and controversial into the sixteenth century." Huot, *Roman de la rose*, 315.

91. Gerson gave a series of sermons, "La série *poenitemini*," in which he criticized the authors of the *Roman de la rose* for encouraging lewd conduct. See Hicks, *Débat*, 179–85.

92. According to Silvio Baridon, there were twenty-two printed editions of the *Roman de la rose* from 1481 to 1538. There were three editions of Molinet's moralized version (the Antoine Verard edition in Paris in 1500, the Balsarin edition in Lyon in 1503, and the Veuve Michel Le Noir edition in Paris in 1521). Seven editions appeared between 1526 and 1538, "le point culminant de la fortune du *Roman de la Rose*" according to Baridon: five were attributed to Marot and the other two to Le Noir and Lotrian, respectively. See Baridon, preface to *Le roman*, 11.

93. See Baridon's discussion of the work's attribution in the preface to Guillaume de Lorris and Jean de Meun, *Attribuée à Clément Marot*, 1:56–80. For the purposes of this chapter, Clément Marot will be called the author of this version, named the "Recension."

94. Andes states, "This 'Preface' to 'Marot's Recension' could well have been written for Molinet's work, and it is quite possible that the inspiration for it came originally from Molinet. At any rate, it contains ideas which are strikingly similar to those which motivated Molinet thirty-five years before." See Andes, introduction to *Le romant*, x.

95. Guillaume de Lorris and Jean de Meun, Attribuée à Clément Marot, 1:89.

96. Guillaume de Lorris and Jean de Meun, Attribuée à Clément Marot, 1:90.

97. Guillaume de Lorris and Jean de Meun, Attribuée à Clément Marot, 1:90–91.

98. Guillaume de Lorris and Jean de Meun, Attribuée à Clément Marot, 1:92.

99. Monahan, "Clément Marot," 91–92.

100. Monahan, "Clément Marot," 92–93.

101. Monahan, "Clément Marot," 94.

3. PLATONIC LOVE, MARRIAGE, AND INFERTILITY

1. All citations are drawn from Kem's critical edition of *La nef des dames vertueuses* (2007), Wilhelmi's critical edition of *La nef des princes* (2002), and Champier, "A Critical Edition"—Phyllis Ann Hall's unpublished edition of *La nef des princes* (1502). Citations from the *Nef des princes* are drawn from Wilhelmi's published

edition, and citations from the unedited works in the *Nef des princes* are taken from the 1502 Guillaume Balsarin edition.

2. Champier published at least 55 works in 100 editions, mostly historical and medical treatises in Latin and French. In 1533, Jérôme Monteux, one of Champier's students, claimed that the Lyonnais physician had written more than 105 volumes, including 35 medical works, 26 histories, 14 pedagogical manuals, 12 theological treatises, 7 tomes on astronomy, 7 collections of correspondence, and 4 apologetic works. See Cooper, "Dernières Années," 26. For a complete bibliography of Champier's works, see Allut, *Etude biographique*, 105–264. Richard Cooper is presently working on a new bibliography; see Cooper, "Symphorien Champier e l'Italia," 242n1; Cooper, "Symphorien Champier et l'Italie," 287n2.

3. For example, Giovanni Tracconaglia states, "We believe that such a change of opinion is due to new or wider readings of Italian authors or to a deeper study of some dialogues of Plato, especially the *Symposium*." See Tracconaglia, *Femminismo e Platonismo*, 12–13.

4. Phyllis Ann Hall characterizes Champier as an "important pioneer in the use of the vernacular" in medical writings, and Brian P. Copenhaver calls him an innovator in the use of the French vernacular in medical writing. Hall, introduction to "A Critical Edition," 27; Copenhaver, *Symphorien Champier*, 76. The same year that the *Nef des dames* appeared, Champier published *Le guidon en français* (1503), purportedly his translation of Guy de Chauliac's surgical treatise, followed by a one-chapter commentary. However, according to Hall, Champier's translation was a revision of Nicholis Panis's earlier translation (published in 1478, 1485, and 1493). Hall, introduction to "A Critical Edition," 27. Champier later translated and summarized his own work, titled *Castigationes seu emendationes pharmacopolarum* (Castigations of pharmacists; Lyon: I. Crespin, 1532), as *Le myrouel des appothiquaires et pharmacopoles* (The mirror of apothecaries and pharmacists; Lyon: Pierre Mareschal, 1532?). See Planchon, preface to *Le myrouel des appothiquaires*, 13. For more on Champier's medical humanism, see Roger, "L'humanisme médical," 261–72; Antonioli, "Un médecin."

5. Champier penned eleven works; Robert de Balsat, or Balsac, composed four. Robert de Balsac (1440?–1503?) was a French nobleman who served under Louis XI and Charles VIII and was made "high commandant" of Pisa in 1495. His name is sometimes spelled "Barsat" and "Balzac." For information on Champier's relationship with Balsac, see Pijoan, "Introductory Note," 118–19.

6. Jacques Robertet was Jean Robertet's third son and became Imperial and Apostolic Protonotary. See Hall, introduction to "A Critical Edition," 42n28.

7. Wilhelmi's 2002 edition of *La nef des princes* includes the prologue, "Le testament de ung vieil prince lequel il laissa à son enfant" (46–77), "Le gouvernement et

regime dung jeune prince" (78–106), "Le dyalogue de noblesse" (107–12), the letter addressed to Jacques Robertet (112–13), and a list of Latin quotes under the title "Opus admodum tornatum corruptos mulierum mores" (113–24). She ends her edition with "La nef des batailles avec le Chemin de lospital" by Robert de Barsat (125–55). In her unpublished critical edition of the *Nef des princes*, Hall includes the first six works, which include, in addition to the prologue, "Le testament de ung vieil prince lequel il laissa à son enfant" (151–93), "Le gouvernement et regime dung jeune prince" (194–238), "Les proverbes des princes" (239–56), "Le doctrinal des princes" (257–70), "La fleur des princes" (271–84), and "Le dyalogue de noblesse" (285–94).

8. Portia [Porcia Catonis], wife of the Roman Marcus Brutus, took her life in 43 BC. Artemisia ruled Caria with her brother and incestuous husband Mausolus in the mid-fourth century BC. Both appear in Boccaccio's *On Famous Women* (*De claris mulieribus*), §82; §57, and the first book of Champier's *Nef des dames*, 71–72, 75.

9. The Menian (Minyan) women also appear in Boccaccio's *De claris mulieribus* (§31) and in the first book of Champier, *Nef des dames* (2007), 78.

10. Champier, *Nef des princes* (2002), 113–21.

11. "*Opus admodum tornatum corruptos mulierum mores in medium memorans ab eruditissimo viro Simphoriano artis peonie professore eximio editum.*" Champier, *Nef des princes* (2002), 113.

12. Plautus (254–184 BC). Champier quotes from the following comedies: *Bacchides, Menaechmus, Mercator, Miles gloriosus, Mostellaria, Persa, Poenulus, Stichus,* and *Truculentus.*

13. Cicero (106–43 BC). Champier cites Cicero's *Tusculan Letters* as well as the pseudo-Ciceronian *Rhetorica ad Herrenium.* The *Tusculan Letters* are cited several times elsewhere in the *Nef des princes.*

14. Ovid (43 BC–AD 17). Champier cites passages from Ovid's *Metamorphoses* and *Amores.*

15. Seneca (4 BC–AD 65). Champier cites Seneca's *Octavia* and *Phaedra.*

16. Valerius Maximus (fl. ca. AD 30). While Champier quotes from Valerius Maximus's *Factorum et dictorum* only once here, he cites the work several times throughout the *Nef des dames.*

17. Juvenal (ca. 60–ca. 140). Champier cites approximately twenty lines from Juvenal's sixth satire.

18. Lactantius (250–ca. 325). Champier depends heavily on Lactantius's *Divine Institutes* in the third book of the *Nef des dames.*

19. Saint Jerome (ca. 347–420). The main work here is the misogynistic *Epistola adversus Jovinianum.*

20. Petrarch (1304–74). There are fourteen quotations from Petrarch's misogynistic *De remediis utriusque fortunae* (*Remedies for Fortune Fair and Foul*) in the *Nef des princes*.

21. Champier, *Nef des princes* (2002), 114. Champier's probable source for Secundus's widely cited definition of woman was Vincent de Beauvais's *Speculum historiale*. Vincent, in turn, borrowed it from the *Gesta secundi philosophi*, also known as the *Altercatio Hadriani Augusti et secundi philosophi*, widely known in the Middle Ages.

22. *Petrarch's Remedies*, 1:65; Champier, *Nef des princes* (2002), 116.

23. "Ou foeillet. xlii. sont contenus plusieurs notables dicts des philosophes a lobprobre des femmes vicieuses et *a lonneur des bonnes*." Champier, *Nef des princes* (1502), xlv; emphasis added.

24. Champier, *Nef des princes* (2002), 114. Champier attributes this quote to Socrates, but it apparently comes from Fulgentius, *Mythologies*, 1.22. It is here that Fulgentius recounts the story of Admetus and Alcestis that Champier cites in "Le livre de vraye amour," the fourth book of the *Nef des dames*.

25. "My, my! Women *do* live under hard conditions, so much more unfair, poor things, than the men's. Why, if a husband has brought home some strumpet, unbeknown to his wife, and she finds it out, the husband goes scot free. But once a wife steps out of the house unbeknownst to her husband, he has his grounds and she's divorced. Oh, I wish there was the same rule for the husband as for the wife! Now a wife, a good wife, is content with just her husband; why should a husband be less content with just his wife? Mercy me, if husbands, too, were taken to task for wenching on the sly, the same way as wanton wives are divorced, I warrant there'd be more lone men about, than there now are women!" Plautus, 3:93; Champier, *Nef des princes* (2002), 118; Plautus, *Mercator*, 4.6.817–29. The speaker here is Syra, an old female slave.

26. Champier, *Nef des princes* (2002), 123; Pamphilus, *De amore*, 259.

27. Bloch, *Medieval Misogyny*, 90.

28. Champier, *Nef des princes* (2002), 117; Petrarch, *De remediis*, 1:69.

29. Bloch, *Medieval Misogyny*, 54.

30. Champier, *Myrouel* (1894), 24, 53.

31. Champier, *Myrouel* (1894), 53.

32. See Champier, *Le myrouel des appotiquaires* (1532), E5v.

33. The *Liber lamentationum Matheoli* had been translated into French by Jehan Le Fèvre de Resson in 1371–72. See Van Hamel, *Les lamentations*.

34. Martin Le Franc also refers to Matheolus as a "bigamist." Le Franc, *Champion*, 2:113, 2:134. Matheolus, a cleric, was considered a bigamist because he married a widow.

35. Champier, *Nef des princes* (1502), 45v–46.

36. Champier, *Nef des princes* (1502), 46.
37. Paul Allut states, "To restore himself in their [women's] good graces, the next year he published *The Ship of Virtuous Ladies*, which is the opposite of this little libel against the feminine sex." Allut, *Etude biographique*, 89; translation mine.
38. Champier, *Nef des dames* (2007), 57.
39. "The woman should be governed by her husband" (La femme doit estre subjecte à son mari). Champier, *Nef des dames* (2007), 134.
40. "And the woman is sometimes and in some things equal to her husband" (Et la femme aulcunement et en aulcune chose est esgalle à son mari). Champier, *Nef des dames* (2007), 134.
41. "And man should treat his wife as his companion and equal" (Et doit l'omme user de sa femme comme de sa compagne et esgale). Champier, *Nef des dames* (2007), 135.
42. See Champier, *Nef des dames* (2007), 131–33, 135, 140–41.
43. Bloch, *Medieval Misogyny*, 58, 57.
44. Champier, *Nef des dames* (2007), 57–58.
45. Champier, *Nef des dames* (2007), 149–50.
46. Champier, *Nef des dames* (2007), 59, 141.
47. See Allut, *Etude biographique*, 69; Tracconaglia, *Femminismo*, 12–13. Copenhaver explains Champier's failure to gain favor from Anne as the result of the unexpected death of Anne's husband, Pierre de Bourbon, in 1503 and the subsequent "marital schemes which were not consonant with the contents of the little *Nefs*."

   More recently, Helen Swift has presented an intriguing thesis about Champier's failed attempt to gain patronage from Anne; she posits that Anne was no doubt already planning to write her *Enseignements*, an educational treatise for her daughter Suzanne, when Champier dedicated the *Nef des dames* to her. Citing Champier's *Apologie* in the *Nef des dames*, addressed to Anne, Swift questions the advisability of Champier's assertion that the female sex "requires a voice to speak on its behalf since women have neither the learning nor the voice, the rhetorical ability nor the opportunity, to defend themselves." She adds that Champier "failed to hit the right note with independent-minded, politically engaged Anne." Swift, *Gender*, 177, 179–80. In a subsequent article, published in 2011, she makes the same claim. See Swift, "Des circuits de pouvoir," 63–65.
48. Christine Hill studied the sources for educational advice in the *Nef des princes*, most of which comes from Aeneas Sylvius Piccolomini's *De liberorum educatione*, and compares it to the scant advice offered in the *Nef des dames*, observing, "It is significant that one who wrote a book in defence of women should say next to nothing about educating them." Hill, "Champier's Views," 332.
49. See Vallambert, *De la manière*.

50. Champier, *Nef des princes* (2002), 103; Champier, *Nef des dames* (2007), 132–33.

51. Champier dedicated the "Gouvernement d'un prince" in the *Nef des princes* to Jean II de Castelnau-Calmont (1465–1505), a nobleman in the service of Louis XI, and to his son Jacques de Castelnau, who married Françoise de La Tour d'Auvergne in 1499.

52. Champier, *Nef des princes* (2002), 81.

53. Champier, *Nef des princes* (2002), 83.

54. Champier, *Nef des princes* (2002), 97.

55. Champier, *Nef des dames* (2007), 160.

56. Champier, *Nef des dames* (2007), 159–60.

57. Hill, "Champier's Views," 324, 332.

58. See note 48 above.

59. Champier, *Nef des dames* (2007)160–62; emphasis added. Cotgrave defines "tripot" as a tennis court and "tripotage" as a "confused jumbling or huddling of things together." Champier appears to be using a euphemism for sexual intercourse.

60. Champier, *Nef des dames* (2007), 164.

61. Champier, *Nef des dames* (2007), 142–43; emphasis added. Acccording to Cotgrave, "dangereuse" can be interpreted as "Dangerous, perilous, ieopardus, full of hazard." The meaning here, in context, appears to be "in danger."

Rhazes, or Razi (Abu Bakr Muhammad ibn Zakariyyā' ar-Rāzī, 865–925), was author of *Liber ad almansorem* (*Kitāb at-Tibb al-Mansūrī*, or The book of medicine dedicated to Mansūr), a short, practical textbook on medicine; its ninth part (*Liber nonus*) formed the basis of medical learning until late in the sixteenth century. The work was translated into Latin by Gerard of Cremona (d. AD 1187).

62. Champier, *Nef des princes* (2002)103; Champier, *Nef des dames* (2007), 133.

63. Champier, *Nef des princes* (2002), 103; Champier, *Nef des dames* (2007), 31.

64. Champier, *Nef des princes* (2002), 137.

65. *History of animals* 3:417–19; Champier, *Nef des dames* (2007), 136nb; Aristotle, *De animalibus*, 7.1.30v.

66. "According to Jerome in *Against Jovinian*, Theophrastus, the philosopher, disciple of Aristotle, asks in *On Marriage*, whether a wise man marries. And after laying down the conditions—that the wife must be fair, of good character, and honest parentage, the husband in good health and of ample means, and after saying that under these circumstances a wise man sometimes enters the state of matrimony, he immediately proceeds thus: 'But all these conditions are seldom satisfied in marriage. A wise man therefore must not take a wife. For in the first place his study of philosophy will be hindered, and it is impossible for anyone to attend to his books and his wife. Matrons want many things, costly dresses, gold, jewels, great outlay, maid-servants, all kinds of furniture [. . .] Then come curtain-lectures

the live-long night: she complains that one lady goes out better dressed than she; that another is looked up to by all; "I am a poor despised nobody at the ladies assemblies. Why did you ogle that creature next door? Why were you talking to the maid? What did you bring from the market? I am not allowed to have a single friend, or companion." She suspects that her husband's love goes the same way as her hate. [. . .] If you give her the management of the whole house, you must yourself be her slave. If you reserve something for yourself, she will not think you are loyal to her; but she will turn to strife and hatred, and unless you quickly take care, she will have the poison ready. *If a woman is fair, it is easy to fall in love, if she is ugly, she is easy to despise.* It is annoying to have what no one thinks worth possessing. But the misery of having an ugly wife is less than that of watching a comely one. Nothing is safe, for which a whole people sighs and longs. But what is the good of even a careful guardian, when an unchaste wife cannot be watched, and a chaste one ought not to be? For necessity is but a faithless keeper of chastity. [. . .] Notice, too, that in the case of a wife you cannot pick and choose: you must take her as you find her. If she has a bad temper, or is a fool, if she has a blemish, or is proud, or has bad breath, whatever her fault may be—all this we learn after marriage. Horses, asses, cattle, even slaves of the smallest worth [. . .] are first tried and then bought; a wife is the only thing that is not shown before she is married, for fear she may not give satisfaction.'" Champier, *Nef des princes* (2002), 113; Jerome, *Select Works*, 383; [Theophrastus,] *Aureolus liber de nuptiis*, 23, col. 277.

Champier has changed the order of the passage and has significantly altered one sentence. Instead of "Pulchra cito adamatur, foeda facile concupiscit" (If a woman is fair, she soon finds lovers; if she is ugly, it is easy to be wanton) he substitutes "Si pulcra est, facile adamat, si feda, facile contempnitur" (If a woman is fair, it is easy to fall in love, if she is ugly, she is easy to despise).

67. Champier, *Nef des dames* (2007), 137.
68. Champier, *Nef des princes* (2002), 89.
69. Champier, *Nef des dames* (2007), 137–39, 139–41.
70. Aristotle's *De animalibus* was considered a medical authority, but Champier also cites the pseudo-Aristotelian *Problems*: "Aristotle, *Problems* 4. Those who abuse the pleasures of love have eyes that are notably hollow, as well as their posteriors." Champier, *Nef des dames* (2007), 138nc; [Aristotle], *Problems*, 4.2.

"Aristotle in the same problem 21. Coital discharges become weaker due to frequency and for this reason many sexual unions weaken the body and cause it to experience all sorts of harmful and painful things." Champier, *Nef des dames* (2007), 138nc. This is a paraphrase of pseudo-Aristotle's *Problems* 4.21.
71. Avicenna, or Ïbn Sīnā (980–1037), was author of *Liber canonis*, a textbook in wide circulation in university and medical circles from the early thirteenth century

onward. For a comprehensive study of Avicenna's influence during the Renaissance, see Siraisi, *Avicenna in Renaissance Italy*. Siraisi cites as evidence of Renaissance interest in Avicenna that more than sixty editions of the complete or partial text of the Latin *Canon* appeared between 1500 and 1674. She also posits that Avicenna drew some of his material from both Rhazes and Haly Abbas. See Siraisi, *Avicenna*, 3, 39–40.

Champier cites three passages from Avicenna on the dangers of too-frequent coitus: "Avicenna, 3, 3, chapter 5. Frequent coitus is very harmful for the eyes." Champier, *Nef des dames* (2007), 137nc; Avicenna, *Liber canonis*, 3.3.1.5.204v.

"The first part of the *Canticles* with the text of commentary 156 and with treatise 23, page 105. Coitus empties the substance of the last meal and thus it leads to a weakness [of the body] that other similar evacuations do not. And it empties the greatest life force because of the pleasure experienced." Champier, *Nef des dames* (2007), 137nd; Avicenna, *Liber Canonis*, 3.20.1.11.352v–353.

"Avicenna in his *Canticles*, with the text of commentary 19. Coitus is not at all allowed for the skinny, the old and the weak." Champier, *Nef des dames* (2007), 139–40nb; Avicenna, *Canticis*, 1.152, in *Liber canonis*, 563.

72. Averroes, or Abu al-Walid ibn Rushd (1126–98), best known for his philosophical writings on Plato and Aristotle, was also a physician and author of the *Kitāb al-Kulliyyāt fi 'ṭ-ṭibb*, known in Latin as the *Colliget*, which discusses the prevention, diagnoses, and cures for diseases. Champier quotes him on sexual or seminal "overabundance" or superfluity.

"Averroes, *Colliget* 5. Hot and humid complexions can tolerate less superfluity and cold and dry are even worse; certainly phlegmatics are in the middle." Champier, *Nef des dames* (2007), 140na; [Averroes?], *Colliget*, 5. Champier believed Averroes the author of this work.

73. "Rhazes, *Almansor*, 4. He who uses coitus often has sunken eyes." Champier, *Nef des dames* (2007), 137nc; Rasis, *Liber ad almansorem* 4.17.19v.

74. "In his true *Theoretics*, Haly Abbas adds in writing that all aid to coitus should only be allowed for those who are adolescent and young, for the sanguine, for those who have rosy complexions and for the healthy. And for this reason old men are delirious when they take girls as if they were women, not for themselves but rather for others, or who unite women, who are still tender and growing [crescentibus], with their sons." Champier, *Nef des dames* (2007), 140nc; Haly Abbas, *Theorice*, a paraphrase of 5.36, 39, and a commentary by Champier.

75. Haly Rodoam, or Alī ibn Ridwān (d. 1061 or 1069), was author of the so-called *Commentum Haly* or *Thegni Galeni*, an Arabic translation of, and commentary on, Galen's *Technē iatrikē*. His commentary, translated into Latin by Gerard of Cremona (d. 1187), was studied at European universities up to the sixteenth century.

"Haly Rodoam, *Tegni* 3, commentary 37. From a great number of sexual encounters, a man becomes old before his time, especially if the complexion of his testicles is cold and dry." Champier, *Nef des dames* (2007), 139nb; Haly Rodoam, *Thegni* 3.3762v.

76. Champier, *Nef des princes* (2002), 105; Champier, *Nef des dames* (2007), 141–42.

77. *Theorice*, 5:36. Haly Abbas, or Alī ibn al-ʿAbbās al-Majūsi (d. 994), a Persian physician surnamed the "Magus," wrote *Theorice* (a commentary on Galen), and *Liber totius medicinae* (a medical survey). His work was the basis of the *Pantegni* of Constantinus Africanus (d. 1087) and was translated by Stephen of Antioch.

"Haly Abbas, 5 *Theorica* 36. If a man full of nourishment and drink engages in coitus, he will weaken. He will have a weakness of the body, a pain in his nerves, an obstruction in his internal organs, and thick humors. If coitus is frequent and assiduous, dropsy will follow, with asthma and tremblings." Champier, *Nef des dames* (2007), 142na; Haly Abbas, *Theorice*, 5:36, 39; translations mine.

78. "Avicenna in the twentieth [fen.] of the third [book], chapter one. Good coitus is that which takes place an hour before evacuation follows superfluity (superfluitam)." Champier, *Nef des dames* (2007), 142nb; Avicenna, *Liber canonis*, 3.20.1.10.352v.

79. Champier, *Nef des dames* (2007), 141–42.

80. Park, *Secrets of Women*, 91.

81. "The same from the same work. Eunuchs have bad morals. Truly, they are stupid, envious, and presumptuous. But he who has not been castrated but was born without testicles, or who has testicles but small ones, might seem a eunuch. It is clear that those born without beards [testicles] are weaker." Champier, *Nef des dames* (2007), 143nb; Rhazes, *Liber ad almansorem* 2.57.10v. This marginal note is missing in the 1531 edition.

82. "Avenzoar, 2 *Theizir*. I say that testicles are among the number of principal organs and their virtue is very great because we see clearly that all eunuchs have delicate voices and they lack much in their way of talking and in manners, and they are without a beard [testicles] and do not have stable judgment and one hardly finds a eunuch endowed with sense and intelligence, or laws. And one never heard of a eunuch with good morals. But perhaps there are some who are somewhat honest and endowed with intellect and excellent reasoning. But that does not come from them but from the education of others, because what comes from their own intellect seems of little or no value. And then, one can deduce reasonably that testicles are principal members. And it happens sometimes that sperm that comes from these same members is not well digested; in this way, they don't produce children because this bad complexion was acquired in the maternal matrix; it is not the work of the doctor. If the bad complexion was acquired after birth, or

as a consequence of an external contusion, or if they had some very unnatural thickness [grossitiem], then they can receive treatment." Champier, *Nef des dames* (2007), 143–44nc; Avenzoar, *Theizir*, 2.3.1.25v.

83. Champier, *Nef des dames* (2007), 145.

84. "Avenzoar in the same work. Generation is hindered by too much dryness, for if the said dryness is not too great, one will produce a male child. Thus everything happens by order of the Creator. If though the dryness is excessive, the man will not produce any child at all. And his treatment is very difficult: But if a man abstains for a long time from sleeping with a woman, it is possible that he will father a child. And if the sperm produced is humid and excessively so, he will father female children. And if it is excessively humid, he will not father any children. And to cure them, one must render their complexion dry. And you will give them a syrup made from lemon rinds in water from hot water springs. And if you do not have this kind of water, boil ordinary water in your best glass vessel until it is half evaporated, and mix the syrup with the water. And it is also useful to eat the lemon rinds." Champier, *Nef des dames* (2007), 145–46nb; Avenzoar, *Theizir*, 2.3.1.26.

"Avenzoar, 2 *Theizir*. If a young man, or a middle-aged man, becomes sterile without a known or evident reason, you can be sure that this does not come from a bad complexion, excessively dry, or cold or humid or dry, or made up of these qualities because they are seen in turn. And, in effect, heat and fever are capable of emerging. And when I was young, I used to eat hot food, and I was sterile and I did not know the cause. Finally, I saw why, and with the aid of glasses [usus fui cucurbitis] I smelled water lily and camphor with fruit. And when I was freed from the fever, I fathered the sons that I have, and others as well. Truly, if one calls it a phenomenon of a cold complexion, you would know that a moderate coldness [frigiditas] hinders generation and we should temper this cold complexion with things that are warm but do no harm to the engendered. And one finds that this is what happens to several old men. And their treatment is to give them for the third time on the third day [tertio in tertium diem] a goldweight or dose of a great tyriaca [an antidote against poison]; but I recommend a greater dose [metridatum] in this case. Give him a diet of boiled pigeons with or without whatever kind of turnips the doctor orders." Champier, *Nef des dames* (2007), 146–47nb; Avenzoar, *Theizir*, 2.3.1.25v–26.

85. "And the prince should refrain from having sex with his wife during menstruation that one calls "flowers", and often the children [from that union] are monsters and weak [defaillans] in their arms and legs; such a thing is infamous for a prince and great man." Champier, *Nef des princes* (2002), 103.

86. Champier published an astonishing number of Latin works on the role of pharmacists and their abuses in Lyon between 1532 and 1534. These include: *Castigationes*

pharmacopolarum (Castigations of pharmacists, 1532), *Hortus gallicus* (The Gallic garden, 1533), *Campus Elysius & Periarchon* (The Elysian fields and the Periarchon, 1533), *Cribratio medicamentorum* (A scrutiny of medicines, 1534), and the *Gallicum pentapharmacum* (The Gallic pentapharmacon, 1534); all condemned bad pharmacists. He had already published the *Officina apothecariorum seu seplasiariorum pharmacopolarum ac iuniorum medicorum* in 1511, but he revised it in 1532. Champier preferred "simples," or uncombined medicines, to concoctions, referred to as "multiples," which he claimed contained questionable ingredients and often resulted in serious injury or even death to the patient.

87. Although Suzanne de Bourbon was Anne's only daughter, in April 1476 Anne had purportedly given birth to a son, Charles, who died soon afterward. See Cluzel, *Anne de France*, 100.

88. Charlotte de Savoie (d. 1483) handed down two medical books to her daughter Anne de Beaujeu. See Green, *Making Women's Medicine Masculine*, 141n69, 141n71.

89. According to Green, "the royal physician Bernard Chaussade completed his *Treatise on Conception and Generation, Especially of Male Children* in 1488 for his patroness and patient, Anne de Beaujeu, former regent of France and current Duchess of Bourbon, who though married for fourteen years had yet to produce an heir." Green, *Making Women's Medicine Masculine*, 264n39.

90. Champier's main patron was Antoine de Calabre, newly made Duke of Lorraine in 1508 at the death of his father, René II. In 1509, Champier became his *primarius medicus* (primary physician) and adviser, and he accompanied the duke in Louis XII's war with the Venetians, distinguishing himself in the battle of Agnadello. After the war, Champier followed the duke back to Nancy, where Champier composed *Le recueil ou croniques des histoires des royaumes d'Austrasie* (A collection or chronicle of histories of the kingdoms of Austrasia), written half in French and half in Latin, and presented it to the duke in 1510. It praises the duke and attributes a fabled origin to the house of Lorraine. From 1510 to 1515, Champier stayed mostly in Nancy as part of the duke's large medical household and worked in the library of almost two hundred books. In 1515, Champier distinguished himself in battle at Marignano and was knighted afterward. Allut, *Etude biographique*, 21. For a discussion of Champier's many other male patrons, see Hall, introduction to "A Critical Edition," 34–47.

91. *Le triumphe du treschrestien Roy de France Loys XII* (1509), *Le recueil ou croniques des hystoires des royaulmes d'austrasie* (1510), *Les grans croniques des gestes des ducz et princes des pays de Savoye et Piemont* (1516), *Les gestes ensemble la vie du preulx chevalier Bayard* (1525), and *L'antiquité de la cité de Lyon. Ensemble la rebeine ou rébellion du populaire* (1529). His most popular work, by far, was *Les gestes ensemble la vie du preulx chevalier Bayard*, which saw thirteen French editions and three

Latin ones in the sixteenth and seventeenth centuries. See Ballard and Pijoan, "A Preliminary Check-List," 184.

92. For bibliographical information, see Allut, *Etude biographique*, 24:198–99; Copenhaver, *Symphorien Champier*, 19. Although Allut and Copenhaver cite the 1517 edition as the original, I found other editions with earlier dates listed on Gallica (Bibliothèque Nationale de France) and WorldCat. Richard Cooper is currently compiling a bibliography of Champier's works. See Cooper, "Symphorien Champier e l'Italia," 242n1; "Symphorien Champier et l'Italie," 287n2.

93. For bibliographical information, see Allut, *Etude biographique*, 22:188–96; Copenhaver, *Symphorien Champier*, 19–20. The 1517 edition cited here is housed at the University of Freiburg.

94. For bibliographical information, see Allut, *Etude biographique*, 39:245–49; Copenhaver, *Symphorien Champier*, 26.

95. According to Copenhaver, Champier viewed syphilis as "an entirely new disease sprung from the wrath of God." Copenhaver, *Symphorien Champier*, 77–78.

96. Isaac Israeli, or Isaac Judaeus (ca. 832–ca. 932), was an Egyptian Jew who composed an important work on pharmacology, translated into Latin under the title *De gradibus simplicum*, that became the foundation for most of the subsequent medieval works on the subject. Avicenna (980–1037) was said to have drawn inspiration from his writings. Constantine Africanus translated some of his works into Latin in the eleventh century.

97. Serapion no doubt refers to Serapion the Younger, author of the twelfth- or thirteenth-century *Book of Simple Medicaments*, probably written in Arabic but translated into Latin in the late thirteenth century.

98. This belief was shared by many of his contemporaries. For example, Jacques Ferrand describes it almost a century later in his *Treatise on Lovesickness* (*Traité de l'essence et guérison de l'amour ou de la mélancolie érotique*; 1610). See also Beecher, "Concerning Sex Changes."

99. Cadden notes that in the Middle Ages, "vulva" was a word often used interchangeably with "vagina" as well as "womb," or to refer to a woman's sexual organs in general. Cadden, *Meanings*, 64.

100. Niccolò da Reggio, or Niccolò di Theoprepos from Reggio in Calabria, translated more than fifty works by Galen in the first half of the fourteenth century. Champier may have discovered him through his work on Guy de Chauliac. See McVaugh, "Niccolò da Reggio's Translations," 275, 278. Lynn Thorndike lists *Passionibus mulierum* as one of the works Niccolò da Reggio translated. See BN 6865, ff. 210va–11rb; Thorndike, "Translations," 228.

101. This work is not to be confused with the *Periarchon Platonicarum*, published around 1515.

102. Another treatise bearing the title *Periarchon* was published around 1515. Copenhaver distinguishes the two treatises by referring to one as the *Periarchon Platonicarum* (1515) and the other simply as *Periarchon* (1533). See Copenhaver, *Symphorien Champier*, 16, 26.

103. Champier, *Periarchon*, 30–31; Albertus Magnus, *On Animals*, 13:1016–18.

104. Cadden, *Meanings*, 138.

105. Albertus Magnus, *On Animals*, 3:418.

106. Albertus Magnus, *On Animals*, 18:1316.

107. Champier, *Periarchon*, 48; Albertus Magnus, *On Animals*, 3:423.

108. Champier, *Periarchon*, 49–50; Albertus Magnus, *On Animals*, 5:510.

109. Albertus Magnus, *On Animals*, 5:514.

110. Champier, *Periarchon*, 50.

111. Champier, *Nef des princes* (2002), 103.

112. Champier, *Periarchon*, 50; Albertus Magnus, *On Animals* 16:1181–82.

113. The pseudo–Albertus Magnus version of *Secrets of Women* appeared in print more than fifty times before 1500.

114. Champier, *Periarchon*, 53; Albertus Magnus, *On Animals*, 9:780.

115. Albertus Magnus, *On Animals*, 18:1293.

116. Albertus Magnus, *On Animals*, 9:783; Champier, *Periarchon*, 53.

117. Albertus Magnus, *On Animals*, 9:783; Champier, *Periarchon*, 53.

118. Albertus Magnus, *On Animals*, 1:216.

119. Albertus Magnus, *On Animals*, 1:220; Champier, *Periarchon*, 52.

120. Celsus, *On Medicine*, 7:28; *Periarchon*, 52.

121. *Periarchon*, 52.

122. *Periarchon*, 62.

123. Albertus Magnus, *On Animals*, 1319.

124. Champier briefly mentions the deleterious effects of intercourse during menstruation in *Nef des princes*, 103. For a discussion of early modern views on menstruation, see McClive, *Menstruation and Procreation*; however, McClive deals mainly with a later period, roughly from the mid-sixteenth century to the eighteenth.

125. In the book titled the *Doctrinal des princes* in the *Nef des princes*, Champier warns about empiricists:

> Doctors who never studied medicine; they abuse it and are worse than highway cutthroats. Because one stays away from robbers and murderers but not from a false and empirical doctor who never read Galen or Avicenna like many apothecaries in France and those "magicians" [enchanteurs]. Often they are more famous than medical doctors. This is a great abuse and problem for two reasons—the first is that the common people are often fooled by them and killed and the second reason is that, because of these

empiricists, learned and wise ones often abandon medicine because sometimes a man, learned and expert in the field of medicine cannot get a patient
to cure or treat. *Nef des princes* (1502), 23v; Hall, "Critical Edition," 263–64.
His invective in the *Nef des dames* is much longer and more detailed. He attacks
not only empirical doctors and apothecaries but also Jewish doctors, for whom
he seemed to have greater antipathy than he did for "Arab" practitioners.

126. Champier, *Practica Nova* (1517), 105.

127. Green, *Making Women's Medicine Masculine*, 280.

128. Green, *Making Women's Medicine Masculine*, 27.

129. For example, Champier urges men repeatedly in the first book of the *Nef des
dames* to love their wives like themselves; Champier, *Nef des dames* (2007), 62–
64. In chapter 5 of the second book, "Le gouvernement de mariage," Champier
promotes love in marriage and condemns divorce: "The wife should love her
husband with all her heart and remain faithful to him. And this for two reasons:
the first because of natural love that should exist between wife and husband and
the second for the sake of lineage. And their love should be so constant that for
no reason the wife should leave her husband nor the husband leave the wife or
go off with another. Thus must they be united without separation, content one
with the other"; Champier, *Nef des dames* (2007), 131. Champier's message in the
Nef des princes is the same: "And the husband should love his wife and the wife
her husband with perfect love and not with carnal concupiscence; he should be
content with his wife and not go off to another carnally. True and perfect love
is with one thing and undivided, while love of several is divided; every thing
divided is corrupted and imperfect. To conclude, it is impossible for a married
man to have love for his wife when he loves another carnally. And if the husband
must be content with his wife, also the wife should be content with her husband";
Champier, *Nef des princes* (2002), 2:4.

130. Tracconaglia, 12–13.

131. Wadsworth, introduction to *Livre de vraye amour*, 13, 14.

132. Wadsworth, introduction to *Livre de vraye amour*, 19; emphasis added.

133. Wadsworth, introduction to *Livre de vraye amour*, 32.

134. In *Renaissance Feminism*, Constance Jordan concludes that the "principal point"
of the *Nef des dames* is that "Legally woman is man's equal in most respects." See
Jordan, *Renaissance Feminism*, 102. However, her conclusion about how Champier
viewed women's legal rights appears based on a mistranslation of a key phrase
in the second book of the *Nef*: "Et la femme aulcunement et en aulcune chose
est esgalle à son mari" (And the woman is sometimes and in some things equal
to her husband). Champier, *Nef des dames* (2007), 134. According to Cotgrave,
"aulcunement" meant "sometimes." This comes in a chapter on how the woman

should be subservient to her husband, so Champier is far from declaring an absolute equality. Without citing the original, Jordan translates the phrase: "And the woman is *always* and *in every respect* equal to the husband." See Jordan, *Renaissance Feminism*, 102; emphasis added. Todd Reeser cites Jordan's study and claims that in book 4 "Champier buttresses his arguments about the equality of women and men made in books 1 and 2, and sidesteps the question of gender inferiority/superiority." Later, he comments that in book 4, Champier "assumes a consistent marriage-based form of heterosexuality to make his nature-centered arguments about male-female equality and to avoid Platonic and classical topoi of male-male relations as inherently superior to those between men and women." See Reeser, *Setting*, 150, 151. It is unclear to which arguments about male-female equality Reeser refers.

135. In both her 2004 article "Marsilio Ficino, Neoplatonism, and the Problem of Sex" and the much-condensed version in 2010 in *The Sexual Culture of the French Renaissance*, Crawford finds Champier's letter infused with "homoerotic attraction" for his fellow physician and claims he thus "undermines the marital message" of the *Nef des dames*. See Crawford, "Marsilio Ficino," 18–22, 34–35; *Sexual Culture*, 117–19.

136. Crawford, "Marsilio Ficino," 22; Reeser, "Redressing," 94.

137. The term "homosocial" comes from Sedgwick, *Between Men*.

138. Wadsworth, introduction to *Livre de vraye amour*, 49. I used Wadworth's transla-tion of the letter since it was the only translation available at this writing. Todd Reeser's translation of Champier's *Nef des dames* is forthcoming.

139. Champier, *Nef des dames* (2007), 48–49.

140. Crawford, "Marsilio Ficino," 20; *Sexual Culture*, 118.

141. Champier, *Nef des dames* (2007), 238.

142. Champier, *Nef des princes* (2002), 111–12; Champier, *Nef des dames* (2007), 75.

143. Crawford, "Marsilio Ficino," 20.

144. Champier, *Nef des dames* (2007), 238.

145. For example, in *Nef des dames* (2007), Champier cites the valor and chivalrous acts of the Amazon Penthesilea and the adroit use of arms and military prowess of Marpesia (65), the war exploits of Thamiris or Tomyris (65–66) and Hysi-cratia (66); the corporeal strength and courage of Arpalice (70–71), the valor, battle exploits, and royal reign of Semiramis (71), the bravery and skill at arms of Hippolyte (76), the noble deeds in arms and "very virile" discourse of Orythia (77), and the courage and prowess of Camilla (79).

146. See Wadsworth, introduction to *Livre de vraye amour*, 54n13.

147. Champier, *Nef des dames* (2007), 242.

148. Champier, *Nef des dames* (2007), 242.

149. Crawford finds the first tale "strange and Champier's second tale "stranger still"; how, she asks, can a story about how love leads to "homicidal violence" demonstrate a civilizing influence? Crawford, "Marsilio Ficino," 20–21.

150. Champier, *Nef des dames* (2007), 237.

151. Champier, *Nef des dames* (2007), 242.

152. Both Crawford and Reeser discuss all three stories in their articles but concentrate only on this story in their respective books.

153. Champier, *Nef des dames* (2007), 243.

154. "Il aimoit mieulx sa vie que tout le monde et qu'il aimoit mieulx perdre sa femme que son amy, car facilement on peult trouver une aultre femme mais non point ung amy." Champier, *Nef des dames* (2007), 244.

155. Reeser claims that the "male-female relations are not soulful, and the male-male relation is not corporeal." *Setting*, 89.

156. Champier, *Nef des dames* (2007), 248, 250.

157. Champier, *Nef des dames* (2007), 249.

158. "Amour n'est aultre chose que desir de chose belle et honneste. Et sont troys manieres de beaulté c'est assavoir beaulté de l'ame, beaulté du corps et beauté de voix. La beaulté de l'ame se congnoist par l'entendement. La beaulté du corps des yeulx: la beaulté de la voix des oreilles. Et pource que amour n'est que desir de beaulté. Amour est contente d'entendement, des yeulx, et des oreilles. *Ne goutement saveurs, senteurs, touchemens elle ne desire ain delaisse aux appetis sensitifz et ainsi amour ne quiert nulz touchemens saveurs ne odeurs mais soy contente des troys dessusditz et l'appetit qui demande aultres sens que entendement ou la voix ou la veue se n'est pas amour mais volupté et enraigement.*" Champier, *Nef des dames* (2007), 236; emphasis added; Ficino, *Commentary*, 1.4; emphasis added.

159. Champier, *Nef des dames* (2007), 249.

160. Champier, *Nef des dames* (2007), 248. See also "How Harmful Vulgar Love Is" (Comment est nuisible l'amour vulgaire) in Ficino, *De amore*, 7:12.

161. Crawford, "Marsilio Ficino," 22.

162. Champier, *Nef des dames* (2007), 248.

163. Reeser, "Redressing," 94.

164. Champier, *Nef des dames* (2007), 251–52.

165. Champier, *Nef des dames* (2007), 247; Ficino, *Commentary*, 2.8.

166. Ficino, *Commentary*, 2.8; Champier, *Nef des dames* (2007), 248.

167. According to Allut, Gonsalvo of Toledo, to whom Champier dedicated a treatise in his *Libelli duo*, was Anne de Bretagne's personal physician. Allut, *Etude biographique*, 143–45.

168. In a letter dated January 17, 1506, published at the end of Champier's treatise *De claris medicine scriptoribus*, Gonsalvo of Toledo wrote:

The book to which you gave the title *Nef des dames* should not be overlooked. The ladies, even the young nubile ones, keep you from pursuing your path. In the city of Lyon you had it published by printers so that through their art (invented by divine power) the work might appear worthy of its public. Thanks to this publication, in which you praise many women described therein, you won the favor of one who is not the least among them. And this woman comes from a beautiful, noble family; so you married this honest young woman and from this beautiful woman I hope to see you very soon father of a posterity. (Et quod silentio involvendum non est: librum cui dominarum navis titulum indidisti. Quem dum usque ad annos nubiles apud te inclusum detinuisses: tandem in civitate lugdunense cholcographis imprimendum tradidisti: ut sic eorundem arte (divinitus inventa) decoratus prodiret in publicum. Quo ex opere: quoniam mulierum plurimas laudes in edo descripseras: non mediocrem earundem benevolentiam tibi conciliasti. Ita ut cuidam ex nobili familia orte pervenuste: perque honeste virgini coniugio copulatus sis: ex qua pulchre sobolis parentem proediem te videre spero.) *Libelli duo*, 40v. See Allut, *Etude biographique*, 16; Copenhaver, *Symphorien Champier*, 53n20. Allut offers the following version:

> Outre un si grand nombre de compositions en latin, il vous a plu de vous exercer dans la langue françoise, et vous avez publié la Nef des princes, Des sybylles et de leurs prophéties. Il ne faut pas oublier non plus la Nef des dames, & que vous avez gardé dans votre cabinet jusqu'au jour où vous avez atteint l'âge du mariage. C'est alors que vous l'avez donné à un libraire de Lyon pour l'imprimer. Ce livre vous a acquis une réputation si grande & une bienveillance telle de la part des nobles dames, dont vous y avez fait l'eloge de main de maître, que les jeunes filles faisoient foule à l'envi pour vous voir & vous connaître, et qu'une gente demoiselle du Dauphiné, des plus considérables par la naissance, la vertu & la beauté, s'est estimée heureuse de vous choisir pour époux. Sans parler des œuvres que vous n'avez pas encore livrées à la presse parce que vous n'avez pas mis la dernière main, quels fruits ne devrions-nous pas attendre de ce que vous avez publié jusqu'à ce jour où vous avez à peine entré dans la trente-troisième année de votre âge! Allut, *Etude biographique*, 145.

In this version, Gonsalvo indicates that Champier held many works in reserve in his "cabinet" and that the young physician published the profemale work when he was ready to marry and hoping to win the hand of his future bride.

169. Lyon: Balsarin, 1502; Paris: Le Noir, 1525. Christine Hill also refers to a manuscript copy of the *Gouvernement et regime* in the *Nef des princes* offered to Louise de

Savoie, which contains a "long disquisition on infant ailments" not included in the print editions. Hill, "Champier's Views," 327.

170. Lyon: Jacques Arnollet, 1503; Paris: Jehan Lagarde, 1515; Paris: Philippe Le Noir, 1531.

171. Copenhaver, *Symphorien Champier*, 66, 76.

172. Reeser, *Setting*, 171–72.

4. LOVE AND DEATH

1. Margaret wrote an epitaph for him in Latin. See Jane de Iongh, *Margaret of Austria*, 135.

2. According to Pierre de Saint Julien, Lemaire died insane: "All those who knew him privately, know that wine added to the weakness of his mind so much that finally he was transported to a hospital where he died insane." *De l'antiquité et origine*, 2:389; cited by Stecher, "Notice," Lemaire, *Œuvres*, 4:87.

3. The three-part work appeared in a collection referred to as *Traictez singuliers*, with works by Chastellain, Crétin, and Molinet. The first poem was attributed to "Seraphin poete Italien," the second and third to Lemaire.

4. In a letter that Lemaire wrote to Margaret of Austria in 1509, he lists the second book of the *Couronne margaritique* as "in final draft" (tout minuté) and that "it remains only to be corrected" (ne reste que le mettre au net), *Œuvres*, 4:395. The "second" book of the *Couronne* has never surfaced. Pierre Jodogne posits that it probably contained the description of Margaret's actual crowning; Jodogne, *Jean Lemaire*, 215n3. Stecher attributes the *Couronne*'s late publication date to the work's anti-French portrayal of Margaret's repudiation by Charles VIII in favor of Anne of Brittany in 1489; he theorizes that it fell victim to a more pro-French political climate after Philibert's death. Stecher, "Notice," in Lemaire, *Œuvres*, 4:31–32.

5. Several critics have decried Lemaire's supposed "domesticity" and his inability to disengage from the constant demands of his two women patrons, Margaret of Austria and Anne of Brittany. See, for example, Thibaut, *Marguerite d'Autriche*, 245–46; Spaak, *Jean Lemaire de Belges*, 66–69; Doutrepont, *Jean Lemaire de Belges*, 380–81, and Jodogne, *Jean Lemaire*, 215.

6. The subsequent parenthetical references in the paragraph come from the critical edition of Lemaire's *Plainte du désiré*.

7. "Mort detestable et immonde. / O Mort mordant, cruelle et furibunde, / ton grant desroy si fort croist et habunde / sur une femme a peu desesperee, / que au monde n'est eloquence ou facunde, / qui sceust puiser en sa sourse fecunde, / tous les fourfaiz dont tu m'as empirée." Lemaire, *Regretz*, 330.

8. Lemaire, *Regretz*, 331.

9. See note 29 below.

10. "Et l'autre estoit sa femme de mesmes, assez et trop congnue par le monde universel, appelee la Mort, lune des trois soeurs, qui nespargnent personne: laquelle les anciens appellerent Atropos, cestadire sans retour." Lemaire, *Œuvres*, 4:20.

11. Lemaire, *Œuvres*, 4:21.

12. In book 1, chapter 5, Boccaccio gives the following etymology for Atropos (Ἄτροπος): "Atropos (from *a*, meaning "without," and *tropos* meaning "turning") refers to "turning away," for everything that is born, when it recognizes that it has come to its predestined end, sinks immediately and plunges toward death, from which there is no natural way to return." Boccaccio, *Genealogy*, I:71. Boccaccio never mentions Atropos's bow and arrows.

13. Lemaire, *Œuvres*, 4:23, 25.

14. Lemaire, *Œuvres*, 4:26.

15. Lemaire, *Œuvres*, 4:26.

16. Lemaire, *Œuvres*, 4:26.

17. Lemaire, *Œuvres*, 4:26–27, 4:27.

18. Lemaire, *Œuvres*, 4:28.

19. See Virgil's *Aeneid*, book 12. Aeneas has been shot by an arrow from an unseen hand. The doctor Iapyx, "girded in the manner of Paeon [i.e., Apollo the Healer]" (Paeonium in morem . . . succinctus, v. 401), finds both herbs and forceps powerless to remove the arrow (12.400–406). Venus brings dittany all the way from Cretan Ida, which Virgil refers to elsewhere as the characteristic location of cypresses: "Hereupon Venus, smitten by her son's cruel pain, with a mother's care plucks from Cretan Ida a dittany stalk, clothed with downy leaves and purple flower; not unknown is that herb to wild goats, when winged arrows have lodged in their flank. . . . And now, following his hand, without constraint, the arrow fell out, and newborn strength returned, as of yore." See Virgil, *Aeneid*, 2.327–29. See also Virgil, *Georgics*, 2.84. Champier states of "dictamnon," "About dictamnon, is it totally unknown to us and grows only in Crete that is called Candie, and is similar to *pulegion*, but has larger leaves." Champier, *Myrouel*, 31.

20. Lemaire, *Œuvres*, 4:30.

21. Boccaccio, *Genealogy*, 4.16.

22. Lemaire, *Œuvres* 4:30; Boccaccio, *Genealogy*, 4.71.

23. "Little by little she showed herself in such a way to the onlookers as does the celestial moon, which, after having suffered a shadowy eclipse of her whole body, repairs her graceful [specieuse] beauty among the wandering clouds and assembles her silvery rays to enrich the taciturn night." Lemaire, *Œuvres*, 4:43.

24. Lemaire, *Temple*, 80, 81.

25. Lemaire, *Temple* 82; emphasis added.

26. Hornik, introduction to *Le temple d'honneur*, 13. The *Nef des dames* was published in Lyon (Jacques Arnollet) in 1503, and *Temple* came out in Paris (Antoine Vérard) in 1504.

27. Lemaire, *Temple*, 43.

28. "Devant mes yeulx se presente ung abisme / confuz, estrange et sans sort unanime / des cas futurs dont de peur je m'effroye; / tout est meslé, n'y a raison ne rime; / tout est en bransle et dangereux estime, / tout sera mis hors de rigle et de roye." Lemaire, *Regretz* 332, 333–34.

29. Lemaire, *Regretz*, 334. In *Jean Lemaire de Belges et la Renaissance* (1934), Georges Doutrepont finds that the rhymes in *Les regretz* are uncharacteristic of Lemaire's careful adherence to versification rules set down by his predecessors and that the strong emotions voiced therein indicate someone else's hand. See Doutrepont, *Jean Lemaire*, 347–48, 351–53. However, he does not go so far as to attribute the poem to Margaret. In his massive volume on Lemaire's life and works (1972), predicated on refuting Doutrepont's theory of Italian influence on the Franco-Burgundian author, Jodogne also questions why Doutrepont still doubts that Lemaire wrote the work. He cites the poem's appearance in a 1509 edition of Lemaire's works and Philipp August Becker's thesis of 1893, "based on external characteristics," as final proofs of Lemaire's authorship. Jodogne, *Jean Lemaire*, 269n2. Becker cites a "double virelay" that Lemaire wrote at the death of Anne of France and claims, "I lamented Savoy and also Castille" (Savoye aussi et Castille plaigny). Becker, *Jean Lemaire de Belges*, 96n2. Yet Becker does not cite the source of the virelay. Subsequent studies of the *Regretz* no longer question the Lemaire attribution. See, for example, Peter Eubanks, "Poetic Self-Assertion," 313.

30. Lemaire, *Œuvres*, 4:42.

31. Lemaire, *Œuvres*, 4:30.

32. Lemaire, *Œuvres*, 4:31.

33. Lemaire, *Œuvres*, 4:32.

34. Lemaire, *Œuvres*, 4:42.

35. Lemaire, *Œuvres*, 4:43.

36. Lemaire, *Œuvres*, 4:116, 136.

37. See Oenone's grief at Paris's death in *Les Illustrations de Gaule et singularitez de Troye*. Lemaire, *Œuvres*, 2:203–6. Oenone collapses at the sight of Paris and dies. Lemaire describes the "extreme distress of her pain" and the cause of her death: "Her heart constricted and broke in her amorous stomach and then she shivered for some time as she gave up her soul." Lemaire, *Œuvres*, 2:207.

38. For a discussion of the history associating women's excessive grief with melancholy and an overabundance of black bile, see Schiesari, *Gendering of Melancholy*, 96–159. According to Ficino, men of letters were thought to suffer from a different, superior

type of melancholy. According to Schiesari, "Ficinian Neoplatonism describes an eros whose content was the nostalgic one of recapturing a lost ideal"; the sufferer was "propelled to the heavens by his amatory anguish." Schiesari, *Gendering*, 115. Yet Ficino's view of the gifts of genius conferred upon melancholics excluded women. Schiesari, *Gendering*, 123–25. Could Lemaire be copying Ficino, consciously or not, by suggesting that through her suffering Margaret, a virago, could also be seen as transcending the corporeal? Michael Randall discusses a possible "plus hault sens," or higher meaning, in the "Neoplatonizing *Couronne*"; see *Building Resemblance*, 84.

39. Lemaire, *Œuvres*, 4:136.

40. See, for example, Galen's writings on passions, available in French (*Galien l'ame et ses passions*) and in English (*Galen: On the Passions and Errors of the Soul*).

41. Jodogne, *Jean Lemaire*, 249.

42. Lemaire, *Œuvres*, 4:62.

43. Arnaud de Villeneuve authored a medical work, *Regimen sanitatis*, published in Latin and in French in Lyon in 1503. See Jodogne, *Jean Lemaire*, 249n3.

44. Jodogne posits that Lemaire became friends with Champier in Lyon prior to 1506. Jodogne, *Jean Lemaire*, 90–92.

45. Lemaire, *Œuvres*, 4:428–30. In a letter written prior to 1507, Lemaire writes of the "physicien" Champier: "For I have already seen enough of his praiseworthy works, printed in Latin and in our gallican tongue," Lemaire, *Œuvres*, 4:428.

46. "Woman is a confounding of man, an insane beast, a continual uneasiness of mind, an incessant fight, a daily hell, an impediment to solitude, the shipwreck of the incontinent man, a vessel of adultery, a pernicious battle, the worse animal, a very heavy burden, an insane viper, human property." See De Beauvais, *Speculum historiale*, quoted in Champier, *Nef des princes* (1502), 42v.

47. Jodogne, *Jean Lemaire*, 229–41.

48. Jodogne, *Jean Lemaire*, 226–29.

49. Virtue asks them simply to "satisfy our desire and clarify our imagination through the dexterity of your high and noble spirits, by making you judges and arbiters of the thing that we proposed, we wait to hear your confirmation or disapproval by the announcement of your judgments" (satisfaire à notre desir, et clarifier nostre imagination par la dexterité de voz hauts et nobles esprits, en vous faisant juges et arbitres de la chose par nous proposee, nous attendons d'en ouyr la confirmation ou improbation par l'arrest de voz sentences); she refers to the crown as "the invention of our imagination" (l'invention comprinse en nostre imaginative). Lemaire, *Œuvres*, 4:62, 58.

50. Jenkins, *Artful Eloquence*, 116.

51. Lemaire, *Œuvres*, 4:171. Parenthetical references in this note come from volume 4 of Lemaire's *Œuvres*; the numbers indicate pages in the volume. The judges use

words to denote judging ("jugement" and "decider"; 63, 141), "determiner" (82), "deducing" (70, 77, 108, 127), "inferring" (80), "concluding" (4:80), explaining ("explanation," "explication," "expliquer," "dilucider," "donner à entendre," and "clarifier"; 108, 121, 152, 115, 77, 62), "demonstrating" ("demonstrant," "exposition," "exemplification"; 77, 120, 152), and narrating ("narration," "collation," "sermocination," "dire," "fourny"; 70 and 152, 78, 96, 140, 82).

52. Lemaire, *Œuvres*, 4:58, 66.

53. Lemaire, *Œuvres*, 4:81, 57.

54. See Chayes, *L'eloquence des pierres*, 237–42.

55. Lemaire, *Œuvres*, 4:63.

56. Lemaire, *Œuvres*, 4:64; emphasis added.

57. Cotgrave defines a "chapelet" as a "garland, wreath for the head."

58. Molinet, *Faictz et dictz*, 1:106.

59. Molinet, *Faictz et dictz*, 1:106, 110. In the paragraph before using the phrase "quelque mystere latent," Lemaire refers to "some hidden meaning" (quelque intelligence occulte). Lemaire, *Œuvres*, 4:57.

60. Molinet, *Faictz et dictz*, 1:44.

61. For example, according to Jodogne, the *Couronne* is "a work of edification aimed at showing the moral strength of Margaret in her unhappiness," and "it has the sole aim, to emphasize Margaret's pain and her great courage." Jodogne, *Jean Lemaire*, 216, 217.

62. Molinet, *Faictz et dictz*, 1:107. According to *Webster's Dictionary*, "basilisks" were mythical lizardlike monsters with supposedly fatal breath and glance, fabled to have been hatched by a serpent from a cock's egg.

63. "Ton fruict, ta fleur et ta racine / Sont medecine / Qui nous donne santé et vie" Molinet, *Faictz et dictz*, 1:113.

64. Molinet, *Faictz et dictz*, 1:111, 113.

65. Molinet, *Faictz et dictz*, 1:114. Cotgrave defines an "electuaire" as a "medicinable composition made of choice drugs, and of substance betweene a syrrope and a conserve, but more enclining to this then [sic] to that." He defines a "cataplasme" as a "poultis" or "soft or moist plaister." Since a "chucas," or "choucas," was a cough, it appears that a "chucade" is a type of cough remedy.

66. Molinet, *Faictz et dictz*, 1:115, 122.

67. Molinet, *Faictz et dictz*, 1:118.

68. These and subsequent parenthetical references come from the *Couronne*; Lemaire, *Œuvres*, vol. 4.

69. Lemaire cites Margaret's repudiation no fewer than ten times in the *Couronne*; Lemaire, *Œuvres*, 4:60–61, 70, 73–75, 87–88, 90, 93, 105–6, 126–27, 132, 136–37.

70. See Lemaire, *Œuvres* 4:69, 72, 73, 77, 128, 134, 146, 148.

NOTES TO PAGES 122–126   227

71. Lemaire, *Œuvres*, 4:146.

72. Boccaccio, *On Famous Women*, 175.

73. Lemaire, *Œuvres*, 4:148.

74. "A 'heroic maiden' is so named because she 'acts like a man' (*vir* + *agere*), that is, she engages in the activities of men and is full of male vigor. The ancients thus would call strong women by that name. But if a woman does manly deeds, then she is correctly called a heroic maiden, like an Amazon." Isidore of Seville, *Etymologies of Isidore*, 242; Isidore of Seville, *Etymologies of Isidore*, 40.2.22.

75. Margaret played on the similarity of the words "serments" (oaths) and "sarments" (vines) to declare that the French king's oath to marry her and French wines were both worthless that year. Lemaire, *Œuvres*, 4:105–6.

76. "Here lies Margot, the gentle damsel, who has two husbands but is still a virgin." See Lemaire's *Couronne margaritique* in *Œuvres*, 4:106. After being repudiated by her first husband, Charles VIII, Margaret joked about drowning on her way to consummating her marriage to Juan de Castille.

77. Lemaire, *Concorde des deux langages*, 4.

78. See Armstrong, "Yearning and Learning"; Brown, "Jean Lemaire's *La concorde*"; Cottrell, "Allegories of Desire"; Fenoaltea, "Doing it with Mirrors"; Griffin, "*La concorde*"; Ménager, "*La concorde*"; Norrell, "L'enigme de *La concorde*"; Randall, "Flamboyant Design"; Randall, *Building Resemblance*; Rigolot, "Jean Lemaire de Belges"; Richter, "Image of the Temple," and Smith, "Scopia."

79. The word "syphilis" comes from a poem by Fracastoro, published in 1530. The *Trois contes* appeared in print for the first time in 1526.

80. For example, Joseph Vianey describes the last two poems as long, heavy, flat, and vulgar: "S'il y a quelque chose de long, et de lourd, et de plat, et de grossier dans les détails, je sais bien que ce sont les deux contes inventés par [Lemaire]." Vianey, *Le Pétrarquisme*, 44.

81. According to Elisabeth Caron in "L'innomable et ses périphrases," Lemaire blames women for the spread of syphilis in these three poems. She bases her accusation on a fleeting reference in the second conte to Cupid's arrow, tainted with Volupté's (menstrual?) blood, which Venus throws into the moat, or "venereal trenches" (fossez veneriques), and which, through a sort of "deadly alchemy" (alchimie funeste), provokes the disease's "first occurrence" (accident primaire) in the metaphorical locus of the female sex organs (138, 142). To support her thesis, Caron interprets words like "chasteau," "fossez veneriques," and "herbettes frisques" (cool/fresh blades of grass) in "the crudest possible manner" (de la façon la plus crue) as, respectively, "a coquettish name for women's sexuality" (une appellation coquette de la sexualité des dames), "the female organ" (l'organe féminin), and "pubic hairs" (poils pubiens; 139–41). Although I do not agree with all of Caron's

Freudian interpretations, I believe that some have merit and that women's humid nature is indeed depicted in this poem. However, I disagree with her thesis that Lemaire blames women more than men for the disease.

82. Jenkins, *Artful Eloquence*, 95.

83. "Comme je ne résoudrai pas la question des attributions, et qu'il y a un net effort de cohérence entre ces trois facéties, je m'en tiendrai à l'opinion du premier imprimeur." Caron, "L'innomable," 135.

84. Lemaire, *Concorde des deux langages*, 4.

85. Becker, *Jean Lemaire*, 372–73.

86. Guy, *Histoire de la poésie*, 1:204; Frappier, "*Concorde des deux langages*," 51–52; Françon, "Note sur Jean Lemaire," 19.

87. Jodogne, *Jean Lemaire*, 465–69.

88. "1520, le first of September, / These trials [grans estats] which I remember / Were assigned to Tours and held there." Lemaire, *Œuvres*, 3:59.

89. Jodogne, *Jean Lemaire*, 463n1. In the absence of a critical edition, all references in this article are taken from the Stecher edition, published over a century ago, which varies little from the 1526 edition and remains the only one readily available.

90. Most critics place Lemaire's birth in 1473, but his death remains a matter of speculation. Frappier states, "It's likely that he did not live much longer after Anne of Brittany"; introduction to *La concorde des deux*, 20–22. Alfred Humpers dates his death around 1515–16, while Kathleen Munn places it as late as 1526. See Humpers, "Quand Jean Lemaire"; Munn, *Contribution*, 82–84. Jodogne summarizes the various viewpoints but, apparently refusing to take part in the controversy, simply states that Lemaire was no longer living in 1526 when the *Trois contes* appeared; *Jean Lemaire*, 139–41.

91. After a detailed comparison of the first poem's word frequency and rhymes with other Lemaire works, Jodogne casts even more doubt on Lemaire as its translator. He blames its scant vocabulary, relative lack of qualifiers, and antithetical style on the requirements of a demanding verse form (terza rima) and fidelity to a now-absent original, but he finds the poem so unlike Lemaire's works that he prefers to attribute it, however tentatively, to an acquaintance or disciple of Lemaire. Jodogne, *Jean Lemaire*, 471–74.

92. Jodogne, *Jean Lemaire*, 469. For a thorough discussion of critics' doubts about the third poem's attribution to Lemaire, see Jodogne, *Jean Lemaire*, 464–65. Like many others, Jodogne finds the third poem too flat and ensconced in forensic rhetoric to be Lemaire's, but his most convincing proof remains the signature at the end of the poem, "coeur à bon droit," the same found at the end of an anonymous poem dated 1520 where the poet describes himself as a young novice. See ms. Paris, Bibl. Nat., fr. 1721, folio 109; cited in Jodogne, *Jean Lemaire*, 464.

93. Cottrell, "Allegories of Desire," 272, 297.

94. Cottrell, "Allegories of Desire, 275.

95. Caron apparently bases this appellation on the choice of verse form, terza rima, in both. Caron, "L'Innomable," 135. In the *Concorde des deux langages*, Lemaire brags about having introduced the Italian verse form into French, but he also wrote parts of the *prosimetrum* work *Le temple d'honneur et de vertus* (1503) in terza rima. See Lemaire, *Concorde des deux langages*, 6; *Temple*, 64–73.

96. Lemaire, *Œuvres*, 3:39.

97. Lemaire, *Œuvres*, 3:39–40.

98. Lemaire, *Œuvres*, 3:40.

99. "Chascun m'adore, et suis Dieu triomphant: / Mais tout chacun te fuit comme le diable / Tu es froide, et je suis eschauffant." Lemaire, *Œuvres*, 3:40.

100. Bloch, *Medieval Misogyny*, 53.

101. Lemaire, *Concorde des deux langages*, 4; emphasis added. Stecher tentatively identifies the defender of the French language as Margaret of Austria, whom Lemaire describes in somewhat similar terms in the *Couronne*. Lemaire, *Œuvres*, 3:99n2. He speaks of her "courage virile" and her "tresprudente audace non feminine," and calls her another Dido, "femme ayant le coeur virile." See Lemaire, *Œuvres* 4:42, 69, 73, 74, 143, 146. In the *Illustrations*, the prudent goddess Pallas claims to have been "produced from her father's head without the aid of the feminine sex." Lemaire, *Œuvres*, 1:240. Consequently, Lemaire contrasts Pallas's "eloquence non vaine" with Venus's "eloquence artificielle," "douce persuasion," and "rhetoriques couleurs." See Lemaire, *Œuvres*, 1:238, 249.

102. Ironically, although eloquence is considered feminine in Lemaire's thought, women do not typically wield that eloquence, and the female Atropos's literal interpretation of the metaphor is a typical female reading.

103. Lemaire, *Œuvres*, 3:41.

104. Lemaire, *Œuvres*, 3:41.

105. Lemaire, *Œuvres*, 3:41.

106. "Et à tous coups que faulse Atropos jette / Elle faisoit homme ou femme amoureux, / Bruslant en flamme, à Cupido subjette. / Maint beau homme alaigre et vigoureux / Y veis je choir, atteint de mortel dard, / Et maint vieillard d'amour tout langoureux." Lemaire, *Œuvres*, 3:42.

107. "Mort et Amour sont lourds et imprudens, / Sans raison nulle, et tous deux aveuglez, / Yvrognes tous, et coquars evidens. / Si Mort est lieffre, et ses faits desreiglez, / Si est Amour dangereux et farouche, / Et tous deux sont d'inconstance accomblez." Lemaire, *Œuvres*, 3:42. For a discussion of the sources, representations, and uses of the androgyne myth, see Rothstein, *Androgyne in Early Modern*.

108. Aristotle, *Poetics*, 1458b.

109. "Death cannot see, and Cupid is cross-eyed" (Mort ne void goute, et Cupido est louche). Lemaire, Œuvres, 3:42.

110. Dionisotti, "Amore et morte," 422–23; Jodogne, Jean Lemaire, 468.

111. Guthke, Gender of Death, 75–77. Guthke provides substantial proof that male and female personifications of death coexisted throughout the Middle Ages. However, male personifications of death dominated because they reflected the conventional religious view of male authority (85). However, literary and artistic depictions of a female Death who either rides on a chariot over her victims, as in Petrarch's "Trionfo della morte" (76–77), or spears them as a bat-winged harpy (78–79) began to appear with greater frequency in the fourteenth and fifteenth centuries. Guthke attributes these female images of Death to the widespread effects of plague in the fourteenth century and the influence of classical antiquity in the fifteenth (38–81).

112. Lemaire, Œuvres, 3:42.

113. Lemaire, Œuvres, 3:45.

114. Lemaire, Œuvres, 3:46.

115. Lemaire, Œuvres, 3:47. According to Randle Cotgrave, a "verrière" is "a glasse-window; and a peece of glasse wherewith a thing is encompassed, or covered."

116. See Kem, "Moral Lessons."

117. "And each of them carries a dead young man; / Behind, and they quickly approach" Lemaire, Œuvres, 3:48.

118. Lemaire, Œuvres, 3:50.

119. Lemaire, Œuvres, 3:51.

120. Lemaire, Œuvres, 3:51.

121. Lemaire, Œuvres, 3:51.

122. "Je vueil aussi que nous changeons de noms, / Et que le nom de l'un l'autre prenons: / Car desormais en tous cris et clamours, / Tu seras dit la Mort, et moy Amours: / Amours seray, et tu la Mort clamé, / De tout un chacun haï, craint et blamé." Lemaire, Œuvres, 3:52.

123. Lemaire clearly blames the spread of the disease on sexual contact, but it does not follow that he blames women more than men for their dalliance in this "plain of lust." Indeed, Lemaire mentions both men and women in the following two verses and seems to place more blame on men: "It was so very pleasing for men and for women / even for men, for which they are more infamous" (Tant fort plaisoit aux hommes et aux femmes / mesmes aux hommes, dont ilz sont plus infames). At the end, he sees both men and women as victims of the disease: "This very great infamy causes such fear / that it creates many a prudent man and many a prudent woman" (Si a la peur de ce tresgrant diffame / Fait maint preudhomme et mainte preudefemme). Lemaire, Œuvres, 3:53, 55.

124. Lemaire, *Concorde des deux langages*, 11.

125. Lemaire, *Œuvres*, 3:53; emphasis added. Lemaire plays on the word "bouton," which, according to Cotgrave, refers to both "a bud of a Vine" and "a pockie botch; or a high and eminent pimple, bursting out in any part of a bodie infected with the pocks."

126. According to Stecher, who credits Jean-Noël Paquot, "Lesbones" refers to "las buas." Lemaire, *Œuvres*, 3:54n2. "Las buas," or "las bubas," was the earliest Spanish name given to the disease and referred to the characteristic skin lesions.

127. Louis Jacques Bégin defines "asaphati" as a type of ringworm or "a term used by Arabists to designate a skin infection which appears similar to mucous tinea" (un terme employé par les Arabistes pour désigner une affection cutanée qui paraît être voisine de la teigne muqueuse). Bégin, *Dictionnaire*, 63.

128. Others, like Molinet, also referred to the onomastic confusion surrounding the disease. In his *Chronicles*, Molinet calls it "la maladie de Naples. . . . les grosses pocques . . . la grande gorre . . . la pancque denarre . . . les fiebvres Sainct-Job," and a form of "mesellerie," or leprosy. See Molinet, *Chroniques*, 5:34, 59. For a discussion of the "male de Santo Job," see Arrizabalaga, Henderson, and French, *Great Pox*, 52–54.

129. Lemaire, *Œuvres*, 3:55n2. The Italians called the disease the "French itch," or *rogna franciosa*. Arrizabalaga, Henderson, and French, *Great Pox*, 24. Avicenna describes scabies in the *Canon medicinae*, iv/vii, tract. iii, cap. vi (De scabie et pruritu) and vii (Du cura [scabiei et pruritus]), 385v–86v; cited in Arrizabalaga, Henderson, and French, *Great Pox*, 314n31.

130. See Jacques de Voragine, *La légende dorée*, 606–9.

131. Eatough, introduction to *Fracastoro's Syphilis*, 1. Girolamo Fracastoro (1478–1553) published the Latin poem *Syphilis sive morbus gallicus*, as well as two treatises on the nature of contagion in 1546 in Venice: *De sympathia* and *De contagione*. For a discussion of his theories on different modes of infection, see Arrizabalaga, Henderson, and French, *Great Pox*, 245–51.

132. Copenhaver, *Symphorien Champier*, 77. In his *Practica nova*, Champier lists over a dozen illnesses that are similar to "morbus gallicus" or "morbus neapolitanus," which he considered a new disease. They include "asaphati" (which he also spells "sahaphati"), "cancer," "elephantiasis," "impetigo," "lepra" (leprosy), "lichen," "mentagra," "pudendagra," and "scabies." Champier, *Practica nova* (1517), 2:12, 11v–12. He cites such medical authorities as Celsus, Galen, Pliny, and Rhazes. He seems to prefer Pliny's description of "lichen." *Natural History*, bk. 26, §1–2. Among the various remedies that Champier recommends is *argentum vivum*, or mercury; he does not mention guaiacum. According to Paul Allut, Champier also deals with the Great Pox in a chapter titled "De

pudendagra" briefly in his *Castigationes* (1532). See Allut, *Etude biographique*, 244. He writes again in the vernacular about *mentagra* and *pudendagra* in the *Lunectes des cyrurgiens* (G1v–G2v). In this lengthy passage, Champier cites Galen, Oribasius, and Pliny. He calls the disease "mal napolitain" (Neapolitan sickness) and "la maladie de Job" (Job's malady), comparing it to mentagra, pudendagra, lichen or "morphée" (a sleeping sickness), and asaphati. Champier claims twice in this passage that the disease is a form of divine punishment for the "sin of lust" and that it is "given to lustful men . . . who outside of marriage want to live like beasts without discretion, for one of the reasons for marriage has been continency and a remedy, and to avoid fornication so that we might not resemble beasts." He ends the passage with a Biblical verse: "Nolite fieri sicut equus & mulus: quibus non est intellectus" (Do not be like the horse or the mule that has no understanding). Psalm 31:9, in Latin Vulgate; Psalm 32:9 (New International Version). It is noteworthy that Champier cites men, and not women, who stray outside of marriage.

133. Arrizabalaga, Henderson, and French, *Great Pox*, 74.

134. Arrizabalaga, Henderson, and French, *Great Pox*, 74.

135. According to Jenkins, "Forensic oratory, which as a general rule predominates in the treatises of ancient rhetoricians, is virtually nonexistent in the works of Jean Lemaire, unless—which seems *unlikely*—the third *Conte de Cupido et d'Atropos* is his composition." Jenkins, *Artful Eloquence*, 113; emphasis added.

136. Lemaire, *Œuvres*, 3:56, 58. Caron associates the words "venimeuse" and "venefique" ("en écho avec le 'venerique' du Second Conte") in the third conte with Venus. Caron, "L'innomable," 143. In fact, the word "venefique" does not appear anywhere in the work. The noun "venefice," though, does, but as an antonym for "benefice," and it is associated with Atropos, not Venus, in the third conte: "Atropos pleine de venefice." Lemaire, *Œuvres*, 3:66.

137. Lemaire, *Œuvres*, 3:62.

138. Lemaire, *Œuvres*, 3:62.

139. "Si l'arc de Mort est triste et doulourex, / Celuy d'Amour est grief et langoureux: / L'un fait acoup du monde trespasser. / L'autre en vivant de mort les traits passer. [. . .] Mieux vaut par mort perdre acoup sa vigueur, / Qu'en amour vivre, et trainer grand langueur." Lemaire, *Œuvres*, 3:63.

140. Lemaire, *Concorde des deux langages*, 45–46.

141. Lemaire, *Œuvres*, 3:65. In what is perhaps an awkward attempt to imitate Lemaire's *Concorde des deux langages*, the author of the third conte uses different forms of the word *concorde* (concordance, discorde, discord, discordante) eight times in just thirty verses. Lemaire, *Œuvres*, 3:64–65.

142. Lemaire, *Œuvres*, 3:66.

143. According to the authors of *The Great Pox*, mercury "had been a resource in the treatment of skin disorders, including *scabies* and lice [pediculi], since the time of Avicenna and Rhazes" and was applied externally as an ointment or lotion once a day in a closed room near a fire for up to thirty days. Arrizabalaga, Henderson, and French, *Great Pox*, 139. Serious side-effects were often blamed on the unqualified practitioner's lack of skill. Arrizabalaga, Henderson, and French, *Great Pox*, 140–42. Lemaire was probably not familiar with guaiacum, a less common and more expensive remedy derived from the wood of a tree indigenous to the West Indies. Arrizabalaga, Henderson, and French, *Great Pox*, 100, 102–3, 187–89. Guaiacum was introduced into Europe in 1508 or earlier and was "in fairly general use in Spain as a medicine" in 1516; it was not known in Italy until 1517 and was known even later in France and the rest of Europe. Munger, "Guaiacum" 201–2. Although guaiacum was found "completely inefficacious in the treatment of syphilis," it had no harmful side-effects, unlike mercury, and allowed the patient's disease to improve on its own. Munger, "Guaiacum," 211.

144. In the 1526 edition, the title ends with an allusion to its moral import: "And this work was written to draw people back from foolish love." Munn, *Contribution*, 122.

145. Ficino was also one of the orators in the *Couronne*.

5. FATAL LOVESICKNESS

1. See Winn, "Témoignage de l'actualité médicale."

2. Cholakian and Cholakian, *Marguerite de Navarre*, 103, 191.

3. Brantôme describes Marguerite's medical intervention in Spain: "When the king was very sick in Spain and held prisoner, she went to visit him like a good sister and friend, with the emperor's blessing and safe conduct. She found her brother in such a pitiful state that if she had not come, he would have died, and since she knew his nature and complexion better than all his doctors, she treated him and had him treated according to what she knew, so well that she cured him." Brantôme, *Œuvres complètes*, 8:119.

4. Beecher, "Received Idea," 78.

5. Beecher also warns against "literal-minded approaches to reading literature, in [the] search for scientific *exempla*" like those of early "incomplete readers," who proved all too "insensitive to the order of ideas and conventions of narrative," or of modern readers, who "impose erroneous clinical readings upon narratives controlled by other conventions." Later he tempers this statement somewhat by adding that to ignore received ideas "is to misread in an equally perilous fashion." See Beecher, "Received Idea," 76, 77.

6. Useful works on lovesickness in the Middle Ages and the Renaissance include Wack, *Lovesickness*; Wells, *Secret Wound*; Allen, "Sex by Prescription: Lovesickness in the Middle Ages," in *Wages of Sin*, 1–24; and Beecher and Ciavolella, "Jacques Ferrand."

7. All references here to *Les quatre dames et les quatre gentilzhommes* come from André Gendre's 2012 critical edition. Arabic numerals preceding the colon indicate the eight parts, and Arabic numerals following the colon indicate the verse number.

8. Jourda finds these poems, as well as *La coche* and four similar letters, awkward, improvised, lacking in art, full of repetitions, monotonous, and conventional. But he adds, "Had she been born fifty years later, she could have competed with Ronsard." Jourda, *Marguerite d'Angoulême*, 533–34. He finds the eight poems of the *Quatre dames* "saved only by the refinement of the psychological analyses." Jourda, *Marguerite d'Angoulême*, 536. Telle damns the eight poems with faint praise; these "monologues," he writes, are "not tiring to read" or "completely devoid of charm or originality." Telle, *L'œuvre de Marguerite d'Angoulême*, 234–35. A more sympathetic reader, Gendre refers charitably to the eight poems as a "work in progress" and glosses several verses as unclear or confusing. Gendre, introduction to *Les quatre dames*, 139.

9. In 1937, Telle spoke of Marguerite's "feminism" and outlined her role in the debate. See Telle, *L'œuvre de Marguerite d'Angoulême*, 396.

10. Several sixteenth-century male writers referred to women's lack of pity in refusing their amorous advances. See, for example, Lemaire's use of the term "gift of pity" (don de mercy) as Oenone gives in to Paris's "gentle rape" (force non forcée). See Kem, *Jean Lemaire de Belges's*, 49.

11. Gendre, introduction to Marguerite de Navarre, *Les quatre dames*, 110.

12. The following quotations up to note 20 are taken from Marguerite de Navarre's *Quatre dames et quatre gentilzhommes* and followed by verse numbers: "maladie" (985), "Mal d'Amour" (995).

13. "Ce fol Amour, qui vous fait insenser" (118), "Perdu as tu sens et entendement" (462), "C'est ta folie" (447), Tu as perdu ... Entendement, raison ..." (468–69), "Quel desplaisant Malheur ... Qui m'a contraint perdre ... Entendement, raison, et congnoissance" (851–52, 854), "Làs, je perdray L'entendement" (917–18), "Hors de raison" (1683).

14. "Qui cause en toy tant de melancolie" (449), "voyant melancolie" (1702).

15. "Mes sens sont morts; mes esperitz reduitz" (1003).

16. "Tu as perdu santé, force, et couleur" (468), "Quel desplaisant malheur, / Qui m'a contraint perdre force, et couleur, / Vie, et puissance" (851–53).

17. "Voz souspirs et vos plaings" (134), "Maintz soupirs, ... larmes, ... criz, ... plaintz" (302–4), "Sans souspirer, sans parler, ne sans plaindre" (907).

18. "Amour ... Ses Traictz pointuz" (1287, 1290), "Pour vous mon corps / Amour met soubs la lame / Par trop couvrir son amoureuse flame" (1333–34), "Ne craingnez point de voir les traitz ardens / De Cupido, dont vient tant d'accidens" (2091–92).

19. "Doux appas ... dangereux repas" (42–43).

20. "Ceste poison, de trop douce liqueur" (245), "O grand douceur, mais plus tost grand poison" (307), "Amour... son amere poison" (1287, 1290). The fourth lady looks for an antidote to love, a "contrepoison" (899).

21. Jourda, *Marguerite d'Angoulême*, 1:537–38.

22. Marguerite de Navarre, *Les quatre dames*, 193n280; Telle, *L'œuvre de Marguerite d'Angoulême*, 231.

23. Marguerite de Navarre, *Les quatre dames*, 9–10. Subsequent references indicate verse numbers in Marguerite de Navarre's *Quatre dames et quatre gentilzhommes*.

24. The lady is suggesting therapeutic intercourse with another, a common remedy for lovesickness: "Assuring you that never will I be upset / That a woman other than me has lordship over you / By whom your pain will be healed." Marguerite de Navarre, *Les quatre dames*, v. 161–63.

25. "You are losing countenance and speech / Your grace and conversation / And I too all pleasure and peace / When I see that life, complexion, and pulse, / Joy and health are failing in you because of me." Marguerite de Navarre, *Les quatre dames*, 59–63.

26. "Mieux vous vaudroit tout nud, ou en pourpoint / Mourir de faim, / Que de languir si beau, si fort, *si sain*." Marguerite de Navarre, *Les quatre dames*, 47–51; emphasis added.

27. Marguerite de Navarre, *Les quatre dames*, 168–70.

28. Marguerite de Navarre, *Les quatre dames*, 172.

29. Marguerite de Navarre, *Les quatre dames*, 248–55.

30. Jourda, 1:537; Marguerite de Navarre, *Les quatre dames*, 159.

31. Gendre in Marguerite de Navarre, *Les quatre dames*, 159n69; emphasis added.

32. Marguerite de Navarre, *Les quatre dames*, 1338–42.

33. Marguerite de Navarre, *Les quatre dames*, 1289–331. Emile Telle explains, somewhat facetiously, the gentleman's demise: "From the physiological point of view of love, it is interesting to note what caused the death of the gentleman: Love, seeing that he had nothing more to gain from remaining in the heart of such a man without the ability to show himself wanted to get out, but unable to do so and, besides, reinforcing himself with a too great abundance of nourishment absorbed through eyes and ears, he could only escape from this prison by the death of the lover... Let's be reassured, love only kills people who would have died anyway during the year, said Oisille. This death ... is a fiction." Telle, *L'Œuvre de Marguerite d'Angoulême*, 229. Marguerite presents a more sophisticated understanding of the physiology of fatal lovesickness in the *Heptaméron*.

34. Marguerite de Navarre, *Les quatre dames*, 1260–75.

35. "*La belle dame sans mercy* nous a apprins à dire: sy gracieuse malladye ne mect gueres de gens à mort." *Heptaméron*, 12:117. Unless otherwise indicated, all

quotations from the *Heptaméron* are taken from Salminen's critical edition, and all translations are the author's. For a discussion of the gendered implications of the word "mercy" and how Marguerite's male devisants use it in the *Heptaméron* as a "strategy of seduction," see Frelick, "Love, Mercy," 325.

36. This section has been expanded, revised, and updated from an earlier version that appeared in 2010 in *Sixteenth Century Journal* under the title "Fatal Lovesickness in Marguerite de Navarre's *Heptaméron*." Nancy Frelick also discusses Marguerite's treatment of lovesickness in two articles, "Love, Mercy" (2010) and "Speech, Silence, and Storytelling" (2013). She examines it, in the former, as a seduction strategy (novella 26) within courtly love discourse and, in the latter, as an example of the "medical benefits of storytelling" (novellas 9 and 50). Frelick, "Speech, Silence, and Storytelling," 70, 76.

37. "Car, si nous n'avons quelque occupation plaisante et vertueuse, nous sommes en danger de *demeurer malades*." Prologue to *Heptaméron*, 8; emphasis added.

38. Prologue to *Heptaméron*, 8; emphasis added.

39. Prologue to *Heptaméron*, 8–9.

40. *Heptaméron*, 40:339.

41. *Heptaméron*, 40:339.

42. *Heptaméron*, 63:457.

43. *Heptaméron*, 63:457.

44. *Heptaméron*, 67:470. See Rezvani, "*Heptaméron*'s 67th Tale."

45. In novella 3, told by Saffredent, a husband cuckolded by the King of Naples suffers from "melancholy" and claims to be dying due to his "hidden" love for the queen. In novella 10, told by Parlamente, Floride's lovesickness, or repressed sexuality, causes the "tears held back in her heart" to produce nosebleeds, an inner psychological or emotional affliction that causes an outward physical manifestation. In novella 13, also told by Parlamente, a young man falls ill due to a hidden love that he reveals in a letter, but he dies in battle. In novella 20, the second told by Saffredent, a gentleman's lovesickness ends when he finds his loved one in the arms of a servant; her unworthy actions defame her and cure him. In novella 22, Géburon indicates that his protagonist's "incurable" lovesickness is feigned and therefore requires no cure. In novella 50, told by Longarine, the lovesick young man suffers from an "opilation de foie," or liver blockage, an affliction caused by lovesickness, but dies from bloodletting, the botched cure. His bandages come undone during a night spent in the arms of his beloved. Some classical and medieval medical authorities believed that erotic melancholy originated in the liver and that this organ eventually generated blackish vapors or humors that result in a potentially fatal condition. See Beecher and Ciavolella, "Jacques Ferrand," 56, 57, 116–17, 128.

46. *Heptaméron*, 65, 268. Several articles and book chapters on novellas 9 and 26 have appeared in the past few years. The most complete analysis of novella 26 to date is Bruno Méniel's "Vertu et l'orgueil," 123–36. Patricia Cholakian devotes a chapter to each in *Rape and Writing*, 79–87, 129–38.

47. Parlamente sets the horizon of expectations by proposing the theme for the third day: "Monstrer qu'il y a des dames qui en leurs amitiez n'ont cherché nulle fin que l'honnesteté" (To show that there are women who in love matters sought no other end than an honest one). *Heptaméron*, 195.

48. Méniel refers to novella 26 as an "educational narrative" or "coming of age narrative" (récit de formation), "Vertu et orgueil," 128.

49. See the chapter titled "Jeux de mémoire: Le fonctionnement d'un texte-écho" in Winn, *L'esthétique du jeu*, 151–76.

50. Winn, *L'esthétique du jeu*, 163.

51. Rothstein, *Reading in the Renaissance*, 62. For a discussion of the long tradition of arts of memory from classical antiquity through the Middle Ages and the Renaissance, see Yates, *Art of Memory*, and Carruthers, *Book of Memory*.

52. *Heptaméron*, 9:60.

53. *Heptaméron*, 9:64.

54. Wack traces therapeutic intercourse for lovesickness to Rufus of Ephesus (born after AD 50). See Wack, *Lovesickness*, 10–11.

55. Beecher and Ciavolella, "Jacques Ferrand," 24.

56. "*Non loquendo, sed moriendo confessi sunt.* J'en ay ouy tant parler, de ces transiz d'amours, mais encores jamais je n'en veidz mourir ung! Et puis que j'en suis eschappé, veu les ennuys que j'en ay portez, je ne pense poinct que jamais autre en puisse mourir." *Heptaméron*, 9:58; emphasis added.

57. "Madame ... pour conforter l'oppinion de Hircain, à laquelle je me tiens, je vous supplye, croyez que Fortune ayde aux *audacieux*, et qu'il n'y a homme que, s'il est aymé d'une dame, mais qu'il la saiche poursuivir *saigement* et affectionnement, que la fin n'en ayt du tout ce qu'il demande ou partie. Mais *l'ignorance et la folle craincte* faict perdre aux hommes beaucoup de bonnes adventures, et fondent leur perte sur la vertu de leur amye, laquelle n'ont jamais experimentée du bout du doid seulement: car oncques place bien assaillye ne fut, qu'elle ne fust prinse." *Heptaméron*, 9:64–65; emphasis added.

58. "Il fut longuement serviteur d'une dame vefve, laquelle il aymoit et reveroit tant que, de la *peur* qu'il avait de perdre sa bonne grâce, ne l'ousoit importuner de ce qu'il desiroit le plus." *Heptaméron*, 20:189; emphasis added.

59. *Heptaméron*, 20:190.

60. Beecher and Ciavolella, "Jacques Ferrand," 67.

61. *Heptaméron*, 20:190, 199.

62. Oisille is the first to pass judgment on the tale: "And if it wasn't that we all swore to tell the truth, I would scarcely believe that a woman of her status would ever be so mean in spirit, keeping in mind God, and in the body, leaving such an honest gentleman for such a vulgar muleteer." *Heptaméron*, 20:191.

63. *Heptaméron*, 26:255.

64. "Vous prandrez l'exemple qu'il vous plaira le mieulx." *Heptaméron*, 26:255. In the manuscript and early printed editions, the summaries before each novella no doubt contributed to the reader's horizon of expectations by signaling a particular focus. Claude Gruget's summary of novella 26 in manuscript 1512 is ambivalent: "Playful discourse of a great lord to have the enjoyment of a lady of Pampelune" (Plaisant discours d'un grand seigneur pour avoir la jouyssance d'une dame de Pampelune). *Heptaméron* (1967), 473n489. It neither names Avannes nor indicates which of the two "dames de Pampelune" he seduced. Randle Cotgrave defines "plaisant" as "pleasant," "joyfull" or "merrie," but also "recreative" or "sportfull" and even "scoffing" and "flowting." The tale appears anything but pleasant, or even "playful," since the wise lady dies; the summary definitely indicates a lack of sympathy for, or identification with, the female protagonist. The De Thou manuscript (ms. fr. 1524) names Avannes as the primary protagonist and the wise lady as his adviser against "foolish love": "By the advice and fraternal affection of a wise lady, the lord of Avannes withdrew from the foolish love that he held for a gentlewoman living in Pampelune" (Par le conseil et affection fraternelle d'une saige dame, le seigneur d'Avannes se retira de la folle amour qu'il portoit à une gentille femme demeurant à Pampelune). *Heptaméron* (1967), 208. It reinforces a reading where the wise lady serves as Avannes's tutor in love matters.

65. *Heptaméron*, 9:60.

66. *Heptaméron*, 26:263; emphasis added. According to Hope Glidden, the mask in the *Heptaméron* "points beyond itself toward role playing, performance, and the carnivalesque," but it also signifies "the ambiguous state of *dissimulation* as both woman's 'nature' and, conjointly, a strategy to hide the appropriation of masculine forms of power." See Glidden, "Gender," 35–36. While she refers to a masked woman in novella 43, Saffredent's ironic use of masks in novella 26 conveys a message about Avannes's dissimulation and use and misuse of masculine power.

67. *Heptaméron*, 16:260, 261.

68. *Heptaméron*, 26:260–61

69. [Aristotle], *Problems*, 4.21, 1:125.

70. Avicenna, *Liber canonis*, 3.20.1.

71. Averroes, *Colliget* in Avenzoar, *Liber theicrisi*, 6.

72. Champier, *Nef des dames* (2007), 139–42. See chapter 3.

73. Alī ibn al-ʿAbbās, *Theorice*, 5.36. Alī ibn al-ʿAbbās (d. 994), or Haly Abbas, wrote a commentary on Galen as well as *Liber totius medicinae*, a general study on medicine.

74. Women were thought sexually insatiable but also passive sex partners who received rather than expended energy. See Berriot-Salvadore, *Un corps, un destin*, 72–74, 113.

75. *Heptaméron*, 9:61.

76. *Heptaméron*, 26:264–65.

77. *Heptaméron*, 26:259–60; emphasis added.

78. Examples include: "Et combien qu'il eût plus volontiers aimé la sage dame que nulle, si est-ce que la *peur* qu'il avait de perdre son amitié, si elle entendait tels propos, le fit taire et s'amuser ailleurs" (And although he would have more willingly loved the wise lady than any other, the *fear* that he would lose her friendship, if she heard such language, made him keep silent and find amusement elsewhere); "Lui, qui la *craignait* et aimait . . ." (He, who *feared* and loved her . . .); and "Il courut au corps mort, duquel vivant *en crainte* il approchait" (He ran up to the dead body, which he would have approached with *fear*, had it been alive). *Heptaméron* 26:260, 261, 269.

79. *Heptaméron*, 9:62.

80. *Heptaméron*, 26:263.

81. *Heptaméron*, 26:265.

82. *Heptaméron*, 9:61.

83. *Heptaméron*, 9:63; emphasis added.

84. "Mais saichés que le *"non"* que si souvent *je vous ay dict* m'a tant faict de mal au prononcer qu'il *est cause de ma mort*, de laquelle je me contante, puis que Dieu m'a faict la grace de n'avoir permis que la violence de mon amour ayt mis tache à ma conscience et renommée . . ." *Heptaméron*, 26:266; emphasis added. Ms. fr. 1512 adds three words: "the grace *to die before* the violence of my love . . ." (La grâce de *mourir premier que* la violence de mon amour . . .). Marguerite de Navarre, *Heptaméron* (1967), 218.

85. "Je vous ay peu declairer mon affection esgalle à la vostre, horsmis que l'honneur des hommes et des femmes n'est pas semblable, vous suppliant, Monsieur, que doresnavant *vous ne craingnez* à vous adresser aux plus grandes et vertueuses dames que vous pourrez, car en telz cueurs habitent les plus fortes passions et *plus saigement conduictes*. Et la grace, beaulté et honnesteté qui est en vous *ne permectra que vostre* amour travaille sans *fruit*." *Heptaméron*, 26:267; emphasis added. Men's and women's different codes of honor, their respective places in society, and the difference between man's law and God's are common motifs in the *Heptaméron*. For example, a lady in novella 15 tells her straying husband, "And as the law of man greatly dishonors women who love someone other than their

husband, so the law of God does not exempt men who love someone other than their wives." *Heptaméron*, 15:152. He responds: "The honor of a woman and of a man are not similar." *Heptaméron*, 15:153. After novella 43, Parlamente speaks of men and women's different views of honor: "Those who are vanquished by pleasure should no longer be called women, but men, whose fury and lust augment their honor . . . But the honor of women has another foundation; it is sweetness, patience, and chastity." *Heptaméron*, 43:365.

86. "L'amour que la damoiselle avoit tousjours cellée se declaira à l'heure si fort que la mere et les serviteurs du mort eurent bien affaire à separer ceste unyon. Mais *à force ousterent la vifve, pis que morte, d'entre les braz du mort*, lequel ilz firent honnorablement enterrer." *Heptaméron*, 9:63; emphasis added.

87. "Et quant il s'apperceut qu'elle estoit morte, il courut au corps mort, duquel vivant *en crainte* il approchait, et le vint embrasser et baiser de telle sorte que *à grant peine le luy peut l'on ouster d'entre les braz.*" *Heptaméron*, 26:268; emphasis added.

88. The text reads, "[He] went away to court where he remained for many years without wanting to see or talk to any woman because he was pining for his lady. And he wore black for two years." *Heptaméron*, 26:268. According to Salminen, the manuscripts are divided on whether it was two years (*deux* ans) or ten (*dix* ans). *Heptaméron*, 734. If two years, his time of grief was short; if ten, it still falls far short of the lady's penance in the ninth novella.

89. *Heptaméron*, 26:268.

90. For a discussion of the importance and probable sources of this most frequently cited example of lovesickness in medical literature, see Wack, *Lovesickness*, 15–18; Beecher and Ciavolella, "Jacques Ferrand," 48–51, 179–80n60.

91. Wack, *Lovesickness*, 17–18.

92. *Heptaméron*, 9:65.

93. *Heptaméron*, 26:255, 257.

94. *Heptaméron*, 26:261.

95. *Heptaméron*, 26:263, 260. Wack recounts the story of Antiochus and Stratonice as well as a popular fifth-century story of lovesickness, *Perdica's Malady* (*Aegritudo perdicae*), in which a young man dies from his incestuous love for his stepmother. Wack notes, "At the root of lovesickness lies an unfulfilled, sometimes unspeakable desire that may be incestuous or otherwise socially unacceptable." Wack, *Lovesickness*, 4–5. Cotgrave translates "fils" not only as "son" but also more generally as "boy," and the *Trésor de la langue française* offers a general meaning: "To be human, placed under the guardianship, the protection of a master" (être humain placé sous la tutelle, la protection d'un maître). Nonetheless, Saffredent's choice of "filz" rather than a synonym for "servant" or "apprentice" seems to allow for a double interpretation and a possible, if not probable, allusion to one of these two early tales of lovesickness.

96. Méniel, "Vertu et orgueil," 124.

97. *Heptaméron*, 26:257. According to Salminen, *fantasticque* means "of an odd nature," (d'humeur fantasque). *Heptaméron*, 802. *Le trésor de la langue française* offers the following definition for *fantastique*: "Qui donne libre cours à son imagination, se forge des chimères" (Someone who gives free rein to his imagination, forges chimeras), which would seem to indicate that the husband was not entirely mentally stable.

98. Méniel finds yet another similarity between the two women: their "mastery of language" (maîtrise du langage) indicated by their use of irony and wordplay. He reads the novella as comic, at least in this respect, and claims that the women are masters of their destiny and "play a leading role in the game from one end to the other" (mènent le jeu de bout en bout). Méniel, "Vertu et orgueil," 125. Cholakian interprets the wise lady's verbal virtuosity with Avannes as more defensive than masterly; she explains that "the female rejects the sex act in favor of the speech act and substitutes discourse for intercourse" in the novellas; *Rape and Writing*, 134, 37.

99. *Heptaméron*, 26:265.

100. *Heptaméron*, 26:268.

101. Mathieu-Castellani, *La conversation conteuse*, 86–89.

102. According to Beecher, novella 26 presents unique problems of interpretation: "The [modern] reader . . . senses that none of the respondents to the story rises to the subtlety of its inflections whether as a tragedy, a study of pathological love, or a study of the ethical ambiguities inherent in love itself. The wandering commentary serves to perpetuate the indeterminacy experienced by the reader—the mixed response of admiration and blame, one that forces us into a reading of the stories *not* written in the place of this one." "Marguerite de Navarre's *Heptaméron*," 76. Méniel finds "a mystery that arises out of this text, that the dialogue of the *devisants* only increases," and a little later, he adds, "the final quote prevents any unambiguous interpretation." Méniel, "Vertu et orgueil," 120, 122. See also Gary Ferguson's discussion of what he calls Saffredent's "volte-face," or "about-face," at the end of the tale in "Gendered Oppositions," 145–51.

103. *Heptaméron*, 26:268–69.

104. Betty J. Davis offers the following explanation for Oisille's wholehearted approval of the story: "She probably does not see the same moral as Saffredent. He does not say which lady he considers wise and which one foolish." Davis, *Storytellers*, 70.

105. Brantôme claimed the wise lady committed suicide in *Œuvres complètes* 9:211, cited in Méniel, "Vertu et orgueil," 133–34.

106. "Pour se monstrer plus vertueuse par dehors qu'elle n'estoit au cueur, et pour *dissimuler* un amour que la raison de nature vouloit qu'elle portast à ung sy honneste

seigneur, *se alla laisser mourir,* par faulte de se donner le plaisir qu'il desiroit *ouvertement* et qu'elle desiroit *couvertement!" Heptaméron,* 26:270; emphasis added.

107. Méniel, "Vertu et orgueil," 133.

108. Cholakian posits that Saffredent "quickly unveils his real intention," which she interprets as a lesson for women to give in to their sexual urges. *Rape and Writing,* 135–36.

109. "Aussy, que leurs *robbes* sont si longues et sy bien tissues de *dissimulation* que l'on ne peult congnoistre ce qui est dessoubz, car, si leur honneur n'en estoit non plus taché que le nostre, *vous trouverriez que nature n'a riens oublyé en elles non plus que en nous." Heptaméron,* 26:269; emphasis added.

110. Berriot-Salvadore, *Un corps, un destin,* 20–22.

111. See note 85 above.

112. In novella 29, Saffredent describes the poor whose women are more natural and less adorned and whose men are less fearful than their noble counterparts: "The meats of the poor are less appetizing, but they have a better appetite, and they are better fed on bread than we are on dainties. They don't have beds as fine or well-made as ours, but they sleep better than we do. They don't have *painted and made-up women* like those we idolize, but they enjoy their pleasures more often than we do, without *fear of words,* but only of the beasts and the birds that see them. What we have, they lack, but in what we lack, they have in abundant supply." *Heptaméron,* 29:279–80; emphasis added. Wack claims that lovesickness was thought more common among the nobility than commoners and cites Jacques Despars's fifteenth-century commentary on Avicenna's *Canon:* "The nobles are more given to leisure and delicately nourished with meat and wine; they frequent dances and often converse with attractive ladies and demoiselles 'who are like darts wounding the mind,'" in Wack, *Lovesickness,* 150.

113. In novella 34, Hircan describes women's vulnerability and compares it to men's: "We men are closer to our salvation than you others because, *not hiding our fruits,* we know our root [true nature]. But you who *dare* not put them *outside* and perform such apparent good works, scarcely would you know the root of your pride that grows under such *fine* coverings." (Entre nous hommes . . . sommes doncq plus près de nostre salut que vous autres car, *ne dissimulant poinct* noz fruictz, congnoissons facilement nostre racine. Mais vous, qui *ne ousez mectre voz fruictz dehors* et qui faictes tant de belles euvres apparantes, à grant peine congnoistrez vous ceste racine d'orgueil, qui croist *soubz sy belles couvertures.) Heptaméron,* 34:309.

114. Wack, *Lovesickness,* 60–61, 150.

115. Wack, *Lovesickness,* 149–50; Ferrand, *Treatise,* 311–12.

116. Lawrence Kritzman, *"Verba erotica,"* 56.

117. Ferrand writes: "According to Galen and his followers, fear and sorrow—the characters and accidents inseparable from the state of melancholy—are traceable to the blackness of humor . . . melancholiacs live in perpetual fear"; *Treatise*, 240. In his *Nef des princes* (first published in 1502), Symphorien Champier urges young princes to avoid fear and sorrow that can result in melancholy: "And fear experienced over a long period makes a man melancholic. And for this reason one should not allow children to be too fearful or sad, or angry, or tearful; happiness leads to a measured life." Champier, *Nef des princes* (2002), 89. Angus Gowland maintains that during the Renaissance, inordinate emotions like fear were thought to cause as well as result from melancholy; *Worlds of Renaissance Melancholy*, 126–27.

118. Wack asserts that the symptoms of lovesickness were thought to "unman" the lover and connoted "feminine and infantile behavior," *Lovesickness*, 151.

CONCLUSION

1. Thysell, *Pleasure of Discernment*, 86ff.

2. See, for example, articles in two special issues of journals: Kem, "Women in the World," and Brownlee and Francis, "Querelles des femmes."

BIBLIOGRAPHY

PRIMARY SOURCES

Agrippa von Nettesheim, Heinrich Cornelius. *Declamation on the Nobility and Pre-eminence of the Female Sex*. Translated and edited with an introduction by Albert Rabil Jr. Chicago: University of Chicago Press, 1996.

——. *De nobilitate et praecellentia foeminei sexus*. Critical edition by Charles Bené, O. Sauvage, and R. Antonioli. Geneva: Droz, 1990.

Albertus Magnus. *On Animals: A Medieval Summa Zoologica*. Translated by Kenneth F. Kitchell Jr. and Irven Michael Resnick. 2 vols. Baltimore: Johns Hopkins University Press, 1999.

——. *Quaestiones super De animalibus*. Edited by Ephrem Filthaut. Monasterii Westfalorum: In Aedibus Aschendorff, 1955.

Albertus Magnus [pseud.]. *De secretis mulierum*. See Lemay, *Women's Secrets*.

Ali ibn al-ʿAbbas. *Theorice*. In *Omnium librorum Halyabatis*. Venice: Jehan le Noir, 1492.

Ali-ibn-Ridwan [Ali-Ben-Rodhouan]. *Antiqua thegni Galeni translatio cum commento Haly Rodoam*. Venice: Jehan le Noir, 1492.

Andes, Raymond N., ed. "*Le romant de la rose moralisé*, by Jean Molinet. A Critical Edition with Notes, Variants, and Glossary." PhD diss., University of North Carolina at Chapel Hill, 1948.

Anne de France. *Les enseignements d'Anne de France, suivis de l'histoire du siège de Brest*. Edited by Tatiana Clavier and Eliane Viennot. Saint-Étienne: Publications de l'Université de Saint-Étienne, 2006.

Aristotle. *De animalibus*. Venice: Bartolomaeus de Zanis for Octavianus Scotus, 1498.

————. *History of Animals*. Translated by A. L. Peck. Vol. 1–2, bk. 1–6. Cambridge MA: Harvard University Press, 1965, 1970.

————. *History of Animals*. Translated by D. M. Balme. Vol. 3, bk. 7–10. Cambridge MA: Harvard University Press, 1991.

————. *On the Generation of Animals*. Translated by A. L. Peck. Cambridge MA: Harvard University Press, 1943.

————. *Poetics*. Cambridge MA: Harvard University Press, 1995.

[Aristotle]. *Problems*. Translated by W. S. Hett. Cambridge MA: Harvard University Press, 1953.

Augustine. *The Trinity*. Translated by Stephen McKenna. The Fathers of the Church 45. Washington DC: Catholic University of America Press, 2010.

Avenzoar. *Liber theicrisi dahalmodana vahaltadabir*. Venice: Gregoriis, 1490.

————. *Liber theizir de morbis omnibus et eorundem remediis; Colliget sive De medicina*. Venice: 1497.

Averroes. *Colliget*. In *Liber theicrisi dahalmodana vahaltadabir*, by Avenzoar. Venice: Gregoriis, 1490.

Avicenna. *The Canon of Medicine* (*Al-qānūn fi 'l-'ṭibb*). Translated by O. Cameron Gruner and Mazar H. Shah and adapted by Laleh Bakhtiar. Chicago: KAZI, 1999.

————. *Liber canonis*. Hildesheim DE: Georg Olms, 1964.

Badius, Josse. *La nef des folles: Stultiferae naves*. Edited by Charles Bené. Grenoble: Publications de l'Universite des langues et lettres de Grenoble, 1979.

Baird, Joseph L., and John R. Kane, eds. *La querelle de la rose: Letters and Documents*. Chapel Hill: University of North Carolina Press, 1978.

Barras, Vincent, Terpischore Birchler, and Anne-France Morand, trans. *Galien: L'ame et ses passions*. Paris: Les Belles Lettres, 1995.

Bernard de Gordon. *Lilio de medicina: Un manual básico de medicina medieval*. Edited by John Cull and Brian Dutton. Madison WI: Hispanic Seminar of Medieval Studies, 1991.

Beroaldo, Filippo. *Orationes et carmina*. Bologna, 1491.

Billon, François de. *Le fort inexpugnable de l'honneur du sexe femenin*. New York: Johnson Reprint Corporation, 1970.

Boccaccio, Giovanni. *Decameron*. Translated by G. H. McWilliam. London: Penguin Books, 2013.

————. *Genealogy of the Pagan Gods*. Vol. 1, bk. 1–4. Edited and translated by Jon Solomon. Cambridge MA: Harvard University Press, 2011.

————. *Famous Women*. Edited and translated by Virginia Brown. Cambridge MA: Harvard University Press, 2001.

Bouchet, Jean. *Le temple de bonne renommée*. Critical edition by Giovanna Bellati. Milan: Vita e Pensiero, 1992.

———. *Le temple de bonne renommée et repos des hommes et femmes illustres*. Paris: Galliot du Pré, 1516.

———. *Les triumphes de la noble et amoureuse dame et l'art d'honnestement aimer, 1563*. Whitefish MT: Kessinger, 2009.

———. *Œuvres complètes I: Le jugement poetic de l'honneur femenin*. Critical edition by Adrian Armstrong. Paris: Honoré Champion, 2006.

Bourbon, Gabrielle de. *Œuvres spirituelles, 1510–1516*. Edited by Evelyne Berriot-Salvadore. Paris: Honoré Champion, 1999.

Brantôme, Seigneur de [Pierre de Bourdeille]. *Œuvres complètes*. 11 vols. Paris: 1875. New York: Johnson Reprint Corporation, 1968.

Braund, Susanna Morton, trans. *Juvenal et Perseus*. Cambridge MA: Harvard University Press, 2004.

Celsus. *On Medicine*. Translated by W. G. Spencer. 3 vols. Cambridge MA: Harvard University Press, 1935–38.

Champier, Symphorien. *Campus Elysius & Periarchon*. In *Hortus gallicus*, by Symphorien Champier. Lyon: Melchior and Gaspar Trechsel, 1533.

———. *Castigationes seu emendationes pharmacopolarum*. Lyon: Crespin, 1532.

———. *Cribratio medicamentorum*. Lyon: Gryphium, 1534.

———. "A Critical Edition of the First Six Books of Symphorien Champier's *La nef des princes*." Critical edition by Phyllis Ann Hall. PhD diss., Columbia University, 1975. Microfilm, 76-12, 811.

———. *Gallicum pentapharmacum*. Lyon: Melchior and Gaspar Trechsel, 1534.

———. *La nef des dames vertueuses*. Critical edition by Judy Kem. Paris: Honoré Champion, 2007.

———. *La nef des dames vertueuses*. Lyon: Jacques Arnollet, 1503.

———. *La nef des dames vertueuses*. Paris: Jehan de La Garde, 1515.

———. *La nef des dames vertueuses*. Paris: Philippe le Noir, 1531.

———. *La nef des princes*. Lyon: Guillaume Balsarin, 1502.

———. *La nef des princes von Symphorien Champier*. Edited by Andrea Wilhelmi. Frankfurt: Peter Lang, 2002.

———. *L'antiquité de la cité de Lyon. Ensemble la rebeine ou rébellion du populaire*. Paris: St. Denys, 1529.

———. *Le livre de vraye amour*. Edited by J. B. Wadsworth. The Hague: Mouton, 1962.

———. *Les gestes ensemble la vie du preulx chevalier Bayard*. Paris: Gilbert de Villiers, 1525.

———. *Les gestes ensemble la vie du preulx chevalier Bayard*. Paris: Payot, 1918.

———. *Les grans croniques des gestes des ducz et princes des pays de Savoye et Piemont*. Paris: Jehan de La Garde, 1516.

———. *Le guidon en français*. Lyon: Jean ler de Vingle pour Etienne Gueynard, 1503.

———. *Les lunectes des cyrurgiens.* See *Le myrouel des appothiquaires,* [1532?].

———. *Le myrouel des appothiquaires et pharmacopoles par lequel est demonstré comment appothiquaires communement errent en plusieurs simples medicines contre l'intention des Grectz.* Edited by Paul Dorveaux. Paris: H. Welter, 1894.

———. *Le myrouel des appothiquaires; Item les lunectes des cyrurgiens & barbiers.* Lyon: Pierre Mareschal, [1532?]

———. *Le recueil ou croniques des hystoires des royaulmes d'Austrasie.* Lyon: Vincent de Portunaris de Trinc, 1510.

———. *Le triumphe du treschrestien Roy de France Loys XII.* Lyon: Claude Davost, 1509.

———. *Hortus gallicus, pro gallis scriptus, veruntamen non minus italis, germanis, & hispanis, quam gallis necessarius.* Lyon: Melchior and Gaspar Trechsel, 1533.

———. *Libelli duo.* Lyon: J. de Campis, 1506.

———. *Medicinale bellum.* Lyon: Simon Vincent, 1516.

———. *Officina apothecariorum.* Lyon: Crespin, 1532.

———. *Periarchon, id est de principiis Platonicarum disciplinarum omniumque.* [Paris?], 1514.

———. *Periarchon, id est de principiis utriusque philosophiae.* Lyon: Melchior and Gaspar Trechsel, 1533.

———. *Practica nova.* Lyon [ca. 1509–ca. 1515]

———. *Practica nova.* Venice: Octavianus Scotus, 1515.

———. *Practica nova.* Paris: Jean Marion, 1517.

———. *Practica nova.* Venice: Ottaviano Scoto, 1522.

———. *Speculum Galeni.* Lyon: Jean de Jonvelle, 1517. http://dl.ub.uni-freiburg.de /diglit/galenus1517.

Chartier, Alain. *The Poetical Works of Alain Chartier.* Edited by J. C. Laidlaw. London: Cambridge University Press, 1974.

Chastellain, Georges. *Oeuvres.* 4 vols. Geneva: Slatkine, 1971.

Christine de Pizan. *The Boke of the Cyte of Ladyes.* London: Henry Pepwell, 1521.

———. *The Boke of the Cyte of Ladyes.* In *Distaves and Dames: Renaissance Treatises for and about Women.* Facsimile reproductions with an introduction by Diane Bornstein. Delmar NY: Scholars' Facsimiles & Reprints, 1978.

———. *The Book of the City of Ladies.* Translated by Earl Jeffrey Richards. New York: Persea Books, 1998.

———. *La cité des dames.* Translated by Eric Hicks and Thérèse Moreau. Paris: Stock, 1986.

———. *La cité des dames.* Edited by Earl Jeffrey Richards. In *La città delle dame,* by Christine de Pizan. Translated by Patrizia Caraffi. Milan: Luni Editrice, 1997.

———. *"Le livre de la cité des dames* of Christine de Pisan: A Critical Edition." Edited by Maureen Cheney Curnow. 2 vols. PhD. diss., Vanderbilt University, 1975.

———. *Le livre des trois vertus*. Critical edition by Eric Hicks. Paris: Champion, 1989.

———. *"Livre de la cité des dames*: Kritische Text-edition auf grund der sieben überlieferten 'manuscrits originaux' des textes."* Edited by M. Lange. PhD. diss., University of Hamburg, 1974.

———. *Œuvres poétiques de Christine de Pisan*. 3 vols. Edited by Maurice Roy. New York: Johnson Reprint Corporation, 1965.

———. *Poems of Cupid, God of Love: Christine de Pizan's "Epistre au dieu d'amours" and "Dit de la rose"; Thomas Hoccleve's "The Letter of Cupid: Editions and Translations,"* with George Sewell's *"The Proclamation of Cupid."* Edited and translated by Thelma S. Fenster and Mary Carpenter Erler. Leiden: Brill, 1990.

———. *The Treasure of the City of Ladies or the Book of the Three Virtues*. Translated by Sarah Lawson. New York: Viking Penguin, 1985.

Cicero. *De amicitia*. In *On Old Age. On Friendship. On Divination*, by Cicero. Translated by W. A. Falconer. Cambridge MA: Harvard University Press, 1923.

———. *The Tuscan Disputations*. Cambridge MA: Harvard University Press, 1927.

[Cicero]. *Rhetorica ad Herennium*. Cambridge MA: Harvard University Press, 1954.

Ciminelli, Serafino. *Le rime de Serafino de Ciminelli dall'Aquila*. 2 vols. Bologna: Romagnoli-dall'Aqua, 1894.

———. *Opere del facundissimo Seraphino Aquilano collecte per Francesco Flavio*. Roma: Ioanni de Besicken, 1502.

———. *Opere del facundissimo Seraphino Aquilano collecte per Francesco Flavio*. Venice: Manfrino de Monfera, 1502.

———. *Opere di Seraphino Aquilano; sonetti C., egloghe III, epistole VII, etc. Di novo consomma diligentia et emendatione*. Fano: Hieronymo Soncino, 1516.

Ciminelli, Serafino, and Jean Lemaire de Belges. *Traictez singuliers contenus ou present opuscule. Les trois comptes intitulez de Cupido et de Atropos, dont le premier fut inventé par Seraphin poete italien. Le second et tiers de l'invention de maistre Jehan Le Maire et a este ceste oeuvres fondee, affin de retirer les gens de folles amours. Les epitaphes de Hector & Achilles avec le jugement de Alexandre le grand composees par Georges Chastelain, dit l'avanturier. Le temple de Mars faict & composé par J. Molinet. Plusieurs chantz royaulx, balades, rondeaulx et epistres composees par . . . maistre Guillaume cretin . . . L'apparition . . .* Paris: Galliot du Pré, 1526.

Cotgrave, Randle. *A Dictionarie of the French and English Tongues*. Columbia: University of South Carolina Press, 1950. http://www.pbm.com/~lindahl/cotgrave/.

Crétin, Guillaume. *Œuvres poétiques de Guillaume Crétin*. Edited by Kathleen Chesney. Paris: Firmin-Didot, 1932.

Dufour, Antoine. *Les vies des femmes celebres*. 1504. Edited by G. Jeanneau. Geneva: Droz, 1970.

Durling, Richard W., ed. *Burgundio of Pisa's Translation of Peri Kraseon, "De complex-ionibus."* Vol. 1 of *Galenus Latinus.* Berlin: Walter de Gruyter, 1976.

Du Pré, Jehan. *Le palais des nobles dames.* Lyon, 1534. Edited by Brenda Dunn-Lardeau. Paris: Honoré Champion, 2007.

Fallopius, Gabriel. *Observationes anatomicae.* Venice: Marco Antonio Ulmo and Gratioso Perchachino, 1561.

Ferrand, Jacques. *A Treatise on Lovesickness.* Edited and translated by Donald A. Beecher and Massimo Ciavolella. Syracuse NY: Syracuse University Press, 1990.

Ficino, Marsilio. *Commentaire sur le banquet de Platon.* Edited by Pierre Laurens. Paris: Les Belles Lettres, 2002.

———. *Commentary on Plato's Symposium on Love.* Translated by Sears Reynolds Jayne. Dallas TX: Spring, 1985.

Fracastoro, Girolamo. *Fracastoro's Syphilis: Introduction, Text, Translation and Notes.* Edited by Geoffrey Eatough. Liverpool: Francis Cairns, 1984.

Gabrielle de Bourbon. *See* Bourbon, Gabrielle de.

Galen, Claudius. *De complexionibus. See* Durling, *Burgundio of Pisa's Translation.*

———. "De locis affectis." In *Claudii Galeni opera omnia,* edited by C. G. Kuhn. Vol. 8 of *Medicorum Graecorum opera qua extant.* Hildesheim: Georg Olms, 1965.

———. *Galen on the Affected Parts.* Translated by Rudolph E. Siegel. Munich: S. Karger, 1976.

———. *On the Usefulness of the Parts of the Body* [Περὶ χρείας μορίων; *De usu partium*]. Vol. 2. Translated by Margaret Tallmadge May. Ithaca NY: Cornell University Press, 1968.

Gournay, Marie de. *Egalité des hommes et des femmes.* 1622. Paris: Côté-Femmes Editions, 1989.

Green, Monica H., trans. *The Trotula: An English Translation of the Medieval Compendium of Women's Medicine.* Philadelphia: University of Pennsylvania Press, 2002.

Guillaume de Lorris, and Jean de Meun. *Le roman de la rose.* Edited by Daniel Poirion. Paris: Garnier-Flammarion, 1974.

———. *Le roman de la rose. Dans la version attribuée à Clément Marot.* Edited by Silvio F. Baridon. 2 vols. Milan: Instituto Editoriale Cisalpino, 1957.

———. *The Romance of the Rose.* Translated by Harry W. Robbins. New York: E. P. Dutton, 1962.

Haly Abbas. *See* Ali ibn al-'Abbas.

Haly Rodoam. *See* Ali-ibn-Ridwan.

Harkins, Paul W., and Walther Riese, trans. *Galen: On the Passions and Errors of the Soul.* Columbus: Ohio State University Press, 1963.

Hélisenne de Crenne. *Les angoysses douloureuses qui procedent d'amours.* Critical edition by Christine de Buzon. Paris: Honoré Champion, 1997.

─────. *Les epistres familieres et invectives de ma dame Hélisenne*. Critical edition by Jean-Philippe Beaulieu and Hannah Fournier. Montréal: Les Presses de l'Université de Montréal, 1995.

Hippocrates. *The Corpus*. New York: Kaplan, 2008.

Isidore of Seville. *The Etymologies of Isidore of Seville*. Translated by Stephen A. Barney. New York: Cambridge University Press, 2006.

Jacques de Voragine. *La légende dorée*. Edited by Jean Batallier. Paris: Honoré Champion, 1997.

Jauss, Hans Robert. *Toward an Aesthetic of Reception*. Translated by Timothy Bahti. Minneapolis: University of Minnesota Press, 1982.

Jerome. *Adversus Jovinianum libri duo*. Vol. 23 of *Patrologia Latina*. Alexandria VA: Chadwyck-Healey, 1996.

─────. *Opera omnia*. Vol. 22–23 of *Patrologia Latina*. Alexandria VA: Chadwyck-Healey, 1996. http://pld.chadwyck.com/all/toc.

─────. *Select Works and Letters. The Principal Works of St. Jerome*. Translated by W. H. Fremantle. The Nicene and Post-Nicene Fathers, 2nd ser., vol. 6. Astor Place NY: J. J. Little, 1893.

Joubert, Laurent. *Popular Errors*. Translated by Gregory de Rocher. Tuscaloosa: University of Alabama Press, 1989.

"Judith." In *The Apocrypha: The Complete Deuterocanonical Texts of the King James Bible*, 138–56. Reseda CA: Enhanced Media Publishing, 2017.

La Sale, Antoine de. *Les quinze joyes de mariage*. Paris: Adamant Media, 2007. *See also Les quinze joyes de mariage*.

Lactantius. *De divinis institutionibus adversus gentes*. Venice: Theodorus de Ragazonibus, 1490. Special Collections, Z. Smith Reynolds Library, Wake Forest University.

─────. *Divinarum institutionem*. Vol. 6 of *Patrologia Latina*. Alexandria VA: Chadwyck-Healey, 1996. http://pld.chadwyck.com/all/toc.

─────. *The Divine Institutes*. Translated by Sister Mary Frances McDonald. Washington DC: Catholic University of America Press, 1964.

─────. *Opera omnia*. Vol. 6 and 7 of *Patrologia Latina*. Alexandria VA: Chadwyck-Healey, 1996. http://pld.chadwyck.com/all/toc.

Lagniet, Jacques. *Recueil des plus illustres proverbes divisés en trois livres*. Paris, 1663.

Hicks, Eric, ed. *Le débat sur le "Roman de la Rose."* Critical edition. Geneva: Slatkine, 1996.

Le Franc, Martin. *Le champion des dames*. Edited by Robert Deschaux. 5 vols. Paris: Honoré Champion, 1999.

─────. *The Trial of Womankind. A Rhyming Translation of Book IV of the Fifteenth-Century "Le Champion des Dames."* Translated by Steven Millen Taylor. Jefferson NC: McFarland, 2005.

Lemaire de Belges, Jean. *Chronique de 1507.* Critical edition by Anne Schoysman. Brussels: Académie Royale de Belgique, 2000.

———. *Couronne margaritique.* Lyon: 1549.

———. *Couronne margaritique.* In *Œuvres,* by Jean Lemaire de Belges, 10–181. Edited by Jean Stecher. Louvain BE, 1882–85. Reprint, Geneva: Slatkine, 1969.

———. *La concorde des deux langages.* Critical edition by Jean Frappier. Paris: Honoré Champion, 1947.

———. *La concorde du genre humain.* Edited by Pierre Jodogne. Brussels: Palais des Académies, 1964.

———. *La plainte du désiré.* Critical edition by Dora Yabsley. Paris: Droz, 1932.

———. *Les epîtres de l'amant vert.* Critical edition by Jean Frappier. Lille: Giard, 1948.

———. *Les illustrations de Gaule et singularitez de Troye, par maistre Jean le Maire de Belges, avec la Couronne margaritique et plusieurs autres oeuvres de luy. [Les trois contes de Cupido et d'Atropos, dont le premier fut inventé par Séraphin, poète Italien, et traduit par Jean Le Maire, le second et tiers de l'invention de maistre Jean Le Maire. Le traicté des différences des schismes et des conciles de l'Eglise. Le traicté nommé La légende des Vénitiens.] Le tout reveu et fidèlement restitué par maistre Antoine Du Moulin.* Lyon: Jean de Tournes, 1549.

———. *Œuvres.* Edited by Jean Stecher. 4 vols. Louvain BE, 1882–85. Reprint, Geneva: Slatkine, 1969.

———. "Les regretz de la dame infortunée." In *Hommages à la Wallonie: Mélanges d'histoire, de littérature et de philologie wallonnes offerts à Maurice A. Arnould et Pierre Ruelle,* edited by Pierre Jodogne, 321–34. Brussels: Editions de l'Université de Bruxelles, 1981.

———. *Le temple d'honneur et de vertus.* Critical edition by Henri Hornik. Geneva: Droz, 1957.

———. *Les trois contes intitulez de Cupido et d'Atropos.* Lyon: Antoine du Moulin, 1549.

Lemay, Helen Rodnite, trans. *Women's Secrets: A Translation of Pseudo-Albertus Magnus's "De secretis mulierum" with Commentaries.* Albany: State University of New York Press, 1992.

Lesnauderie, Pierre de. *La louenge de mariage et recueil des hystoires des bonnes, vertueuses et illustres dames.* Paris: F. Regnault, 1523.

Le triumphe de très haulte dame Verolle royne du Puy d'Amours, nouvellement composé par l'inventeur de menus plaisirs honestes. Paris: Alain Lotrian, 1540.

Magnus Hundt. *Antropologium de hominis dignitate, natura, et proprietatibus; De elementis. partibus et membris humani corporis.* Leipzig: Wolfgang Monacensem, 1501.

Marconville, Jean de. *De la bonté et mauvaistié des femmes.* Critical edition by Richard A. Carr. Paris: Honoré Champion, 2000.

Marguerite de Navarre. *Heptaméron*. Critical edition by Renja Salminen. Geneva: Droz, 1999.

———. *Heptaméron*. Edited by M. François. Paris: Garnier, 1967.

———. *The Heptameron*. Translated by Paul A. Chilton. London: Penguin, 2004.

———. *Le mallade*. Critical edition by Geneviève Hasenohr and Olivier Millet. In *Théâtre*, edited by Nicole Cazauran, 231–59. Vol. 4 of *Œuvres completes*. Textes de la Renaissance. Paris: Honoré Champion, 2001.

———. *Les quatre dames et les quatre gentilzhommes*. Critical edition by André Gendre. In *L'histoire des satyres, et nymphes de Dyane. Les quatre dames et les quatre gentilzhommes. La coche*, edited by Nicole Cazauran, 147–266. Vol. 5 of *Œuvres complètes*. Textes de la Renaissance. Paris: Honoré Champion, 2012.

———. *Théâtre*. Critical edition by Geneviève Hasenohr and Olivier Millet. Vol. 4 of *Œuvres complètes*, edited by Nicole Cazauran. Paris: Honoré Champion, 2001.

Marot, Clément. "Exposition Moralle du Roman de la Rose." In Lorris and de Meun, *Attribuée à Clément Marot*, 1:89–92.

———. *Œuvres poétiques complètes*. 2 vols. Edited by Gérard Defaux. Paris: Bordas, 1990.

Marot, Jehan [Jean]. *Les deux recueils*. Critical edition by Gérard Defaux and Thierry Mantovani. Geneva: Droz, 1999.

———. *Le doctrinal des princesses et nobles dames*. In *Les deux recueils*. Critical edition by Gérard Defaux and Thierry Mantovani. Geneva: Droz, 1999. 4–19.

———. *La vraye disant advocate des dames*. In *Les deux receuils*. Critical edition by Gérard Defaux and Thierry Mantovani. Geneva: Droz, 1999. 93–119.

McRae, Joan E., ed. *Alain Chartier: The Quarrel of the "Belle dame sans mercy."* New York: Routledge, 2004.

McWebb, Christine, ed. *Debating the "Roman de la Rose": A Critical Anthology*. With an introduction and Latin translations by Earl Jeffrey Richards. New York: Routledge, 2007.

Meschinot, Jean. *Edition des lunettes des princes de Jean Meschinot*. Edited by Christine Martineau-Genieys. Geneva: Droz, 1972.

Molinet, Jean. "Art de rhétorique vulgaire." In *Recueil d'arts de seconde rhétorique*, edited by Ernest Langlois. Paris: Imprimerie Nationale, 1902.

———. *Chroniques de Jean Molinet*. Edited by J. A. Buchon. 5 vols. Paris: Verdière, 1827–28.

———. *Les faictz et dictz de Jean Molinet*. 3 vols. Paris: Société des Anciens Textes Français, 1936–39.

[Molinet, Jean?]. *Le mystère de Judith et Holofernés: Une édition critique de l'une des parties du "Mistere du viel testament."* Critical edition by Graham A. Runnalls. Geneva: Droz, 1995.

———. *Le romant de la rose moralisé cler et net*. The Hague: Koninklijke Bibliotheek, MS 128-C-5.

———. *Le romant de la rose moralisé cler et net*. Paris: Vérard, 1500.

———. *Le romant de la rose moralisé cler et net*. Lyon: Balsarin, 1503.

———. *Le romant de la rose moralisé cler et net*. Paris: Veuve Michel le Noir, 1521.

Ovid. *Héroïdes and Amores*. Translated by Grant Showerman. London: William Heinemann, 1925.

———. *Metamorphoses*. Vol. 1–2 of *Ovid in Six Volumes*, translated by Frank Justus Miller. Cambridge MA: Harvard University Press, 1984.

———. *Tristia: Ex ponto*. Translated by Arthur Leslie Wheeler. Cambridge MA: Harvard University Press, 1988.

Pamphilus. *De amore*. In *Seven Medieval Latin Comedies*, translated by Alison Goddard Elliott, 1–25. New York: Garland, 1984.

Paracelsus. *Selected Writings*. Edited by Jolande Jacobi. Princeton NJ: Princeton University Press, 1988.

Paré, Ambroise. *Œuvres complètes d'Ambroise Paré revues et collationnées sur toutes les éditions, avec les variantes: ornées de 217 planches et du portrait de l'auteur: accompagnées de notes historiques et critiques: et precédées d'une introduction sur l'origine et les progrès de la chirurgie en Occident du sixième au seizième siècle, et sur la vie et les ouvrages, d'Ambroise Paré*. Paris: J. P. Baillière, 1840.

———. *Œuvres de M. Ambroise Paré*. Paris: Chez Gabriel Buon, 1575.

———. *Œuvres de M. Ambroise Paré*. Paris: Chez Gabriel Buon, 1598.

Petrarch, Francesco. *De remediis utriusque fortunae*. Assen NL: Van Gorcum, 1968.

———. *Petrarch's Remedies for Fortune Fair and Foul*. Translated by Conrad H. Rawski. 5 vols. Bloomington: Indiana University Press, 1991.

Philippe de Clèves, seigneur de Ravestein. *L'instruction de toutes manières de guerroyer […] sur mer. Edition critique du manuscrit français 1244 de la Bibliothèque nationale de France*. Edited by Jacques Paviot. Paris: Honoré Champion, 1997.

Pietro d'Abano. *Conciliator differentiarum philosophorum et praecipue medicorum*. Mantua IT, 1472.

Plato. *The Collected Dialogues Including the Letters*. Edited by Edith Hamilton and Huntington Cairns. Princeton NJ: Princeton University Press, 1996.

Plautus. Translated by Paul Nixon. 5 vols. London: Heinemann, 1916–38.

Pliny. Vol. 7, bk. 24–27 of *Natural History*, edited by Jeffrey Henderson. Translated by W. H. S. Jones. Cambridge MA: Harvard University Press, 2014.

Poullain de la Barre, François. *De l'egalité des deux sexes*. Paris: J. Vrin, 2011.

Rabanus Maurus. *De institute clericorum*. Pforzheim DE: Thomas Anshelm of Baden, 1504.

———. *De rerum naturis*. Cassino IT: Università degli studi di Cassino, 1996.

Rabelais, François. *The Complete Works of François Rabelais*. Translated by Donald M. Frame. Berkeley: University of California Press, 1991.

———. *Le tiers livre*. Critical edition by Jean Céard. Paris: Librairie Générale Française, 1995.

———. *Œuvres complètes*. Edited by Pierre Jourda. 2 vols. Paris: Garnier Frères, 1962.

Rhazes [Abu Bakr Mohammed ibn Zakarija]. *Liber ad almansorem*. Venice: Bergomensem, 1497.

———. *Liber Rasis de secretis in medicina qui liber amphorismorum appellatur*. Bologna, 1489.

Rasis. *See* Rhazes.

Robertet, Jean. *Œuvres*. Edited by Margaret Zsuppàn. Geneva: Droz, 1970.

Romieu, Marie de. "Brief Discours que l'excellence de la femme surpasse celle de l'homme, autant recreatif que plein de beaux exemples." In *Les premières oeuvres poétiques*, edited by André Winandy, 12–25. Geneva: Droz, 1972.

Rychner, Jean, ed. *Les XV joies de mariage*. Geneva: Droz, 1967.

Sacchi, Bartolomeo, dit Platine. *Le Platine en français ou "De honesta voluptate et valetudine," d'après l'édition de 1505*. Paris: Editions Manucius, 2003.

Saint-Gelais, Octavien de. *Le séjour d'honneur*. Edited by Joseph Alston James. Chapel Hill: University of North Carolina Press, 1977.

Seneca. *Letters on Ethics: To Lucilius*. Translated by Margaret Graver and A. A. Long. Chicago: University of Chicago Press, 2015.

———. *Seneca's Tragedies*. Vol. 1–2 of *Seneca in Nine Volumes*, translated by Frank Justus Miller. Cambridge MA: Harvard University Press, 1968.

Steber, Bartholomäeus. *A malafranczos morbo Gallorum praeservation ac cura*. Vienna: Johann Winterburg, 1498.

Sylvius Piccolomini, Aeneas. "The Treatise of Aeneas Sylvius Piccolomini . . . *De liberorum educatione*." Translated by William Harrison Woodward. In *Vittorino da Feltre and Other Humanist Educators: Essays and Versions, an Introduction to the History of Classical Education*, by William Harrison Woodward, 134–58. Cambridge MA: Cambridge University Press, 1912.

———. *The Tale of the Two Lovers*. Translated by Flora Grierson. London: Constable, 1929.

[Theophrastus]. *Liber aureolus de nuptiis* [The golden book of marriage]. In *Epistola adversus Jovinianum* [Letter against Jovinian], by Jerome, 1.47. *Patrologia Latina* 23: 276–78.

Torella, Gaspare. *Tractatus com consiliis contra pudendagram seu morbum gallicum*. In *The Earliest Printed Literature on Syphilis*, edited by Karl Sudhoff. Florence: R. Lier, 1925.

Valerius Maximus. *Factorum et dictorum memorabilium*. Stuttgart: Teubner, 1966.

———. *Memorable Deeds and Sayings: One Thousand Tales from Ancient Rome*. Translated by Henry J. Walker. Indianapolis IN: Hackett, 2004.

Vallambert, Simon de. *De la manière de nourrir et gouverner les enfans dès leur naissance.* Critical edition by Colette H. Winn. Geneva: Droz, 2005.

Van Hamel, A. G., ed. *Les lamentations de Matheolus et le livre de leesce de Jehan Le Fevre de Resson (poèmes français du xivème siècle).* Critical edition by A. G. Van Hamel. Paris: Bouillon, 1892–1905.

Vésale, André. *Résumé de ses livres sur la fabrique du corps humain* [*Andreae Vesalii Bruxellensis suorum de humani corporis fabrica librorum epitome*]. Translated by Jacqueline Vons. Paris: Les Belles Lettres, 2008.

Vincentius Bellovacensis. *Speculum historiale.* Duaci: Baltazaris Belleri, 1624. Reprint, Graz: Akademische Druck-u. Verlagsanstalt, 1964.

Virgil. *Aeneid.* In *Virgil, Eclogues, Georgics, Aeneid 1–6* and *Aeneid 7–12, The Minor Poems,* translated by H. R. Fairclough. Cambridge MA: Harvard University Press, 1978.

Wallis, Faith, ed. *Medieval Medicine: A Reader.* Toronto: University of Toronto Press, 2010.

Whitbread, Leslie George, trans. *Fulgentius the Mythographer.* Columbus: Ohio State University Press, 1971.

William of Saliceto. *The Surgery of William of Saliceto.* Translated by Leonard D. Rosenman. Philadelphia: Xlibris, 2002.

Worth-Stylianou, Valérie, ed. *Les traités d'obstétrique en langue française au seuil de la modernité: Bibliographie critique des "Divers travaulx" d'Euchaire Rösslin (1536) à l'"Apologie de Louyse Bourgeois sage femme" (1627).* Geneva: Droz, 2007.

Zumthor, Paul, ed. *Anthologie des Grands Rhétoriqueurs.* Paris: Union Générale des Editions, 1978.

SECONDARY SOURCES

Adams, Alison. *Webs of Allusion: French Protestant Emblem Books of the Sixteenth Century.* Geneva: Droz, 2003.

Adams, Tracy, and Glenn Rechtschaffen. "Isabeau of Bavaria, Anne of France, and the History of Female Regency in France." *Early Modern Women* 8 (October 2013): 119–47.

Allen, Peter Lewis. *The Wages of Sin: Sex and Disease, Past and Present.* Chicago: University of Chicago Press, 2000.

Allut, Paul. *Etude biographique et bibliographique sur Symphorien Champier.* Nieuwkoop NL: HES & De Graaf, 1972.

Altmann, Barbara K., and Deborah L. McGrady, eds. *Christine de Pizan: A Casebook.* New York: Routledge, 2003.

Analyse et Traitement Informatique de la Langue Française. *Trésor de la langue française.* http://atilf.atilf.fr/.

Andes, Raymond N. Introduction to *"Le romant de la rose moralisé*, by Jean Molinet. A Critical Edition with Notes, Variants, and Glossary," iv–xxxiii. Edited by Raymond N. Andes. PhD diss., University of North Carolina at Chapel Hill, 1948.

Antonioli, Roland. *Rabelais et la médecine*. Études rabelaisiennes 12. Geneva: Droz, 1976.

———. "Un médecin lecteur du *Timée*, S. Champier." In *Actes du Colloque sur l'Humanisme Lyonnais au XVIe Siècle, mai 1972*, 53–62. Grenoble: Presses Universitaires de Grenoble, 1974.

Arden, Heather M. "Le duc des vrais amans? Christine de Pizan ré-écrit le *Roman de la Rose*." In *De la rose: Texte, Image, Fortune*, edited by Catherine Bel et Herman Braet, 411–20. Louvain BE: Peeters, 2006

———. *The Romance of the Rose*. Boston: Twayne, 1987.

———. *The "Roman de la rose": An Annotated Bibliography*. New York: Garland, 1993.

Armstrong, Adrian. "Yearning and Learning: Spaces of Desire in Jean Lemaire de Belges's *Concorde des deux langages* (1511)." In *The Erotics of Consolation: Desire and Distance in the Late Middle Ages*, edited by Catherine E. Léglu and Stephen J. Milner, 79–94. New York: Palgrave Macmillan, 2008.

Arrizabalaga, Jon, John Henderson, and Roger French. *The Great Pox: The French Disease in Renaissance Europe*. New Haven CT: Yale University Press, 1997.

Baader, Renate, and Margarete Zimmermann. "Querelle des femmes." *Lendemains: Études comparées sur la France* 16, no. 61 (1991): 9–37.

Badel, Pierre-Yves. *Le roman de la rose au XIV' siècle. Etude de la réception de l'œuvre*. Geneva: Droz, 1980.

Baird, Joseph L. "Pierre Col and the Querelle de la Rose." *Philological Quarterly* 60, no. 3 (Summer 1981): 273–86.

Baird, Joseph L., and John R. Kane. "*La querelle de la rose*: In Defense of the Opponents." *French Review* 48, no. 2 (1974): 298–307.

Ballard, James F., and Michel Pijoan. "A Preliminary Check-List of the Writings of Symphorien Champier, 1472–1539." *Bulletin of the Medical Library Association* 28, no. 4 (1940): 182–88.

Baridon, Silvio F. Preface to *Le roman de la rose dans la version attribuée à Clément Marot*, by Lorris and de Meun, 1:11–86.

Bauschatz, Cathleen M. "Rabelais and Marguerite de Navarre on Sixteenth-Century Views of Clandestine Marriage." *Sixteenth Century Journal* 34, no. 2 (2003): 395–408.

Becker, Philipp August. *Jean Lemaire de Belges, der erste humanistische Dichter Frankreichs*. Strasbourg: Karl J. Trübner, 1893. Reprint, Geneva: Slatkine, 1970.

Beecher, Donald A. "Concerning Sex Changes: The Cultural Significance of a Renaissance Polemic." *Sixteenth Century Journal* 36, no. 4 (2005): 991–1016.

———. "Marguerite de Navarre's *Heptaméron* and the Received Idea: The Problematics of Lovesickness." In *International Colloquium Celebrating the 500th Anniversary of the Birth of Marguerite de Navarre*, edited by Régine Reynolds-Cornell, 71–78. Birmingham AL: Summa, 1995.

————. "Windows on Contagion." In *Imagining Contagion in Early Modern Europe*, edited by Claire L. Carlin, 32–46. Basingstoke: Palgrave Macmillan, 2005.

Beecher, Donald A., and Massimo Ciavolella. "Jacques Ferrand and the Tradition of Erotic Melancholy in Western Culture." In *Treatise on Lovesickness*, by Jacques Ferrand, 3–202. Edited and translated by Donald A. Beecher and Massimo Ciavolella. Syracuse NY: Syracuse University Press, 1990.

Bégin, Louis Jacques. *Dictionnaire des termes de médecine, de chirurgie, art vétérinaire, pharmacie, histoire naturelle, botanique, physique, chimie*. Paris: Crevot, Béchet, Baillière, 1823.

Bell, Susan Groag. *The Lost Tapestries of the City of Ladies: Christine de Pizan's Renaissance Legacy*. Berkeley: University of California Press, 2004.

————. "A Lost Tapestry: Margaret of Austria's 'Cité des dames.'" In *Une femme de lettres au Moyen Age: Etudes autour de Christine de Pizan*, edited by Liliane Dulac and Bernard Ribémont, 449–67. Orléans FR: Editions Paradigme, 1995.

————. "A New Approach to the Influence of Christine de Pizan: The Lost Tapestries of the 'City of Ladies.'" In *Sur le chemin de longue étude: Actes du colloque d'Orléans, juillet 1995*, edited by Bernard Ribémont, 7–11. Paris: Honoré Champion, 1998.

Berriot-Salvadore, Evelyne. *Les femmes dans la société française de la Renaissance*. Geneva: Droz, 1990.

————. *Un corps, un destin: La femme dans la médecine de la Renaissance*. Paris: Honoré Champion, 1993.

Blaylock, Joshua M. "International Echoes: Emblems, Rabelais, and *Heptaméron* 13." In "Women in the World and Works of Marguerite de Navarre," edited by Judy Kem. Special issue, *L'esprit créateur* 57, no. 3 (2017): 79–92.

Bloch, R. Howard. *Medieval Misogyny and the Invention of Western Romantic Love*. Chicago: Chicago University Press, 1991.

Bock, Gisela, and Margarete Zimmerman. "The European *Querelle des femmes*." In *Medieval Forms of Argument: Disputation and Debate*, edited by Georgianna Donavin, Carol Poster, and Richard Utz, 127–56. Eugene OR: Wipf and Stock, 2002.

Boucher, Alain. "Les années médicales lyonnaises de Rabelais." *Histoire des sciences médicales* 26, no. 3 (1992): 197–206.

————. "L'Héritage lyonnais d'Hippocrate." *Histoire des sciences médicales* 29, no. 3 (1995): 219–26.

Bourdillon, F. W. *The Early Editions of the Roman de la Rose*. London: Chiswick Press, 1906.

Britnell, Jennifer. *Jean Bouchet*. Edinburgh: Edinburgh University Press, 1986.

Brown, Cynthia J. "Jean Lemaire's *La concorde des deux langaiges*: The Merging of Politics, Language, and Poetry." *Fifteenth-Century Studies* 3 (January 1988): 29–39.

———. "The Reconstruction of an Author in Print: Christine de Pizan in the Fifteenth and Sixteenth Centuries." In *Christine de Pizan and the Categories of Difference*, edited by Marilynn Desmond, 215–35. Minneapolis: University of Minnesota Press, 1998.

Brown-Grant, Rosalind. *Christine de Pizan and the Moral Defence of Women: Reading Beyond Gender*. Cambridge: Cambridge University Press, 1999.

———. "Christine de Pizan as a Defender of Women." In *Christine de Pizan: A Casebook*, edited by Barbara K. Altmann and Deborah L. McGrady, 81–100. New York and London: Routledge, 2003.

Brownlee, Kevin, and Scott Francis, eds. "Querelles des femmes: French Women Writers of the 15th and 16th Centuries." Special issue, *French Forum* 42. no. 3 (Winter 2017).

Brownlee, Kevin, and Sylvia Huot, eds. *Rethinking the Romance of the Rose*. Philadelphia: University of Pennsylvania Press, 1992.

Cadden, Joan. *Meanings of Sex Difference in the Middle Ages: Medicine, Science, and Culture*. Cambridge: Cambridge University Press, 1993.

Campbell, John, and Nadia Margolis, eds. *Christine de Pizan 2000: Studies on Christine de Pizan in Honour of Angus J. Kennedy*. Amsterdam: Editions Rodopi, 2000.

Campbell, Julie D. "The *Querelle des femmes*." In *The Ashgate Research Companion to Women*, edited by Allyson M. Poska, Jane Couchman, and Katherine A. McIver, 362–79. Farnham UK: Ashgate, 2013.

Campbell, P. G. C. "Christine de Pisan en Angleterre." *Revue de littérature comparée* 5 (January 1925): 663–65.

Carlino, Andrea. *Books of the Body: Anatomical Ritual and Renaissance Learning*. Translated by John Tedeschi and Anne C. Tedeschi. Chicago: University of Chicago Press, 1999.

Caron, Elisabeth. "L'innomable et ses périphrases dans les *Contes de Cupido et d'Atropos*." *Le moyen français* 39–41 (1997): 135–49.

Carruthers, Mary. *The Book of Memory: A Study of Memory in Medieval Culture*. Cambridge: Cambridge University Press, 1990.

Cayley, Emma. *Debate and Dialogue: Alain Chartier in His Cultural Context*. Oxford: Clarendon Press, 2006.

Chayes, Evelien. *L'eloquence des pierres précieuses: De Marbode de Rennes à Alard d'Amsterdam et Remy Belleau; Sur quelques lapidaires du XVIe siècle*. Paris: Honoré Champion, 2010.

Cholakian, Patricia. *Rape and Writing in the "Heptaméron" of Marguerite de Navarre*. Carbondale: Southern Illinois University Press, 1991.

Cholakian, Patricia, and Rouben Cholakian. *Marguerite de Navarre: Mother of the Renaissance*. New York: Columbia University Press, 2006.

Classen, Albrecht, ed. *Sexuality in the Middle Ages and Early Modern Times: New Approaches to a Fundamental Cultural-Historical and Literary-Anthropological Theme.* Berlin: Walter de Gruyter, 2008.

Clavier, Tatiana, and Eliane Viennot. Introduction to *Les enseignements d'Anne de France, suivis de l'histoire du siège de Brest,* edited by Tatiana Clavier and Eliane Viennot, 7–35. Saint-Étienne: Publications de l'Université de Saint-Etienne, 2006.

Cluzel, Jean. *Anne de France: Fille de Louis XI, duchesse de Bourbon.* Paris: Fayard, 2002.

Cooper, Richard. "Les Dernières Années de Champier." *Réforme, humanisme, Renaissance* 47, no. 1 (December 1998): 25–50.

———. "Symphorien Champier e l'Italia." In *L'aube de la Renaissance,* edited by D. Cecchetti, L. Sozzi, and L. Terreaux, 233–45. Geneva: Slatkine, 1991.

———. "Symphorien Champier et l'Italie." In *Litteræ in tempore belli: Etudes sur les relations littéraires italo-françaises pendant les guerres d'Italie,* edited by Richard Cooper, 287–302. Geneva: Droz, 1997.

Copenhaver, Brian P. *Symphorien Champier and the Reception of the Occultist Tradition in Renaissance France.* The Hague: Mouton, 1978.

Cottrell, Robert. "Allegories of Desire in Lemaire's *Concorde des deux langages.*" *French Forum* 23, no. 3 (September 1998): 261–300.

———. "Spirit, Body, and Flesh in Marguerite de Navarre's *Heptaméron.*" In *Heroic Virtue, Comic Infidelity: Reassessing Marguerite de Navarre's Heptaméron,* edited by Dora E. Polachek, 23–27. Amherst: Hestia Press, 1993.

Crawford, Katherine. "Marsilio Ficino, Neoplatonism, and the Problem of Sex." *Renaissance and Reformation / Renaissance et réforme,* n.s., 28, no. 2 (Spring 2004): 3–35.

——— *The Sexual Culture of the French Renaissance.* Cambridge: Cambridge University Press, 2010.

Croft, Claire M. "Pygmalion and the Metamorphosis of Meaning in Jean Molinet's *Roman de la Rose Moralisé.*" *French Studies* 59, no. 4 (2005): 453–66.

Curnow, Maureen Cheney. "*The Boke of the Cyte of Ladyes,* an English Translation of Christine de Pizan's *Le livre de la cité des dames.*" *Les bonnes feuilles* 3 (1974): 116–37.

Davis, Betty J. *The Storytellers in Marguerite de Navarre's Heptaméron.* Lexington KY: French Forum, 1978.

Delogu, Daisy. "A Fair Lady Takes on 'Maistre Allain': Anne de Graville's *Belle dame sans mercy.*" In "Querelles des femmes: French Women Writers of the 15th and 16th Centuries," edited by Kevin Brownlee and Scott Francis. Special issue, *French Forum* 42, no. 3 (Winter 2017): 471–91.

Delsaux, Olivier. "Le Pin de Jean Castel, fils d'Étienne Castel et de Christine de Pizan." *Archives d'histoire doctrinale et littéraires du Moyen Âge* 78, no. 1 (2011): 335–75.

Deschaux, Robert. Introduction to *Le champion des dames,* by Martin Le Franc, 1:vii–xliii. Edited by Robert Deschaux. Paris: Honoré Champion, 1999.

Desmond, Marilynn, ed. *Christine de Pizan and the Categories of Difference.* Minneapolis: University of Minnesota Press, 1998.

———. "The *Querelle de la rose* and the Ethics of Reading." In *Christine de Pizan: A Casebook*, edited by Barbara K. Altmann and Deborah L. McGrady, 167–80. New York: Routledge, 2003.

Devaux, Jean. "De l'amour profane à l'amour sacré: Jean Molinet et sa version moralisée du *Roman de la rose*." In *Image et mémoire du Hainaut médiéval. Actes du colloque organisé par le* CAMELIA *(Valenciennes, 28–29 Novembre 2002)*, edited by Jean-Charles Herbin, 21–32. Valenciennes FR: Presses Universitaires de Valenciennes, 2004.

———. *Jean Molinet indiciaire bourguignon.* Paris: Honoré Champion, 1996.

———. "Pour plus fresche memoire: La fonction didactique de l'histoire dans le *Roman de la rose moralisé*." *Le moyen age* 112, no. 3 (2006): 557–73.

———. "Tradition textuelle et techniques de réécriture: *Le roman de la rose moralisé* et Jean Molinet." In *De la rose: texte, image, fortune*, edited by Catherine Bel and Herman Braet, 377–91. Louvain BE: Peeters, 2006.

Dionisotti, Carlo. "Amore et morte." *Italia medioevale e umanistica* (1958): 419–26.

Doutrepont, Georges. *Jean Lemaire de Belges et la Renaissance.* Brussels: Lamertin, 1934.

Dupire, Noël. *Jean Molinet. La vie—les œuvres.* Paris: Droz, 1932.

Durling, Richard. *A Dictionary of Medical Terms in Galen.* Leiden: E. J. Brill, 1993.

Dusenberry, Maya. *Doing Harm.* New York: Harper, 2018.

Eatough, Geoffrey. Introduction to *Fracastoro's Syphilis: Introduction, Text, Translation and Notes*, by Girolamo Fracastoro, 1–2. Liverpool: Francis Cairns, 1984.

Eubanks, Peter Jared. "Poetic Self-Assertion in Jean Lemaire de Belges's 1506 *Les regretz de la dame infortunée*." *Romance Notes* 47, no. 3 (Spring 2007): 313–21.

Fenoaltea, Doranne. "Doing it with Mirrors: Architecture and Textual Construction in Jean Lemaire's *Concorde des deux langages*." In *Lapidary Inscriptions: Renaissance Essays for Donald A. Stone, Jr*, edited by Barbara C. Bowen and Jerry C. Nash, 21-33. Lexington KY: French Forum, 1991.

Fenster, Thelma. "'Perdre son latin': Christine de Pizan and Vernacular Humanism." In *Christine de Pizan and the Categories of Difference*, edited by Marilynn Desmond, 91–107. Minneapolis: University of Minnesota Press, 1998.

Ferguson, Gary. "Gendered Oppositions in Marguerite de Navarre's *Heptameron*: The Rhetoric of Seduction and Resistance in Narrative and Society." In *Renaissance Women Writers: French Texts/American Contexts*, edited by Anne R. Larsen and Colette H. Winn, 143–59. Detroit MI: Wayne State University Press, 1994.

Ferguson, Gary, and Mary B. McKinley, eds. *A Companion to Marguerite de Navarre.* Boston: Brill, 2013.

———. "The *Heptaméron*: Word, Spirit, World." In *A Companion to Marguerite de Navarre*, edited by Gary Ferguson and Mary B. McKinley, 323–71. Boston: Brill, 2013.

Fetterley, Judith. *The Resisting Reader: A Feminist Approach to American Fiction*. Bloomington: Indiana University Press, 1978.

Françon, Marcel. "Note sur Jean Lemaire de Belges et Seraphino dall'Aquila." *Italica* 28, no. 1 (1951): 19–22.

Frappier, Jean. Introduction to *La concorde des deux langages*, by Jean Lemaire de Belges, vii–lxviii. Critical edition by Jean Frappier. Paris: Droz, 1947.

Frelick, Nancy. "Contagions of Love: Textual Transmission." In *Imagining Contagion in Early Modern Europe*, edited by Claire L. Carlin, 47–62. Basingstoke: Palgrave Macmillan, 2005.

———. "Love, Mercy, and Courtly Discourse: Marguerite de Navarre Reads Alain Chartier." In *Mythes à la cour, mythes pour la cour*, edited by A. Corbellari, Y. Foehr-Janssens, J. C. Mühlethaler, J. Y. Tilliette, and B. Wahlen, 325–36. Geneva: Droz, 2010.

———. "Mirroring Discourses of Difference: Marguerite de Navarre's *Heptaméron* and the *Querelle des femmes*." In *Querelles des femmes: French Women Writers of the 15th and 16th Centuries*, edited by Kevin Brownlee and Scott Francis. Special issue, *French Forum* 42, no. 3 (Winter 2017): 375–92.

———. "Speech, Silence, and Storytelling: Marguerite de Navarre's "Heptameron" and Narrative Therapy." *Renaissance and Reformation / Renaissance et réforme* 36, no. 1 (Winter 2013): 69–92.

Gendre, André. Introduction to *Les quatre dames et les quatre gentilzhommes*, by Marguerite de Navarre. Critical edition by André Gendre. In Vol. 5 of *Œuvres complètes*, by Marguerite de Navarre, 103–45. Edited by Nicole Cazauran. Paris: Honoré Champion, 2012.

Gerulaitis, Leonardas V. "Incunabula on Syphilis." *Fifteenth-Century Studies* 29 (2004): 80–96.

Glidden, Hope H. "Gender, Essence, and the Feminine (*Heptaméron* 43)." In *Critical Tales: New Studies of the Heptaméron and Early Modern Culture*, edited by D. Lyons and Mary B. McKinley, 25–40. Philadelphia: University of Pennsylvania Press, 1993.

———. "Marot's *Le roman de la rose* and Evangelical Poetics." In *Translation and Transmission of Culture Between 1300 and 1600*, edited by Jeanette Beer and Kenneth Lloyd-Jones, 143–74. Kalamazoo MI: Medieval Institute Publications, 1995.

Gowland, Angus. *The Worlds of Renaissance Melancholy*. Cambridge: Cambridge University Press, 2006.

Green, Monica H. *Making Women's Medicine Masculine: The Rise of Male Authority in Pre-modern Gynaecology*. Oxford: Oxford University Press, 2008.

Griffin, Robert. "*La concorde des deux langages: Discordia concors*." In *Literature and the Arts in the Reign of Francis I: Essays Presented to C. A. Mayer*, edited by Pauline M. Smith and I. D. McFarlane, 54–81. Lexington KY: French Forum, 1985.

Guthke, Karl S. *The Gender of Death: A Cultural History in Art and Literature.* Cambridge: Cambridge University Press, 1999.

Guy, Henri. *Histoire de la poésie française au XVI ' siècle.* 2 vols. Paris: Honoré Champion, 1910.

Hall, Phyllis Ann. Introduction to "A Critical Edition of the First Six Books of Symphorien Champier's *La nef des princes*," 1–132. Critical edition by Phyllis Ann Hall. PhD diss., Columbia University, 1975.

Hawkins, Joyce. *Oxford Universal Dictionary.* New York: Smithmark, 1985.

Hill, Christine. "Symphorien Champier's Views on Education in the *Nef des princes* and the *Nef des dames vertueuses.*" *French Studies* 7 (1953): 323–34.

Hillman, David, and Carla Mazzio, eds. *The Body in Parts: Fantasies of Corporeality in Early Modern Europe.* New York: Routledge, 1997.

Hornik, Henri. Introduction to *Le temple d'honneur et de vertus,* by Jean Lemaire de Belges, 7–40. Edited by Henri Hornik. Geneva: Droz; Paris: Minard, 1957.

Huchon, Mireille. *Louise Labé: Une créature de papier.* Geneva: Droz, 2006.

———. *Rabelais.* Paris: Gallimard, 2011.

Hult, David F. "The *Roman de la Rose,* Christine de Pizan, and the *Querelle des femmes.*" In *The Cambridge Companion to Medieval Women's Writing,* edited by Carolyn Dinshaw and David Wallace, 184–94. Cambridge: Cambridge University Press, 2003.

Humpers, Alfred. "Quand Jean Lemaire est-il mort?" *Bulletin de l'Académie royale de Belgique* (1913): 408–21.

Huot, Sylvia. *The Romance of the Rose and Its Medieval Readers: Interpretation, Reception and Manuscript Transmission.* Cambridge: Cambridge University Press, 1993.

Iongh, Jane de. *Margaret of Austria, Regent of the Netherlands.* Translated by M. D. Herter Norton. New York: W. W. Norton, 1953.

Jacquart, Danielle, and Claude Thomasset. *Sexuality and Medicine in the Middle Ages.* Translated by Matthew Adamson. Princeton NJ: Princteon University Press, 1988.

Jenkins, Michael F. O. *Artful Eloquence: Jean Lemaire de Belges and the Rhetorical Tradition.* Chapel Hill: University of North Carolina Department of Romance Languages, 1980.

Jodogne, Pierre. *Jean Lemaire de Belges: Écrivain franco-bourguignon.* Brussels: Palais des Académies, 1972.

Johnston, Ian. *Galen: On Diseases and Symptoms.* Cambridge: Cambridge University Press, 2006.

Jordan, Constance. *Renaissance Feminism: Literary Texts and Political Models.* Ithaca NY: Cornell University Press, 1990.

Joukovsky, Françoise. "Querelle des femmes." *Magazine littéraire* 319 (1994): 51–52.

Jourda, Pierre. *Marguerite d'Angoulême duchesse d'Alençon, reine de Navarre, étude biographique et littéraire.* 2 vols. Paris: Honoré Champion, 1930. Reprint, Bottega d'Erasmo, 1966.

Kelly, Joan. "Early Feminist Theory and the *Querelle des femmes, 1400–1789.*" *Signs* 8, no. 1 (Autumn 1982): 4–28.

Kem, Judy. "Fatal Lovesickness in Marguerite de Navarre's *Heptaméron.*" *Sixteenth-Century Journal* 41, no. 2 (Summer 2010): 355–70.

———. *Jean Lemaire de Belges's "Les illustrations de Gaule et singularitez de Troye": The Trojan Legend in the Middle Ages and Early Renaissance.* New York: Peter Lang, 1994.

———. "'Malebouche,' Metaphors of Misreadings, and the 'Querelle des Femmes' in Jean Molinet's *Roman de la rose moralisé* (1500)." *Fifteenth-Century Studies* 31 (April 2006): 123–43.

———. "Marguerite de Navarre and the Querelle des Femmes." In "Women in the World and Works of Marguerite de Navarre," edited by Judy Kem. Special issue, *L'esprit créateur* 57, no. 3 (2017): 1–7.

———. "Moral Lessons for Women Readers of *Les illustrations de Gaule et singularitez de Troye.*" *Journal of the Rocky Mountain Medieval and Renaissance Society* 13 (1992): 67–83.

———. "Symphorien Champier." In *Sixteenth-Century French Writers,* edited by Megan Conway, 98–104. Vol. 327 of *Dictionary of Literary Biography.* Detroit MI: Bruccoli Clark Layman, 2006.

———. "Symphorien Champier and Christine de Pizan's *Livre de la cité des dames.*" *Romance Notes* 45, no. 2 (Winter 2005): 225–34.

———, ed. "Women in the World and Works of Marguerite de Navarre." Special issue, *L'esprit créateur* 57, no. 3 (Fall 2017).

Kennedy, Angus J. *Christine de Pizan: A Bibliographical Guide.* London: Grant & Cutler, 1984.

———. *Christine de Pizan: A Bibliographical Guide. Supplement I.* London: Grant & Cutler, 1994.

———. *Christine de Pizan: A Bibliographical Guide. Supplement II.* Woodbridge UK: Tamesis, 2004.

Kritzman, Lawrence. *The Rhetoric of Sexuality and the Literature of the French Renaissance.* Cambridge: Cambridge University Press, 1991.

Laqueur, Thomas. *Making Sex: Body and Gender from the Greeks to Freud.* Cambridge MA: Harvard University Press, 1990.

Lefranc, Abel. "L'identification de Raminagrobis." *Revue des études rabelaisiennes* 9 (March–April 1911): 144–47.

Lemay, Helen Rodnite. Introduction to *Women's Secrets: A Translation of Pseudo-Albertus Magnus's "De secretis mulierum" with Commentaries,* 1–58. Albany: State University of New York Press, 1992.

Maclean, Ian. *The Renaissance Notion of Woman: A Study in the Fortunes of Scholasticism and Medical Science in European Intellectual Life.* Cambridge: Cambridge University Press, 1980.

Mathieu-Castellani, Gisèle. *La conversation conteuse: Les nouvelles de Marguerite de Navarre.* Paris: Presses Universitaires Françaises, 1992.

————. *La quenouille et la lyre.* Paris: Librairie José Corti, 1998.

Mazzio, Carla. "Sins of the Tongue." In *The Body in Parts: Fantasies of Corporeality in Early Modern Europe,* edited by David Hillman and Carla Mazzio, 53–79. New York: Routledge, 1997.

McClive, Cathy. *Menstruation and Procreation in Early Modern France.* New York: Routledge, 2015.

McLeod, Glenda K. Introduction to *The Reception of Christine de Pizan from the Fifteenth through the Nineteenth Centuries: Visitors to the City,* edited by Glenda K. McLeod, i–xi. Lewiston NY: Edwin Mellen, 1991.

————, ed. *The Reception of Christine de Pizan from the Fifteenth through the Nineteenth Centuries: Visitors to the City.* Lewiston NY: Edwin Mellen, 1991.

————. *Virtue and Venom: Catalogs of Women from Antiquity to the Renaissance.* Ann Arbor: University of Michigan Press, 1991.

McVaugh, Michael R. "Niccolò da Reggio's Translations of Galen and Their Reception in France." *Early Science and Medicine* 11, no. 3 (2006): 275–301.

Ménager, Daniel. "*La concorde des deux langages*: Vers et prose chez Jean Lemaire de Belges." In *Prose et prosateurs de la Renaissance: Mélanges offerts à Robert Aulotte,* 15–25. Paris: SEDES, 1988.

Méniel, Bruno. "La vertu et l'orgueil, étude littéraire de la nouvelle 26." In *Lire "L'Heptaméron" de Marguerite de Navarre,* edited by Dominique Bertrand, 123–36. Clermont-Ferrand FR: Presses Universitaires Blaise Pascal, 2005.

Monahan, Jennifer. "Clément Marot, the *Roman de la rose,* and Poetic Identity." *Medievalia et humanistica,* n.s., 31 (2005): 83–99.

Munger, Robert S. "Guaiacum, the Holy Wood from the New World." *Journal of the History of Medicine* (Spring 1949): 196–229.

Munn, Kathleen. *A Contribution to the Study of Jean Lemaire de Belges.* New York: Menonnite, 1936.

Murphy, James J. *Rhetoric in the Middle Ages: A History of Rhetorical Theory from St. Augustine to the Renaissance.* Berkeley: University of California Press, 1974.

Neri, Ferdinando. *Letture francesi secolo XVI (Rabelais–Louis Labé).* Torino: Edizioni de l'Erma, 1931.

Norrell, Renée. "L'enigme de *La concorde des deux langages.*" *Revue des langues romanes* 83 (1978): 151–55.

Oriel, J. David. *The Scars of Venus: A History of Venereology.* London: Springer-Verlag, 1994.

Park, Katharine. *Secrets of Women. Gender, Generation, and the Origins of Human Dissection.* New York: Zone Books, 2006.

Pijoan, Michel. Introductory note to "L'Hôpital by Robert de Balsac," 118–25. Translated by Michel Pijoan. *Bulletin of the Institute of the History of Medicine* 1, no. 3 (April 1933): 118–25.

Planchon, G. Preface to *Le myrouel des appothiquaires et pharmacopoles par lequel est demonstré comment appothiquaires communement errent en plusieurs simples medicines contre l'intention des Grectz*, edited by Paul Dorveaux, 5–18. Paris: H. Welter, 1894.

Poirier, Guy. "A Contagion at the Source of Discourse on Sexualities: Syphilis during the French Renaissance." In *Imagining Contagion in Early Modern Europe*, edited by Claire L. Carlin, 157–76. Basingstoke: Palgrave Macmillan, 2005.

Pomata, Gianna. "Was There a Querelle des Femmes in Early Modern Medicine?" *Arenal: Revista de historia de las mujeres* 20, no. 2 (July–December 2013): 313–41.

Pormann, Peter E., and Emilie Savage-Smith. *Medieval Islamic Medicine*. Washington DC: Georgetown University Press, 2007.

Quilligan, Maureen. *The Allegory of Female Authority: Christine de Pizan's Cité des dames*. Ithaca NY: Cornell University Press, 1991.

Rabil, Albert. "Agrippa and the Feminist Tradition." In *Declamation on the Nobility and Preeminence of the Female Sex*, by Henricus Cornelius Agrippa, 3–37. Chicago: University of Chicago Press, 1996.

Radden, Jennifer, ed. *The Nature of Melancholy: From Aristotle to Kristeva*. Oxford: Oxford University Press, 2000.

Randall, Catharine. *Earthly Treasures: Material Culture and Metaphysics in the Heptaméron*. West Lafayette IN: Purdue University Press, 2007.

Randall, Michael. *Building Resemblance: Analogical Imagery in the Early French Renaissance*. Baltimore: Johns Hopkins University Press, 1996.

Reeser, Todd. "Redressing Ficino, Redeeming Desire: Symphorien Champier's *La nef des dames vertueuses*." In *Men and Women Making Friends in Early Modern France*, edited by Lewis C. Seifert and Rebecca M. Wilkin, 81–98. Farnham UK: Ashgate, 2015.

———. *Setting Plato Straight*. Chicago: University of Chicago Press, 2015.

Regalado, Nancy Freeman. "Le *Romant de la rose moralisé* de Jean Molinet: Alchimie d'une lecture méditative." In *Mouvances et jointures: Du manuscrit au texte médiéval*, edited by Milena Mikhaïlova, 99–117. Orléans: Paradigme, 2005.

Resnick, Irven M. *Marks of Distinction: Christian Perceptions of Jews in the High Middle Ages*. Washington DC: Catholic University of America Press, 2012.

Reynolds-Cornell, Régine. *Witnessing an Era: Georgette de Montenay and the Emblèmes ou devises Chrestiennes*. Birmingham AL: Summa, 1987.

Rezvani, Leanna Bridge. "The *Heptaméron*'s 67th Tale: Marguerite de Navarre's Humble Heroine Confronts the *Querelle des femmes* and Catholic Tradition." *Romance Notes* 52, no. 1 (2012): 43–50.

Richards, Earl Jeffrey. "Christine de Pizan and Jean Gerson: An Intellectual Friendship." In *Christine de Pizan 2000: Studies on Christine de Pizan in Honour of Angus J. Kennedy*, edited by John Campbell and Nadia Margolis, 197–208. Amsterdam: Editions Rodopi, 2000.

―――, ed. *Reinterpreting Christine de Pizan*. Athens: University of Georgia Press, 1992.

Richter, Bodo. L. O. "The Image of the Temple in the Works of Jean Lemaire de Belges." *Mediaevalia* 12 (1989): 305–38.

Rigolot, François. "The Invention of Female Authorship in Early Modern France." In *Teaching French Women Writers of the Renaissance and Reformation*, edited by Colette H. Winn, 84–89. New York: Modern Language Association of America, 2011.

―――. "Jean Lemaire de Belges: Concorde ou discorde des deux langages?" *Journal of Medieval and Renaissance Studies* 3, no. 2 (Fall 1973): 165–75.

Roger, Jacques. "L'humanisme médical de Symphorien Champier." In *L'humanisme français au début de la Renaissance*, 261–72. Paris: J. Vrin, 1973.

Rothstein, Marian. *The Androgyne in Early Modern France: Contextualizing the Power of Gender*. Basingstoke: Palgrave Macmillan, 2015.

―――. *Reading in the Renaissance:* Amadis de Gaule *and the Lessons of Memory*. Newark: University of Delaware Press, 1999.

Runnalls, Graham A. Introduction to *Le mystère de Judith et Holophernés, une édition critique de l'une des parties du "Mistere du viel testament,"* by [Jean Molinet?], 59–78. Critical edition by Graham A. Runnalls. Geneva: Droz, 1995.

Schaefer, Jacqueline Thibaut. "Jean Molinet Rhétoriqueur et le recyclage du *Roman de la Rose*." In *De la rose: Texte, image, fortune*, edited by Catherine Bel and Herman Braet, 393–410. Louvain BE: Peeters, 2006.

Schiesari, Juliana. *The Gendering of Melancholy: Feminism, Psychoanalysis, and the Symbolics of Loss in Renaissance Literature*. Ithaca NY: Cornell University Press, 1992.

Schleiner, Winifred. "Infection and Cure through Women: Renaissance Constructions of Syphilis." *Journal of Medieval and Renaissance Studies* 24, no. 3 (Fall 1994): 499–517.

―――. "Moral Attitudes toward Syphilis and Its Prevention in the Renaissance." *Bulletin of the History of Medicine* 68 (1994): 389–410.

Sedgwick, Eve Kosofsky. *Between Men: English Literature and Male Homosocial Desire*. New York: Columbia University Press, 1985.

Silver, Isidore. "Plato and Ficino in the Work of Symphorien Champier." *Bibliothèque d'humanisme et Renaissance* 55, no. 2 (1993): 271–80.

Siraisi, Nancy G. *Avicenna in Renaissance Italy: The Canon and Medical Teaching in Italian Universities after 1500*. Princeton NJ: Princeton University Press, 1987.

―――. *Medieval and Early Renaissance Medicine: An Introduction to Knowledge and Practice*. Chicago: University of Chicago Press, 1990.

Smith, Alan. K. "Scopia: Visual and Oral Fantasies of Self-Invention in *La concorde des deux langages.*" In *Repossessions: Psychoanalysis and the Phantasms of Early Modern Culture*, edited by Timothy Murphy and Alan K. Smith, 111–41. Minneapolis: University of Minnesota Press, 1998.

Sommers, Paula. "Marguerite de Navarre as Reader of Christine de Pizan." In *The Reception of Christine de Pizan from the Fifteenth through the Nineteenth Centuries: Visitors to the City*, edited by Glenda K. McLeod, 71–82. Lewiston NY: Edwin Mellen, 1991.

Sournia, Jean-Charles. *Histoire de la médecine.* Paris: La Découverte, 1997.

Spaak, Paul. *Jean Lemaire de Belges: Sa vie, son œuvre et ses meilleures pages.* Brussels: Lamertin; Paris: Honoré Champion, 1926.

Stecher, Jean. "Notice sur la vie et les œuvres de Jean Lemaire de Belges." In *Œuvres*, by Jean Lemaire de Belges, 4:i–cvii. Louvain BE, 1882–85. Reprint, Geneva: Slatkine, 1969.

Sullivan, Karen. "At the Limit of Feminist Theory: An Architectonics of the Querelle de la Rose." *Exemplaria: A Journal of Theory in Medieval and Renaissance Studies* 3, no. 2 (1991): 435–66.

Suranyi, Anna. "A Fifteenth-Century Woman's Pathway to Fame: The 'Querelle de la Rose' and the Literary Career of Christine de Pizan." *Fifteenth-Century Studies* 23 (1997): 204–21.

Swift, Helen J. "Des circuits de pouvoir: Un modèle pour la relecture des rapports poète-mécène dans les apologies du sexe féminin de la fin du Moyen Âge." *Études françaises* 47, no. 3 (2011): 55–69.

———. *Gender, Writing, and Performance: Men Defending Women in Late Medieval France, 1440–1538.* Oxford: Clarendon Press, 2008.

———. "'Pourquoi appellerions nous ces choses differentes, qu'une heure, un moment, un mouvement peuvent rendre du tout semblables?': Representing Gender Identity in the Late Medieval French *Querelle des femmes.*" In *Representing Medieval Genders and Sexualities in Europe: Construction, Transformation, and Subversion*, edited by Elizabeth L'Estrange and Alison More, 89–106. Farnham UK: Ashgate, 2011.

Telle, Emile V. *L'œuvre de Marguerite d'Angoulême, reine de Navarre et la querelle des femmes.* Toulouse: Lion et Fils, 1937.

Tétel, Marcel. *Marguerite de Navarre's "Heptameron": Themes, Language, and Structure.* Durham NC: Duke University Press, 1973.

Theureau, Louis. *Etude sur la vie et les œuvres de Jean Marot.* Geneva: Slatkine Reprints, 1970.

Thibaut, Francisque. *Marguerite d'Autriche et Jehan Lemaire de Belges: ou, De la littérature et des arts aux Pays-Bas sous Marguerite d'Autriche.* Paris: E. Leroux, 1888.

Thiry, Claude. "Rhétoriqueurs de Bourgogne, Rhétoriqueurs de France: Convergences, Divergences?" In *Rhetoric-Rhétoriqueurs-Rederijkers*, edited by Jelle Koopmans, Mark A. Meadow, Kees Meerhoff, and Marijke Spies, 101–16. Amsterdam: North Holland, 1995.

Thorndike, Lynn. "Translations of Works of Galen from the Greek by Niccolò da Reggio (c. 1308–1345)." *Byzantina-Metabyzantina, A Journal of Byzantine and Modern Greek Studies* 1 (1946): 213–35.

Thysell, Carol. *The Pleasure of Discernment: Marguerite de Navarre as Theologian*. Oxford: Oxford University Press, 2000.

Tracconaglia, Giovanni. *Femminismo e Platonismo in un libro raro del 1503: "La nef des dames" di Symphorien Champier*. Lodi IT: C. Dell'Avo, 1922.

Tuve, Rosemond. *Allegorical Imagery*. Princeton NJ: Princeton University Press, 1966.

Van Orden, Kate. "Female 'Complaintes': Laments of Venus, Queens, and City Women in Late Sixteenth-Century France." *Renaissance Quarterly* 54, no. 3 (Autumn, 2001): 801–45.

Vianey, Joseph. *Le Pétrarquisme en France au XVIᵉ siècle*. Montpellier: Coulet et fils, 1909.

Wack, Mary Frances. *Lovesickness in the Middle Ages: "The Viaticum" and Its Commentaries*. Philadelphia: University of Pennsylvania Press, 1990.

Wadsworth, James. Introduction to *Le livre de vraye amour*, by Symphorien Champier, 11–35. The Hague: Mouton, 1962.

———. "Les Alibantes of Rabelais." *Modern Language Notes* 71, no. 8 (December 1956): 584–87.

Warner, Lyndan. *The Ideas of Man and Woman in Renaissance France: Print, Rhetoric, and Law*. Farnham UK: Ashgate, 2011.

———. "The Querelle des Femmes." In *The Ideas of Man and Woman in Renaissance France: Print, Rhetoric, and Law*, 93–119. Farnham UK: Ashgate, 2011.

Wells, Marion A. *The Secret Wound: Love-Melancholy and Early Modern Romance*. Stanford CA: Stanford University Press, 2007.

Wickersheimer, Ernest. "Sur la syphilis aux XVᵉ et XVIᵉ siècles." *Bibliothèque d'humanisme et Renaissance* 4 (1937): 157–207.

Willard, Charity Cannon. "Anne de France, Reader of Christine de Pizan." In *The Reception of Christine de Pizan from the Fifteenth through the Nineteenth Centuries: Visitors to the City*, edited by Glenda K. McLeod, 59–70. Lewiston NY: Edwin Mellen Press, 1991.

———. *Christine de Pizan: Her Life and Works*. New York: Persea Press, 1984.

———. "Margaret of Austria: Regent of the Netherlands." In *Women Writers of the Renaissance and Reformation*, edited by Katharina Wilson, 350–62. Athens: University of Georgia Press, 1987.

Winn, Colette. *L'esthétique du jeu dans "L'Heptaméron" de Marguerite de Navarre*. Paris: J. Vrin, 1993.

———. "Témoignage de l'actualité médicale du temps: *Le mallade* de Marguerite de Navarre (c. 1535)." *Renaissance and Reformation / Renaissance et Réforme* 26, no. 4 (2002): 91–111.

Yates, Frances A. *The Art of Memory*. Chicago: University of Chicago Press, 1966.

Zegura, Elizabeth Chesney. "Gender and Patriarchy: A Many-Sided View." Chap. 3 in *Marguerite de Navarre's Shifting Gaze: Perspectives on Gender, Class, and Politics in the Heptaméron*. Abingdon UK: Routledge, 2017.

Zimmermann, Margarete. "Christine de Pizan: Memory's Architect." In *Christine de Pizan: A Casebook*, edited by Barbara K. Altmann and Deborah L. McGrady, 57–77. New York: Routledge, 2003.

———. "The Querelle des Femmes as a Cultural Paradigm." In *Time, Space, and Women's Lives in Early Modern Europe*, edited by Anne Jacobson Schutte, Thomas Kuehn, and Silvana Seidel Menchi, 17–28. Kirksville MO: Truman State University Press, 2001.

Zsuppan, C. M. "Jean Robertet's Life and Career: A Reassessment." *Bibliothèque d'humanisme et Renaissance* 31, no. 2 (1969): 332–42.

Zumthor, Paul. *Le masque et la lumière*. Paris: Editions du Seuil, 1978.

INDEX

Anne of France (*continued*)
of, 113; lament for, 225n29; and *Nef des
dames*, 195n76; physician to, 169; as
reader, 39, 93, 216n88, 216n89; and Symphorien Champier, 38, 77, 84, 93, 210n47
Anslay, Brian, 194n58
Antiochus, 161–62, 241n95
Antoine de Calabre, 216n90
Anvers (Antwerp), 50
apostrophe, 84
Arabs, 91, 94, 95, 111, 154, 232n127
Aristotle: associates of, 211n66; background of, 177; on excessive sexual
activity, 90, 212n70; on love, 108; on
menstrual blood, 95; misogynistic
writing of, 23, 27, 28; on procreation,
5, 88, 96; on soul as blank slate, 67; on
sperm quality, 9; on women's charac-
teristics, 14; writings on, 213n72
Arnaud de Villeneuve, 121, 180–81, 226n43
Arras, treaties of, 49, 200n15
L'art de chevalerie selon vegece, 195n70
Artemisia, 79, 105, 208n8
Artful Eloquence (Jenkins), 128
Asclepius, 124
astrology, 191n26
Atropos, 114–16, 130–35, 137–41, 224n12,
230n102, 233n136
Augustine, 51
Avenzoar, 91, 92, 179, 214n82, 215n84
Averroes, 90, 157–58, 179, 213n72
Avicenna: background of, 178; on cure
for lovesickness, 154–56; on excessive
sexual activity, 90, 157; influence of, 94,
95, 101, 212n71; influences on, 217n96;
on sexual activity, 214n78; on skin
disorders, 232n129, 234n143

Bade, Josse, 84
Balsac, Robert de, 207n5

"Barbarie" (Barbary Coast), 55
Baridon, Silvio, 206n92
Bayard, Pierre de, 93, 111, 216n91
Bayezid II, 201n39
Beau, Philibert le, Duke of Savoy, 16
Beaujeu, Anne de. *See* Anne of France
Beauvais, Vincent de, 122
Becker, Philipp August, 129, 225n29
Beecher, Donald A., 143, 185n3, 234n5,
234n6, 242n102
Bégin, Louis Jacques, 232n127
Bell, Susan Groag, 197n88
La belle dame sans mercy (Chartier), 15,
30–31, 37, 109, 144, 149, 192n41
Benzi, Ugo, 182
Bernard de Gordon, 181
Beroaldo, Filippo, 105
Berriot-Salvadore, Evelyne, 2, 8, 36, 190n1,
190n60
Bible: as cure for sadness, 150; on
immoral women, 13–14, 59, 60; Jean
Lemaire's references to, 122, 137; Jean
Molinet's references to, 65, 66, 123,
196n82, 205n81; on murmuring, 60–
61; name "Abra" in, 205n80; physical
strength through, 152; reading of, 44;
Symphorien Champier's quotation of,
232n132. *See also* Matthew, book of
bile, black, 2, 3, 8–9, 120, 157, 164, 170, 225n38
bile, yellow, 2, 3, 55
Billon, François de, 198n118
Bloch, Howard, 80, 83, 131, 203n70
blood, 2, 3, 116. *See also* menstruation
Boccaccio, Giovanni: account of Dido,
126; attitude toward women, 119,
208nn8–9; in *Couronne*, 121; deaths in
works of, 150; on etymology for Atropos, 224n12; influence of, 37, 38, 105,
106, 115, 122, 128; on Phebe, 116; readers
of, 106; tragic love story by, 52

Bock, Gisela, 190n1
Boleyn, Anne, 194n58
The Book of the City of Ladies (Christine). See *Le livre de la cité des dames* (Christine)
Boucher, Alain, 188n47
Bouchet, Jean, 41, 43–46, 196n82, 197n109, 198n112
Bourbon court, 38
Brant, Sebastian, 38, 84
Brantôme, 143, 234n3
Briau, André, 103, 104
British Museum, 194n58
Brou (Bourg-en-Bresse), 16
Brown, Cynthia Jane, 194n69, 195n70
Brussels, 50
Burgundio of Pisa, 179
Burgundy, 39, 49, 129

Cadden, Joan, 2, 96–97, 187n15, 217n99
Calabre, Antoine de, Duke of Lorraine, 17
Campbell, P. G. C., 194n58
Campi clysteriorum (Champier), 16
Caraffi, Patricia, 193n57
Caria, 208n8
Caron, Elisabeth, 128, 138, 140, 228n81, 230n95, 233n136
Carthage, 94, 126
Castel, Jean, 33, 44, 193n48, 197n109
Castigationes seu emendationes pharmacopolarum (Champier), 80, 81, 207n4, 232n132
Cato, 33
Cayley, Emily, 27, 30–31, 190n1
Celsus, 100–101, 232n132
Chalcidius, 187n22
Champier, Symphorien: advice to men in, 44; and Anne of France, 84, 93, 117, 210n47; audience of, 204n72; background of, 182; defense of women,

18, 45–46, 80, 82–83, 104, 110–12, 119, 169, 221n168; on dittany, 224n119; on fear and melancholy, 244n117; friends of, 16, 17, 140, 188n44, 188n47, 221n167, 226nn44–45; goals of, 101–2, 169; influences on, 17, 37–39, 79, 95, 121, 195n73, 208nn12–19, 209nn20–21, 212n71, 213n72; on lovesickness, 108; male patrons of, 93, 216n90; marriage of, 111; misogynistic writing of, 78–79, 81, 103, 107, 110, 111; on motherhood, 86–88; role in querelle des femmes, 19, 20, 75, 77, 84, 110, 111; on sexual overindulgence, 158; on syphilis, 94, 138, 217n95, 232n132; works of, 2, 15, 77, 93, 207n2, 207nn4–5, 215n86, 216n91; writing style of, 83–85, 211n59
Champion, 33–34, 193n51
Champion, Pierre, 47
Champion des dames (Le Franc), 18, 27, 31–34, 53, 121
Chappelet des dames (Molinet), 41, 57, 119, 123–25
Charles V, 191n26
Charles VII, 200n15
Charles VIII, 10, 49, 118, 126, 127, 200n15, 223n4, 228n75
Charlotte de Savoie, 216n88
Chartier, Alain, 15, 17, 30, 32, 37, 144, 149, 192n41
Chastellain, Georges, 45, 121, 196n82, 223n3
Chaussade, Bernard, 216n89
Chayes, Evelien, 123
Le chemin de long estude (Christine), 195n70
childbirth, 124, 137. *See also* reproduction
childlike disposition, 28, 63, 168
child rearing, 85–86
Chilton, Paul A., 194n67

Cholakian, Patricia, 143, 238n46, 242n98, 243n108
Cholakian, Rouben, 143
choleric temperament, 3, 17–18, 55, 56, 169
Christianity: of Albertus Magnus, 28; in *Couronne*, 121, 122, 141; and cure for lovesickness, 154, 165; and infertility, 91; Jean Molinet on Mohammed's damage to, 54–55; and love, 53, 54, 110; in *Romant de la rose moralisé*, 49, 74; temperament associated with, 18, 56, 169; view of women in, 80
Christine de Pizan: on equality of sexes, 112; father of, 191n26; influence of, 30, 32–33, 36–43, 46, 193n55, 195n73; language of, 192n46; portrayal of death, 133; praise of women, 119; reputation of, 34–36, 38–39, 194n58, 194n69, 195n70; role in querelle de la rose and des femmes, 17–19, 23–27, 33–35, 45, 46, 61–63, 167, 168, 171–72, 190n1; on women's minds and bodies, 1, 2, 43; writers' opinions of, 25, 26, 44, 63, 69, 170, 203n71, 204n72
Chroniques (Molinet), 50, 54, 200n17, 201n39, 232n128
Chrysostom, John, 98
Ciavolella, Massimo, 234n6
Cibele, 102
Cicero, 33, 51, 79, 105, 208n13
Ciminelli dall'Aquila, Serafino, 133, 140, 141; poem by, 128–30
De claris medicine scriptoribus (Champier), 16, 221n168
De claris mulieribus (Boccaccio), 37, 38, 119, 121, 208n9
clergy, 19, 61, 67, 69, 71, 91, 205n81
Clèves, Philippe de, Duke of Ravenstein, 19, 48–51, 54, 169, 200n17
Col, Pierre, 24, 26

Colliget (Averroes), 213n72
Compendium (Gaguin), 121
complaintes, 113–14, 117, 196n82, 225n29
De complexionibus (Galen). See *De temperamentis* (Galen)
concorde, 122–23, 233n141
La concorde des deux langages (Lemaire): content of, 130, 197n90, 230n95; defender of French language in, 131; on harmony through eloquence, 127, 139; influences on, 17, 196n82; meaning of title, 122; study of, 128; Venus in, 133, 136
La concorde du genre humain (Lemaire), 122, 196n82
Constantine the African, 8, 101, 179, 214n77, 217n96
Contes amoureux (Flore), 171
Copenhaver, Brian P., 111, 137–38, 207n4, 210n47, 217n95, 218n102
Il corbaccio (Boccaccio), 121
Un corps, un destin (Berriot-Salvadore), 2
Cotgrave, Randle: on concorde, 122; on fatuite, 201n31; on fils, 241n95; on Jean Lemaire's wordplay, 232n125; on Jean Molinet's word choices, 205n81; on lovesickness, 54; on medicinal preparations, 227n65; on Symphorien Champier's word choices, 211n59, 211n61, 219n134; on women's dissimulation, 14
Cottrell, Robert, 130
La couronne margaritique (Lemaire): Atropos in, 133; concorde and virtue in, 122–23; content of, 20, 41, 119, 121, 140, 141; Death in, 114, 115; defender of French language in, 230n101; gems as therapy in, 125–26; influences on, 17, 121–22, 190n57; purpose of, 124, 227n61; role in querelle des femmes, 114, 169, 170; writing and publication of, 113, 114, 223n4

Crawford, Katherine, 104, 105, 108, 220n135, 221n149, 221n152

Crétin, Guillaume, 196n82, 223n3

Cupid, 23, 104, 145. See also *Temple de cupido* (Marot); *Les trois contes de Cupido et d'Atropos* (Lemaire)

Cura pastoralis (Gregory the Great), 205n83

Cymon, 105–6

Dante, 17, 128, 196n82

death: in *Heptaméron*, 150–53, 160–63; Jean Lemaire's portrayal of, 114–16, 133, 141; and love, 109–10, 114, 131, 135, 139–41; Margaret of Austria's threat of, 119–20, 127; personifications of, 231n111; preferred to lovesickness, 144–45. See also lovesickness: fatality of

Debate and Dialogue (Cayley), 27

Decameron (Boccaccio), 52, 105, 106, 150

Declamation on the Nobility and Preeminence of the Female Sex (Agrippa), 193n52

de Meun, Jean: admiration and defense of, 17, 25–26, 34, 39, 42, 43, 60, 63–64, 71, 72, 196n82; character based on, 31, 32; Christine de Pizan's attacks on, 23, 24, 25, 27, 194n67; criticism of, 18, 43, 57, 61, 62, 69, 167; influence of, 37; Jean Molinet's disagreement with, 70, 199n11; plow metaphor of, 65, 67, 68; portrayal of death, 133; on "reign of Jupiter," 54; *Roman de la rose* continuation by, 187n15, 190n4; vulgarity of, 24, 25, 26

Denis the Aeropagite, 51, 200n23

Devaux, Jean, 48, 49, 50, 200n17

Dido, 81, 126, 127, 230n101

Dionisotti, Carlo, 129, 132, 133

dittany, 116, 224n119

Divine Names (Denis the Aeropagite), 51, 200n23

Le doctrinal des princesses et nobles dames (Marot), 42

Doutrepont, Georges, 225n29

Dufour, Alain, 38

Dupire, Jean, 48, 49

Dupire, Noël, 39–40, 198n1, 199n11

Du Pré, Galliot, 129

Du Pré, Jehan, 39

Dyogenes, 108

earth (element), 2

Eclogues (Virgil), 52

Elizabeth I, 194n58

eloquence. *See* rhetoric

England, 194n58

English language, 36, 187n15, 193n56, 194n58, 195n70

Enseignements à sa fille, Suzanne de Bourbon (Anne of France), 36, 210n47

Epistola adversus Jovinianum (Saint Jerome), 89

"L'epistre au dieu d'amours" (Christine), 23–24, 30

Epistres familières et invectives de ma dame Hélisenne (Hélisenne de Crenne), 36

Epistulae morales ad lucilium (Seneca the Younger), 51

Epître d'Othéa (Christine), 133

Les epîtres de l'amant vert (Lemaire), 122

erotomania. *See* lovesickness

Etymologies (Isidore), 122

eunuchs, 90, 214nn81–82

exclamatio, 84

Exposition morale (Marot), 73

Factorum et dictorum memorabilium (Valerius Maximus), 51

Les faictz et ditz (Dupire), 40

Fallopius, Gabriel, 183

fear: as cause of lovesickness, 155, 156, 165; as feminine trait, 148; in *Heptaméron*, 158, 160–62, 164, 165, 244n117; in *Quatre dames*, 148–49

Fenster, Thelma, 192n46

Ferrand, Jacques, 8, 24, 164, 184, 217n98, 244n117

fertility. *See* reproduction

Fetterley, Judith, 106

Ficino, Marsilio: background of, 182; in *Couronne*, 121, 234n145; influence of, 18, 103, 111, 140; on lovesickness, 8, 108, 110; on melancholy, 225n38; on Platonism, 19–20, 75, 78; on senses and love, 106, 107, 109

fire (element), 2

Flanders, 49–50

Flore, Jeanne, 168, 171

flowers, 124–25, 135–36

Fort inexpugnable du sexe feminin (Billon), 198n118

Fracastoro, Girolamo, 10, 137, 182, 232n131

France: authors in court of, 39, 113, 129, 197n88; Christine de Pizan's reputation in, 34–37, 194n69, 195n70; Jean de Meun praised in, 196n82; Jean Molinet's hopes for, 49; origin of querelle des femmes in, 23; Platonism in, 75, 78, 103, 121; reception of *Couronne* in, 223n4; syphilis in, 9, 234n143; and treaty of Arras, 200n15; in war with Italy, 50; women's status in, 2, 6, 21, 46, 104, 172

Francis I, 17, 143, 192n41, 234n3

Françoise de La Tour d'Auvergne, 211n51

Françoise de Luxembourg, 49, 51

Françon, Marcel, 129

Frappier, Jean, 129, 229n90

Frelick, Nancy, 185n3, 192n41, 237n36

French disease. *See* syphilis

French language: Christine de Pizan's work in, 36, 44, 45, 192n46, 193n57, 194n58; defender of, 230n101; difference from Italian, 130; medical writings in, 77, 78, 80–81, 92, 93; prevalence of, 21; and querelle de la rose, 26, 27; in *Romant de la rose moralisé*, 47; *De secretis mulierum* in, 187n15; Symphorien Champier's use of, 75, 89, 91–92, 103, 110, 111, 121, 207n2, 207n4, 216nn90–91; "syphilis" in, 137; in *Trois contes*, 132–33

Fulgentius, 209n24

Gabrielle de Bourbon, 35, 36

Gaguin, Robert, 121, 122

Gaillarde, Jeanne, 45, 198n118

Galen of Pergamum: background of, 177; on consequences of sex, 9; on fear and melancholy, 164, 244n117; on hysteria, 8; influence of, 85, 90, 93–95, 97, 98, 102, 186n6, 213n75, 214n77, 217n100, 240n73; on syphilis, 232n132; on temperaments, 2–3; on women's anatomy, 3–5, 100, 164

Gargantua (Rabelais), 188n47

Gellius, Aulus, 105

gems, 123, 125–27, 141

gender equality: Christine de Pizan on, 38, 112; in querelle des femmes, 168, 172; Symphorien Champier on, 18, 38, 82–83, 103, 104, 219n134. *See also* men: superiority of

The Gender of Death (Guthke), 133

Gendre, André, 144, 148, 235n9

Genealogia deorum (Boccaccio), 115, 116, 122

Geneviève, Sainte, 102

Gerard of Cremona, 179, 213n75

German language, 137, 187n15

Germans, 44

Les lunectes des cirurgiens (Champier), 81
Lunettes des princes (Meschinot), 196n82
Lyon: authors in, 45, 140; books printed
   in, 37, 38, 39, 93, 198n1, 206n92; Jean
   Lemaire in, 16, 140, 226n43; medicine
   in, 16, 215n86; poetry published in, 129;
   riots in, 93; women's status in, 110–11

Maclean, Ian, 14, 60, 68
madness, 120, 146, 153, 223n2
Maimonides, 180
A malafranczos morbo Gallorum preserva-
   tio ac cura (Steber), 10, 11
Malebouche: Clément Marot's characterization of, 73; Jean Molinet's
   characterization of, 66, 69, 71, 202n62,
   204n73; Martin Le Franc's characterization of, 31; and slanderers, 41, 43, 63
"La malice des femmes" (Champier),
   78–79, 81–82
Malines (Mechelen), 50
Le mallade (Marguerite de Navarre), 143
Marcus Brutus, 79, 208n8
Margaret of Austria: book promised to,
   169; childlessness of, 116; Christine
   de Pizan's influence on, 35, 46, 193n55,
   197n88; crown of, 121–23, 126, 127, 141,
   223n4; dedication to, 193n52; employ-
   ees of, 16; Jean Lemaire's attitude
   toward, 18, 20, 41, 74, 117, 119–20, 127,
   170, 225n38, 230n101; Jean Lemaire's
   writing for, 15, 113, 115, 118, 123, 223n5,
   227n61; Jean Molinet's writing for,
   15, 50; marriage and repudiation of,
   49, 126, 127, 200n15, 223n4, 227n69,
   228n75; as reader, 39, 197n83
Marguerite, lady of La Rivière. *See* La
   Rivière, Marguerite de
Marguerite de Navarre: acquaintances of,
   15, 16, 17; characters of, 148, 164, 193n51,

194n67; influences on, 17, 35–37,
   190n58, 192n41; on lovesickness, 2, 18,
   20–21, 151, 164–66, 237n36; and moral
   in *Heptaméron*, 163, 165; praise of,
   198n118; as reader, 39; role in querelle
   des femmes, 1, 34, 144, 170–72, 235n9;
   suffering of, 152; treatment of Francis
   I, 143, 234n3; works of, 15
Marguerite de Navarre, Mother of the
   Renaissance (Cholakian and Cholakian), 143
"Marguerite de Navarre as Reader of
   Christine de Pizan" (Sommers), 36–37
Marie de Bourgogne, 123
Marignano, 216n90
Marot, Clément, 19, 45, 46, 71–74, 206n90,
   206nn92–94
Marot, Jean, 41–43, 45, 46, 197n92
marriage: counseled by the Champion,
   32; in *Heptaméron*, 162; of Muslims,
   54, 55, 56; to prevent hysteria, 8;
   Symphorien Champier's stance on, 20,
   78, 79, 84–86, 88–89, 102–4, 110, 169,
   211n66, 219n129, 219n134, 232n132
Mary of Burgundy, 57
Matheolus (Mathieu de Boulogne), 27,
   42, 78, 81, 82, 110, 209n34
Mathieu-Castellani, Gisèle, 163
Matthew, book of, 98. *See also* Bible
Maurus, Rabanus, 51, 200n22
Mausolus, 79, 105, 208n8
Maximilian I, 48–50, 200n15, 200n17
Mazzio, Carla, 64–65, 69
McClive, Cathy, 218n124
McLeod, Glenda, 35–37, 195n73
Medea, 81
medical ideas: authorities of, 102, 177–84,
   215n86, 218n125; books about, 93, 94,
   211n61, 212n71, 215n86, 216n88, 217n96;
   about disease names, 138; about gems,

123–27; about herbs and flowers, 123–24, 135–36, 227n65; influences on, 191n26; Jean Lemaire's interest in, 117, 121, 122, 132, 140; in Jean Molinet's works, 124–25; about lovesickness, 8–9, 153–55, 157–58, 163–66; about madness, 120; Marguerite de Navarre's interest in, 143, 144, 165; about obstetrics and procreation, 5, 6, 91, 187n22; role in querelle des femmes, 1–2, 15, 17, 21, 77, 114, 121, 168, 172; of Symphorien Champier, 19, 80–81, 83–84, 92–93, 102, 111, 207n4, 218n125; about syphilis, 10; about women's fear, 148; about women's secrets, 27–28. *See also* illness

De medicina (Celsus), 100–101

Medieval Misogyny (Bloch), 80

Mehmed II, 50

melancholic temperament: characteristics of, 3; cures for, 124–25; as illness, 150; and lovesickness, 120, 153, 164, 244n117; religion associated with, 55, 56; and sexual activity, 91; women's tendency toward, 14, 117, 170. *See also* grief

memory, 126, 127, 141, 153

men: books written for, 93, 94; as death, 231n111; differences from women, 20, 42–44, 112, 170; dissimulation by, 148–49, 165, 171, 239n66; Jean Molinet's ideas about, 56, 71; language skills of, 131; literature for, 28; love for women, 102–5, 107, 109, 219n129; lovesickness of, 8–9, 23–24, 153, 155, 164, 165; Martin Le Franc's portrayal of, 31–32; melancholy of, 225n38; minds and bodies of, 152; moralizing by, 69, 71, 107; relationships with men, 103, 104, 106, 107, 161, 220n135; role in procreation, 5, 6–7, 78, 85, 91, 92, 99, 101–2, 214n82, 215n84; role in querelle de la rose, 27;

role in querelle des femmes, 39, 172; sexual activity of, 9, 60–61, 78, 89–92, 94, 158, 165; sperm production by, 98; superiority of, 3–6, 17, 33–34, 58–59, 74, 78, 81–84, 87, 88, 96, 99–102, 110, 121, 164, 193n52, 219n134; syphilis blamed on, 231n123; women as conscience of, 70–71

Méniel, Bruno, 162, 163, 242n98, 242n102

menstruation: comparison to hemorrhoids, 56; effects on procreation, 100, 101; as imperfection, 5, 6, 34, 95, 97; moon's regulation of, 117; and sexual activity, 13, 218n124; Symphorien Champier's ideas about, 92, 102, 218n124. *See also* blood

mercury (element), 10–13, *11, 12,* 20, 130, 140, 232n132, 234n143

Mercury (god), 130, 138, 140, 141

Meschinot, Jean, 196n82

Metamorphoses (Ovid), 52

Middle Ages: diseases in, 137; medical ideas from, 5, 154, 164, 187n22, 217n96; personifications of death in, 231n111; querelle des femmes in, 190n1; rhetorical texts in, 83; stories of heroines in, 105; views of women in, 15, 80, 203n70, 209n21; women's medicine in, 91, 217n99; works on lovesickness in, 234n6

Milan, 51

De mineralibus (Albertus), 122

Mohammed, 54–55

Molinet, Jean: attitude toward women, 57–59, 67, 68, 70–71, 123–24, 199n11; and Christine de Pizan, 204n72; criticism of, 47; on dangers of love, 51–53; defense of *Roman de la rose,* 19, 58–59, 61–64, 168; friends and family of, 15–16; humoral theory of religion, 55–56, 56t; influence of, 45, 123–25; influences on, 17, 39–43, 196n82; on Islam, 54–55,

Molinet, Jean (*continued*)
201n39, 201n43; on name of syphilis,
232n128; on rhetorical and sexual
performance, 65–68; on spiritual
love, 17–18, 46; support of Philippe
de Clèves, 50, 200n17; translation of
Roman de la rose, 48–49, 71–74; works
of, 15, 57, 66, 119, 205n79, 206n94, 223n3
Monahan, Jennifer, 73
Montenay, Georgette de, 35, 36
Monteux, Jérôme, 207n2
Montpellier, 16, 186n6, 188n47
Montreuil, Jean de, 24–27, 41
moon, 116–17
Moulin, Antoine du, 129
Munn, Kathleen, 229n90
murmurers, 60–61, 63, 65, 69, 71, 74, 168,
202n62, 204n73. *See also* tongues;
women: loquaciousness of
Murphy, James J., 205n83
Muslims, 17–18, 55–56, 74, 169, 201n39. *See
also* Islam
*Le myrouel des appothiquaires et pharmaco-
poles* (Champier), 80, 81, 93, 207n4
Le mystère de Judith et Holoférnes, 66,
205n79
Mytilene, 50

Nancy, France, 216n90
Das Narrenschiff (Brant), 38, 84
Nef des dames vertueuses (Champier):
advice to men in, 44; Christine de
Pizan acknowledged in, 195n73; content of, 17, 208nn8–9, 221n149, 221n152;
dedication to Anne of France, 117,
210n47; defense of women in, 18, 37,
38, 46, 78, 80, 82, 119, 210n37, 219n134,
220n145; goal of, 78, 169; influence
of, 121; influences on, 37–39, 195n76,
208n16, 208n18; language of, 78, 89, 92,

102; marital advice in, 102–5, 219n129;
medical advice in, 84, 86, 88–93; reproductive and child rearing advice in,
86, 101; on sexual overindulgence, 158;
tone and style of, 19, 75, 77, 83, 85, 103–
4, 106, 110, 111, 221n168; writing and
publication of, 77, 85, 93, 111, 220n138
Nef des folles (Bade), 84
Nef des fous (Brant). See *Das Narrenschiff*
(Brant)
Nef des princes (Champier): dedications
in, 211n51; influences on, 208n13,
209n20, 209n24, 210n48; language of,
92, 102; marital advice in, 102–3, 105,
219n129; medical advice in, 84, 85,
88–90, 92–93, 244n117; on medical
practitioners, 218n125; misogyny in,
78–79, 81–82, 103, 110; reproductive
and child rearing advice in, 86, 98–99;
tone of, 75, 77, 80, 85, 87, 88, 111; writing
and publication of, 77, 85, 111, 222n169
Neri, Ferdinando, 129, 133
Niccolò da Reggio, 95, 181, 217n100

Ockeghem, Johannes, 196n82
oeuvres (Lemaire), 226n51
oeuvres (Paré), 4–5
Œuvres spirituelles 1510–1516 (Gabrielle de
Bourbon), 36
On Famous Women (Boccaccio), 208n8
On the Usefulness of the Parts of the Body
(Galen), 3
Ordre de la chevalerie (Champier), 16
Oribasius, 177, 232n132
Oriel, J. David, 10
Orpheus, 109
Ovid, 23, 27, 51, 52, 79, 190n4, 208n14
Ovide moralisé, 52, 73
Oxford University, 194n58

of continuation of, 187n15. *See also* querelle de la rose

Le romant de la rose moralisé (Molinet): attacks on murmurers in, 63, 204n73; audience of, 68; content of, 19, 203n67; criticism of, 41, 47–48, 199n2, 199n7; influences on, 196n82; metaphors in, 65–68; Philippe de Clèves in, 49–51; purposes of, 57, 71, 74, 168; tragic love stories in, 52–53; on women's nature, 80; writing and publication of, 198n1

rose, 72–73

Rothstein, Marian, 154

Rufus of Ephesus, 238n54

Runnalls, Graham A., 205n79, 205n80

Sacchi, Bartolomeo, dit Platina, 182

Sainte Reine, 137

Saint-Gelais, Octavien de, 196n82

Saint Julien, Pierre de, 223n2

Saint Margaret of Antioch, 137

Saint Victor library, 16

Salamanca, 10

Salic law, 6

Salminen, Renja, 242n97

sanguine temperament, 3, 18, 55, 56, 91, 169

Sappho, 39

Schaefer, Jacqueline, 199n2

Schiesari, Juliana, 225n38

De secretis mulierum (pseudo-Albertus Magnus): challenging of ideas in, 27–28, 171; as literary type, 14; on menstrual cycle, 5, 102; misogynistic writing in, 101, 121; popularity of, 187n15, 218n113; on women's sexuality, 13

secrets of women, 99, 100, 111, 172. See also *De secretis mulierum* (pseudo-Albertus Magnus); women

Secundus, 79, 209n21

Séjour d'honneur (Saint-Gelais), 196n82

semen, 5, 95–98, 101, 157–58. *See also* sperm

Semiramis, 81

Seneca, 79, 208n15

Seneca the Younger, 51

senses, 63, 106–8, 203n70

Serapion the Younger, 94, 180, 217n97

Serres, Louis de, 184

sex: within bonds of marriage, 78, 104, 110; comparison to rhetoric, 65–68, 74; as cure for lovesickness, 154–55, 158, 163–65, 238n54; deprivation of, 8, 157; diseases spread by, 9, 94; effects on women, 13, 88–89, 240n74; excessive, 9, 78, 84, 89–92, 94, 101, 157–58, 166, 171, 212nn70–71, 214n77; ideal time for, 90, 214n78; inability to perform, 60–61, 100–101; medical books about, 96–97

sex difference: loss of, 18, 20, 135, 141, 170; Marguerite de Navarre on, 144, 165; Symphorien Champier on, 19; in *Trois contes*, 131, 135, 140, 141

Ship of Fools (Brant). See *Das Narrenschiff* (Brant)

Siraisi, Nancy, 2, 186n6, 212n71

slanderers: of Jean de Meun, 57; Jean Molinet's characterization of, 56, 60, 63, 66, 74, 168; misogynists as, 42, 43, 81, 82, 84; women as, 41, 60, 70–71

Socrates, 108, 209n24

Sommers, Paula, 36–37

souls, 150–52, 163. *See also* love, spiritual

Spain, 10, 126, 143, 234n3, 234n143

Spanish language, 137, 232n126

Speculum Galeni (Champier), 78, 93, 95–96

Speculum historiale (Vincent de Beauvais), 209n21

Speculum morale (Beauvais), 122

sperm, 8–9, 96–100, 158. *See also* semen

Steber, Bartholomaeus, 10, *11*

Vianey, Joseph, 228n80
Viaticum (Constantine the African), 8
Vienna, 10
Les vies des femmes célèbres (Dufour), 38
Vincent de Beauvais, 121–22, 209n21
virago. *See* women: virility of
Virgil, 52, 70, 126, 224n19
Virgin Mary, 65, 66, 72, 73
Virtue. *See also* women: virtues of
virtue, 122–24, 226n49
De virtutibus lapidem (Albertus), 122
La vraye disant advocate des dames
  (Marot), 41–42

Wack, Mary Frances, 234n6, 238n54,
  241n95, 244n118
Wadsworth, James, 16, 103, 105, 220n138
water (element), 2
Webs of Allusion (Adams), 36
Wells, Marion A., 234n6
Willard, Charity Cannon, 30, 32, 34–37,
  191n26
William of Saliceto, 180
Winn, Colette, 143, 153
Winterburg, Johann, 10
Witnessing an Era (Reynolds-Cornell), 36
wives, 79, 80, 85, 86, 88–89, 102, 219n129.
  See also women
women: accounts of Menian, 79, 208n9;
  condemnation of all, 24, 25; dangers

of, 78–82; as Death, 133, 231n111; dissimulation by, 154–56, 159–65, 239n66;
fear felt by, 148; humors of, 3, 9, 10, 13,
14, 56, 68, 74, 90, 95, 116–17, 120, 140,
141, 164, 215n84, 225n38, 228n81; immorality of, 13–14, 19, 29, 48, 78, 89, 92,
103–4, 108–9, 168–69; loquaciousness
of, 13, 19, 42, 60, 66, 80, 83, 86; love for
men, 104–5, 107, 109, 134; in medical
profession, 102; minds and bodies of,
1–6, 14, 17, 29, 58–59, 88, 94, 95, 100,
117, 119–21, 152, 164, 167, 186n9, 217n99;
role in procreation, 5–7, 92, 99–101,
111, 215n84; sexual activity of, 8, 9, 13,
42, 88–91, 158, 165, 240n74; syphilis
blamed on, 9–10, 134, 136, 228n81,
231n123; virility of, 105, 121, 126, 127, 131,
170, 220n145, 228n74, 230n101; virtues
of, 14–15, 29, 33–34, 37–38, 42–46, 79,
81, 82, 106, 112, 120–21, 127, 160, 161, 163,
165, 193n52, 198n118, 230n101; wise and
foolish, 153–65; as writers and readers,
21, 26, 28, 31, 34–39, 41, 44–46, 54–58,
62, 69, 70, 71, 74, 78, 80–82, 84, 89, 91,
106, 111–12, 127, 148, 167–68, 171, 172,
194n69, 198n118. *See also* gender equality; secrets of women; wives

Zeuxis, 59
Zimmerman, Margarete, 35, 190n1, 193n55

In the Women and Gender in the Early Modern World series:

Women's Life Writing and Early Modern Ireland
Edited by Julie A. Eckerle and Naomi McAreavey

Pathologies of Love: Medicine and the Woman Question in Early Modern France
By Judy Kem

The Politics of Female Alliance in Early Modern England
Edited by Christina Luckyj and Niamh J. O'Leary

To order or obtain more information on these or other University
of Nebraska Press titles, visit nebraskapress.unl.edu.

CPSIA information can be obtained
at www.ICGtesting.com
Printed in the USA
LVHW090757171019
634475LV00006BA/64/P